Confronting Global Gender Justice

Confronting Global Gender Justice contains a unique, interdisciplinary collection of essays that address some of the most complex and demanding challenges facing theorists, activists, analysts, and educators engaged in the tasks of defining and researching women's rights as human rights, and fighting to make these rights realities in women's lives.

With thematic parts on Complicating the discourses of victimhood, interrogating practices of representation, mobilizing strategies of engagement, and crossing legal landscapes, this volume offers both specific case studies and more general theoretical interventions. Contributors examine and assess current understandings of gender justice, and offer new paradigms and strategies for dealing with the complexities of gender and human rights as they arise across local and international contexts. In addition, it offers a particularly timely assessment of the effectiveness and limits of international rights instruments, governmental and non-governmental organization activities, grassroots and customary practices, and narrative and photographic representations.

This book is a valuable resource for both undergraduate and graduate students in disciplines such as Gender or Women's Studies, Human Rights, Cultural Studies, Anthropology, and Sociology, as well as researchers and professionals working in related fields.

Debra Bergoffen is Emeritus Professor of Philosophy at George Mason University.

Paula Ruth Gilbert is Professor of French, Canadian, and Women and Gender Studies at George Mason University.

Tamara Harvey is Associate Professor of English at George Mason University.

Connie L. McNeely received the Ph.D. in Sociology from Stanford University and is currently on the faculty of the School of Public Policy at George Mason University.

Confronting Global Gender Justice

Women's lives, human rights

Edited by Debra Bergoffen,
Paula Ruth Gilbert, Tamara Harvey,
and Connie L. McNeely

 Routledge
Taylor & Francis Group

LONDON AND NEW YORK

First published 2011
by Routledge
2 Park Square, Milton Park, Abingdon, Oxon, OX14 4RN

Simultaneously published in the USA and Canada
by Routledge
711 Third Avenue, New York, NY 10017

Routledge is an imprint of the Taylor & Francis Group, an informa business

© 2011 Debra Bergoffen, Paula Ruth Gilbert, Tamara Harvey,
and Connie L. McNeely; individual chapters, the contributors

The right of Debra Bergoffen, Paula Ruth Gilbert, Tamara Harvey,
and Connie L. McNeely to be identified as editors of this work has been
asserted by them in accordance with the Copyright, Designs and Patent
Act 1988.

Typeset in Baskerville
by Keystroke, Tettenhall, Wolverhampton

British Library Cataloguing in Publication Data
A catalogue record for this book is available from the British Library

Library of Congress Cataloging in Publication Data
Confronting global gender justice : women's lives, human rights /
Debra Bergoffen{...}[et al.].
    p. cm.
Includes bibliographical references.
1. Women's rights. 2. Human rights. 3. Women—Social conditions.
4. Feminism. I. Bergoffen, Debra B.
HQ1236.C626 2010
305.42—dc22
2010021197

ISBN: 978-0-415-78078-0 (hbk)
ISBN: 978-0-415-78079-7 (pbk)
ISBN: 978-0-203-83859-4 (ebk)

For Lucinda Peach

Contents

Acknowledgments

There are many colleagues, students, and staff at George Mason University who have helped us with this project, starting with those participants in our Gender Justice Research Community, those who worked with us in organizing a 2008 symposium on Global Gender Justice where some of the chapters in this book originated, and the faculty, students, and staff of the Women and Gender Studies Program and Center. We would like to single out: Nancy Hanrahan, Suzanne Scott, Vicki Kirsch, Susan Miller, Karen Wolf, Burcu Borhan, and Marjorie Agosín, our guest speaker at the symposium. We also acknowledge the financial support of a number of units at George Mason University for this symposium.

We would like to recognize the difficult and sometimes tedious editing done by Jennifer Dean who worked tirelessly to make all of the essays uniform and in compliance with the required style.

The co-editors would also like to thank the editorial team at Routledge for their encouragement of this project and for their assistance in the preparation of this volume for publication. We would specifically like to thank Gerhard Boomgaarden for his support and Jennifer Dodd for her prompt attention to details.

We appreciate the research assistance provided by Shelley Harshe of the Department of Philosophy and Religion at American University on Chapter 4 by Lucinda Peach.

We acknowledge the permission from Kay Chernush to reproduce the photographs that accompany her chapter in this volume and from Marjorie Agosín for the use of her poems in Chapter 7.

And finally, we would each like to acknowledge and thank our families who supported and encouraged us during this collaborative project.

Notes on contributors

Debra Bergoffen is Emeritus Professor of Philosophy at George Mason University. Her areas of research and interest are continental philosophy (including the psychoanalytic theories of Freud, Lacan, Kristeva, and Irigaray), feminist theory, and human rights. She is the author of *The Philosophy of Simone de Beauvoir: Gendered Phenomenologies, Erotic Generosities* (1997). As co-director of the Society for Phenomenology and Existential Philosophy (SPEP) she co-edited *Remembrance and Responsibility,* and *Other Openings.* She is also the co-editor of *Continental and Post Modern Perspectives in the Philosophy of Science,* and a special issue of *New Nietzsche Studies* titled *Nietzsche and the Jews.* Her recent articles include "Exploiting the Dignity of the Vulnerable Body: Rape as a Weapon of War," *Philosophical Papers* (2009), and "Nietzsche and the Enemy: Nietzsche's New Politics," in *Nietzsche , Power, Politics: Rethinking Nietzsche's Legacy for Political Thought* (edited by H. W. Siemens and V. Roodt, 2008). She is currently working on a book tentatively titled, *Vulnerable Bodies: Genocidal Rape and the Human Right to Sexual Self Determination.*

Nitza Berkovitch is Associate Professor in the Department of Sociology and Anthropology at Ben Gurion University (Israel). She is the author of *From Motherhood to Citizenship: Women's Rights and International Organizations* (1999) and co-editor of a special volume of *Social Politics* entitled *Feminist Challenges in the Middle East* (1999). She is also the co-editor of *Women of the Space Periphery and Gender* (2005) and *In/Equality* (2006). She is currently co-directing sociological research on the role played by nongovernmental organizations in the re-organization of welfare-to-work programs directed towards women in Israel (with Adriana Kemp).

Kum-Kum Bhavnani, Scholar, Activist, and Filmmaker, is Professor of Sociology and Chair of the Women, Culture, and Development program at the University of California, Santa Barbara. In addition to her numerous books and articles, she has published important collections on race and gender in their complex dimensions and intersections with politics, youth culture, and feminism, and, in 2006, released her award-winning feature documentary, *The Shape of Water.*

Nancy Chi Cantalupo is the Assistant Dean for Clinical Programs at Georgetown University Law Center, where she teaches "Rule of Law Promotion and Civil Society in China: Implications for Women and Girls." She has also taught "International Women's Human Rights" at the George Washington University's Law School and "Gender, Oppression, Liberation and Global Laws" with Georgetown's Women's and Gender Studies Program. She participated in a team fact-finding mission and wrote a report entitled *Domestic Violence in Ghana: The Open Secret* (published in 2006 by the *Georgetown Journal on Gender & the Law*). She has served on the board of the Asian/Pacific Islander Domestic Violence Resource Project and the National Women's Alliance.

Kay Chernush is a leading U.S. photographer with 30 years of experience in commercial and fine art photography. She has photographed more than 50 feature stories for *Smithsonian Magazine* and shot for many other national and international publications, major corporations and foundations. Her interest in issues related to human trafficking began with an assignment for the State Department in 2005, resulting in exhibitions at the United Nations in New York and Vienna, the World Bank, and Princeton's Woodrow Wilson Center. More recently, working with a group of trafficking survivors, she created an award-winning series of transformational images and narratives that has been exhibited in The Hague and Amsterdam and that will travel to other European cities. Other projects include "Self-Examination," a meditation in images and words on her experience of breast cancer, and "The US and The They," a series of portraits that explores prejudice and empathy. Her work may be viewed at www.kaychernush.com

Louise du Toit is Senior Lecturer in the Department of Philosophy at the University of Stellenbosch in South Africa. She is the author of *A Philosophical Investigation of Rape: the Making and Unmaking of the Feminine Self* (Routledge, 2009) and guest editor of the special edition of *Philosophical Papers* on "Rape, and its Meanings (November 2009). She has published widely on the topic of rape within contexts of transitional justice, feminism, legal theory, and phenomenological analysis. She also works within the fields of literature, hermeneutics, and feminist philosophy of religion.

Paula Ruth Gilbert is Professor of French, Canadian, and Women and Gender Studies at George Mason University. She specializes in Québec Studies and French and Francophone women writers, nineteenth-century French Studies and the study of Paris, gender and violence (and violent women), and gender/human rights and narrative. She has written or edited several books, including: *The Aesthetics of Stéphane Mallarmé in Relation to His Public*; *The Literary Vision of Gabrielle Roy: An Analysis of Her Works*; *Traditionalism, Nationalism, and Feminism: Women Writers of Québec*; *Women Writing in Québec: Essays in Honor of Jeanne Kissner*; *Doing Gender: Franco-Canadian Women Writers of the 1990s*; *Violence and Gender: An Interdisciplinary Reader*; *Violence and the Female Imagination: Québec's Women Writers Re-frame Gender in North American Cultures*; and *Translatlantic Passages:*

Literary and Cultural Relations between Québec and Francophone Europe along with numerous articles. She is currently completing work on a book-length study, "Narrating Female Lives: Human Rights Violations against Women and Girls."

Tamara Harvey is Associate Professor of English at George Mason University. She is author of *Figuring Modesty in Feminist Discourse Across the Americas, 1633–1700* (2008) and co-editor with Greg O'Brien of *George Washington's South* (2003). Her research focuses on women and early America with an emphasis on hemispheric studies. She is also working on a project comparing seventeenth- and twenty-first-century feminisms' uneasy relationship to rights discourse.

Amy L. Hill is a digital storytelling instructor, documentary filmmaker, and public health/community development consultant. After receiving her MA in Social Sciences in Education/Gender Studies from Stanford University, she spent twelve years coordinating women's health and violence prevention projects throughout California. This experience, coupled with life-long interests in narrative and visual arts, led her to founding *Silence Speaks*, an international digital, story-telling initiative that blends oral history, participatory media-making, and popular education in workshops to support the telling and public sharing of personal stories that document injustice and promote gender inequality, women's health and human rights. Amy continues to manage *Silence Speaks* in her current role as Director of Programs at the Center for Digital Storytelling in Berkeley, California.

Saida Hodžić is Assistant Professor of Women and Gender Studies at George Mason University. She received her Ph.D. in Medical Anthropology at University of California, Berkeley and University of California, San Francisco and a Designated Emphasis certificate from the Department of Gender and Women's Studies at University of California, Berkeley. This chapter complements her articles on women's rights and Ghanaian advocacy for the Domestic Violence Bill published in *Ethnos* and *Domestic Violence and the Law in Colonial and Postcolonial Africa* (2010). Her current work on a manuscript titled *Of Rebels, Spirits, and Social Engineers: The Awkward Ending of Female Genital Cutting* has been supported by a research and writing grant from the Harry Frank Guggenheim Foundation.

Adriana Kemp is Associate Professor in the Department of Sociology and Anthropology, Tel Aviv University, and a researcher at the Van Leer Institute of Jerusalem. She is the co-author of *Foreigners and Workers: The Political Economy of Labor Migration in Israel* (2008) and the co-editor of *Israelis in Conflict: Hegemonies, Identities, Challenges* (2004), and *Citizenship Gaps in Israel* (2008). She is currently co-directing sociological research on the role played by nongovernmental organizations in the reorganization of welfare-to-work programs directed towards women in Israel (with Nitza Berkovitch).

Donna K. Maeda is Professor in the Department of Critical Theory & Social Justice at Occidental College in Los Angeles, California. Dr. Maeda's research and teaching interests focus on interactions between legal and social discourses in the production and transformation of race, gender, culture, and other forms of "difference." Dr. Maeda has served as Special Assistant to the President, developing strategies to address issues of diversity, equity, and campus climate. She has also served as Academic Director for Occidental's Multicultural Summer Institute.

Connie L. McNeely received the Ph.D. in Sociology from Stanford University and is currently on the faculty of the School of Public Policy at George Mason University. She is active in several professional associations, serves as a reviewer and evaluator in a variety of programs and venues, and sits on several editorial and advisory boards and committees. Her teaching and research address various aspects of race, ethnicity, nation, gender, culture, politics, and complex organizations. Dr. McNeely has numerous publications, including a variety of articles and chapters engaging questions related to women in science and technology, diversity, and polity participation. She also is working as part of a larger international initiative on democratizing education, development, and human rights.

Valentine M. Moghadam joined Purdue University in January 2007 as Professor of Sociology and Women's Studies, and Director of the Women's Studies Program. From May 2004 to December 2006 she was Chief of the Section for Gender Equality and Development, of the Social and Human Sciences Sector of UNESCO, in Paris, France. Dr. Moghadam is author of *Modernizing Women: Gender and Social Change in the Middle East* (first published 1993; updated second edition 2003), and *Women, Work and Economic Reform in the Middle East and North Africa* (1998). Her third book *Globalizing Women: Transnational Feminist Networks*, won the APSA's Victoria Schuck Award for the best book on women and politics in 2005. Dr. Moghadam's areas of research are globalization, transnational feminist networks, civil society and citizenship, and women's employment in the Middle East.

Deirdre M. Moloney, Princeton University, a U.S. historian, is author of *American Catholic Lay Groups and Transatlantic Social Reform Movements in the Progressive Era* (2002) and "Women, Sexual Morality, and Economic Dependency in Early Deportation Policy," *Journal of Women's History* (2006). Her current book project, undertaken as a Fellow at the Woodrow Wilson International Center, is titled "National Insecurities: Immigrants and U.S. Deportation Policy."

Lucinda Peach, (1956–2008). Lucinda Joy Peach was Associate Professor at American University, where she co-directed the M.A. Program in Ethics, Peace, and Global Affairs. Her publications include *Legislating Morality: Religious Identity and Moral Pluralism* and three edited volumes: *Women and World Religions*; *Women in Culture: A Women's Studies Anthology*; and *Ethics and Global Affairs: An Active Learning Sourcebook*, as well as articles on topics ranging from the ethics of women in military combat, reproductive rights, women's human rights, sex trafficking, women in Buddhism, gender ideology, law and religion, and global ethics.

Joanna R. Quinn is Associate Professor in the Department of Political Science, and Director of the Centre for Transitional Justice and Post-Conflict Reconstruction at The University of Western Ontario. Her current research looks at traditional mechanisms of acknowledgment and reconciliation in Uganda, following on an earlier study of the ability of truth commissions in Uganda and Haiti to bring about societal acknowledgment.

Louise Shelley is the founder and Director of the Terrorism, Transnational Crime and Corruption Center (TraCCC). She is a leading expert on transnational crime and terrorism with a particular focus on the former Soviet Union. She is the recipient of Guggenheim, NEH, IREX, Kennan Institute, and Fulbright Fellowships and received a MacArthur Grant to establish the Russian Organized Crime Study Centers. Dr. Shelley is the author of *Policing Soviet Society* (Routledge, 1996), *Lawyers in Soviet Worklife* and *Crime and Modernization* and an editor (with Sally Stoecker) of *Human Traffic and Transnational Crime: Eurasian and American Perspectives.*

Laura Sjoberg is Assistant Professor of Political Science at the University of Florida. Her research focuses on feminist theorizing of national security. She is the author of *Gender, Justice, and the Wars in Iraq* (2006) and *Mothers, Monsters, Whores: Women's Violence in Global Politics* (with Caron Gentry, 2007). She is the editor of *Rethinking 21st Century Security: New Problems, Old Solutions* (with Amy Eckert, 2009) and *Gender and International Security: Feminist Perspectives* (Routledge, 2009).

Mary Michael Tamia works as an HIV/AIDS educator for Community Based Health Care (CBHC), an NGO based in Tari, Southern Highlands Province, Papua New Guinea, which works to improve health and promote sustainable development. She is currently undertaking a project that will focus on the needs of AIDS widows and orphans in order to reduce stigma and to enable HIV-affected children to remain in school. She is also trying to establish a small AIDS hospice for people who have been rejected by their families and have nowhere else to go. She may be contacted at marymichael@rocketmail.com.

Ricardo F. Vivancos Pérez is Assistant Professor at George Mason University. He specializes in Latina/o studies, Latin American studies, Exile studies, and Feminist and Queer theories. His book manuscript is entitled *'Dangerous Beasts': Contemporary Chicana Poetics,* and his most recent works include essays on exiled and displaced Spanish novelists in the U.S.

Julie Walters is Assistant Professor of Political Science at Oakland University, Rochester, Michigan. Her teaching and research interests involve issues concerning complex organizations and institutional analysis, law and public policy, and social stratification.

Holly Wardlow is Associate Professor of Anthropology at University of Toronto. She is the author of *Wayward Women: Sexuality and Agency in a New Guinea Society,* which uses the life-histories of "passenger women" (the local term for women who exchange sex for money) to problematize dominant academic discourses about sex work. She has co-edited two books: *The Making of Global and Local Modernities in Melanesia: Humiliation, Transformation and the Nature of Cultural Change* (co-editor, Joel Robbins) and *Modern Loves: The Anthropology of Romantic Courtship and Companionate Marriage* (co-editor, Jennifer Hirsch). Her most recent research examines male labor migration and married women's risk for HIV, and she will soon begin a new project on the rollout of antiretroviral therapies in Papua New Guinea.

Amy T. Wilson is the Program Director of the International Development Programs at Gallaudet University and teaches research and courses related to international development with people with disabilities in developing countries. Her research focuses on how Northern organizations can best bring development assistance to disabled people living in developing countries. Her work is published in journals such as *American Annals of the Deaf* and *Deaf Worlds,* and in books including *Sex Equity and Disabled Students* and *Deaf Way II.* She recently completed a two-year study in 9 countries of an American NGO's work with children with multiple disabilities.

Introduction

Women's lives, human rights

Debra Bergoffen, Paula Ruth Gilbert, and Tamara Harvey

The social contract theorists of the sixteenth and seventeenth centuries began their political reflections by referring to a mythical state of nature where all men were endowed with natural rights and lived among each other as equals. This state of nature and its respect for natural rights were the standards against which the legitimacy of sovereign states was weighed. In the eighteenth century, the American and French revolutionaries transformed the mythical natural rights of the social contract theorists into political instruments. Before taking military action, the Americans legitimated their rebellion in the name of the inalienable human rights of life, liberty, and the pursuit of happiness. Where the Americans published their Declaration of Independence in advance of their attack, the French published their Declaration of the Rights of Man and Citizen after their triumph. Justifying their revolution after the fact, they sealed their victory by distinguishing the human rights principles that would ground their government from the principles of the illegitimate state they overthrew. Whether they justified their rebellions before or after the fact, however, the Americans and the French legitimated their particular political grievances in terms of universal human rights principles. They claimed that their battles were waged in the name of all human beings and that others had the right to oppose any government that deprived them of the rights of man.

It did not take long for women to exercise this right. They were quick to notice the gap between the universal claims of the American and French revolutionaries and the concrete realities of their lives. They did not enjoy the inalienable rights of man. By simply substituting the phrase "men and women" for the word "man," the women who wrote the Seneca Falls Declaration, exposed the gender biases of the Declaration of Independence. The word "man" only seemed to refer to all human beings. Their substitution created a scandal because man meant men. The men who fought for the rights of man fought against the idea of women's suffrage. They would not repeal laws that made married women the property of their husbands. Protective of their masculine privileges, they fought to maintain the gendered status quo. They argued that the natural law of women's subordination took precedence over women's inalienable human rights—specifically the right to equality under the law and the right to exercise their power as citizens. Here the women found a theoretical ally (if not a material ally) in the French, for though the American Declaration of Independence was silent on the relationship between inalienable human rights and citizenship rights, the French Declaration of the Rights of Man and Citizen was not. According to the French Declaration, it is as citizens that men are equal and possess inalienable rights. Political rights are the ground of human rights. Suffrage rights were the necessary condition of human rights.

Ultimately women gained the right to vote. They learned, however, that as a necessary condition of human rights, suffrage rights are not a sufficient condition for guaranteeing inalienable rights. Securing the rights of citizenship did not make women equal before the law or in the eyes of the state. To be meaningful, to make a difference in people's lives, human rights declarations must confront the ways in which social, economic, and cultural practices affect the ways in which the idea of human rights is lived and the ways in which the laws which guarantee rights can be undermined by social norms—even to the point of becoming an instrument of oppression.

In the eighteenth century, human rights were treated as internal and gender neutral affairs. A government that violated them risked inciting rebellion. A government that recognized them would secure the loyalty of its people. In either case, the people who mattered were men. In the twentieth and twenty-first centuries we have come to understand that human rights are of international concern and that women matter. One of the bitter lessons of World War II was that a state that nullifies the human rights and humanity of its own citizens threatens us all. One of the bitter lessons of the genocides in Rwanda and the former Yugoslavia is that when men feel entitled to use women's bodies in times of peace, women's bodies will become tools of destruction in times of war.

The United Nations Declaration of Human Rights reflects these hard won insights. In its "recognition of the inherent dignity and of the equal and inalienable rights of members of the human family in the foundation of freedom, justice and peace in the world," it made human rights a global issue. Further, in speaking of the rights of human beings, rather than the rights of man, and in specifically affirming "the equal rights of men and women" when it reaffirmed its "faith in the fundamental human rights, in the dignity and worth of the human person," it specifically addressed the issue of gender inequality. As the abstract principles of the eighteenth-century declarations exposed the injustices of kings and provided grounds for concrete political action, the United Nations' affirmation of the equal rights of men and women in its twentieth-century declaration exposed the injustices women suffer because they are women. It provided grounds for demanding that specific laws and concrete practices that support these injustices be challenged and changed.

The essays in this volume take up this challenge. They address some of the most complex and demanding issues facing scholars and analysts theorizing and researching women's rights issues. They identify the difficulties faced by activists and educators fighting to make women's rights realities in women's lives. They examine the effectiveness and limits of international rights instruments, governmental and nongovernmental organization activities, grassroots and customary practices, and narrative and photographic representations. Their specific case studies and theoretical interventions ask us to reassess familiar claims about causes of and solutions to gendered human rights' abuses around the world. In alerting us to the limits of human rights laws, instruments, and discourses, these essays also alert us to the ways in which appeals to human rights can become powerful forces for change. Thus, though they recognize that human rights protocols' cannot by themselves guarantee that women will be treated with the dignity they deserve, the authors of these essays are committed to the idea that human rights claims' can be fruitfully invoked in local, national, and international efforts to ensure that women be recognized as fully human.

As editors we share this commitment. We also believe that creating a human rights global culture will require a close working relationship among theorists across the disciplines and practitioners around the world. This volume reflects this belief. It creates a dialogue between theorists who tackle the complexities of human rights ideas and activists who deal with the challenges of rectifying concrete injustices. In creating this dialogue we are reaffirming the feminist commitment to the marriage of theory and practice. Further, in marrying theory and practice in a volume titled *Confronting Global Gender Justice: Women's Lives, Human Rights,* we are staging a confrontation between the idea that all human beings are equally entitled to certain inalienable rights and the reality that some human beings, because they are women, are routinely deprived of these rights. We do this not to denigrate the idea of human rights, but to point to their promissory nature. We see human rights laws and protocols as one of the ways in which the dignity of all human beings is recognized and protected. We find, however, that though human rights laws and protocols declare that these rights already exist, they do not. Or, more precisely, they exist as moral imperatives not as empirical realities. Like all promises, human rights declarations speak about the future, and like all promises, whether or not the future they envision will come into existence depends on our actions in the present. Whether or not the promise of women's rights as human rights is realized is our responsibility.

As promises, human rights laws and protocols are also tools. To be effective tools for global gender justice they must recognize the ways in which gender power structures abet the abuse of women. They must be used to challenge the denigration of women at the individual and structural level. For example, it is not enough to prosecute sex traffickers; we must also critique the ways in which women's gendered status makes them vulnerable to being trafficked. We must not only condemn genocidal rape as a crime against humanity; we must also critique the ways in which the ideals of masculinity and femininity make women's bodies available as weapons of war.

We must, however, be careful when we wield these human rights tools, for if in insisting that human rights must deal with sex/gender differences and if in focusing on the unique vulnerability of women to human rights abuses we push the idea of difference and vulnerability too far, we may find ourselves inadvertently reinforcing the very stereotypes that justified the abuse of women in the first place. The challenge lies in finding the right balance between insisting that sex differences matter and in recognizing that these differences do not, however, negate the common bond of humanity that men and women share, for the power of human rights discourses lies in the idea that it is because we share a common human bond that we are morally obliged to recognize and protect each other's inalienable right to be treated with dignity and respect.

This collection of essays seeks to achieve that balance by recognizing that questions of women's rights cannot be divorced from questions of human rights. To speak of human rights as a matter of gender justice means that achieving human rights for women requires that we attend to the concrete and complex conditions of women's private and public lives. It means that we must understand the cultural and institutional logics that support the inequities endured by women and must counter the logic that supports these inequities at the local and global levels. It also means that men must be looked upon as allies, for in framing women's rights as a human rights issue, we are arguing that neither men's nor women's human rights will be secured so long as the logic that justifies the denial of human rights to women endures, for this logic, insofar as it holds that some human beings are less human than others, poses a threat to all human beings.

Overview

We have divided this volume into five thematic parts: "Complicating the discourses of victimhood"; "Interrogating practices of representation"; "Mobilizing strategies of engagement"; "Crossing legal Landscapes"; and "Confronting global gender justice." Contributors to each part examine and assess current understandings of gender justice and offer new paradigms and strategies for dealing with the complexities of gender and human rights as they arise in international and local contexts. Our first part, "Complicating discourses of victimhood," treats issues of women's agency, motivation, and complicity with regard to a range of human rights abuses. The chapters in "Interrogating practices of representation" examine the tensions between local and international agendas as they explore the possibilities and limitations of representing human rights abuses for a global audience. The chapters grouped together as "Mobilizing strategies of engagement" discuss activist practices while considering the ways in which the effectiveness of these tactics, discourses, and organizational structures are often threatened by competing interests and demands. The chapters in our fourth thematic group, "Crossing legal landscapes," analyze the often vexed relationship between local and international legal mechanisms around the world (including the U.S.). In the final part "Confronting global gender justice," we conclude the volume with an interview with scholar, activist, and filmmaker Kum-Kum Bhavnani, titled "Configuring feminisms, transforming paradigms," not in order to bring these discussions to a close but to open them up to further reflection.

Part I: Complicating the discourses of victimhood

In some crimes victims are chosen at random; in others they are not. The crimes of sex trafficking and wartime/genocidal rape belong to this second category of crimes. The victims are predominately women and girls. There are cases where young boys are trafficked for sex and times when men who are tortured are also raped, but these cases are (to date and as far as we know) relatively rare. The statistics are clear. The customer who buys the criminally trafficked woman is a heterosexual man. The genocidal rapist is a male soldier. In both peacetime and wartime women are the specific targets of sex crimes. That women have been victimized by peacetime sex merchants and wartime rapists does not mean, however, that women are always and only victims. Here the facts are also clear. Women as well as men profit from trafficking women and girls. Women as well as men have given and enforced orders to use women's bodies as weapons of war. In combating the pandemic of violence against women it is important to ensure that exposing this victimization of women does not reinforce stereotypes of woman as victim, for, if we allow this to happen, we will ignore the resilience and agency of women who have been victimized, and we will either see women who traffic other women as pawns in a man's game or as exceptions to the codes of womanhood rather than as criminals who are part of the problem.

Reporters covering the March 29, 2010 suicide bombing in the Moscow subway revealed the power of the myth of woman as victim. The headline in the *New York Times* read: "Female suicide bombers strike at Moscow subway." Were the bombers male, it would not warrant mention. The following day one of the women bombers was portrayed as having been lured from her mother by a radical Islamic man whom she later married, and as having converted to Islam under his influence. Her suicidal act was described as an emotional response to her husband's murder by Russian authorities. It is never suggested that this act was a result of her decision, her politics, or her religious convictions. Her agency is muted if not ignored. Her crime was not so much that she killed innocent people in killing herself, but a matter of having been led astray by a radical terrorist man. Though he is already dead, her husband is the criminal here. However attractive the myth of the peaceful woman may sometimes seem (isn't it better to be seen as a passive victim of a man's influence than as actively responsible for a suicide bombing?), we need to see that whatever the circumstances, when women are deprived of their agency they are deprived of their full humanity.

The chapters in this part take up the task of combating the stereotype of the passive female victim by complicating the discourses of victimhood in two ways. First they insist on the difference between being targeted as a victim and being defined as a victim. Second they alert us to the fact that though it is women who are the primary victims of sex trafficking and genocidal rape campaigns, it is not always the case that it is men who perpetrate these crimes. Men may be the customers, but women, as well as men, capitalize on the sex trade. Trafficking is the only area of organized crime where significant numbers of women are perpetrators. Male soldiers may do the raping, but women as well as men give the orders to rape. Thus, the International Criminal Tribunal for the Former Yugoslavia (ICTY) accused Biljana Plavic, the Acting President of the Serb Republic of masterminding the Serbian genocidal rape strategy; and the International Criminal Tribunal for Rwanda (ICTR) charged Pauline Nyirmasuhuko, Minister for Family and the Advancement of Women, with ordering genocidal rape.

The first two chapters in this part, Laura Sjoberg's "Women and the genocidal rape of women: the gender dynamics of gendered war crimes" and Louise Shelley's "Human trafficking: why is it such an important women's issue?," alert us to these facts and to the ways that they have been represented in the law, the media, and the social imaginary. They note the ways in which confronting the fact of women exploiting women and of women using women's bodies as weapons of war belies our vision of women as nurturing, protective, peaceful, and passive. They ask us to confront a basic question: Will these facts disrupt the myth of femininity, or will they be represented in ways that reinforce the myth of woman as victim? They make it clear that this is not an academic question. The meaning we give to these facts has a direct impact on women's lives. They argue that, however uncomfortable it may be, the facts must be given their due.

In Chapter 1, Sjoberg finds that to date, the facts have been manipulated to support the myths. She notes that the accounts of women who have been responsible for genocidal rape campaigns first depict these women as monsters and then strip them of their agency. Once they are identified as active criminals (the fact), they are stigmatized as abnormal women. The fact is not denied—this woman committed this crime—but it is not allowed to disturb the myth of woman, since only an abnormal woman would do this. Representing the women in this way also legitimates myths of masculinity. It reinforces the idea that men are naturally aggressive, for though it is recognized as a crime, men raping women is not considered abnormal. Sjoberg argues that we will not do justice to the facts or to the women victims of genocidal rape campaigns unless we appeal to the theory of relational autonomy and situated agency to account for women's roles as perpetrators of genocidal rape. Women who organize rape campaigns are neither monsters nor unnatural; they are women who, like men who have access to power, have determined that women's bodies can be used to further their political agendas. Identifying this fact allows us to focus on another fact: genocidal rape campaigns, unlike domestic rapes, are not attacks on women per se; they are attacks on the women's ethnic and political communities.

Shelley's chapter shifts attention from rape as a means of fostering nationalist objectives, to the peacetime phenomenon of trafficking in women. Here women are targeted because they are women who can be profitably sold as pleasure objects. Asking us to consider trafficking in women as analogous to the slave trade, Shelley alerts us to the fact that, like slaves, trafficked women are considered an economic resource. She shows us that just as the image of the savage was used to justify slavery, the image of the passive woman is used to increase the value of the trafficked woman—she will do whatever you ask. Where Sjoberg showed us how the fact of women perpetrators undermines the myth of the passive woman, Shelley shows us how women activists refuse to accept their position as victims.

She describes the work of feminists in the 1990s in the Netherlands and Belgium on behalf of trafficked East European women and notes that in creating forums for women to testify against their traffickers, in launching sustainability programs, and in using the media to document the brutal conditions of trafficked women, women have made it clear that they will not stand by while other women are victimized and that they will use their power to empower other women. A victim who demands justice is no longer simply a victim. By demanding accountability, she shatters the silence that enforces the image of woman as victim.

Where Shelley documents the activist work of women supporting women, Donna K. Maeda in Chapter 3, "Transforming the representable: Asian women in anti-trafficking discourse," examines the tension between representing women as passive victims or active criminals through the lens of two cases: the Golden Venture Case and the El Monte Case, and the U.S. Trafficked Victims Protection Act (TVPA). Maeda argues that the discourses surrounding these cases, and the legislation inspired by them, unreflectively deploy Western liberal understandings of agency to solidify the opposition between victims, those who are trafficked, and criminals, those who are smuggled. With this distinction in place, the trafficked person is identified as worthy of our sympathy, support, and sometimes a chance to become a U.S. citizen. The smuggled person, however, is identified as a criminal and deported. Further, the prostitute, like the smuggled person, is also seen as having chosen her fate and also treated as a criminal. So long as this binary grid is in place, there will be no room for understanding the complex situation of the smuggled person or the prostitute. Maeda does not object to seeing the trafficked person as a victim. The problem is that the trafficked person must maintain her victim status to receive support and justice. This problem is complicated by the ways in which the image of the trafficked woman is racialized, for the trafficked woman is invariably imaged as an Asian woman who is seen as doubly victimized: once by her trafficker and again by her culture and religion. Our sympathy for the woman entails demonizing her culture. Maeda finds that an empowerment model of coalition work that examines the complexities of transnationality can serve as an antidote to this use of Asian women's bodies as signifiers of women's victimhood.

Lucinda Peach's chapter, "Sin, salvation, or starvation? The problematic role of religious morality in U.S. anti-sex trafficking policy," also examines the TVPA for its effects on women in general and Asian women in particular. Unlike Maeda, however, who finds that the language of the Act and the ways in which it is implemented demonize Asian cultures and racialize the image of the trafficked woman, in Chapter 4 Peach accuses the TVPA of distorting the problem of trafficking by seeing it in terms of Western liberal accounts of victims and criminals and conservative Christian attitudes toward the sexual body. This would be problematic enough if this law only affected the United States, but, given U.S. political and economic power the problem is intensified, for the conservative Christian attitude toward women's sexuality is at odds with Buddhist and Hindu understandings of prostitution. Where conservative Christians see prostitution as sinful, degrading, and immoral, Buddhists do not. They find that it can sometimes be justified; and though they see it as carrying negative karma, they do not vilify it. Older Hindu traditions were also more tolerant of prostitutes. Peach shows us the ways in which these religious differences have material consequences for women. Given the influence of conservative Christian groups, recipients of U.S. aid cannot employ prostitutes in the battle against AIDS and cannot use U.S. funds to support programs that protect prostitutes from becoming infected with AIDS. Further, these U.S. programs support raid and rescue missions that indiscriminately target women who are victims of trafficking and women who have chosen to work as prostitutes. Arguing that these moralist U.S. policies do not serve women's needs, Peach asks us to reexamine these policies so that the crime of trafficking can be addressed in ways that take account of the different religious values of non-Christian cultures and that recognize the difference between trafficked women whose bodies are criminally exploited and prostitutes who view selling their bodies as a legitimate form of work.

Part II: Interrogating practices of representation

Where the first part of this collection examines the question of the representation of women within the context of the specific issues of genocidal rape and trafficking, this second part takes up the broad question of the representation of women per se. The humanities and human rights scholar, Elizabeth Goldberg, suggests that "after the grave violations of human rights have occurred, the realm of representation is precisely the ground upon which the struggle for justice in legal, emotional, and cultural terms is waged" (Goldberg 2007: 26). In other words, after the actual event, all we have left is the representation, not as a replica of the past outrage but as a purposeful disturbance of the real. But what kind of representation? Does fiction, for example, have its own set of issues not applicable to the truth claims of factual and philosophical representation? Are at least some of the factual truth claims present in fiction filtered through distance, space, memory, and language? Is there a difference between literarily constructed texts (fiction, poetry, and theater) and the constructed stories that find their way into memoirs and testimonies, between texts authored by women rather than by men about women (or about men)? Is there an advantage to reading about the outrages of human rights violations as opposed to a strictly historical account and to other representations and expressions of violence against women in news and police reports, oral accounts, and documents produced by human rights organizations? How does "giving an account" of gendered human rights violations differ from "telling a story"? Do painting, photography, and other creative arts speak to the viewer more powerfully than the written or spoken word?

The philosopher Maria Pia Lara makes a compelling case for the need to utilize stories in order to understand the world better and to deepen our understanding of what constitutes a moral wrong. For Lara, reflective judgment is the result of using a moral filter (the narrative) to make the connection between a specific violation and the integrity of a human being. Authors are the ones who use creative language to articulate their judgment, but such judgments must then be validated by the public. Authors allow us to "express the unimaginable by creating linguistic terminologies that can convey the means to express what is unsayable" (Lara 2007: 14), provide us with a moral sense, and "provide new ways of interpreting human complexity" (16). Ultimately, "the literary effect of metaphors and of naming can disclose . . . hidden truths . . . as morally compelling signs that require all our attention" (18).

One of the problems that can arise with representations of violence, however, is that what film and cultural studies theorist Theresa de Lauretis (1989) calls a "standard frame of visibility" or "representability" can and does change over time, according to who is looking, at whom, when, and where. Susanne Kappeler had in 1986 already made a similar observation, finding that representation is too often interpreted merely as a reflection of reality, and people neglect to ask: "Who is holding the mirror, for whose benefit, and from what angle?" (Kappeler 1986: 2):

> Representations are not just a matter of mirrors, reflections, key-holes. Somebody is making them, and somebody is looking at them, through a complex array of means and conventions. Nor do representations simply exist on canvas, in books, on photographic paper or on screens. They have a continued existence in reality as objects of exchange; they have a genesis in material production. They are more 'real' than the reality they are said to represent or reflect. All of these factors somehow straddle the commonsense divide between fiction and fact, fantasy and reality.
>
> (Kappeler 1986: 3)

But even if one accepts to read fiction alongside of reality, is it at all possible to speak of violence and human rights—and any representation of violence and human rights—without discussing gender? De Lauretis, makes herself clear on issues of violence, representation, the body, and gender: "I . . . contend . . . that the representation of violence is inseparable from the notion of gender, even when the latter is explicitly 'deconstructed' or, more exactly, indicated as 'ideology.' I contend, in short, that violence is en-gendered in representation" (De Lauretis 1989: 240). Discourse analysis—as any form of representation—can no longer assume a gender-neutral position.

This second part of the collection, "Interrogating practices of representation," explores these issues of the interplay between "the real" and "the representational," between global gender justice/human rights violations and their representation in how they are read, how they are photographed, how they are written, and how they are told.

Louise du Toit interrogates the meaning of rape in South Africa in Chapter 5, "How not to give rape political significance." She explores possible meanings of the continuing high levels of rape throughout the past fourteen years of democratization. She supplements a Girardian frame for understanding violence with both phenomenological-feminist insights into the use of rape to bolster a threatened regime, as well as postcolonial theory which helps explain the expected turmoil involved in the foundation or establishment of modern, Western-styled states. For this postcolonial, Girardian reading of rape in post-apartheid South Africa, she uses South African philosopher Leonhard Praeg's framework developed in *The Geometry of Violence* for a comparative analysis of the forms of violence involved in the Rwandan genocide and "necklace" murders and familicide in transitional South Africa.

Independent photographer Kay Chernush troubles us with her photographs from Southeast Asia in "Human trafficking: a photographic essay." Human trafficking is fueled by extreme poverty and the economic dependence of women (and therefore children) on the one hand, and by cultural norms that devalue and commodify women on the other. It is also fueled by a seemingly insatiable demand for exploitive sex and cheap labor. It exists in every country and is a growth industry internationally, ranked along with drug trafficking and arms smuggling. In each country it takes different forms, but the general outlines are remarkably similar. The State Department estimates that 600,000 to 800,000 individuals are trafficked across international borders annually, a statistic that does not take into account the millions more who are enslaved within national borders, trafficked from countryside to cities, or the numbers involved in peripheral activities that feed the trade in human beings. In making photographs of human trafficking in its many different guises, Chernush puts a disturbing face on the statistics and headlines and tells the stories behind them.

But she also gives us some hope in her final photographs and in her closing remarks: "It is heartening and inspiring to see the heroic efforts of individuals and organizations that are fighting this scourge." She shows us images of grassroots efforts to combat child labor practices and modern-day slavery; she introduces us to charities that work to aid young runaways. And she ends with a marvelous photograph of young girls playing at a community-based intervention program. The representation of women and girls as resilient and hopeful clearly counters their more common representation as victims.

Ricardo F. Vivancos-Pérez writes about "Marjorie Agosín's poetics of memory: human rights, feminism, and literary forms" in Chapter 7, in which he explores the complex relations among Marjorie Agosín's essays, poems, and work as an editor of Latin American literary texts in the U.S. He first locates her work from the perspective of Latino Studies and Latina feminisms. Is she a Latina (feminist) writer? Although Agosín prefers to identify herself as a Latin American (Chilean) writer rather than Latina, her works are clearly linked to a Latino literary tradition that focuses on the interconnection between literature and social justice. He analyzes how Agosín occupies a unique position among U.S. Latino writers who choose to denounce and publicize human rights violations in Latin America and the U.S. Agosín's case leads Vivancos-Pérez to a second and more general question regarding human rights and literary forms: How can we, as cultural critics, read the literature of human rights? He proposes a de-centered position that moves across disciplines and structures of power in academia and the publishing market and that blurs the distinction between cultural criticism and creative writing. He bases his proposal on Agosín's own strategic solutions to these matters.

We end this second part with Chapter 8, "Digital storytelling for gender justice: exploring the challenges of participation and the limits of polyvocality," by Amy L. Hill of the Center for Digital Storytelling. In her essay, Hill describes *Silence Speaks*, an international digital storytelling initiative that provides survivors and witnesses of gender-based violence and other human rights' violations with a safe, supportive environment in which to tell their stories. Participatory workshops, which place control over content in the hands of the storytellers, result in short videos that have the capacity to challenge journalistic legacies of voyeurism and naturalized representation. And yet, *Silence Speaks* stories, like other cultural forms, must be viewed as having been shaped by and having contributed to the constellation of larger discourses that circulate and produce understandings about trauma. This raises important questions about the processes through which stories are produced, as well as the environments in which they are shared. Hill complicates opaque notions of "participation" by exploring some of the ways that power and authorship play out in the context of *Silence Speaks*. She also explores work done in South Africa, as a way of critically examining the practice of sharing stories in public arenas without careful consideration of the spaces in which they are heard.

Part III: Mobilizing strategies of engagement

Throughout her interview at the end of this volume, Kum-Kum Bhavnani stresses "movement and fluidity" in thinking about categories used to identify individual subject positions, disciplinary divides, globalization, and the workings of development. At her most optimistic, she asks whether it "is possible to dance a passionate dance of development, to turn development into a means for social justice for all?" The chapters in this part all treat in some manner the "dance of development," stressing complex individual negotiations as well as the broad figures traced on the global stage as these strategies of engagement are used, influenced, and interpreted by local and international forces.

Arguably, the U.N. International Women's Decade from 1975–1985 marked the beginning of what Radhika Coomaraswamy has called "the fourth generation [of human rights], radically challenging the private-public distinction in international human rights law and pushing for the rights of sexual autonomy" (Coomaraswamy 1999: 178). Inarguably, the mantra "Women's Rights are Human Rights" that took root over the course of a series of international conferences beginning in the mid-1970s has shaped the rhetoric, strategies, and policies of grassroot and international endeavors to address human rights and well-being. Manisha Desai has traced the narrowing gap between universalist and particularist claims within women's human rights debates from the International Women's Decade, through the 1993 Second World Conference on Human Rights in Vienna, to the 1995 Fourth World Conference on Women in Beijing. She, like Bhavnani, uses playful tropes of performance ("the Viennese Waltz," "the Beijing Opera") to describe the accommodations, arguments, and rhetorical strategies used to bring women's human rights to the fore such that, writing in the late 1990s, she can conclude that on

> a practical level, the international women's human rights movement has, almost single-handedly, made 'human rights' a household word throughout the world. From being a discourse of international agencies, academics, and some committed activists, human rights have become a 'power tool' available to thousands of grassroots groups for local organizing.
>
> (Desai 1999: 193)

In language echoed by Bhavnani, she insists that human rights movements are only effective when grounded on "a participatory, communicative process" and "a dynamic relationship" between "historically grounded universal[s]" and "negotiated, historical particulars" (193). What remains to be addressed effectively, she acknowledges, are the mechanisms of accountability (194).

The chapters in this part all enter the dance in some way, stressing strategic negotiations which are at once practical and idealistic, interested and compassionate. They also look more carefully at the mechanisms by which specific wrongs are addressed and both state and non-state actors are and are not held accountable. In them we see continuing efforts to work out strategies of engagement while maintaining a clear-eyed attention to the costs of these engagements.

The collaboration between Holly Wardlow and Mary Michael Tamia in facilitating AIDS prevention in the Tari area of Papua New Guinea has yielded a qualified success that in many ways resonates with Bhavnani's call for a "passionate dance." Addressing "Sweet Heart Sister Holly," Tamia writes optimistically that the AIDS awareness program she and Wardlow nurtured despite cultural resistance and financial difficulties will continue, but she also reports that "AIDS is becoming like a bush fire," taking two of her cousins among the victims. In describing their collaboration, Wardlow explains her efforts to do justice to Tamia's voice and perspective while acknowledging the practical factors that limited their ability to collaborate more fully on writing Chapter 9, "'Sweet electrical greetings': women, HIV, and the evolution of an intervention project in Papua New Guinea." Expedience and commitment informed Wardlow's and Tamia's involvement in this program as well as that of those organizations providing support, initially Porgera Joint Venture (PJV), a gold mine currently owned by Barrick Gold, and now a small NGO run by the Nazarene Church called Community-Based Health Care (CBHC). For her part, Wardlow writes that her initial participation was informed by a desire to provide a service to people who "felt abandoned by their civil servants, missionaries, and political representatives" such that they "would be less likely to consider me a valid target for crime and more inclined to protect me." PJV became involved at a time when their operations were especially threatened by sabotage in an effort to improve community relations. Rather than foregrounding sexual behavior and the use of condoms, Wardlow stressed the socio-economic situations that contribute to extramarital sexuality in ways that only implied the need for practicing safe sex. More recently, Tamia has put more energy into working with people living with HIV/AIDS, in doing so rethinking dominant discourses that read this epidemic as evidence of moral decline. Thus, the negotiations of this chapter attend to economic realities as well as cultural and moral discourses in ways that bring effective education and care to those in need.

Microfinance projects in their current form are the product of both local efforts to provide women with access to capital and global movements mobilized through the UN Decade of Women and similar international conventions. Since 1997, the year of the Microcredit Summit Campaign, the amounts of money invested in microcredit operations and the number of people reached have increased enormously; the 2006 Nobel Peace Prize awarded to Muhammad Yunus and the Grameen Bank are a hallmark of both the success and increased visibility of this approach to development. As Nitza Berkovitch and Adriana Kemp observe in Chapter 10, "Economic empowerment of women as a global project: economic rights in the neo-liberal era," focusing on women "help[s] mobilize legitimacy and support" because women both symbolize the very poor and have come to be associated with social change, suggesting that this is one way that the international summits focusing on women throughout the late twentieth century have led to mechanisms that bring about real change while demanding some measure of accountability both from donor agencies and recipients. Yet, while bracketing debates about the true efficacy of these programs in terms of the long-term well-being of clients, Berkovitch and Kemp observe a curious rhetoric of inevitability and natural forces shaping the increasing marketization of microcredit projects. In the last ten years, far more of these projects are undertaken by commercial banks, both because of the greater flexibility they can exercise compared to NGOs and because these are profitable endeavors. In the process, market dynamics begin to be the measure of social effectiveness even as more money goes into the pockets of for-profit consultants rather than NGOs and training programs become increasingly driven by profitability. Indeed, this emerging market in some ways depends on the continued oppression of women to the degree that their desirability as reliable borrowers is linked to restrictions in their lives that make it less likely that they will simply abscond. Neither an argument for nor against microfinance programs, the analysis of Berkovitch and Kemp reminds us that the frequently extolled dynamic nature of putting development to work rarely yields results that are simply positive.

Using social movement theory as a framework, in Chapter 11, "Algerian women in movement: three waves of feminist activism," Valentine M. Moghadam discusses women's activism in Algeria since the 1980s, first in resistance to conservative efforts after the death of President Houari Boumédienne to institute a strict family code that would limit women's freedom of movement and their family rights; then against the Islamist movement and the *terrorisme* that came with it; and finally post-*terrorisme* efforts to address issues related to amnesty and reconciliation, family law reform, and methods for addressing domestic violence, family abuse, and workplace harassment. By attending to the "political opportunity structure," Moghadam is able to trace a range of ways in which activists have been able to mount effective challenges to the state and other powerful forces within Algeria while providing a sense of the strikingly secular and leftist grounding of much of this activism. However, these women's movements cannot be understood solely in terms of dynamics within the state. Moghadam's discussion of the ways in which women's groups have drawn on the global women's rights agenda and transnational networks provides further examples of mobilizing strategies that negotiate discourses, movements, and opportunities at both the national and global level simultaneously.

The foundational assumption of the pedagogical strategies Nancy Chi Cantalupo outlines in Chapter 12, "Using law and education to make human rights real in women's real lives," is that "human rights law [is] an instrument of beneficial change for women, although not the only or a perfect one." While the undergraduates she teaches benefit from a more complete understanding of how the law shapes their lives, law students frequently need to be reminded of extralegal forces that shape the law and its implementation. All of her students in the United States benefit from a greater understanding of both the particularities and limitations of U.S. law and first-hand experiences of legal issues and strategies in other countries in order to develop comparative and international research projects. Cantalupo helps illuminate the limitations of U.S. law and situate it within an international context through her use of the *Gonzales v. United States* case, which is currently being considered by the Inter-American Commission as this volume goes to press in 2010. This case draws on the same theory of state responsibility that has been used to find the government of Honduras responsible for implicitly condoning disappearances carried out by its military to argue that the U.S. is likewise responsible when insufficient protections are provided in domestic abuse cases. In addition to a number of assignments aimed at providing students with a more nuanced understanding of both political and legal practices in the U.S., Cantalupo discusses some approaches to comparative legal studies, particularly through experiential learning abroad.

Part IV: Crossing legal landscapes

The title of this book, *Confronting Global Gender Justice: Women's Lives, Human Rights*, may be read as a question: Does the pursuit of gender justice through human rights mechanisms make a difference in women's lives? The chapters in this fourth part address this problem by examining the trickle-down effect of human rights laws, protocols, conventions, courts, and trials. They closely examine concrete case histories and analyze the ways in which human rights laws are, and are not, implemented, to interrogate the relationship between what the law promises and what it actually delivers.

As the first part of this collection challenges the stereotype of woman as victim, this section challenges the assumption that human rights instruments are unambiguously beneficial. We use the metaphor of the landscape to capture this ambiguity, for like a landscape which is always seen against the background of its horizon, the law operates within the horizons of time and place. It cannot be understood in isolation from the parameters which frame it. Different boundaries support different laws. The same laws have distinct effects in diverse social, cultural, historical, and economic contexts. Where Amy T. Wilson, for example, finds that the fact finding requirements of the Convention on the Elimination of Discrimination Against Women (CEDAW) are critical for securing the rights of women with disabilities, Saida Hodčić finds that the information requirements of CEDAW divert attention and resources from programs that actually assist abused women.

The law, especially human rights law, makes universal claims. To be meaningful, however, these claims need to resonate locally. Negotiating the terrain between the universal and the local is an ongoing challenge for those pursuing global gender justice. The chapters in this part examine the diverse ways in which this challenge is being met. Saida Hodžić in Chapter 13, "Seduced by information, contaminated by power: women's rights as a global panopticon," analyzes the interactions between the UN CEDAW committee, the Ghanaian state, and Ghanaian activists. She finds that the UN CEDAW committee does not support Ghanaian women's rights due to a disconnect between official state and activist politics, the inequalities of the global economy, and its focus on fact finding rather than effective action. Though she accuses the UN of creating a disciplinary regime where the production of truth takes precedence over support for rights activism and argues that the UN system of monitoring forecloses dialogue rather than encouraging it, Hodžić also finds that in its recent shift from asking for information about laws to asking for information about achievements in implementing laws, the UN is taking a step in the right direction. She warns us, however, that in assessing the effects of human rights instruments, we must remain attentive to the ways in which these instruments are contaminated by power.

Where Hodžić is critical of what she terms the fetish of information, Amy T. Wilson, in Chapter 14, "Human rights of women and girls with disabilities in developing countries," bemoans the fact of too little information. She notes that though CEDAW requires states to report on the situation of women with disabilities, little reporting is actually done. Lacking information, we do not know how, or if, women with disabilities benefit from CEDAW. The information gathered from the Convention on the Rights of Persons with Disabilities (CRPWD), however, gives us a picture of the scope of those affected by disability, the effects of negative attitudes toward those with disabilities, and the unique discrimination suffered by women with disabilities. Wilson uses this information to alert us to the ways in which women with disabilities are more likely to suffer from the effects of poverty, inadequate health care, armed conflict, and gender biased cultural practices. Though Wilson applauds CRPWD for the ways in which it has made the problem of women with disabilities visible, she finds hope for change in the lives of women with disabilities not in UN conventions but in a paradigm shift in the industrialized world where the focus has changed from what the disabled person cannot do to what she can do. Wilson finds this shift spreading globally and argues that with this shift societies are examining the ways in which they impose limitations on persons with disabilities, and persons with disabilities are engaging in local activism to ensure that this examination produces results.

Turning from issues raised by UN conventions, Joanna R. Quinn's chapter, "Gender and customary mechanisms of justice in Uganda," directs our attention to the limitations of human rights trials and truth and reconciliation commissions. Noting that these approaches often fail to heal the wounds of transitional societies and often lack the authority to take up the task of rebuilding societies recovering from violent conflicts and political repression, Quinn finds that customary mechanisms, that is mechanisms that draw on local customs and traditions, when used either in conjunction with or in place of official practices have been effective transitional justice instruments. In Chapter 15, she analyzes the implications of her qualitative investigations of the ways in which these customary mechanisms are used. Two of her findings compel our attention. First, though women have little voice in these customary mechanisms, they support the use of them if they contribute to establishing peace. Second, though these mechanisms draw on local traditions, these traditions are not static. In being called on to address current concerns, they respond by changing and adapting. These changes may create opportunities for women's voices to be heard.

The final two chapters in this part remind us that it is not only women in Africa and the developing world who experience the ambiguity of the law when it comes to confronting violence and discrimination. Women in the United States and Europe also find that the law can either support traditions that legitimate violence against them or challenge established patterns of discrimination. Deirdre M. Moloney's chapter, "Policing bodies and borders: women, prostitution, and the differential regulation of U.S. immigration policy," cites the parallels and notes the differences between early twentieth-century and contemporary attitudes toward and responses to violence along the Cuidad Juárez/El Paso border. Chapter 16 returns us to the questions of trafficking and race, for it documents the different narratives constructed around the women trafficked from Europe and Mexico. Where the plight of European trafficked women was seen through the lens of slavery and the women were sympathetically imaged as naive, gullible, and powerless, trafficked Mexican women were not seen as victims of the "white slave trade" and were unsympathetically figured as sexually exotic and seductive. In the early nineteenth century, however, it was the European trafficked women who caught the attention of immigration authorities, not the Mexican trafficked women, for they, not the Mexicans, were seen as a threat to the moral fabric of the United States. Immigration agents targeted European prostitutes for deportation but were fairly indifferent to the operations of traffickers who dealt with Mexican women. They did not investigate reports of rape and violence inflicted on these women. Though the racism of this different implementation of immigration law cannot be ignored, what also bears noting is that European prostitutes were seen as a threat, whereas Mexican prostitutes were not, because it was feared that the European women would stay in the U.S., and it was assumed that the Mexican women would return to Mexico. Much of U.S. anti-immigration activism today is fueled by this same fear, that is, that illegal immigrants (whatever their occupation) will become part of the American body politic. Now, however, this fear is directed toward Mexicans not Europeans.

Julie Walters' chapter, "The institutionalization of domestic violence against Women in the United States," brings this part to a close by turning from the violence inflicted on the trafficked woman to the violence women are exposed to in the course of their daily lives. She finds that the best way to understand the pervasiveness of this violence is to think of domestic violence as an institution. Drawing on the work of Max Weber and Emile Durkeim, Walters argues that by looking at domestic violence as an institution, that is, as a multifaceted system of meanings, values, rules, and symbols that appear to be impersonal and objective and that have the effect of stabilizing social behavior, we can better see the difficulties of dealing with violence against women and eliminating it. Her close reading of European and U.S. law over the past several decades shows how legal definitions of domestic violence shape and regulate people's behavior, and her analyses of common law, religious traditions, social norms, media coverage, and language reveal the ways in which an institutional approach to domestic violence captures its complexity. This integrative approach to domestic violence, in revealing and critiquing the regulative, normative, and cognitive structures that support domestic violence, also gives us the tools to dismantle it.

Part V: Confronting global gender justice

We thought it fitting to give a human rights theorist and activist the last words. In Chapter 18, Kum-Kum Bhavnani, interviewed by our co-editor Connie L. McNeeley, reveals the complex ways in which the personal is political. In weaving the story of her life with the story of her development as a scholar, and filmmaker activist, Kum-Kum Bhavnani shows us the ways in which universal human rights ideas and ideals can be translated into deeds that make a difference in women's lives.

Bibliography

Coomaraswamy, R. (1999) "Reinventing International Law: Women's Rights as Human Rights in the International Community," in P. Van Ness (ed.) *Debating Human Rights*, New York: Routledge.

De Lauretis, T. (1989) "The Violence of Rhetoric: Considerations on Representation and Gender," in N. Armstrong and L. Tennenhouse (eds) *Violence of Representation: Literature and the History of Violence*, New York: Routledge.

Desai, M. (1999) "From Vienna to Beijing: Women's Human Rights Activism and the Human Rights Community," in P. Van Ness (ed.) *Debating Human Rights*, New York: Routledge.

Goldberg, E. (2007) *Beyond Terror: Gender, Narrative, Human Rights*, New Brunswick, NJ: Rutgers University Press.

Kappeler, S. (1986) *The Pornography of Representation*, Cambridge, England: Polity Press/Oxford, England: Blackwell.

Lara, M. P. (2007) *Narrating Evil: A Postmetaphysical Theory of Reflective Judgment*, New York: Columbia University Press.

Part I

Complicating the discourses of victimhood

1 Women and the genocidal rape of women

The gender dynamics of gendered war crimes[1]

Laura Sjoberg

Since the end of the Cold War, rape and violence against women have been increasingly recognized as war crimes in international law (MacKinnon 2001: 897). While there had previously been an inconsistent history of the punishment of wartime rape (e.g., MacKinnon 2001), the 1990s saw jurisprudence classifying it as a war crime. Courts have also recently begun to recognize that *rape* and *genocidal rape* are different war crimes, where rape is a crime against its victim and women generally, and genocidal rape is such a crime used as a weapon against an ethnic or national group, attacking racial purity, national pride, or both.

This distinction has been made in litigation concerning the Bosnian conflict, where genocidal rape was defined as rape "with the specific intent of destroying ethnic-religious groups" (*Kadic v. Karadzic* 2nd Cir 1995: 70 F.3d 232). The International Criminal Tribunal for Rwanda also found that instances of rape can "constitute genocide in the same way as any other so long as they were committed with the specific intent to destroy, in whole or in part, a particular group, targeted as such" (*Prosecutor v. Akayesu* 1998: Case No. ICTR 96 4 T, 694). Accordingly, the court found that "the rape of Tutsi women was systematic and was perpetrated against all Tutsi women and solely against them" (*Akayesu*, ICTR 96 4 T, 694, 731).

Given the proliferation of rape as a weapon of genocide in the 1990s, scholars have begun analyzing the relationship between rape and racial extermination (Card 2003). This work, more often than not, defines genocidal rape as a crime where men are the perpetrators and women are the victims. As Frances Pilch describes, "the revolutionary changes that have taken place in this area of the law in large part reflect the growing mobilization and influence of non-governmental organizations articulating the importance of the rights of women" (Pilch 2002: 4). Similarly, Todd Salzman has characterized genocidal rape as "an assault against the female gender, violating her body and its reproductive capabilities as a 'weapon of war'" (Salzman 1998: 349).

The observations of genocidal rape as a gendered tactic are important and accurate. Wartime rape is an experience which is almost exclusively reserved for those persons biologically classifiable as female, and exclusively for those who are gendered female (and feminized) in political and social relations. Several feminist scholars have identified genocidal rape as a key threat to women's security (Hansen 2001: 59). Judith Gardam explains that "it is difficult to find any support for the view that non-combatant immunity at any time in its development has included [effective] protection from rape" (Gardam 1993: 359). Gardam contends that this is a linchpin of gender subordination because "nowhere is women's marginalization more evident than in the attitude of the law of armed conflict to rape, an experience limited to women" (Gardam 1993: 358–59). She notes, therefore, "in one sense, rape is never truly individual, but an integral part of the system ensuring the maintenance of the subordination of women" (Gardam 1993: 363–64).

The puzzle that this chapter seeks to address is one that, in some ways, interrupts the discourse of genocidal rape as a crime that men commit against women. While that characterization is, as detailed above, largely accurate, women have participated in, encouraged, and led genocidal rape. If genocidal rape is the most extreme site of women's marginalization, a key threat to women's security, a communication of domination, and an integral part of the system ensuring the maintenance of the subordination of women, how can we make sense of women's perpetration of such an act? Why do women commit an act that subordinates women?

With this question comes a whole host of other questions about women who commit genocidal rape. Why are they largely invisible in the international media and legal discourses surrounding genocidal rape? When women accused of or involved with genocidal rape do appear in politics, the media, and the courts, how are they characterized? How is the apparent contradiction between their participation in genocidal rape and its gender-subordinating implications resolved in those narratives, if it is?

This chapter looks at the dynamics of women's participation in the war crime of genocidal rape against other women. It asks both why women participate in genocidal rape and how their participation is consumed and presented in media and scholarly accounts. The chapter looks at these questions by exploring three cases of women's (alleged) commission of the war crime of genocidal rape. It concludes with a reformulated approach to the laws and norms against genocidal rape in the international community, taking account of women's roles in the crime not only as (often) victims but also as (sometime) perpetrators.

Women's purported motivations for perpetration of genocidal rape

Scholarly and media accounts present a number of reasons that women participate in political violence generally and genocidal rape specifically. In previous work, Caron Gentry and I have identified these as the mother, monster, and whore narratives (Sjoberg and Gentry 2007). The mother narratives feature women's motherhood as a key motivator for their participation in violence. The mother narrative has two general strands. The first portrays women perpetrators of genocide as nurturing mothers, whose role in the conflict is to take care of and provide for *their men*. The fact that those men happen to be participating in genocide (and therefore nurturing them is too) does not change the women's role in society or perception of their familial duty. The other strand of the mother narrative portrays women who commit genocide as vengeful mothers—avenging the deaths of their husbands, brothers, or fathers at the hands of those on the other side of the conflict.

The second narrative we have identified is the monster narrative. This story of women's motivation for involvement in genocide frames women perpetrators as severely psychologically disturbed. These stories portray women perpetrators as crazier and more monstrous than the men that they act with or alongside. Women's monstrosity, in these stories, comes from the sort of irrational anger only women could have, or feelings of personal inadequacy coming from the inability to marry or have children. The final narrative we have identified is the whore narrative. In the whore narrative, women's participation in genocide is either defined by erotomania or erotic dysfunction. The erotomania story tells of women sexually obsessed with and therefore controlled by men—of women's sexuality gone wrong and out of control. These women are portrayed as having committed genocide because their sex drive had gone out of control, and female sexuality at its worst is violent and brutal. The story of erotic dysfunction tells a story of a woman who has turned to violence because she is either unwilling to or unable to please men. These women are portrayed as having turned to violence because they were unable to function/serve as real women, which requires getting married and having children.

All of these stories about why women commit genocide share several things. First, they assume that the problem of why women commit genocide is a problem separate from the question of why men commit genocide (or even the question of why people generally commit genocide). Second, they preserve a distinction between women who are capable of violence and real or normal women who remain, as we have always assumed, more peaceful than men. Third, though real or normal women are seen as more peaceful than men, these stories depict women's violence as the result of the excesses of femininity. Finally, these narratives imply that women cannot both be victims of genocide (as a class) and perpetrators of genocide (as individuals or as a group)—it has to be one or the other. Often, both in the public eye and in the academic literature, the identification of women as perpetrators has been traded off against the recognition of women as victims.

This is all the more true because, if it seems *unnatural* for women to perpetrate war violence and genocide, it seems even more unnatural for women to participate in, lead, encourage, and plan the sexual violation of other women. If, after all, as argued above, rape is a cornerstone of women's oppression, women's participation in rape is a perpetration of gendered oppression—*by the oppressed*. Certainly, this has happened in the past (Jews who participated in the Holocaust, Tutsis who participated in the Rwandan genocide, etc.). Still, there is something all the more unsettling about it when the violations discussed are specifically sexual in nature. There seems to be an assumed consensus that women *would not* rape women, much less do so in the context of a genocidal conflict.

In the empirical snapshots of women alleged to have committed genocidal rape in this chapter, we will not find stories of women who are more peaceful than, more reserved than, or more sensitive than men. But we will also not find women held equal to men, even when they are committing similar crimes for the same political purposes. Instead, we will find women framed as instances of femininity gone awry—examples of why other women should control their impulses and stay within the mold of accepted femininity. In each of these stories, we will see the double move of sensationalizing *that women rape women* and distancing women rapists both from agency in their own actions and from normal femininity.

The LGBT (lesbian, gay, bisexual, and transgender) community in the United States has done a substantial amount to document and research violence that women commit towards women. As Lori Girshick explains, "woman-to-woman sexual violence is an invisible form of sexual violation because of our denial that women are sexual perpetrators" (Girshick 2002). In this context, while some "take comfort in statistics showing how rare woman-on-woman assault is" (Marlowe 1999: 401), others see the recognition of woman-on-woman sexual violence as a reason to reevaluate our understandings of what women are (and what they are capable of), of the meaning of gender subordination, and of laws about violence.

Taking a page from that analysis, we can see that currently the international relations community generally and those scholars engaged in the study of genocide specifically can be described as taking comfort in how rare woman-on-woman genocide and/or genocidal rape is. Those accounts that do recognize women's participation in genocide explain their actions in terms of the mother, monster, and whore narratives discussed above—in terms of the extreme expression of femininity gone wrong—while maintaining a space for the innocence of real or normal women. Several accounts have also read women's perpetration of genocide, genocidal rape, and other sexual crimes as a *reversal* of gender sub-ordination—where women have become the perpetrators, and are therefore no longer the victims.[2]

Three snapshots: women accused of genocidal rape

Biljana Plavsic: rape as a tool of ethnic cleansing

Biljana Plavsic was Acting President of the Serb Republic in 1992 and again between 1996 and 1998 (Mudis 2003). Throughout her academic (she was a biologist) and political careers, Plavsic had given many speeches advocating ethnic cleansing, sometimes even implying that rape was an appropriate method to achieve political goals (BBC News 2003). She "used her knowledge of biology to convince people to share her ethnic hatred" and argued that "Bosnian Muslims were 'genetically deformed Serbs'" (Sjoberg and Gentry 2007: 151; Fitzpatrick 2000). After the conflict, the International Criminal Tribunal for the Former Yugoslavia accused her of "genocide, crimes against humanity, and war crimes for a series of crimes, including rape crimes, committed by the Serb military, political, and government authorities" under her command (Askin 2003: 513–514).

Specifically, she was accused of masterminding and overseeing the Serbian genocidal rape strategy.

Accounts of Plavsic's participation in and leadership of genocide have consistently featured sexual language and sexualized stories, including allegations that she has sexual relationships with a number of Serbian warlords (BBC News 2003; Suljagic 2003). Her violence is also attributed to her maternal instinct to challenge men into masculinity, "goading" men into committing rape and other violence (Ansah 2005). Plavsic's involvement in genocidal rape was also blamed on her (apparent) madness, as she was labeled a "female Mengele" by Slobodan Milosevic (BBC News 2003). Another place where gender was prominent in stories about Plavsic was in discussions of her sentencing in which witnesses used her womanhood to point out her humanity and argue for mitigating circumstances and a lighter sentence (Mudis 2003: 717).

Pauline Nyiramasuhuko: first woman charged with genocidal rape

In 1997, "the ICTR established an incredible precedent by being the first tribunal ever to charge a woman with genocide and rape" (Balthazar 2006: 46; Harman 2003). Pauline Nyiramasuhuko, who had held the cabinet position of Minister for the Family and Advancement of Women during the Rwandan genocide, "was charged with two charges of rape: one as a crime against humanity and the other as a violation of the Geneva conventions on war crimes" (Balthazar 2006: 47). As a member of the Council of Ministers, Nyiramasuhuko "had been open and frank at cabinet meetings, saying that she personally was in favor of getting rid of all Tutsi" (Melvern 2004: 229).

The allegations against Nyiramasuhuko include being a key planner of the genocide (Wood 2004), instigating the strategy of genocidal rape in the conflict (Landesman 2002b), directly commanding troops to rape women before they killed them (Landesman 2002a), establishing a system of sexual slavery (Landesman 2002b), and creating new tactics of sexual and other torture to inflict on the victims of the genocide prior to their death (Landesman 2002a).

News stories and academic accounts about Nyiramasuhuko's alleged leadership of genocidal rape emphasize the special atrocity of woman-on-woman sexual violence. While explanations of her behavior are careful to distinguish her from regular or normal women who are seen as incapable of this sort of violence, they also refer to her atrocities as a case of her motherhood and sexuality gone wrong— womanhood at its worst. Her case has been especially sensationalized, appearing in the mainstream media a decade after the alleged atrocities took place. Miller argues that the case has received so much attention since "this sort of crime committed by a woman seems almost unfathomable because, historically, it is men who commit or instigate rape" (Miller 2003: 373). Several theorists have argued that Nyiramasuhuko's behavior debunks myths of "the special victimization of women" (Sperling 2006: 638), but Nyiramasuhuko has argued that it is exactly women's pacifism and victimization that proves her innocence, contending that "if there is a person who says that a woman—a mother—killed, then I'll confront that person" (Landesman 2002a).

Nazi women's violation of women prisoners

It is well known that several women served the Third Reich in Germany as prison guards, and that many of them were complicit in or actively involved in the terrible things that happened in concentration camps leading up to and during the Second World War. A less-emphasized element of these women's involvement, however, is the allegation that several of them committed sex-based and sexual crimes against women held at those camps. Two women particularly have been accused of crimes that constitute the personal and sexual violation of women prisoners: Ilse Koch and Dorothea Binz.

Ilse Koch was the wife of Commandant Karl Koch at the Buchenwald concentration camp, where she became a guard and allegedly participated in a substantial amount of torture and terror in her role there. The most infamous stories about her cruelty chronicle her collecting tattoos from the skin of women prisoners and using those pieces of human skin to decorate her house, creating lampshades and other decorations (Weber 2003). Even apart from that accusation (which has been contested), Koch's reputation was one of sadism and cruelty towards prisoners, whom she is alleged to have abused physically and sexually (Przyrembel 2001). Accounts of her torture of women prisoners were a key factor in her receiving a life sentence at the end of the war.

Another woman accused of sadistic and sexual violence against women was Dorothea Binz, who was a guard at Auschwitz. Binz's guard duties included watching over around 50,000 women and children prisoners and training other guards (Christie 2006). She is "said to have supervised gas chamber killings, shootings, starvations and freezings" (Sjoberg and Gentry 2007: 62; Brown 2002). She was accused, among other things, of beating, shooting, whipping, and sexually abusing women prisoners (Christie 2006).

The women who perpetrated war crimes in Nazi Germany were often characterized as the pawns of their husbands (who were often SS members), or as carefree teens who were unaware that their actions were wrong or had broader consequences. The ones who were given any agency in their violence were characterized as sick, demented, or emotionally unstable. One narrative blames feminine creativity (an intense desire to decorate?) for Ilse Koch's actions. These women, like other women in this chapter, were characterized as, on the one hand, having committed crimes that constituted genocide and sexual assault (genocidal rape was not yet a recognized war crime) and, on the other hand, as both incapable of the sort of intentionality that made this sort of thing a crime *and* anomalous among women.

Women's motivations for genocidal rape and sex-based violence

These stories about women's participation in genocide and/or genocidal rape tell different tales of different women in different contexts, but they share, as mentioned above, several elements. First, these stories classify women perpetrators of genocide and genocidal rape as separate, different, and often more violent than men who commit similar or the same crimes. In tales of Pauline Nyiramasuhuko, her crimes are framed as especially terrible because she was not only a woman but the minister for women and family affairs. Wight and Myers explain that a violent woman's gender is "the primary explanation or mitigating factor offered up in any attempt to understand her crime" (Wight and Myers 1996: xii). A woman's "sex is the lens through which all of her actions are seen and understood" when she commits violence (Wight and Myers 1996: xi).

As such, the question of why *women* commit violence generally and genocide specifically is treated as a different question than the question of why men commit such violence. Women's violence is often almost exclusively explained by gender-specific theories or gender-specified versions of traditional theories of individual violence. In addition to distinctions between women's commission of genocide and genocidal rape and men's commission of similar war crimes, women who commit genocide are distinguished from other, "real," women. "Real" or "normal" women are seen as incapable of committing genocide generally and the sexual violation of women specifically. "Real" women are peaceful, conservative, virtuous, and restrained; violent women ignore those boundaries of womanhood. Instead, the women on the pages of this chapter are the enemy from whom others, often innocent women, need protection. Their stories contradict the dominant narrative about what a woman is generally and about women's capacity for violence specifically. Because their stories do not resonate with these inherited images of femininity, violent women are marginalized in political discourse. Their choices are rarely seen as choices, and, when they are, they are characterized as apolitical.

Those with a political interest in the gender order cannot hear or tell those stories of women's participation in genocidal rape; instead, stories are produced and reproduced where women's agency in their violence is denied and violent women are characterized as singular and aberrant. Stories about women's participation in genocide "become systems of signification which are productive (or reproductive) of their subject women" specifically and women more generally (Sjoberg and Gentry 2007: 57). If violent women are seen as different from what *women as women* should be, then their existence can be explained away without interrogating the fundamental problems with the stereotypical understanding of what women are—peaceful, virtuous, non-violent, etc.

This problem is all the more clear in the treatment of women's *sexual* violence against women. If there is anything that women have in common, some assume, it should be reluctance to participate in the very sexual violence that many consider the linchpin of gender subordination. The ideal-typical woman is either asexual or sexually conservative; women who are sexual or use sexuality as violence are to be distinguished from normal women.

Even though women who commit genocide or genocidal rape are framed as aberrations to femininity, they are aberrations not because they have traits that women usually do not have, but instead because they are the dangerous result of femininity uncontrolled and taken to extremes. In other words, the excesses of femininity are blamed for these women's crimes—women could be genociders and rapists *if characteristics associated with femininity are allowed to get out of control.* H. H. A. Cooper writes that violent women possess an "intractable" and "cold rage . . . that even the most alienated of men seem quite incapable of emulating" (Cooper 1979: 150). In these accounts, women's violence is worse (and to be feared more) than men's violence because women are naturally emotional and unpredictable as opposed to men's presumed rationality and consistency, even in the commission of crimes.

Traits associated exclusively with femininity permeate the snapshots earlier in this chapter. The women who encouraged genocidal rape in Darfur were described as "singing" their support, a trait traditionally associated with femininity but gone terribly wrong in this situation. Biljana Plavsic's alleged leading role in the genocidal rape in the Republica Srpska is associated with her oedipal attraction to warlords in the conflict. Pauline Nyiramasuhuko's alleged commands to have women raped and killed are often related to her feminine jealousy, her maternal relationship with her son (a participant in the genocide under her command), and female monstrosity. The women who participated in sexual abuse of prisoners at Nazi concentration camps were framed in much the same way—their feminine desires (to please men or to decorate their homes) were carried out in extreme ways (by violence and abuse, making lampshades out of human skin). Women who sold women into sexual slavery in the Armenian genocide were characterized as doing so, at least in part, to shore up their positions as the only wives in their households. Therefore, though they are a blight on the purity of femininity, women who commit genocidal rape or other sex-based crimes in genocide are described as being motivated by things that could only come from their status as women—what is abnormal to women is not their femininity, it is its uncontrolled status and extreme expression.

Finally, these stories of women's participation in genocidal rape are similar in that they either argue or imply that women's perpetration of genocidal rape against women disrupts narratives of female victimhood. El Basri has argued that the case of Pauline Nyiramasuhuko brings us "the problem of misogyny with a feminine name" (El Basri 2004). Others have argued that her story demonstrates that women are no longer the victims of armed conflict (Drumbl 2005: 11). Barbara Ehrenreich has argued, using Abu Ghraib as an example, that women's participation in sexual violence demonstrates that feminism has worked—that women are now equal to men and do not need to be seen as victims of men's violence, but instead as potential perpetrators on an equal playing field with men (Ehrenreich 2004). In other words, there are those who argue that women's participation in violence signals the end of women's victimization in war and genocide. Still, many of the women who were discussed in the snapshots above *sexually* victimized women *on the basis of gender*. In other words, they perpetrated gender subordination.

Even if there was not gender subordination in these women's actions, women's participation as agents of genocide (or any other political violence) does not necessarily mean that women are not victimized in genocide or by genocidal rape. Instead, the media and academic community's difficulties in reacting to and understanding women's participation in sexual violence related to genocide demonstrate a need to reevaluate our understandings of what women are (and what they are capable of), of gender subordination, and of violence and laws about violence.

A reformulated approach to genocidal rape

Women's commission of genocidal rape invites a reconsideration of our under-standings of gender roles. The shock and surprise of women's involvement in such crimes comes in part from the inherited notion that women are incapable of violence and in part from the expectation that, even were women capable of violence, the last realm of violence that they would enter is the realm which combines gender subordination and cultural extermination. While there are so many realms in which we have come to see women as equally capable with men (e.g., intellectual capacity, competence in certain workplaces), the realm of personal or political violence is one where many people still see women as less capable than men. The women in this chapter prove that (at least in their individual lives) no stereotype could be further from the truth.

Stories of women's participation in genocide show that narratives about women's violence are often fraught with gender stereotypes and negative sensationalizations of femininity. They are, for that reason, inaccurate and gender-subordinating as they apply to empirical observations of women's behavior, which includes participating in genocide and genocidal rape. This is not to say that men *and* women do not commit their violence in a gendered world with a number of gendered influences and gendered implications. Instead, it is to say that we should think twice when we assume women's participation in genocide and/or genocidal rape is unnatural or anomalous.

Discovering that women commit (sexual) violence in war and genocide tells us that the stereotype that women are necessarily more peaceful than men is not an accurate one. As such, it invites a reconsideration of what it means to be a woman—if "women" do not (necessarily) have characteristics traditionally associated with femininity. Womanhood, if not bound by essential social charac-teristics, can be read as bound by living in a world defined by gender expectations and gender stereotypes. Gender is a set of discourses that set, shape, and define social and political life based on perceived membership in social classes. Being gendered female, then, as Catherine MacKinnon explained, is a subordination that can happen to anyone—it is only that we assume that it is natural for it to happen to those people we understand as women (MacKinnon 1994).

Along with the implied naturalness of women's subordination and the assumption of women's incapability, we can see in the stereotyped reactions to women's commission of sexual violence not only that women are expected not to violate other women—but also that there is some normalness to men's sexual violation of women. While rape generally and genocidal rape specifically are subject to some sense of taboo, the increased sensationalization of women's participation in genocidal rape demonstrates that there is some sense in which men sexually victimizing women has come to be expected or can be seen as business as usual. These realizations invite a reevaluation of our understandings of gender subordination.

Lori Girshick, writing about woman-on-woman domestic violence, explains "that same-sex abuse between women exists does not mean that we have to throw out our feminist analysis of rape and battering. However, seeing a framework where male privilege is just one aspect of the broader hierarchical power-over is more useful" (Girshick 2002: 15). The reason that women's violence seems so impossible to understand *with* gender subordination is that we have an over-simplified understanding of what gender subordination is. Women's violence seems to end or change gender subordination because and only because we understand gender subordination as something that all men do to all women. While feminist theory has been trying to complicate these ideas by highlighting differences among women[3] and demonstrating that gendering is something that happens both to men and women,[4] observations of and narratives about women's subordination of women ask us to articulate a more sophisticated understanding of gender subordination.

First, gender subordination is based on perceived membership in and relation-ship with, rather than some sort of absolute and actual membership in, sex classes. There is not just one femininity and one masculinity. Instead, there are ideal-types of masculinity and femininity based on class, culture, religion, race, ethnicity, and time—and other masculinities and femininities related to those ideal-types. Those multiple masculinities and femininities come together to set boundaries for what women should be and what men should be, situated in sociocultural contexts. These boundaries provide the content of perceived membership in sex classes.

Second, the impact of perceived membership in and relationship with sex classes only registers because gender subordination is fundamentally a power relationship in which those perceived as female/feminine are made less power-ful than those perceived as masculine/male. This power relationship extends through the perceived possession of gendered traits and the gendering of perceived behaviors and actions. A woman who commits sexual violence, then, is seen as at once "not a normal woman" in terms of her disassociation with traditional feminine behavior and an example of "femininity out of control" because that discourse can be at once disempowering and othering. Gender subordination, then, is not something men *do to* women or women *do to* women, but the result of a systemic discursive framework of expectations and power relationships based on perceived membership in sex categories. As such, women can be (and are) perpetrators of a crime that disempowers and subjugates women individually and as a class. Women's participation in genocide and genocidal rape does not negate the gendered impacts of genocide and genocidal rape.

The third step, then, is to reformulate international legal approaches to genocidal rape to accommodate the possibility of women perpetrators while still preserving the understanding that women are, as a class, victimized by genocidal rape based on gender. As Girshick explains, "the law presumes heterosexuality, and assumes a female victim and a male perpetrator" (Girshick 2002: 22). While the law does not explicitly label men as perpetrators, the frequent identification of women as victims sets up a presumed opposition with men as perpetrators—the implication is that if women *as women* are victims, then men *as men* are the persons doing the victimizing. The realization that women *as women* can victimize women *as women* (which is much more commonly accepted in everyday life than in genocide) offers the law two directions in terms of reformulation.

First, the law can change the assumed gender of the perpetrator by adopting a more nuanced understanding of gender subordination—maintaining the focus of the gendered impact of genocidal rape while making it clear that women can, and do, participate in it and should, and will, be punished for that participation. Second, our understandings of what genocidal rape is can change with the realization that women can and do participate in it. Instead of trying to add or fit women to theories, the terms of which were set before women's violence was considered, we could see the international law of genocidal rape understand the phenomenon of perpetration *as if* women as *both* perpetrators and victims mattered in theoretical formulation.

Perhaps feminist theory can lend a hand here. One of the primary concerns of feminist theory is the reconciliation of women's lives and masculinist interpretation of key concepts like interpersonal relations, the state, and the international system. The women in this chapter committed proscribed violence—specifically genocide and genocidal rape. Feminist theory asks why women are systematically excluded from explanations for individual (sexual) violence. Women are not usually present in these theories, and when they are, one of two discursively exclusive moves is made. First, women are included in a theory that defines individual violence in reference to masculine standards of individual conduct. More often, though, women are included *but gender differentiated* in these theories of individual violence.

In *Mothers, Monsters, Whores* (2007), Caron Gentry and I argued that a relational autonomy framework provides a basis for us to move beyond these problems. According to a feminist understanding of relational autonomy, human choice is never entirely free, but it is also never entirely constrained. Thus, the radical denial of agency in the mother, monster, and whore narratives is both gendered and unwarranted, but the (masculine) theories at the other end of the spectrum (including rational choice, psychoanalytic, or frustration-aggression theories) are also incomplete explanations.

Any move towards a gender-conscious theory of women's (or men's) perpetration of genocide would need at once to account for political and social motivations, gendered context, and individuality. Including previously hidden gender inequalities in the analysis of individual violence in global politics "allows us to see how many of the insecurities affecting us all, women and men alike, are gendered in their historical origins, their conventional definitions, and their contemporary manifestations" (Tickner 1992: 129). Recognizing that women sometimes commit genocide and genocidal rape, this perspective argues, is insufficient.

Instead, the problem will not be fixed until we reach a point where both the people and values associated with femininity are "more universally valued in public life" and "women's agency in their decisions is as recognized as men's agency in theirs" (Tickner 1992: 141). The beginning of this re-visioning is the recognition of human interdependence and relational autonomy, which shows that all decisions are contextual and contingent, not only women's, and all decisions are made, not only men's.

Feminist theory provides a way forward for the creation of such an understanding of individual violence in global politics. Kathy Ferguson explains that "praxis feminisms focus on affirmative intersubjective connections between persons rather than on autonomous or combative selves," which would cause them to suggest that individual violence be discussed in relational, rather than abstract, terms (Ferguson 1993: 69). An intersubjective theory of individual violence in global politics would account for both context and individual choice.

This could be operationalized in legal terms by a description of gender subordination as a socially fluid but systematic force of discrimination on the basis of perceived membership in categories inscribed with gendered power, and an understanding that human perpetration and victimization exist in a world where there is both relational autonomy (incomplete independence) and unequal power (gender subordination). As such, women, individually and collectively, can be seen as victims of women's perpetration of genocidal rape, while women, individually and collectively, are not robbed of agency by their classification as victims.

Notes

1   It is important to note here that this chapter is *not* arguing that women are statistically as violent as men, nor that women are in some way uniquely responsible for the sexual assaults on the basis of their gender. Women perpetrators are a *small* minority of participants in genocide generally and genocidal rape specifically, as far as the research can reveal. The Rwandan conflict is the only one in which there is any indication that even a critical mass of women participated in genocide; still, very few of those female perpetrators are alleged to have engaged in woman-on-woman sexual violence. It is also important to note that the empirical evidence surrounding whether or not the women discussed in this chapter actually committed the violence of which they were accused is vulnerable in each case, some more than others. As such, this chapter does not claim to explore women who *committed* genocidal rape, but instead women who are alleged to have done so.
2   See, for example, the work of Adam Jones (2002) and (2004).
3   E.g., the work of Chandra Mohanty (1988) and (2003).
4   E.g., Zalewski and Parpart (1998); Hooper (2001).

Bibliography

Ansah, T. (2005) "Genocide and the Eroticization of Death: law, violence, and moral purity," *Southern California Interdisciplinary Law Journal*, 14.

Askin, K. D. (2003) "The Quest for Post-Conflict Gender Justice," *Columbia Journal of Transnational Law*, 41.

Balthazar, S. (2006) "Fulfilling the Legacy: international justice 60 years after Nuremberg,"*Gonzaga Journal of International Law*, 10.

BBC News. (2003) "Biljana Plavsic: Serbian Iron Lady," 27 Febraury. Online. HTTP: <http://news.bbc.co.uk/go/pr/fr/-/1/hi/world/europe/1108604.stm >(accessed 1 January 2007).

Bloom, M. (2005) *Dying to Kill: the allure of suicide terror*, New York: Columbia University Press.

Brown, D. P. (2002) *The Camp Women: the SS Auxiliaries, who assisted the SS in running the Nazi concentration camp system*, London: Schiffer.

Card, C. (2003) "Genocide and Social Death," *Hypatia*, 18: 1.

Christie, A. (2006) "Guarding the Truth," *Washington Post*, W08, 26 February.

Cooper, H. H. A. (1979) "Woman as Terrorist," in F. Adler and R. J. Simon (eds) *The Criminology of Deviant Women*, Boston: Houghton Mifflin.

Drumbl, M. A. (2005) "The ICTR and Justice for Rwandan Women," *New England Journal of International and Comparative Law*, 12.

Ehrenreich, B. (2004) "Prison Abuse: feminism's assumptions upended: a uterus is not a substitute for a conscience," *Los Angeles Times*, 16 May.

El Basri, A. (2004) "Not so Innocent," *Liberation Daily*, 19 January. Online. HTTP: <http://www.voicesunabridged.org/article2.php?is_ss_article=196&id_rub=1&sous_rub=violence&numero=1. >(accessed 1 January 2007).

Ferguson, K. E. (1993) *The Man Question: visions of subjectivity in feminist theory*, Berkeley: University of California Press.

Fitzpatrick, P. (2000) "It Isn't Easy Being Biljana," *Central Europe Review*, 22: 2.

Gardam, J. G. (1993) "Gender and Non-combatant Immunity," *Transnational Law and Contemporary Problems*, 3: 345.

Girshick, L. (2002) *Woman-to-Woman Sexual Violence: does she call it rape?* Boston: Northeastern University Press.

Hansen, L. (2001) "Gender, Nation, Rape: Bosnia and the construction of security," *International Feminist Journal of Politics*, 3: 1.

Harman, D. (2003) "A Woman on Trial for Rwanda's Massacre," *Christian Science Monitor*, 7 March. Online. HTTP: <http://www.csmonitor.com/2003/0307/p09s01-woaf.html >(accessed 1 January 2007).

Hooper, C. (2001) *Manly States: masculinities, international relations, and gender politics*, New York: Columbia University Press.

Jones, A. (ed.) (2004) *Gender and Genocide*, Nashville, TN: Vanderbilt University Press.

— (2002) "Gendercide and Genocide in Rwanda," *Journal of Genocide Studies*, 4.

Landesman, P. (2002a) "A Woman's Work," *New York Times Magazine*, 15 September.

— (2002b) "The Minister of Rape," *Toronto Star*, 21 September.

MacKinnon, C. (2001) *Sex Equality*, New York: Thomson-West.

— (1994) "Rape, Genocide, and Women's Human Rights," *Harvard Women's Law Journal*, 17.

Marlowe, E. (1999) "Five Thousand Lesbians and No Police Force," *Feminism and Psychology*, 9.

Melvern, L. (2004) *Conspiracy to Murder: planning the Rwandan Genocide*, London: Verso Books.

Miller, A. A. (2003) "From the International Criminal Tribunal for Rwanda to the International Criminal Court: expanding the definition of genocide to include rape," *Pennsylvania State Law Review*, 108.

Mohanty, C. (2003) *Feminism without Borders*, Durham, NC: Duke University Press.

— (1988) "Under Western Eyes: feminist scholarship and colonial discourses," *Feminist Review*, 30: 61–88.

Mudis, D. A. (2003) "Current Developments and the Ad Hoc International Criminal Tribunals," *Journal of International Criminal Justice*, 4(3): 623–658.

Pape, R. (2005) *Dying to Win: the strategic logic of suicide terrorism*, New York: Random House.

Pilch, F. (2002) "Rape as Genocide: the legal response to sexual violence," Working Paper, Center for Global Security and Democracy, Rutgers University, available on CIAO Online.

Przyrembel, A. (2001) "Transfixed by an Image: Ilse Koch, the 'Kommandeuse of Buchenwald,'" *German History*, 19(3): 369–398.

Salzman, T. (1998) "Rape Camps as a Means of Ethnic Cleansing: religious, cultural, and ethical responses to rape victims in the former Yugoslavia," *Human Rights Quarterly*, 20.

Sjoberg, L. and Gentry, C. (2007) *Mothers, Monsters, Whores: women's violence in global politics*, London: Zed Books.

Sperling, C. (2006) "Mother of All Atrocities: Pauline Nyiramasuhuko's role in the Rwandan Genocide," *Fordham Urban Law Journal*, 33.

Suljagic, E. (2003) "Kisses as Bosnian War Kicked Off," *Institute for War and Peace Reporting*. Online. HTTP: <http://www.iwpr.net/?p=tri&s=f&o=163907&apc_state=henitri 2003> (accessed 1 January 2007).

Tickner, J. A. (1992) *Gender in International Relations: feminist perspectives on achieving global security*, New York: Columbia University Press.

Weber, M. (2003) "'Extermination' Camp Propaganda Myths," in E. Gauss (ed.) *Dissecting the Holocaust*, Berlin: Theses and Dissertation Press.

Wight, S. and Myers, A. (1996) "Introduction" in A. Myers and S. Wight (eds) *No Angels: women who commit violence*, London: HarperCollins.

Wood, S. (2004) "A Woman Scorned for the 'Least Condemned' War Crime: precedent and problems with prosecuting rape as a serious war crime in the International Criminal Tribubal for Rwanda," *Columbia Journal of Gender and the Law*, 12.

Zalewski, M. and Parpart, J. (eds) (1998) *The "Man" Question in International Relations*, Boulder, CO: Westview Press.

2 Human trafficking

Why is it such an important women's issue?

Louise Shelley

Human trafficking is an international problem that affects all regions of the world. Countries on all continents are integrated into this global trade. This is much more than a crime and law enforcement problem. Rather, human trafficking results from fundamental economic, political, and social problems in the contemporary world. The increasing economic and demographic disparities between the developing and developed world, along with the feminization of poverty and the marginalization of many rural communities, have all contributed to the increase in trafficking. Globalization has also resulted in the tremendous growth of tourism that has enabled pedophiles to travel and many to engage in sex tourism.

Trafficking has also expanded because the transportation infrastructure is there and transportation costs have declined. The end of the Cold War resulted in the rise of regional conflicts and the decline of borders, leading to an increased number of economic and political refugees. Furthermore, many rebel groups turned to illicit activity, including human trafficking, to fund their military actions and obtain soldiers. Demand has also increased as producers depend more on trafficked and exploited labor to stay competitive in a global economy in which consumers seek cheap goods and services, including easily available and accessible sexual services.

Human trafficking is an important gender issue because it is the only area of transnational crime in which women are significantly represented. Women are disproportionately the victims of human trafficking, particularly trafficking for sexual exploitation, domestic servitude, and marriage. Men and boys are more often trafficked as laborers and male children as child soldiers. Unfortunately, women are also all too often perpetrators and facilitators of human trafficking. Yet at the same time, women are increasingly mobilizing on the regional, national, and international level to combat human trafficking through nongovernmental organizations (NGOs), as well as by using the political process to push for prevention programs, the development of anti-trafficking legislation, and effective responses by the state to the perpetrators and the victims of trafficking.

Unfortunately for women and girls, human trafficking is the most rapidly growing form of transnational crime; for, in addition to being sexually exploited, women and girls are frequently trafficked for domestic servitude and other forms of labor exploitation. They are also trafficked for marriages and are forced to become child soldiers (Everts 2003: 149–58). Although the drug trade generates greater profits and is a more prominent activity of international crime groups, human trafficking is affecting ever larger numbers of people and every region of the world. The growth of human trafficking has been increasingly recognized as an international security challenge that has consequences transcending the political arena, as societies suffer demographically, and the profits of human trafficking are used by criminal and terrorist groups to sustain their activities. The relationship between trafficking and these threats to security and stability has made human trafficking more than a women's issue. Women activists have used the national security challenges resulting from trafficking as a way to mobilize male legislators and policy makers to action.[1]

Victimization occurs in all regions of the world. The greatest likelihood of trafficking occurs where women and girls are denied property rights, access to education, economic rights, and participation in the political process. Women and female children are particularly vulnerable to trafficking because of their low social status and the lack of investment in girls. The view in some societies that females can be used to help a family economically results in girls in many societies being sold off to repay a family's debt, provide cash for a medical emergency, or compensate for an absence of revenue when crops have failed. Often women are expected to go abroad to send remittances home to their families. Discrimination against women and girls is a major causal factor of trafficking not only in Asia, where it is most pervasive, but also in Latin America, Africa, and the Middle East where it is also prevalent.

In the recent past, much trafficking was internal to countries and regions. But with globalization, increased communications, and greater movement of goods and people, women and girls are trafficked greater distances to their point of exploitation. This recalls the slavery of the past where slaves could expect never to see their country again once they had been shipped from their homeland.

The rapid growth of trafficking is explained by several simultaneous developments internationally. First, globalization has not only increased the mobility of goods and people but has also enhanced the economic disparity between the developed and developing world. This disparity has been further exacerbated by the global financial crisis that began in late 2008. Women and children have been among the largest financial losers of globalization and the recent economic crisis.

Coinciding with globalization was the end of the Cold War. The end of the superpower conflict that characterized the Cold War has resulted in the rise of violent conflicts worldwide. As a consequence of the post-Cold War conflicts, millions of people have been impoverished. Women and children, displaced by these conflicts, become vulnerable to trafficking as impoverished refugees; for having lost male family members, they often have no protection from predatory traffickers. Traffickers in conflict regions can thus traffic many women and girls who have lost the protection of their families as child soldiers, laborers, and prostitutes ("Child Soldier Use 2003"; Interact 2004). One form of victimization often leads to others.

Peacekeepers brought in to stabilize these numerous conflicts often merely try to impose order and do little to assist the victims. When peacekeepers brought in to control the conflicts become active customers of brothels that spring up right outside their bases, they become part of the problem. In some countries, the organizations supplying or supervising the peacekeepers traffic women to provide "services" to the men (Mendelson 2005; Picarelli 2002). In refugee camps in conflict regions, some children are forced to exchange sex with the peacekeepers to obtain food that they need for their daily survival (*New York Times* 2007; *The Economist* 2008).

Defining the problem

In the year 2000, the United Nations adopted the Convention on Transnational Organized Crime (UN General Assembly 2001). Accompanying this convention were two protocols addressing human smuggling and trafficking. As of September 2008, there were 117 signatories to the Trafficking Protocol that came into force on Christmas Day in 2003 (UNODC 2000a). The Protocol Against Smuggling of Migrants by Land, Sea and Air had 112 signatories as of September 2008 and came into force in late January 2004, once it had the requisite forty signatories (UNODC 2000b).

The United Nations protocols on human smuggling and trafficking provide a common international definition of these phenomena. The United Nations' transnational crime definition provides the overarching framework for the protocols. It addresses the size, duration, and multi-jurisdictional aspects of the acts of crime and the groups that commit these crimes. Furthermore, it provides the flexibility to examine transnational organized crime outside of such traditional ethnic groups as Russian-speaking organized crime groups, Colombian drug cartels, Chinese Triads, Japanese Yakuza, and Italian Mafia families.

The Convention defined a transnational criminal organization as follows:

"Organized criminal group" shall mean a structured group of three or more persons, existing for a period of time and acting in concert with the aim of committing one or more serious crimes or offences established in accordance with this Convention, in order to obtain, directly or indirectly, a financial or other material benefit. "Serious crime" shall mean conduct constituting an offence punishable by a maximum deprivation of liberty of at least four years or a more serious penalty. "Structured group" shall mean a group that is not randomly formed for the immediate commission of an offence and that does not need to have formally defined roles for its members, continuity of its membership or a developed structure. . . . [A]n offence is transnational in nature if: (a) It is committed in more than one state; (b) It is committed in one state but a substantial part of its preparation, planning, direction or control takes place in another state; (c) It is committed in one state but involves an organized criminal group that engages in criminal activities in more than one state; or (d) It is committed in one state but has substantial effects in another state.

(UN General Assembly 2001)

The Convention and its protocols set the problem of trafficking and smuggling within a criminal context. This definition ignored the difference between women who are trafficked and women who, some women activists assert, engage in voluntary sex work.[2] Even though there was extensive debate before the protocol was adopted as to "whether prostitution *per se* is slavery and therefore equivalent to trafficking in persons" (Ditmore and Wijers 2003),[3] in the end there was international consensus on a definition that only examined the criminal elements of trafficking into prostitution.

The definition of trafficking in article 3a of the anti-trafficking protocol attached to the Convention defines the problem in the following way:

> The recruitment, transportation, transfer, harbouring or receipt of persons, by means of the threat or use of force or other forms of coercion, of abduction, or fraud, of deception, of the abuse of power or of a position of vulnerability or the giving or receiving of payments or benefits to achieve the consent of a person having control over another person, for the purpose of exploitation. Exploitation shall include, at a minimum, the exploitation or the prostitution of others or other forms of sexual exploitation, forced labour or services, slavery or practices similar to slavery, servitude or the removal of organs.
>
> (UNCJIN, 2001)

This broad definition of trafficking includes sex trafficking as well as trafficking into exploitative work situations such as domestic help, agricultural workers, and workers in dangerous industries as well as those trafficked as child soldiers. It also includes trafficking for adoptions, marriage, children forced to beg on the streets by their traffickers, as well as individuals who sell or are coerced into providing their organs for transplants. Of these trafficking offenses, only the organ trade, begging, child soldiers, and adoptions have many male victims. Yet women also are victims. Women suffer when they are forced to surrender their babies to traffickers or have their babies stolen from them. Women sometimes sell their kidneys to provide for their children without realizing that they will be crippled by this surgery.

Scale of the problem

In 2004 the U.S. government estimated that some 600,000 to 800,000 people were trafficked worldwide, of whom 80 percent were female, 50 percent were minors, and 70 percent were trafficked for sexual exploitation. The GAO (Government Accountability Office) criticized these estimates for not being based on adequate data. In 2006 the Trafficking in Persons Report (TIP), issued annually by the

U.S. State Department, attempted to provide alternative statistics citing data of the International Labour Organization (ILO) that includes trafficking both across borders and within individual countries. According to their data, 12.3 million people worldwide are in forced bonded labor, forced child labor, and sexual servitude (U.S. Department of State 2006: 6). Their report, "A Global Alliance Against Forced Labor," states that "9.8 million are exploited by private agents and 2.5 million are forced to work by the state or by military groups" (ILO 2005). The most numerous victims are in the Asian region, estimated by the ILO to number 9.5 million. They estimated that 2.45 million are victims of human trafficking, of whom about two-thirds are women and children trafficked into commercial sexual exploitation. But at least one-third are also trafficked for other forms of economic exploitation. These victims are more often men and boys (ILO 2005). UNICEF has estimated that 300,000 children under 18 are trafficked to serve in armed conflicts worldwide (U.S. Department of State 2007: 26). Those trafficked as child soldiers are most often male but not exclusively.

Forms and consequences of victimization

The consequences for women and girls who are trafficked are severe and diverse. Once women and girls have been trafficked, their future opportunities in life are often very limited. Trafficked children are deprived of the opportunity of getting an education at a crucial age. In many societies teenagers of both sexes and women who have been trafficked for sex and labor are sometimes deprived of the opportunity of marriage or of having children.

Women are often dehumanized and perceived as objects as a result of trafficking. Women who have been trafficked are often ostracized by their community if they are returned home even though their victimization is not their fault. As sexual services become more available in the commercial market, and as more men take advantage of them, the quality of relations in the family and in couples that have yet to be married is negatively affected. Families that have lost victims to traffickers may be permanently traumatized. Moreover, many trafficked women and girls suffer major health and psychological problems. Still others die prematurely of AIDs, venereal disease, other infectious diseases, drug overdoses, suicide, and homicide. In the United States, the FBI estimates that trafficking victims survive seven years after they enter prostitution because of the previously identified causes of death (FBI). Children of women trafficked into prostitution, particularly girls in India and other parts of Asia, may themselves be forced to become prostitutes as a result of their mothers' deaths or debts to the traffickers. This results in intergenerational prostitution (Gupta 2005).

Today, few female victims of sexual trafficking are repatriated after having been trafficked because of the limited chances of rescue and the significant costs for transport to their home communities. Those who are sent home or are able to return may only go home to die or they may be so psychologically damaged that they become an enormous burden to their home communities. This is especially true in rural areas where trafficking victims return from the fast-paced life of cities where they have often become addicted to alcohol and drugs. Without treatment programs for their addictions in their home communities, the victims may spread the problem of drug abuse.

Trafficking also affects the financial welfare of low income women generally. Women trafficked into domestic servitude reduce the salary levels of other women and the quality of their work environment because many employers know they have access to a cheaper and more malleable work force. Women and girls who have been trafficked often work in the most dangerous sectors of the economy where scant attention is paid to health and safety conditions. As a result there are much higher risks of accident and permanent injury because of the limited access of trafficking victims to any form of medical care.

Women and girls who are sexually trafficked suffer a wide range of victimization. Many young women who resist their traffickers die each year; for example, the dozens of skeletons of young women found in a pit in 2007 in Nizhyi Tagil in the Urals region of Russia (*Komsomolskaya Pravada* 2007). Before being sold to clients, women and girls may be beaten and tortured by their traffickers to break their will. In some countries, girls who refuse to serve sexual clients even though the girls are ill may be subject to torture. This has been documented in Cambodia where young girls are subjected to electric shock in basements of brothels, at times dying from this abuse (Kristof 2009). Eastern European criminals have tortured women and girls to death in front of others to induce compliance.

Once engaged in prostitution, trafficked women and girls in brothels in many countries may be forced to serve as many as thirty clients a day during a 12 to 14-hour work day without any days off for menstruation or illness. Unlike the women who work in the regulated brothels of some Western European countries where their clients are required to use condoms, trafficked women are often denied the right to protect themselves. Young girls are especially vulnerable to lesions that compound the likelihood of sexually transmitted diseases and AIDS infection. Girls and women who become pregnant can be forced to have sex while pregnant, whereas others are forced to have abortions. In some cases, multiple abortions make trafficking victims sterile.

In certain regions of the world, such as India and Africa where rates of HIV transmission are particularly high among sex workers, mortality often occurs at a very young age (Farr 2005: 228–30). Often the trafficked women leave behind young children whose mothers' early deaths leave them no means of survival outside of the brothels where they are raised. Falling into the hands of the brothel keepers or pimps who controlled their now deceased mothers, these children have no futures outside of the world of begging, forced prostitution, or crime.

Many who have been sexually trafficked, if they survive, are permanently psychologically damaged suffering post-traumatic stress, painful flashbacks, anxiety, fear, sleep disorders, and panic attacks as a result of the conditions described above. For many others there are common problems of loss of appetite and controlling aggression, self-blame, thoughts of suicide, self-harm, and constant crying. One woman articulately summed this up: "I feel like they have taken my smile and I can never have it back" (Zimmerman et al. 2006).

Violent abuse is not limited to women trafficked into sexual servitude. Women sold into domestic servitude may be subject to severe beatings and food deprivation, and may be locked inside homes for years on end. They may be forced to work long hours without breaks. They may also be subject to sexual abuse by male family members of the households in which they work. In many parts of the world, exploited women have no recourse against exploitation either because there are no labor laws to protect them or because their illegal status deprives them of any access to justice.

Women may be trafficked into marriage to men they do not want to marry. For example, women who escape from North Korea into China may be trafficked into marriages with Chinese men who will buy women because of the sexual imbalance that presently exists in China as a result of the one child policy (CECC 2006). In the United States, Hmong refugees import women to the United States as second wives (MOJP/MSAC 2006). In both the Chinese and the American cases, these women are not really wives but often merely domestic slaves who are vehicles for reproduction.

Women are also trafficked to work in factories where they can be locked in at night to prevent their escape. Physical abuse is meted out to women who fail to produce goods at the high production norms established by the factory owners. Often they work in factories with unsafe equipment or with toxic fumes that can later result in fatal illnesses (Bales 1999: 202).

Female children are trafficked into particular industries where their small size allows them to perform more effectively. For example, girls are trafficked into the carpet industry in Nepal. While engaged in carpet weaving, they may be sexually abused (ILO/IPEC 2004). Therefore, the labor trafficking may be only the initial form of exploitation as they may be subsequently trafficked into full-time sexual slavery when they are older.

Male and female children are trafficked as beggars. Their traffickers beat them and deprive them of food if they do not bring home sufficient money each day. In India, the beggar mafia deliberately maims children to make them better beggars, often with the complicity of members of the medical profession.[4] This phenomenon has also recently been observed in Great Britain with beggar children from Eastern Europe (Harvey 2008).

In Africa and Latin America, girls, like boys, have been trafficked as child soldiers. Forced to bear arms and even kill family members, they are traumatized by the violence to which they are exposed and in which they are forced to participate.

Women and girls may suffer secondary victimization even if they are rescued from those who originally exploited them. Despite the adoption of the UN protocol that defines trafficked people as "victims," many individual states, even advanced Western democracies, have not changed their laws or procedures sufficiently to protect the rights of trafficked persons. In many countries, the resources and the enforcement mechanisms are inadequate to protect the victims. In some countries, protection is possible only if the victim agrees to participate in a criminal investigation against her or his traffickers. Many states have inadequate witness protection programs and make no provisions to protect the families of the trafficking victims, often in the home country, who may be endangered by the testimony that is given abroad by their exploited family member. Moreover, many countries make no provisions to grant residence permits to those who have testified against their traffickers. Therefore, the trafficking victim remains a vulnerable individual who may subsequently face deportation and even imprisonment. The victim's courageous act of testifying against his/her traffickers, which serves the interests of the host country, may subsequently result in the victim's death at the hand of crime groups or even that of his or her family members.

Women as traffickers

There are a great variety of human traffickers. These include criminal groups and their corrupt government collaborators, corporations seeking cheap labor who contract with human smugglers and traffickers, warlords, insurgents, and terrorists who fund their struggles through human trafficking. Yet this is the only area of organized and transnational crime in which women are significant perpetrators. Most often, women work with crime groups in moving people and are less involved in recruitment of labor victims for factories or with the trafficking associated with warlords and terrorists (Aronowitz 2009: 52–55).

Women are involved in all stages of trafficking—as recruiters, entrepreneurs, and managers of brothels or escort services. Women play an especially important role in human smuggling and trafficking in Asia where organized crime assumes such a large role. In China, some women are significant human smugglers. Women have been identified as active recruiters in the exploitation of girls and women in brothels in India, Cambodia, and Indonesia. Women become socialized into the culture of exploitation and seek to strive to achieve the status of a trafficker. The following quotation illustrates this phenomenon:

> In India, with its numerous brothels and victims, there is a specific name for the women who recruit and control the trafficked girls. The *nayika*, a term equivalent to boss lady, occupies a role absolutely pivotal to the brothel system. Usually older ex-prostitutes, they have survived by saving money and gradually acquiring girls of their own. Several *nayikas* might rent space in one brothel; the organizational effect of this is akin to cell structures used in spy networks to isolate individual operatives and frustrate outside penetration. The girls are not only physically and psychologically cut off from the outside world, but they are also divided amongst themselves by the pressure of competition with girls working for other *nayikas*.
>
> (*The Hindu* 2006)

Elsewhere in Asia, women are also important in the smuggling and trafficking business. The notorious chief of an entire Chinese smuggling organization, Sister Ping, was recently sentenced to thirty-five years' imprisonment for conspiracy to commit alien smuggling, other smuggling charges, and money laundering (ICE).

Her smuggling operations resulted in deaths on a vessel named the *Golden Venture*. After years of careful investigative work on several continents, it was determined that she ran a multinational smuggling organization with tens of millions of dollars in profits. The profit level of her business would be acceptable for a mid-sized drug trafficker (Bernstein 2006). Zhang, Chin, and Miller suggest that Chinese women make such successful smugglers because there is limited violence in Chinese smuggling and women excel at networks that are the key to Chinese recruitment (Zhang et al. 2007: 699).

Yet the role of women in human trafficking is not limited to Asia. Women often function as trafficking recruiters in Nigeria and other parts of Africa, in Eastern Europe and the former Soviet Union, as well as in Latin America. Participation in trafficking as a trafficker may seem a rational choice for a woman in a desperate situation as was the case after the collapse of the USSR when many women were trafficked to Turkey.[5] Often it is older women who no longer can function as prostitutes who recruit the next generation. For others, a visit home is paid for by their traffickers on the condition that they bring back other women to serve the trafficker. Because so much trafficking is done within circles of acquaintances, the trust that women and families have in women they know facilitates the trafficking.

Women as activists

Mobilization against organized crime is rarely gender specific. The anti-Mafia movement in Italy was led by men and women. Community efforts to combat the drug trade involve different sectors of society. But the rise of human trafficking in the past two decades has provoked a strong reaction among women in many countries and diverse cultures.[6] It is this aspect of transnational crime that has mobilized women to stand up to organized crime.

Female activism against human trafficking rarely assumes the form of mass public protests. Instead, women have used the legislative process at the national level, pressured multilateral organizations and formed nongovernmental organizations in many countries to help victims and to mobilize anti-trafficking activism. Women have organized in both advanced Western democracies, transitional countries from the socialist system, poor developing countries, and even in some highly authoritarian countries where any form of activism involves great personal risk and courage.

The most visible mobilization against transnational trafficking occurred in the early 1990s when women's groups in the Netherlands and in Belgium began to pressure government to act against the rise in sexual trafficking of women from Eastern Europe to their countries. Appalled by the violence experienced by these women, they got the Belgian parliament to hold hearings in 1992.[7] These hearings tried to assess the extent of the problem and initiate a governmental response.

Female mobilization against trafficking has been particularly focused on the phenomenal growth in women and girls trafficked for sexual exploitation. Much less attention has been paid to other forms of exploitation such as labor trafficking, forced marriages, trafficking for adoptions, and organ trafficking. Women of diverse religions, cultures and political views have often united on the national and international level to press for governmental action. For example, in the United States, the Victims of Trafficking and Violence Protection Act was passed in 2000 at the impetus of a coalition of conservative Christian and liberal members of Congress.[8] A similarly diverse international coalition of women was instrumental in securing passage of the Protocol on Trafficking at the level of the United Nations and pushing for the subsequent concerted UN strategy against human trafficking.

The rise of service-oriented NGOs, often run by women in many countries around the world, has helped to run prevention campaigns to educate potential victims and to assist the victims of traffickers. Women in many regions of the world have gone into schools and local communities trying to raise awareness of what trafficking is and to warn of the ploys used by the traffickers against the socially vulnerable.

Women running these programs have often undertaken Herculean efforts to find funds to sustain their programs. These programs are invaluable as they provide training that will allow women to survive financially and prevent retrafficking. Some programs in Asia have even managed to secure computer training for former trafficking victims (Step Up Program; Gupta 2008). The activism and energy of these women working against enormous obstacles recalls the anti-slavery activists of the nineteenth century.

Working in the brothels of India, among runaway girls who have been trafficked into prostitution in Los Angeles, California, or with women who have been trafficked to Eastern Europe, women have developed sustainable programs to assist victims recovering from the psychological damage of trafficking and to equip them for new lives.[9] Women in other instances work with victims, helping them prepare testimony that will be presented in cases against the traffickers.

Women cinematographers have used their skills to produce emotionally moving films that help convey the suffering of sexual trafficking victims, thereby mobilizing women to action. Among the most notable of these are *Sex Slaves* produced by a Canadian filmmaker who documents trafficking between Moldova, Ukraine, and Turkey. Ruchira Gupta's prizewinning film examined trafficking between Nepal and India and within the brothels of India. *Born into Brothels* documents the empowerment of young people raised in Indian brothels. *Chants of Lotus*, an Indonesian film based on a typical situation, shows the recruitment of a young girl into sexual slavery by a friend of her mother. These films, which have reached wide audiences, have been important tools for galvanizing anti-trafficking efforts and for making policy makers understand the complexity of countering these problems that are affected by poverty, caste, class, political conflict, and gender discrimination.

Women have done far less to protect the millions of victims of labor trafficking who are probably the most numerous of victims, particularly in Asia where they may represent as much as three-quarters of all victims. It is sexual slavery today that has mobilized women as did the state-sanctioned slavery of past centuries.

Conclusion

Human trafficking has grown phenomenally in recent decades and has affected millions of women and girls in every region of the world. Despite greater attention to this problem on the international arena, the problem continues to grow as a result of current economic and political problems of the world and the low status of women that makes women particularly vulnerable to exploitation. Exploitation is particularly acute in societies where women are seen as a means of contributing to the financial security of the family and the community. Large numbers of girls and women are trafficked into labor, sexual exploitation, and forced marriages and serve as child soldiers. There is no region in the world where women do not suffer this exploitation. The consequences are devastating for women—acute physical and mental suffering and, often, premature death. But there are also costs for the larger society that include serious health problems, demographic declines, and the entrenchment of organized crime within the community and the perpetuation of conflict.

Human trafficking has devastating consequences in many regions of the world. In populations with low birthrates, the consequences are more apparent than in regions where the high birthrate contributes to the trafficking. The demographic consequences are most severe in the former communist countries and in China. Because of the large-scale human smuggling from Fukian and other southern provinces of China to the United States and Western Europe, there are now villages that are literally drained of people (Keefe 2009). Trafficking deprives communities in other regions of a significant proportion of their women. In the communities of the Hill Tribes in Northern Thailand, a favorite source of Thai trafficking, there are almost no young women between ages 16 and 25.[10]

The situation is also acute in many of the former socialist states that are epicenters of trafficking. Moldova, Ukraine, and Russia, which have lost hundreds of thousands of women to sexual and labor trafficking, were already facing an acute demographic crisis. The women who are trafficked are generally in the 18 to 25 age range; therefore, their loss compounds the problems of low birthrates. These women do not give birth to children in their own countries, and many of them are unlikely to return, or if they do, may not prove to be suitable and effective mothers because of the psychological damage they have incurred.

The health consequences are devastating for girls and women as well as the rest of society. Sex trafficking infects many women and their customers with HIV and venereal diseases, but those trafficked into labor may also spread tuberculosis, scabies, and other infectious diseases. Those who are trafficked into sexual labor face particular risks because they cannot protect themselves (Beyrer and Stachowiak 2003: 105–17).

The trafficking of children as child soldiers helps perpetuate conflict by providing disposable foot soldiers for wars. The trafficking of women in conflict regions provides financial support for the criminal organizations that embed themselves in the society in periods of societal chaos.

Women, as much as they are victims, are also facilitators of this human trade. In China, women often head large smuggling operations. But more often, women who have aged as prostitutes, recruit the next generation of trafficking victims. This is the only area of organized crime in which women assume a major role. They recruit women, exploit them, often through violent means, and can sometimes profit significantly from this trade. This is a gender aspect of human trafficking that is all too rarely mentioned. Women's exploitation of other women must be addressed if we are to break the cycle of trafficking.

Women have mobilized to combat sexual trafficking. Women's sense of horror at the sexual exploitation of girls and other women seems to be an important element of their desire to mobilize. Female activism has been directed at prevention, policy response, and treatment of the victim. Women have also worked, where possible, with law enforcement to seek prosecutions against the traffickers. This is one area of anti-organized crime activity in which women assume a significant role, because without the emotional, physical, and financial support provided to victims, women are unable and often unwilling to testify against their traffickers. Therefore, in the United States, Europe, and in some other locales, non-governmental organizations staffed by women work with the police to help punish the traffickers.

Despite this activism on the part of many dedicated women and the greater commitment of the international community to act, there is little that is stemming the growth in trafficking because of the enormous demand. Society must work on many levels to stem the demand for sexual and labor trafficking, child soldiers, and other exploited women mentioned in this essay. Toward this end we must work to create conditions that foster gender equality and respect for women. We must not, however, neglect the economic side of the equation.

The economic crisis that began in 2008 will exacerbate the trafficking problem in the future. Although it has temporarily suppressed demand for trafficked people for sexual exploitation as men have less disposable income, as well as people to engage in cheap industrial production because of the reduced demand for consumer goods, the long-term prognosis for demand reduction is situational rather than tied to a long-term strategy to reduce trafficking.

Because so much of trafficking is caused by poverty, the economic crisis has exacerbated the causes of trafficking. This crisis has especially hit the poor in the world who lack a social safety net. This has resulted in many girls being pulled out of school, given less to eat, and forced to work at young ages to support their families.[11] Without the skills to survive in the world, these girls will be especially vulnerable to traffickers in the future. The continued and increasing economic demand and ready supply of women and girls lead to the unfortunate conclusion that there will be an increase in trafficking in the future.

Notes

1 See for example the discussion of Russia in Pridemore, W. A. (ed.) "Russia's Efforts to Combat Human Trafficking: efficient crime groups versus irresolute societies and uncoordinated states," in *Ruling Russia: law, crime and justice in a changing society*, Lanham, MD: Rowman and Littlefield, 2005, 167–82.

2 For example(s) see Kempadoo, K., Sanghera, J., and Pattanail, S. (eds) (2005) *Trafficking and Prostitution Reconsidered: new perspectives on migration, sex work and human rights*, Boulder, CO: Paradigm; Kempadoo, K., and Dozema, J. (1998) *Global Sex Workers: Rights, Resistance and Redefinition*, New York and London: Routledge; Truong, T., Wieringa, S., and Chhachhi, A. (2006) *Engendering Human Security: feminist perspectives*, London and New York: Zed Books; Gallagher, A. (2001) "Human Rights and the New UN Protocols on Trafficking and Migrant Smuggling: a preliminary analysis," *Human Rights Quarterly*, 23: 975–1004.

3 For further discussion of this see Dozema, J. (2002) "Who Gets to Choose? Coercion, consent and the UN trafficking protocol," *Gender and Development*, 10:1, March, 20–42.

4 "CNN-IBN and DIG exposes the Beggar Mafia in India," 31 July 2006. Online. http://www.indiantelevision.com/release/y2k6/july/julyrel67.htm (accessed 19 May 2009). Discussion of Indian doctors caught on film offering to maim children and adults for begging with payment offered by the begging mafia. Online. http://www.bio-medicine.org/medicine-news/Maimed-Conscience—and-Maimed-Beggars—28Medical-Ethics-in-India-29—u2013-Part—12794-4 (accessed 18 August 2008).

5 For a discussion of trafficking in Turkey see Agathangelou, A. M. (2004) *The Global Political Economy of Sex: desire, violence, and insecurity in Mediterranean nation states*, New York: Palgrave Macmillan: 130–36; Janssens, S. and Arsovska, J. (2008) "Human Trafficking Networks in Turkey," *Jane's Intelligence Review*, 20: 12.

6 See Johnston, M. (ed.) (2005) "Preface: Mobilizing Citizens for Reform," in *Civil Society and Corruption: Mobilizing for Reform*, Lanham, MD: University Press of America: xi–xviii.

7 On 26 November 1992 the Belgian parliament held hearings on human trafficking. Online. http://en.wikipedia.org/wiki/Parliamentary_inquiries_by_the_Belgian_Federal _Parliament (accessed 19 May 2009).

8 The document is available at: www.state.gov/documents/organization/10492.pdf (accessed 19 May 2009).

9 Examples of these would be La Strada in Eastern Europe and Ukraine, Children of the Night in Los Angeles, and Apnea Aap in India.

10 The author observed this when she traveled for five days with an anthropologist through the hill communities of Northern Thailand in 1998.

11 Discussion with Save the Children official on field reports from the countries in which they work, April 2009, Washington, D.C.

Bibliography

Aronowitz, A. (2009) *Human Trafficking, Human Misery: the global trade in human beings*, London: Preager, 52–55.

Bales, K. (1999) *Disposable People: new slavery in the global economy*, Berkeley: University of California Press, 202.

Bernstein, N. (2006) "Making It Ashore and Still Chasing the U.S. Dream," *New York Times*, 9 April, A1.

Beyrer, C. and Stachowiak, J. (2003) "Health Consequences of Trafficking of Women and Girls in Southeast Asia," *Brown Journal of World Affairs*, X: I, 105–17.

Blinova, V. "Proshchanie" (2007) *Ogonek*, 7: 12–18 February, 18–20.

"Child Soldier Use 2003," Coalition to Stop the Use of Child Soldiers. Online. www.child-soldiers.org.

Congressional-Executive Commission on China (CECC) (2006) Statement of Ambassador John Miller, "Combating Human Trafficking in China: domestic and international efforts," 6 March. Online. http://www.cecc.gov/pages/hearings/2006/20060306/JohnMiller.php (accessed 18 August 2008).

Ditmore, M. and Wijers, M. (2003) "The Negotiations on the UN Protocol on Trafficking in Persons," *Nemesis* 4, 80.

The Economist (2008) "Peacekeeping and Sex Abuse: who will watch the watchmen?" 29 May. Online. http://www.economist.com/world/international/displaystory.cfm?story_id=11458241 (accessed 19 May 2009).

Everts, D. (2003) "Human Trafficking: the ruthless trade in human misery," *Brown Journal of World Affairs*, 10: 1 (Summer/Fall), 149–58.

Farr, K. (2005) *Sex-Trafficking: the global market in women and children*, New York: Worth Publishers, 228–30.

FBI. "Innocence Lost Initiative," (powerpoint) Online. http://courts.michigan.gov/scao/services/CWS/AWOLP/FBI.pdfwebsite (accessed 17 August 2008).

Gallagher, A. (2001) "Human Rights and the New UN Protocols on Trafficking and Migrant Smuggling: a preliminary analysis," *Human Rights Quarterly*, 23, 975–1004.

Global Report on Child Soldiers (2008). Online. http://www.childsoldiersglobalreport.org/overview-and-benchmarks (accessed 13 September 2008).

Gupta, R. (2005) "Interview," *Satya*, January. Online. http://www.satyamag.com/jan05/gupta.html (accessed 5 June 2006).

—. (2008) "NGO Briefing on Release on Trafficking in Persons Report," U.S. State Department, Washington, D.C. 6 June 2008.

Harvey, S. (2008) "A Europol Perspective on Criminal Profits and Money Laundering Linked to Trafficking in Human Beings," OSCE-UNODC-Cyprus Regional Operational Meeting in Combating Human Trafficking and Money Laundering in the Mediterranean Rim Region, Larnaca, Cyprus, 18–19 September.

The Hindu (2006) "Woman Held for Human Trafficking," 22 August. Online. http://www.hindu.com/2006/08/22/stories/2006082222330300.htm (accessed 20 May 2008).

ICE. (2006) "Sister Ping Sentenced to 35 years in Prison for Alien Smuggling, Hostage Taking, Money Laundering and Ransom Proceeds Conspiracy," (news release), http://www.ice.gov/pi/news/newsreleases/articles/060316newyork.htm (accessed 16 March 2006).

ILO/IPEC (2004) "Helping Hands or Shackled Lives: understanding domestic child labour and responses to it," June. Online. http://www.ilo.org/public/libdoc/ilo/2004/104B09_138.engl.pdf (accessed 11 January 2009).

Interact (2004) "Children in Armed Conflict Review and Evaluation Workshop," Pretoria, South Africa, Institute for Security Studies, 22 June. Online. http://www.iss.co.za/pubs/CReports/2004/interactjun.pdf (accessed 13 September 2008).

International Labour Organization (ILO) (2005) Report of the Director General, *A Global Alliance Against Forced Labor*, 10–12. Online. http://www.ilo.org/wcmsp5/groups/public/—dgreports/—dcomm/documents/publication/kd00012.pdf (accessed 27 August 2008).

Keefe, P.R. (2009) *The Snakehead: an epic tale of the Chinatown underworld and the American dream*, New York: Doubleday.

Kempadoo, K. and Dozema, J. (1998) *Global Sex Workers, Rights, Resistance and Redefinition*, New York and London: Routledge.

Kempadoo, K, Sanghera, J., and Pattanaik, B. (eds) (2005) *Trafficking and Prostitution Reconsidered: new perspectives on migration, sex work and human rights*, Boulder, CO: Paradigm.

Komsomolskaya Pravada (2007) "Na Urale nashli tainoe zahoronenie seks-rabyn," 2 February. Online. http://kp.ru/daily/23848.4/62919/ (accessed 5 February 2007).

Kristof, N.D. (2009) "The Evil Behind the Smiles," *New York Times*, 1 January, A21.

Mendelson, S.E. (2005) *Barracks and Brothels: peacekeepers and human trafficking in the Balkans*, Washington, D.C.: CSIS.

Minnesota Office of Justice Programs and Minnesota Statistical Analysis Center (MOJP/MSAC) (2006) "Human Trafficking in Minnesota: a report to the Minnesota legislature," September.

New York Times (2007) "UN Ousts Peacekeepers in Sex Case," November 3. Online. http://query.nytimes.com/gst/fullpage.html?res=9800E5D61439F930A35752C1A96 19C8B63&fta=y (accessed 19 May 2009).

Picarelli, J.T. (rapporteur) (2002) "Trafficking, Slavery and Peacekeeping: the need for a comprehensive training program," report on conference in Turin, Italy, hosted by Interregional Crime and Justice Research Institute, 9–10 May (UNICRI Report).

Step Up Program, Microsoft. Online. http://www.microsoft.com/philippines/citizen ship/stepup.aspx (accessed 19 May 2009).

Truong, T., Wieringa, S., and Chhachhi, A. (2006) *Engendering Human Security: feminist perspectives*, London and New York: Zed Books.

UN General Assembly (2001) "Convention against Transnational Organized Crime," 2 November, New York: United Nations Publications, 25–26.

United Nations Crime and Justice Information Network (UNCJIN). (2001) Online. http://www.uncjin.org/Documents/Conventions/dcatoc/final_documents_2/convent ion_%20traff_eng.pdf (accessed 7 September 2008).

United Nations Office On Drugs and Crime (UNODC) (2000a) "Protocol to Prevent, Suppress and Punish Trafficking in Persons, Especially Women and Children, Supplementing the United Nations Convention against Transnational Organized Crime," 15 November. Online. http://www.unodc.org/unodc/en/treaties/CTOC/ countrylist-traffickingprotocol.html (accessed 7 September 2008).

— (2000b) "Protocol against the Smuggling of Migrants by Land, Sea and Air, Supplementing the United Nations Convention against Transnational Organized Crime," 15 November. Online. http://www.unodc.org/unodc/en/treaties/CTOC/ countrylist-migrantsmugglingprotocol.html (accessed 7 September 2008).

U.S. Department of State (2006) "Trafficking in Persons Report," Washington, D.C., 6.

— (2007) "Trafficking in Persons Report," Washington, D.C., 26.

Zhang, S.X., Chin, K. and Miller, J. (2007) "Women's Participation in Chinese Transnational Human Smuggling: a gendered market perspective," *Criminology*, 45: 3, August, 699.

Zimmerman, C., Yun, K., and Watts, C. (2006) "Stolen Smiles: a summary report on the physical and psychological health consequences of women and adolescents trafficking in Europe," London: London School of Hygiene and Tropical Medicine. Online. http://www.eaves4women.co.uk/POPPY_Project/Documents/Recent_Reports/Stole n%20smiles-OSCE%20version%20Final.pdf (accessed 19 May 2008).

3 Transforming the representable

Asian women in anti-trafficking discourse

Donna K. Maeda

Introduction

Narrative I

In June 1993, the *Golden Venture*, a ship carrying nearly three hundred un-documented immigrants from China, ran aground near Queens, New York. Ten migrants drowned; survivors were detained by the Immigration and Naturalization Service. The migrants had paid approximately $5000, with a promise to pay an additional $30,000 in labor, to a "snakehead" (smuggling) operation (Pienciak 2003). Cheng Chui Ping, the head of the smuggling operation also known as "Sister Ping," was captured in 2000 in Hong Kong; she was returned to New York after a three-year extradition battle (Gearty 2005: 5). Sister Ping was convicted on charges of conspiracy, money laundering and trafficking in ransom proceeds (Feuer 2005: 3).

Approximately forty-five of the surviving migrants were granted asylum, while nearly two hundred were deported to China and other countries. In 1997, by special order of then-President Bill Clinton, the remaining migrants were released from detention pending final determination of their immigration status (Pienciak 2003: 8). As of September 2008, these migrants had still not received final determination of their status (O'Shaughnessy 2008: 24). Some of the migrants who remain in the United States have been trapped into working for the snake-head by debt still owed and lack of legal status (Pienciak 2003; Arai 1995).

Narrative II

On August 2, 1995, police raided an apartment complex in El Monte, California, that housed an illegal sweatshop in which seventy-two undocumented Thai workers lived and worked. Workers had been in the complex for up to seventeen years with no days off; eight to ten lived in rooms designed for two. The workers were not allowed to leave the complex; they were held by the operators to pay off travel debts, as well as costs of room and board. The workers were allowed to purchase food, toiletries, and other necessities only from the factory operators (Su 1998: 406).

The El Monte garment factory was run by a Thai woman with three of her sons and three other men. After the resolution of criminal and civil cases, the ringleader, Suni Manasurangkun, was sentenced to seven years in prison; her three sons were sentenced to six years. Others who guarded the workers received shorter sentences (*New York Times* 1996). One hundred nine garment workers (including Latinas who worked in other factories run by the operation) won $1.1 million in back wages (Jablon 1996). The ringleader and two of her sons were also ordered to pay $4.5 million in restitution to the workers (*New York Times* 1996).

Initially detained by immigration authorities, the Thai workers were assisted by a coalition of community organizations, including the Asian Pacific American Legal Center (APALC), the Thai Community Development Center (Thai CDC), and the Korean Immigrant Workers Advocates (KIWA) (Su 1998). Many of the garment workers eventually received visas to stay in the U.S.; several obtained U.S. citizenship in 2008 (Watanabe 2008).

Widespread publicity about both of these cases, including news articles providing updates on the migrants' status, raised public awareness about practices that threaten the lives of migrants who come to the United States without legal papers. These cases represent what are now classified as "smuggling" and "trafficking in persons," as defined by the Trafficking Victims Protection Act (TVPA) of 2000. While similarities can be seen in the cases, migrants like those in the *Golden Venture* case are considered to be smuggled persons who chose to participate in illegal activity by engaging with criminal smugglers; the El Monte garment workers became model victims of criminal traffickers in the development of the TVPA.

Even while great attention is paid in the U.S. to migrations from Mexico, stories of mass migrations from Asia contribute to the shaping of categorizing practices surrounding movements of people without papers across national borders. The practices and experiences involved in the *Golden Venture* and El Monte cases represent the core distinction: trafficking involves victimhood due to "force, fraud or coercion" related to labor and sexual exploitation, while smuggling involves free engagement in criminal activity. This chapter argues that while images of Asian immigration shape attitudes and treatments of different practices related to migration, it is the unnamed figure of the Asian woman in particular that elicits ideologies that enable stark distinctions to be made between such practices. Images of Asian women serve in discourses around "agency" in which they are represented as submissive—hence victims of both their own cultures and "western" masculinity—or articulate resisters whose agency is granted through western acknowledgment. Often it is the unremarked race and gender of the Asian women figures that enable the usefulness of their bodies as simply "women's" bodies, over which discourses of choice, agency, and victimhood are produced.

Definitions and frameworks for anti-trafficking efforts

In 2000, largely as the result of increasing concern over cases like that of the El Monte sweatshop, the U.S. Congress passed the Trafficking Victims Protection Act (TVPA) that seeks to end the international criminal practice of trafficking and to provide support for victims (DeStefano 2007).

According to the TVPA (U.S. Congress 2000), severe forms of trafficking are defined as:

1. sex trafficking in which a commercial sex act is induced by force, fraud, or coercion, or in which the person induced to perform such an act has not attained 18 years of age; or
2. the recruitment, harboring, transportation, provision, or obtaining of a person for labor or services, through the use of force, fraud, or coercion for the purpose of subjection to involuntary servitude, peonage, debt bondage, or slavery.

Key to this definition is the repetition of the phrase "force, fraud, or coercion." Trafficking victims are distinguished from smuggled persons and other "illegal immigrants" because of criminal acts that result in loss of free choice and agency.

Also in 2000, the United Nations adopted a Protocol to Prevent, Suppress, and Punish Trafficking in Persons, Especially Women and Children. The definition of trafficking in persons in the Protocol is

> the recruitment, transportation, transfer, harbouring or receipt of persons, by means of the threat or use of force or other forms of coercion, of abduction, of fraud, of deception, of the abuse of power or of a position of vulnerability or of the giving or receiving of payments or benefits to achieve the consent of a person having control over another person, for the purpose of exploitation.
>
> (United Nations 2000)

Both the TVPA and UN Protocol treat trafficking primarily as a criminal matter, focusing on the need to end the international criminal practice that victimizes some migrants; the UN Protocol is a supplement to the UN Convention against Transnational Organized Crime. Necessarily related to the criminal framework of trafficking is the concept of the trafficked person as victim, who, under humanitarian concerns, deserves sympathy and benefits as a victim of crime. Under the TVPA, persons formally certified as trafficked persons are eligible for benefits if they are willing to cooperate with the investigation and prosecution of the traffickers. Benefits include the same cash assistance as that received by refugees, health care (including medical, dental, and mental health care), work authorization, job retraining and job search assistance, victim assistance, and witness protection. Importantly, certified trafficked persons who are willing to cooperate with law enforcement in the investigation and prosecution of the traffickers are also eligible to apply for a T Visa and derivative visas for immediate family members, to apply for adjustment to legal permanent resident status three years after receiving the T Visa, and citizenship in an additional five years (U.S. Congress 2000).

Although trafficked persons are eligible for such support, the TVPA does not provide personnel or infrastructure for the provision of services. The Office to Monitor and Combat Trafficking in Persons, under the U.S. Department of State, coordinates domestic and international anti-trafficking efforts, while relying on nongovernmental organizations to provide services, including overall case management that coordinates the services to meet the many needs of trafficking survivors.

Sympathy for victims of crime

As noted above, the presentation of trafficked persons as victims of crime is central to the criminal trafficking model. As the structure and content of the TVPA show, the crucial characteristic of severe forms of trafficking, "force, fraud, or coercion," determines that the trafficked person is someone deserving of support; failure to qualify as a victim of trafficking carries the consequence of being treated as a criminal prostitute or illegal immigrant. Success in the process that determines victimhood results in eligibility for benefits to meet basic needs.

This distinction between victim and criminal relies on wide representational strategies. Narrative and pictorial representations of trafficking victims show them as abject, deserving of pity and needing rescue by those who embody agency. For example, the *Trafficking in Persons Report*, published annually as a requirement of the TVPA, uses photographs and narratives that represent the victimhood of trafficked persons. The *Report* intends to offer "the most comprehensive worldwide report on the efforts of governments to combat severe forms of trafficking in persons" (Office to Monitor and Combat Trafficking in Persons 2008: 8). It claims to provide reliable information on the different forms of trafficking and the diverse needs of survivors. While the *Report* notes that there are many forms of trafficking, its photographs emphasize sexual exploitation of women or young children. All of the photographs are depictions of destitution, shame, fear, or extreme vulnerability, through downcast eyes, gestures that hide faces, or proximity to potentially threatening persons. Significantly, a statement about the *Report*'s profiles of victims notes that many of the photographs "are not images of con-firmed trafficking victims, but are provided to show the myriad forms of exploitation that help define trafficking" (Office to Monitor and Combat Trafficking in Persons 2008: 4). In other words, the photographs have been intentionally chosen to represent a particular image of trafficking. They are being used to construct an image of victimhood that justifies sympathetic treatment of trafficked persons and that distinguishes the victims of trafficking from smuggled persons and prostitutes who, because they are understood to have chosen to participate in illegal activity, deserve to be treated as criminals and deported.

Representing the agent/victim binary through the focus on prostitution

The distinction between agency and victimhood is important in all prostitution and labor trafficking cases. Yet it is the figure of the prostitute, not the image of the laborer, that gives life to the victim/criminal agent dichotomy. Feminist discourses around prostitution engage these categories through varying representations of "women's" agency, the meanings of "choice," and the realities of the embodied constraints women encounter in different geographic and economic spaces.

On the one hand, abolitionists such as Kathleen Barry and the Coalition Against Trafficking in Women (CATW) argue that prostitution is inherently oppressive to women and, thus, participation cannot ever be "chosen" with free agency. CATW's philosophy states that "all prostitution exploits women, regardless of women's consent" (CATW). In this view, "consent" is so constrained by circumstances that it cannot be a matter of freedom or agency. Kara Abramson calls this a protectionist argument (Abramson 2003: 489). In this view, women need protection from the exploitation that constitutes prostitution.

On the other hand, feminists who advocate for sex workers' rights argue that women can, and do, choose sex work as a way to make a living and that the abolitionist or protectionist approach takes away such choices. Allison Murray argues that it is "the moral hypocrisy of global capitalism and sexual repression, including the criminalization of prostitutes, which creates the space for exploitation, discrimination and negative attitudes toward female sexuality" (Murray 1998: 54). For Murray, sex workers make full choices to engage in a particular kind of work. It is those who seek to end prostitution who create the repressive conditions that make this work dangerous by forcing it underground. Murray criticizes the representation of sex workers as victimized. She notes that distinguishing forms of prostitution as "trafficking" relies on the idea of "third parties coercing women into prostitution: if any money is offered to the women or their parents it should be as pitiful as possible, whereas the profits being made from their sexual labor should be as enormous as possible" (Murray 1998: 59). Anti-trafficking rhetoric rests on the abolitionist creation of victims as "others" to "enforce the moral condemnation of prostitution, with broad implications for all sex trade workers" (Murray 1998: 59). For Murray, the trafficking paradigm reflects hysteria over sexuality. Rather than focusing on "protection" that results in the repression of embodied labor, she advocates the creation of safer working conditions and the eradication of the inequalities and discriminations that lead to the harmful forms of sex work (Murray 1998: 63–64).

Following up with the focus on agency, Jo Doezema advocates focusing on the human rights of sex workers rather than attempting to draw a line between "consent" and "coercion." Doezema notes the historical connection between concerns over trafficking and the moral and bodily purity of *some* women (Doezema 1998: 35). The social purity movements that lobbied to enact the 1864 Contagious Diseases Act in Britain regulating prostitutes set the stage for campaigns against the "white slave trade" that bred panic about pure (white) females kidnapped by (dark) immigrants for sexual slavery (Doezema 1998: 35–36). According to Doezema, both the policing of prostitutes and the panic over stories of white slavery were based on concerns over maintaining "proper" sexual behavior: men needed to be protected from the enticements of impure women while pure women needed protection from the dangers of those who desired to turn them into impure objects. Doezema situates the 1949 United Nations Convention for the Suppression of the Traffic in Persons and the Exploitation of the Prostitution of Others within this history. The 1949 Convention serves, in turn, as the forerunner to the 2000 UN Protocol to Prevent, Suppress, and Punish Trafficking in Persons, Especially Women and Children (Doezema 1998: 36).

Doezema pays greater attention than Murray to the danger and violence connected with forced prostitution. Doezema argues that attempts to distinguish forced from voluntary prostitution, however, detract from a primary focus on the human rights of all women, including sex workers. Such a distinction fosters the moralistic regulation of women's sexuality instead of focusing on improving practical human rights concerns, such as safety and humane work settings.

Racialized representations of victimhood and erased race of agency

Behind this feminist discourse regarding women's agency and women's choice lie figures of women whose racial difference is both erased and employed. Even when feminist discourses acknowledge the ways that race figures into analyses of trafficking and prostitution, they still present the trafficked woman as a mere shadow whose agency needs to be recuperated—as someone who needs to be granted agency, by being rescued or by being "recognized." This agency is asserted to be real *in place of* the absent presence; "other" women's agency is measured by "ours."

Often considered to be the "expert" or model scholar-activist fighting against trafficking and new forms of slavery, Kevin Bales argues forcefully for exposing practices of slavery around the world.[1] He argues that "race" is no longer a salient factor in the new forms of slavery or trafficking, even while he pays special attention to practices in Asia, Africa, and Latin America.

Significant in his analysis is this attention, under erasure, to the practices of "other" peoples that ignores racialized readings of "culture." Bales's analysis of sex slavery in Thailand illustrates this simultaneous erasure and racialization of the gendered "other." Bales asserts that the major reasons that young Thai girls are sold into sex slavery are Thai culture, Thai Buddhism, and Thai family desires for material goods. Bales writes,

> Religion help[s] provide . . . important justifications for . . . sales of daughters. Within the type of Buddhism followed in Thailand, women are regarded as distinctly inferior to men. . . . [In this type of Buddhism there] is no notion of sex as a sin; instead, sex is seen as an attachment to the physical and natural

world. . . . The implication is that if you must have sex, have it as impersonally as possible. Thai Buddhism also carries a central message of acceptance and resignation in the face of life's pain and suffering.

(Bales 1999: 38–39)

Bales also comments that "a religious belief in the inferiority of girls is not the only cultural rule pressing them into slavery. Thai children, especially girls, owe their parents a profound debt, an obligation both cosmic and physical" (Bales 1999: 39). Bales connects the "traditional obligations" of children to their parents to contemporary desires of their parents to account for the new forms of slavery. Thai parents, according to Bales, are seduced by "a flood of consumer goods— refrigerators, televisions, cars and trucks, rice cookers, air conditioners—all of which are extremely tempting . . ." "As it happens, the cost of participating in [the] consumer boom can be met from an old source, one that has also become much more profitable: the sale of children" (Bales 1999: 40).

Bales's unacknowledged but highly racialized interpretation of culture and his fundamentalist view of religion rely on and perpetuate notions of Asian passivity and lack of normative agency. In this orientalist view, Asian women and girls are especially victimized because their culture embodies gendered oppression. The young girl that Bales profiles becomes resigned to violent treatment, after having been broken down by beatings. Yet in Bales's interpretation, which erases the role of violent suppression, she is already prone to resignation because of Thai religion. For Bales, interpretations of culture and religion have nothing to do with "race," as he remains blind to racializations of cultural "difference," in which the Asian "other" is interpreted through the framework of normative "western" culture, behavior, and agency. While devaluation of girls in many countries is a constant feminist concern, the scrutiny of Asian locations reproduces the uncomplicated, unidimensional notions of culture based on what the West is "not." Instead of focusing on the effects of economic globalization or the growth of the sex industry around U.S. military bases and their centers for rest and recreation (see Enloe 2001), Bales uses orientalized notions of culture and religion to provide explanatory frameworks that rely on representations of difference from, and inferiority to, the "West" (see Said 1994).

Such images of Asian women float throughout discourses on trafficking, especially, but not limited to, sex trafficking. This constant use of the racialized, cultural other as a signifier of the victim in trafficking indicates the significance of the Asian woman figure in the discourses of choice, agency, and victimhood.

In "Sex for Sale: Prostitution, Trafficking, and Cultural Amnesia: what we must not know in order to keep the business of sexual exploitation running smoothly," Melissa Farley presents the Asian woman as passive and agent-less, even when she explicitly attempts to assert agency. Farley displays the figure of Grace Quek, who, under the name "Annabel Chong," performed "The World's Biggest Gang Bang" (Farley 2006: 127). For Farley, Quek epitomizes the abject, sexually exploited woman whose lack of agency is erased by attempts to give value to sex work. She selects reviews of the performance that represent Quek in a particular way: "[o]ne reviewer . . . viewed Quek as 'the new feminist icon who provokes and is not ashamed . . . to be viewed as nothing more than an object'" (Farley 2006: 135, quoting Bila-Gunther). Farley continues, "[s]he seemed 'empty' to one observer who noted that she 'came across like a puppet terrified of disappointing her commanders. There was no sign of the much-vaunted empowerment or control in her frantic displays, just someone that had sadly become less than human'" (Farley 2006: 135, quoting Kakmi). Calling forth Quek's identity as a Chinese immigrant from Singapore, Farley notes that Quek had been gang-raped before entering into prostitution and subsequently moving to Los Angeles to perform in hard-core pornography (Farley 2006: 134–35).

In Quek, Farley has clearly found a troublesome example that raises questions about choice and agency in sex work. Yet in highlighting this story, Farley employs Quek as a figure for her own argument about the inherent exploitation of sex work. Rather than giving context or a fuller presentation of the woman, Farley takes pieces of Quek's life, identity, and behavior that are useful for her own narrative and erases those that are not. Farley's article does not attempt to present Quek's perspectives about her own life, choices, work, or ideas as a performance artist. As she presents Quek as the unknowing victim with no consciousness of what is "really" happening to her, Farley deploys the readily-available figure of the submissive, agent-less Asian immigrant woman. In marking Quek's identity as "a Chinese immigrant from Singapore" without providing elements of Quek's story that do not fit the victim narrative, Farley calls forth a figure that is easily deployable as always already a victim. Pointing to Quek's history as a victim of a gang rape (Farley 2006: 134) who is called a "babbling idiot" (135) and preyed on by the pornography industry's "predators . . . [who] exploit[ed] her dissociative vulnerability" (135), Farley represents Quek as *only* a victim who is unaware of her victimization even as she attempts to make choices to perform in pornography. Farley's selection and representation of Quek positions the Chinese woman in a narrative in which the Asian victim is already a known figure. Similar to Bales's story of the young Thai prostitute, Farley deploys the figure of the pitiable, sexualized Asian woman. While Bales presents the Asian woman as victim to her culture, religion, and her own people, Farley takes a figure that is read by some as a marker of agency, a worker who chooses to work in sex, and re-presents her as the always already agent-less Asian victim. These representations reproduce the image of the racialized, sexualized Asian woman victim across ethnicities.

On the "other side" of the victim/agent binary, Allison Murray calls on the Asian woman as she argues for the recognition of women's choice and agency. *Even* the Asian woman must be understood to have choice and agency, regardless of circumstance. If the Asian woman is presumed to be the face of victimhood, it is she who especially must be recuperated as an indicator of "women's" agency. Murray disputes reports of Burmese women trafficked into Thailand for forced prostitution, claiming that most of the women chose this work as a way to leave Burma (Murray 1998: 56). Murray criticizes reports of Burmese women lured or tricked back into prostitution when deported because of lack of legal status in Thailand for, in effect, calling the women "stupid" (Murray 1998: 56). Rather than considering circumstances that place migrants in danger, Murray insists on reading the situation simply as a matter of women's choice. Murray reproduces the false binary of agency or victimhood; the Asian women must be read as agents, not victims, thereby disregarding conditions of potentially violent constraint. Her binary reading reproduces the image of the Asian woman as passive; for it is Murray's interpretation that reads an agency based on choice into the Asian women in opposition to victimhood. It is the woman most stereotypically presumed to be a victim whose agency of choice must be rescued for the sake of this type of feminist interpretation.

In these discourses around sex work and trafficking, Asian women appear as figures who are used to support the positions of those who would author her. As she interrogates more complex positionalities within the category "women," Ratna Kapur demonstrates how such representations reproduce the post-colonial sexual subaltern. In her critique of the anti-trafficking approach of the United States and the United Nations, Kapur holds a position that seems at first similar to sex worker advocates such as Doezema and Murray. Kapur points to the paternalistic approach that emphasizes women's lack of agency or choice in prostitution (Kapur 2001: 876). Yet Kapur interrogates ways that the sex worker in postcolonial India disrupts the binary of agency and victimhood (Kapur 2001: 879). Unlike Doezema and Murray, Kapur looks at how the particularity of the sex worker who is positioned as a sexual subaltern in postcolonial conditions also challenges economic, sexual, and cultural assumptions upon which such binaries are based (Kapur 2001: 879). The sexual subaltern claims agency by moving between the "first" and "third" worlds. She claims the right to be a market actor, engaging directly in economic exchanges, thereby challenging imperialist constructions of the sexual subject in the third world as always only abject (Kapur 2001: 879–80). While Kapur turns to the notion of consent, she does not attach the concept to a western, "first world" notion of the consent of the free agent. Rather, Kapur argues that

> [T]he sexual subaltern subject creates the possibility of crossing sexual, cultural and geographic boundaries. But her agency is not free and unfettered. She is constantly negotiating the experiences of violence, racism, and marginality, negotiating hegemonic feminist constructions of feminist sisterhood and the imperialist maneuvers that deny her subjectivity. Yet, by focusing on the marginal location of the postcolonial sex worker, the third space, we come to understand the disruptive potential of this subject, through her agency, her mobility, and the pursuit of her desires.
>
> (Kapur 2001: 885)

Kapur calls for a strategy that "can create the possibility of a more liberatory and emancipatory politics" through the recuperation of desire (Kapur 2001: 884). Such a politics requires a subversion of binaries that require agency to be attached to "woman" in opposition to "victim." Agency, then, attaches to the sexual subaltern who consents as a practice to conditions that may be construed as acceptable or unacceptable to the western subject. Yet rather than merely consenting under this binary, the sexual subaltern's position calls forth the construction of conditions under which some women may be read as "choosers" while others are interpreted as "victims." Under postcolonial conditions of globalized economics, the sexual subaltern "inserts herself" into this script of choice, challenging the binary and "creating the possibility of revisioning the sex worker as a complex subject who is simultaneously exploited by normative arrangements and is disruptive of these arrangements" (Kapur 2001: 879). Kapur, like Doezema and Murray, points to the damaging effects of a legal approach to anti-trafficking that paternalistically takes a position of determining when a woman acts with choice (and, as an agent prostitute, is thus criminalized) and when she is a victim (and, as a victim prostitute, is thus given assistance). However, her analysis not only challenges stereotypical, racialized representations of some women as already prone to victimhood, but more importantly, points to the histories, politics, and economics that place them in such conditions. Rather than perpetuating narratives of victimhood or agency, Kapur writes of subaltern subjectivity that necessarily calls for a simultaneous critique of the production of such conditions in "feminist" discourse and recognition of subjecthood that is not quite/not the same as the western agent of choice (see also Trinh 1991).

Subverting binaries: coalitional constitutions of embodied subjects

While Kapur writes to recuperate agency of the postcolonial sexual subaltern rather than returning to the issue of human trafficking, the transnational collaborative/coalitional work of nongovernmental organizations points to other ways of conceiving of anti-trafficking work that does not center on the agent/victim binary. This coalitional work fosters agency of trafficked persons while also working to change the conditions, and thus the terms, of victimhood and agency.

The following two sections consider a collection of Los Angeles-area NGOs whose work reframes the trafficking and agency debate by engaging in politically transformational anti-trafficking work. This coalitional work pushes possibilities for fuller human agency. While members of organizations working with trafficked persons must consider questions of choice and consent because of the requirements of the TVPA, that work is tactical, not defined by the law's concept of agency. Leading up to and continuing after the passage of the TVPA, the organizations work from an empowerment model that begins with an understanding of the complex factors that contribute to the constitution of racialized, gendered subjects under conditions of economic globalization.

As noted above, the TVPA is oriented toward criminal law in order to focus on pursuing traffickers. While the TVPA provides benefits for trafficked persons who qualify as "victims of a severe form of trafficking," support for trafficked persons relies on the work of nongovernmental organizations. Meeting the immediate and long-term needs of trafficked persons requires a collaborative/coalitional approach. No single organization can provide all of the support needed by trafficked persons across the broad range of types of trafficking, across different communities. Rather than focusing on the binary between agency and victimhood as defined by the legal anti-trafficking framework, the empowerment model subverts the binary. Similar to Kapur, this model multiplies and differentiates the actual subjects of the agency–victim discourse in order to change its terms. In what follows I examine the ways in which the NGOs' transnational collective work fosters the creation of subject positions that challenge the assumptions of the theoretical debates and provide practical tools for empowerment.

Crafting an empowerment model before the TVPA

As it occurred before the existence of an anti-trafficking law, drawing attention to the existence of "new forms of slavery," the El Monte sweatshop case pointed to the need for an approach that provided support for persons leaving a trafficking situation in addition to the need for prosecuting traffickers. After the raid on the El Monte sweatshop, the workers were initially put into detention by immigration authorities as "illegal immigrants." Images of persons taken out of conditions of enslavement and put into jail highlighted the need for a new approach. Yet authorities were ill-equipped to handle the multiple issues faced by the workers who had been held as captives. Local community organizations, including the Asian Pacific American Legal Center (APALC), the Thai Community Development Center (Thai CDC), and the Korean Immigrant Workers Advocates (KIWA) crafted an approach on the ground, in the moment, to meet the workers' immediate needs.

Persons emerging from a trafficking situation typically have immediate needs for health care (physical, dental, and mental), housing, personal items for daily living, job assistance and retraining, and protection from threats of traffickers. Because of the transnational nature of many trafficking cases, those who assist trafficked persons must have knowledge about survivors' language and culture. Knowledge about conditions in the survivors' home country and the local ethnic community is also necessary in order to address threats to family members and factors affecting adjustment in the U.S. or repatriation to the home country. Trafficked persons may have little knowledge about U.S. laws and procedures but may need to deal with criminal and civil legal issues that involve local law enforcement, a U.S. Attorney's office, the Federal Bureau of Investigation, Department of Labor, and Immigration and Customs Enforcement.

In the El Monte case, the community-based organizations needed to craft an approach that would assist in all of these areas. The lead attorney in the El Monte case, Julie Su from APALC,[2] organized this coalitional work using an empowerment model that challenges traditional legal work and the primary focus of attorneys on narrowly legal arguments. Su writes about talking with the workers "not just in terms of legal rights, but in terms of basic human dignity. . . . Human dignity must be the measure of what we recognize as legal rights" (Su 1998: 412–13). For Su, advocacy entails ensuring that workers understand the system so that they can be empowered to make their own decisions about their case and to become advocates for themselves on the range of issues that affect their lives. She notes,

> The workers . . . [learned] that mere access to the legal system and to lawyers does not ensure that justice will be served. No one will give you a social and economic structure governed by principles of compassion and equality over corporate profit, particularly if you are poor, non-English speaking, an immigrant, a woman of color, a garment worker—unless you fight for it yourself.
>
> (Su 1998: 411)

Rather than conceiving of the case as requiring an expert legal authority, Su worked with other NGOs and used an organizing approach to foster the voices and decision-making of survivors. Rather than focusing primarily on the technical framework of law through which claims are made, Su privileged advocacy that leads to the workers' empowerment.

Importantly, Su brought Latina/o garment workers employed in factories owned by those who ran the El Monte sweatshop into a legal case contesting structures of the industry so that practices in those factories would not simply be "normalized" in contrast to the El Monte factory (Su 1998: 410–11). Su's efforts with immigrant workers across lines of race, language, and national origin call attention to particular conditions that shape possibilities for fuller agency. As an Asian American attorney, Su recognized the need to constantly consider her own positionalities and to develop skills to work across lines, especially when Latina/o workers reacted to her racial similarity to the owners of the garment factories in which they worked. Su's participation in coalitional work not only challenged standards for legal advocacy but also built possibilities for transformations of labor "rights" across racialized immigrant communities.

For the El Monte case, Thai CDC contributed to the provision of culturally appropriate services and the knowledge base for addressing concerns of the Thai workers across national borders. Ethnic communities are complex in their local and transnational politics; some community members understand the need to expose trafficking in order to end the practice, while others fear the publicity that can feed negative attitudes toward racialized peoples. In addition, policies and practices needed to support laborers in transnational ethnic communities do not always fit the strategies of ethnic entrepreneurs. However, when the El Monte case broke, Thai CDC already had a history of focusing on the needs of economically disadvantaged, low-wage workers within the immigrant community. As it works on a range of issues related to community economic development, Thai CDC uses a human rights orientation that enables a focus on the rights of low-income immigrant workers. The organization's stated goals include:

> [e]mpowering and improving working conditions for low-income Thais and other exploited workers, especially those working in sweatshops and other inhumane conditions; [p]romoting the rights of Thai Americans as well as

advocating for more humane labor and immigration policies; [p]roviding and ensuring access to culturally sensitive human and social services; and [d]eveloping leadership among Thai Americans through community service.

(Thai CDC)

As Thai CDC contributed to assisting the Thai workers by providing knowledge of language, cultural, and migration contexts, KIWA shared in the human rights orientation to the needs of workers. As an organization, KIWA works "to empower low wage immigrant workers and to develop a progressive constituency and leadership among low wage immigrant workers in Los Angeles that can join the struggle in solidarity with other underrepresented communities for social change and justice" (KIWA). KIWA brought its history of organizing for immigrant and workers' rights across racial/ethnic lines to the coalitional work with APALC and Thai CDC. All three organizations work from an understanding of how globalization shapes flows of migration and creates subordinated classes of gendered and racialized laborers.

The coalition of organizations working with the El Monte workers focused on an organizing model that fostered empowerment rather than simply treating the trafficked persons within a framework that asks where the workers fit in the binary model of victimhood and agency. Even while the coalition used legal tactics, these were a set of tools that were useful but needed to be deployed in a broader empowerment strategy. Because U.S. and international laws around immigration, labor, and crime do not focus primarily on the lives and needs of low-income women around the globe, an empowerment strategy looks toward changing conditions, including legal ones, that create vulnerability to exploitation. These organizations work from the understanding that agency must be negotiated and produced within, against, and beyond the confines of gendered and racialized bodies of subaltern transnational communities shaped by economic globalization.

Commitment to an empowerment model beyond the TVPA

The Coalition to Abolish Slavery & Trafficking (CAST) was formed in 1998 out of the El Monte case. While the founders of CAST were developing a sustainable comprehensive services model as well as national and international networks of organizational partners, they also advocated for the passage of the TVPA. Similar to APALC, CAST considers the tools to support trafficked persons created by the TVPA to be important, even while both organizations see the need for broader transformations in the treatments of migrants and workers in the U.S. CAST utilizes a social services model that includes case management, in-house legal services, and a housing program that includes the first shelter in the country dedicated to trafficked persons. CAST also works with networks of attorneys at other organizations, including APALC, and organizations in many immigrant communities. In addition, CAST holds workshops and trainings for law enforcement agencies, NGOs and faith-based organizations, educational institutions, attorneys and others who may come into contact with trafficked persons. CAST also engages in public and legislative advocacy.

Importantly, while both are connected historically to the El Monte sweatshop case, APALC and CAST have not taken the same direction on trafficking, although the organizations still work together on particular cases. While CAST was formed to work specifically on developing a comprehensive approach for working with trafficked persons from many countries, APALC works on trafficking issues within the context of immigrant and workers' rights, focusing on Asian and Pacific Islander communities, but also working in coalition with other communities' organizations. CAST distinguishes trafficking as a new form of slavery, not simply another form of exploitative practices around labor and prostitution, while APALC orients its work toward seeing connections between the forms of exploitation of labor and bodies. Yet such differences do not prevent collaborative work because, coming from different orientations, both connect trafficking issues to politics around shared understandings of the effects of transnational economic practices on the racialized, gendered lives in immigrant communities. Both organizations connect needs of particular trafficked persons to these broader politics rather than to de-racialized notions of agency or victimhood. For all of the NGOs, agency requires the fostering of empowerment of lives shaped by gender and race under global economic conditions, which are themselves shaped by effects of racialized colonial histories.

Conclusion: agency of the subverted binary

The coalitional work with trafficking survivors and political work around trafficking and the human rights of immigrants/workers/women inserts the racialized, gendered bodies of persons whose lives are shaped by postcolonial and transnationalized economies into discourses of agency in ways that subvert, and thus transform, their categorization. Rather than arguing for "agency" as an opposition to "victimhood," this work supports and implements Kapur's analyses by recognizing the differential positioning of the individual subjects who are subsumed in the categories of "woman," "migrant," and "worker." By working together, though not always in agreement, the coalitional collaborative connects issues of the exploitation of bodies to transnational economies and politics. Trafficking, then, is confronted as one issue among many for women/immigrants/workers in racialized communities. Although the TVPA provides tools for assisting trafficked persons, neither the work nor the goals of these groups are defined solely by the availability of the anti-trafficking tools or framework. The larger politics of the coalitional work attends to conditions that foster trafficking, smuggling, and other forms of exploitation. Although CAST distinguishes these practices from each other, the organization also aligns with other NGOs to support the longer-term politics of working for the human rights of all immigrants/women/workers.

Looking through the lens of the coalitional work that considers transnationality focuses on limiting effects of the subjectivity of western liberal modernity. Rather than relying on the agency of that subject, the coalitional work subverts its opposition to victimhood. Such work inserts the multiple subjectivities of gendered, racialized bodies of Asian women and other "others" into discourses of agency to transform its terms and practices. The NGOs' coalitional work fosters the empowerment of actual "other" women rather than using their bodies as empty figures. These multiple subjectivities displace the terms of liberal agency discourse and create a radical, liberatory politics that opens up, rather than forecloses, the movements of embodied subjects.

Notes

1   Bales's book, *Disposable People: New Slavery in the Global Economy* was nominated for the Pulitzer Prize. He has received several human rights awards. His work was named one of the top "100 World-Changing Discoveries" by the Association of British Universities. He has been a consultant to the United Nations Global Program on Trafficking of Human Beings and has advised the U.S., British, Irish, Norwegian, and Nepali governments, as well as the governments of the Economic Community of Western African States (Free the Slaves).
2   For her innovative work, Su received a 2001 MacArthur Foundation "genius" grant (MacArthur Foundation).

Bibliography

Abramson, K. (2003) "Beyond Consent, Toward Safeguarding Human Rights: implementing the United Nations trafficking protocol," *Harvard International Law Journal*, 44: 473–502.

Arai, H. (1995) "The Price the Golden Venture Passengers Paid: The Snake Road—Fuzhou to New York via Hong Kong," *Nineties Magazine*, Aug.–Nov. Online. http://www.geocities.com/heartland/cabin/4716/newyork.html (accessed 5 April 2009).

Bales, K. (1999) *Disposable People: new slavery in the global economy*, Berkeley: University of California Press.

Coalition Against Trafficking in Women (CATW). Online. http://www.catwinternational.org/about/index.php (accessed 5 April 2009).

Coalition to Abolish Slavery & Trafficking (CAST). Online. http://www.castla.org/aboutus/history.htm (accessed 6 April 2009).

DeStefano, A. M. (2007) *The War on Human Trafficking: U.S. policy assessed*, New Brunswick, NJ: Rutgers University Press.

Doezema, J. (1998) "Forced to Choose: beyond the voluntary v. forced prostitution dichotomy," in K. Kempadoo and J. Doezema (eds) *Global Sex Workers: rights, resistance and redefinition*, New York: Routledge, 34–39.

Enloe, C. (2001) *Bananas, Beaches and Bases: making feminist sense of international politics*, Berkeley: University of California Press.

Farley, M. (2006) "Sex for Sale: Prostitution, Trafficking and Cultural Amnesia: what we must not know in order to keep the business of sexual exploitation running smoothly," *Yale Journal of Law & Feminism*, 18: 109–44.

Feuer, A. (2005) "Businesswoman Known as Sister Ping Is Found Guilty on Federal Conspiracy Charges," *New York Times*, 23 June: 3.

Free the Slaves. Online. http://www.freetheslaves.net/Page.aspx?pid=382 (accessed 6 April 2009).

Gearty, R. (2005) "Immigrants' Smuggler Iced: Golden Venture Big faces 35 Years," *New York Daily News*, June 23: 5.

Jablon, R. (1996) "Sweatshop Workers Split $1.1 Million in Back Wages," *Associated Press*, 8 March.

Kapur, R. (2001) "Post-Colonial Economies of Desire: legal representations of the sexual subaltern," *Denver University Law Review*, 78: 855–85.

Korean Immigrant Workers Advocates (KIWA). Online. http://www.kiwa.org/e/homefr. htm (accessed 5 April 2009).

MacArthur Foundation. Online. http://www.macfound.org/site/c.lkLXJ8MQKrH/ b.1142731/k.6679/Fellows_List—October_2001.htm (accessed 6 April 2009).

Murray, A. (1998) "Debt-Bondage and Trafficking: don't believe the hype," in K. Kempadoo and J. Doezema (eds) *Global Sex Workers: rights, resistance and redefinition*, New York: Routledge, 51–64.

New York Times (1996) "4 Draw Prison Terms in Sweatshop Case," 8 May, 21.

Office to Monitor and Combat Trafficking in Persons (2008) *Trafficking in Persons Report 2008*. U.S. Department of State. Online. http://www.state.gov/g/tip/rls/tiprpt/2008/ (accessed 5 April 2009).

O'Shaughnessy, P. (2008) "From Hell at Sea to the American Dream: fifteen years after the Golden Venture Tragedy, one man tells his story," *New York Daily News*, 8 June: 24.

Pienciak, R. T. (2003) "Refugees Still Held Captive by Red Tape: amnesty fight lasts a decade," *New York Daily News*, 1 June: 8.

Said, E. (1994) *Orientalism*, New York: Vintage Books.

Su, J. S. (1998) "Making the Invisible Visible: the garment industry's dirty laundry," *Journal of Gender, Race and Justice*, Spring: 405–17.

Thai Community Development Center (Thai CDC). Online. http://www.thaicdchome. org/cms/goals/ (accessed 5 April 2009).

Trinh, T. M. (1991) *When the Moon Waxes Red: representation, gender and cultural politics*, New York: Routledge.

United Nations (2000) *Protocol to Prevent, Suppress, and Punish Trafficking in Persons, Especially Women and Children*. Online. http://www.uncjin.org/Documents/Conventions/dcatoc/ final_documents_2/convention_%20traff_eng.pdf (accessed 5 April 2009).

U.S. Congress (2000) *Trafficking Victims Protection Act (TVPA)* Publ. Law 106–386. Online. http://www.state.gov/documents/organization/10492.pdf (accessed 5 April 2009).

Watanabe, T. (2008) "Thai Slave Laborers Freed in El Monte Become U.S. Citizens," *Los Angeles Times*, 14 August: 1.

4   Sin, salvation, or starvation?

The problematic role of religious morality in U.S. anti-sex trafficking policy[1]

Lucinda Peach

Introduction

In recent years, the United States government has promoted the view that prostitution and other forms of sex work must be eliminated as "inherently harmful and dehumanizing" (US Department of State 2007: 28). This "abolitionist" agenda is incorporated in several federal laws and policies which are imposed on other nations, especially through policies and practices regarding human trafficking and HIV/AIDS. In particular, the Trafficking Victims Protection Reauthorization Act (TVPRA) conflates prostitution with sex trafficking (defined in international law as requiring fraud, coercion, deceit, kidnapping, etc.),[2] and so prohibits US funding to foreign organizations which have not stated in their grant applications that they do "not promote, support or advocate the legalization or practice of prostitution" (US Congress 2003: Sec. 7 (2)). The Global AIDS Act also conflates prostitution with sex trafficking and contains similar "loyalty oath" or "prostitution pledge" provisions.[3]

The US Department of State rates countries (143 in the 2007 report) on how well they are making efforts to combat human trafficking in its annual *Trafficking in Persons Report (TIPS Report)* and threatens sanctions to those that fail to comply with the US's unilaterally designated standards (US Department of State 2006).[4] These policies, by conflating prostitution with sex trafficking, and in their blanket condemnation of prostitution, are problematic in themselves. They are especially problematic when imposed on non-western cultures, for they reflect a particular hegemonic and culturally imperialistic perspective on the sexual body that is rooted in conservative Christian understandings of sexuality and prostitution as sinful, and the prostitute as either an "innocent victim" or a "sinful whore." These Christian understandings are at sharp variance with both Hindu and Buddhist understandings of prostitution. When applied to such countries as India and Thailand, countries which have a significant problem with sex trafficking, these Christian-oriented policies create problems for women working as prostitutes and hamper efforts to stop sex trafficking.

Before I begin my discussion, a few qualifications are in order. First, human trafficking is an egregious human rights violation, whether it be for sex or other forms of exploitation. My aim in critiquing current U.S. policies is not to diminish the severity of trafficking crimes but, rather, to argue that there are more appropriate and less harmful ways of addressing trafficking than the US's current policies. In particular, where these policies portray trafficked women exclusively as "victims," the reality is far more complex. Policies that took account of these complexities would have a better chance of success.

Second, while it is important to keep in mind that, though gay and straight men as well as bisexual and transgender persons also engage in prostitution, most prostitutes are women. In view of the widespread understanding that the vast majority of persons trafficked for sex and working in the sex industry are female, and the different considerations that come into play in dealing with children, this paper will focus on the effects of current US prostitution and trafficking policies on adult women.

Third, I use the terms "prostitute," "sex worker," and "women in prostitution" interchangeably, while recognizing their sometimes highly politicized valences. And finally, the term "prostitution" itself encompasses a variety of different practices, ranging from high-class call girls to street walkers and brothel prostitution to a spectrum of different roles and activities in between these. For purposes of this paper, these differentiations are less important than the ways in which commercial sex is perceived and regulated.

Christian elements of US anti-prostitution policy

From the early days of Christian theology, sex has been viewed as embodying sin (see Brock 2000: 256). Even though Jesus places prostitutes, along with tax collectors, ahead of the acknowledged religious leadership, as more worthy of entering the Kingdom of God (see Countryman 1988: 88), and the Gospel of Matthew is similarly radical in including two "harlots" among those whom Jesus befriended,[5] Paul's sexual ethics includes the directive that "The body, however, is not for *porneia*, but for the Lord and the Lord for the body" (quoted in Countryman 1988: 104–105). Etymologically, the term *porneia* meant fornication or prostitution (Collins 2000: 82). This interpretation is reinforced in 1 Thessalonians, where Paul writes: "This is God's will, your sanctification—for you to keep away from harlotry (*porneia*), for each of you to know how to possess his own vessel in holiness and honor, not in a passion of desire" (quoted in Countryman 1988: 105). Paul also insisted that having intercourse with a prostitute was destructive of one's spirit, that is, one's relation to Christ and to God:

> Flee from harlotry. Every sin that a person commits is outside the body, but the man who uses harlots is sinning against his own body. Or do you not know that your body is the temple of the Holy Spirit that is in you, which you have from God, and you do not belong to yourselves? For you were bought at a price; so glorify God with your body.
>
> (Countryman 1988: 204, quoting 1 Corinthians 6:18–20)

In 1 Corinthians (6:9–10), Paul says that sexually immoral persons will fail to enter the kingdom of God (see Collins 2000: 189). Thus, anti-prostitution attitudes in early Christianity appear to have been institutionalized by the Apostle Paul and not by Jesus himself. For the former, "the use of prostitutes was . . . something to be shunned under the rubric of avoiding sexual immorality" (Collins 2000: 185).

In medieval Christian theology, St. Augustine viewed prostitution as a necessary evil. Prostitutes were viewed as sinners, but also as necessary to preserve the integrity of the family. By permitting male lust from escalating out of control, prostitutes were seen as protecting the "'good' women of the family from the demands of male sin" (Brock 2000: 246; see Brock and Thistlethwaite 1996: 236). Thus, prostitution was accepted as the price of social purity for righteous Christian women, a price that would have to be paid until men could live up to Christian ideals of morality (Bullough and Bullough 1987: 73).

Though Christian writers emphasized the degradation of prostitution, they also argued that the prostitute herself might be "saved" through Christian charity. There are a number of early Christian stories about famous courtesans, "but the moral of these stories is the conversion of the lost and forsaken, and their ultimate salvation" (Bullough and Bullough 1987: 78). In more recent Christian history, prostitution was seen as immoral and inherently demeaning and degrading as well as sinful. As feminist theologian Rita Nagashima Brock notes: "The dominant American culture is shaped by the legacy of Christian religious dualism, which projects blame for prostitution on females" (Brock 2000: 248).

The approach of many contemporary "faith-based" organizations (FBOs) (which, at least in the US, are overwhelmingly Christian) reflects this traditional Christian understanding of prostitution as sinful, degrading, or immoral. For example, a position paper on "Sexuality: Some Common Convictions" by the Evangelical Lutheran Church in America (ELCA) explicitly states: "Prostitution is sinful because it involves the casual buying and selling of 'sex,' often in demeaning and exploitative ways" (ELCA 1996: 6). The ELCA also refers to prostitution as a "social sin, a structure of evil that shapes and snares persons" and "corrupts God's wonderful gift of sexuality by reducing it to a marketable item" (ELCA 2001: 4). To similar effect is the Salvation Army's statement that "prostitution is sexual exploitation sustained over time" (Salvation Army 2009).

The influence of such Christian ideas on US anti-trafficking policy and practice has been significant. Members of the Christian right lobbied for the legislation that eventually led Congress to pass the Trafficking Victims Protection Act (TVPA) in 2000 and for a Cabinet-level agency to address trafficking, which became the Interagency Task Force to Monitor and Combat Trafficking in Persons in 2002 (see Soderlund 2005: 68, 73–75). Most notably, faith-based groups helped to initiate the "prostitution policy pledge," which prohibits federal funding to non-US organizations that work with sex workers (see Soderlund 2005: 79–81). At the same time, the US Government has directed an increasing level of funding to "faith-based organizations," some of which engage in ethically problematic "raid and rescue missions" that I will discuss later (see Hoenig 2004: 1; McKelvey 2004: 3).

As the following discussion will reveal, such religious views of prostitution undergirding US anti-trafficking and HIV/AIDS policy significantly diverge from those present in other cultural contexts subject to US policy prescriptions, including Thailand and India.

US anti-prostitution policy in cross-cultural perspective

The example of Thailand

Prostitutes have existed in Thailand for many centuries, although in earlier times often in specialized roles as courtesans or "temporary wives" rather than as the commercial sex workers that predominate in that country today (see Kapur-Fic 1998: 454; Jeffrey 2002: 5–14). Polygamy was legal until 1935 and most high status men had several wives. Commercial prostitution first appeared in Southeast Asia in the late 1600s and was legalized under the "Three Seals Law" of 1805. Although originating in the colonial period, the sex trade in Thailand began to take its modern form with the influx of US armed servicemen coming to Thailand for "rest and recreation" ("R&R") from the Vietnam War in the 1960s and 1970s. The sex industry in Thailand has continued to thrive and grow since that era, becoming a major hub for sex tourism and a significant contributor to the Thai economy.

As a Theravada Buddhist country, the ethics of the orthodox Buddhist religion play a significant role in people's attitudes regarding prostitution in Thailand (Bhikkhu 2003: 1). While prostitution is believed to accumulate negative karma by reinforcing craving and attachment to the sensual world of desire (which perpetuates bondage to this world of *samsara* or suffering), throughout Buddhist history it has not been considered a "sin" or violation of fundamental religious laws, as it has been in Christianity (see Brock and Thistlethwaite 1996: 62–63; Murcott 1991: 119–121; Keyes 1984: 236). In fact, Mettanando Bhikkhu suggests that "Westerners may be surprised that in Thailand, Buddhism has so little problem with prostitution—especially when the profession was legal [before 1986]. In Bangkok, some brothels stand side by side with temples" (Bhikkhu 2003: 1).

According to traditional Buddhist teachings, prostitution can be interpreted as running afoul of the prohibition of sexual misconduct, one of the basic five precepts taken by lay Buddhists as well as monks (along with not killing, stealing, lying, or drinking alcohol). However, the sexual misconduct referred to in the precept is more often thought of as referring to "unskillful" rather than "sinful" conduct, since sex itself is not viewed as a sin (*bap*), only as a form of bodily attachment and craving which must be abandoned in order to attain liberation (Satha-Anand 1999: 197–198; Kapur-Fic 1998: 420, citing Horner 1930: 94; Brock and Thistlethwaite 1996: 196; Khin Thitsa 1980: 23). In addition, Buddhist views of impermanence mean that having worked as a prostitute does not leave any permanent or irrevocable mark on one's identity.

Indeed, according to some interpretations, Buddhist principles of "merit making" and karma actually justify prostitution, at least on a temporary basis. Merit making is a traditional Buddhist principle according to which good deeds, such as acts of generosity and kindness, can "accrue" to the benefit of persons other than the recipient. Children have a strong filial obligation to make merit on behalf of their parents. Lacking other options for merit making, women's work in the sex industry, if temporary, is viewed as justified and remedied based on understandings of karma. Some Thai Buddhists believe that the negative karmic impact of prostitution is counteracted by the merit women are able to make for themselves and their families from their earnings. Thus, family members may willfully neglect to inquire how the money that their daughters send home has been earned, especially as it can be used to make merit by giving lavish donations to the local temple (Kapur-Fic 1998: 457; Skrobanek et al. 1997: 69–78; Vichit-Vadakan 1994: 518). By accepting such donations, these institutions lend some legitimacy to the way the money is earned (*see* Skrobanek et al. 1997: 74).

In addition, although the all-male Sangha today does not condone the sexual exploitation of women through trafficking and coerced prostitution, it has not formally opposed the practice either. As the authors of a study on trafficking in Thailand observe, even though "Buddhist monks should in principle be opposed to prostitution, there has been little evidence of their involvement in activities to change the attitudes of the people" (Skrobanek et al. 1997: 77–78; Kapur-Fic 1998: 454–455; Kabilsingh 1991: 80–81). In order to provide an opportunity for prostitutes to work out their bad karma by making merit, monks accept alms from them and do not expel them from the temples (see Kapur-Fic 1998: 420; Kabilsingh 1991: 83).

Nor, as Penny van Esterik puts it, does Buddhism "irrevocably damn prostitutes as evil beings" (van Esterik 2000: 170). In fact, the Patimokha Laws of the *Vinaya* can be interpreted as sanctioning prostitution by listing ten kinds of wives, including a *Dhanakita*, "a woman bought with money for the purpose of sexual pleasure," and a *Muhuttiya*, "a temporary wife, a wife for the moment" (Murcott 1991: 96; also Keyes 1984: 224; Truong 1990: 136). In early Buddhist texts, courtesans (or "*sobhini*"—meaning "praise" or "beautiful") are described (or describe themselves) as beautiful, of high social status, and able to command huge fees from their "clients." They are depicted as having tremendous spiritual power in addition to their secular power of having accumulated great wealth and renown.[6]

Several stories of courtesans or prostitutes are featured in the *Therigatha* ("Songs of the Nuns"), a chronicle of the initial generation of female Buddhists, as well as in other early Buddhist texts (see Kapur-Fic 1998: 451, 453; Horner 1930: 86–94, 184–193; Law 1981: 25–34; Rhys Davids and Norman 1989: 201–202; Murcott 1991: 131–134). The *Therigatha* poem of Ambapali, for example, tells the story of a courtesan who donates a pleasure garden to the Sangha and renounces worldly life to become a nun once she realizes the transience of her beauty. At least four courtesans attained enlightenment at some point during the Buddha's lifetime in this account (see Sponberg 1992: 4; Horner 1930: 89).

Furthermore, none of the "*ganika*" or prostitutes who served the general public are criticized or viewed negatively in the texts. Although the Pali Canon describes the Buddha as referring to the frequenting of prostitutes as a vice of the men, he never criticizes prostitutes for their immoral acts. Instead, he gives them many opportunities to discuss their behavior with him (Bhikkhu 2003: 1; Kabilsingh 1991: 81; Horner 1930: 86–94, 184–193; Law 1981: 25–34). In sum, although religion in Thailand does not promote or valorize sex work or sex workers, neither does it condemn prostitution as sinful nor prostitutes as irredeemable sinners as Christianity has done.

The example of India

Although mainstream attitudes towards prostitution in India today are similar to those in the United States, we find evidence of markedly more positive perspectives in the period prior to British colonialism, when many men had established relationships with women in addition to their initial or primary wives. A variety of early texts in Indian history reveal a more accepted place for the prostitute's body (as well as for sexuality in general)[7] than today. Among the myriad images of the prostitute's body in the Indian past,[8] some have been quite positive, particularly prior to British colonialism, which brought with it Christian moralistic views about non-marital sex as sinful and the women who engaged in it as sinners. In general, however, even in the colonial encounter, prostitutes were neither pitied nor condemned in the same way they have been throughout the history of Christianity (see Ballhatchet 1980: 20).[9]

There are many prostitutes mentioned in both of the great Indian epics *The Ramayana* and *The Mahabharata* as well as the *Smrtis* (especially the *Manusmrti* or *Laws of Manu*), the *Agamas,* the *Arthasastra*[10] and, of course, the *Kamasutra.*[11] Prostitution came to be legally regulated by the state sometime in the first millennium, and the *Smrtis* contain a number of rules about how prostitution was to be conducted (Kotiswaran 2001: 197). Evidence suggests that prostitution continued to be well organized and regulated by the state under Muslim rule in India during the Mughal period.[12] Certain classes of prostitutes entertained kings and brahmans (Srinivasan 2006: 166).

A brief look at three different social organizations of prostitution, the *ganika,* the *devadasi,* and the *tawa'if,* and the British response to them, gives us some sense of the ways in which the British applied the Christian concept of sinful to all forms of prostitution in order to de-legitimatize long-standing Hindu practices. It should be noted, however, that though Hindus regarded prostitutes differently than the colonists, only some prostitutes were highly regarded. Hindus, like their Christian counterparts, considered the wife, but not the prostitute, to be pure. Further, the lives of certain types of Hindu prostitutes look hauntingly like the lives of today's trafficked women. But in refusing to note the difference among prostitutes, British policies may be seen as setting the stage for current US policies which conflate all forms of prostitution with sexual slavery.

1. The Ganika: *Ganikas* or courtesans are typically described in early Sanskrit literature as beautiful, well educated (as few women were), and accomplished in singing, dancing, and the other arts. In contrast, the *vesya* were women who lacked the *ganika*'s skills. The *Kamasutra*'s description of how a *vesya* can enhance her status by gaining proficiency in the high arts and skills of the courtesan and, through becoming a *ganika*, can receive "a seat of honour in the assembly of men," discourse with men as their equal, and become "an object of universal regard" (quoted in Srinivasan 2006: 162), suggests that a certain social mobility from lower to more respected strata of prostitution was possible. In addition, there were lower-ranked *pumscali* and *dasis* (literally "slaves"). The latter category included *devadasis* ("slaves of God"), discussed further below, and *kumbhadasis* ("pots-and-pans" prostitutes) (Srinivasan 2006: 162). As already noted, early Buddhist texts suggest that courtesans were socially accepted within the different strata of Hindu society.

Even among courtesans, however, historically there have been differences in status. For example, the Muslim *baijis* were highly respected in nineteenth century colonial Bengal, in contrast to the Hindu *khemtawalis*, who were not. Even in ancient India, however, the wife had more esteem with respect to sexual purity than even the courtesan, no matter how learned the latter might be, since the wife's sexual purity was necessary to insure the positive *dharma* of the husband and his offspring. Thus, in relation to the wife, the courtesan was deemed sexually impure and compromised, even in ancient India.

2. Devadasi: *Devadasis* (literally "slaves of god" or "temple women") are a group of females who historically have been dedicated to the service of gods in particular regions of India, especially in southern states like Karnataka and Tamil Nadu. *Devadasis* played a respected and important social role within their local communities.[13] Whereas prostitution may have been only incidental, if present at all, in the traditional roles some *devadasis* performed, the British Parliament used information about the *devadasi* system as evidence of "debauched primitiveness" and referred to *devadasis* as "prostitutes" as part of its campaign to justify paternalistic British rule to "civilize" India in the nineteenth century (see Nataraj 2003: 4; Orr 2000: 199 n.28). British missionaries supported reformers' requests to have *devadasis* legally declared prostitutes so that their roles could be de-legitimized (Orr 2000: 15).

Aside from objections by some *devadasis* to the characterization of themselves as victims of violence and coercion, there was mostly only a reaction of embarrassment by Indians to such portrayals (Orr 2000: 14).[14] Both colonial and nationalist reformers denounced the *devadasi* as inconsistent with the idealized image of Indian womanhood as chaste, pure, married, domestic, and self-sacrificing (Orr 2000: 13),[15] leading to the ironic result that many *devadasis* today in regions where the practice is still extant (despite several regional laws banning the practice), have been reduced to little more than common prostitutes as in the case of women dedicated to temples of the goddess Yellamma on the Karnataka-Maharashtra border (Orr 2000: 199 n.28).[16]

3. Tawa'if: From at least the beginning of the nineteenth century until after Indian Independence, courtesan singer-dancers (*tawa'if*) were at the center of elite entertainment in feudal and mercantile-colonial milieux of India, performing at courts and presiding over reenactments of court assemblies in salons that became the first public venue for Hindustani art music (Qureshi 2006: 312).[17] Along with *devadasi, tawai'if* were considered to be the holders of traditional Indian art, culture, and religion.[18] *Tawa'if* came from both Hindu and Muslim families. Veena Talwar Oldenburg's landmark study of *tawa'if* in Lucknow indicates that many *tawai'if* held positions that were relatively more affluent and independent than those of their "chaste" or married counterparts (Oldenburg 1990). Similar to the *devadasi*, the *tawai'if* and her dance became morally stigmatized by missionaries and both British and Indian middle-class social reformers, resulting in the "resignification of courtesans as fallen women" (Qureshi 2006: 319–320)[19] and the undesirable "Other."

This brief review of Hindu *ganika, devadasi,* and *tawa'if* traditions is intended to demonstrate that there are important strands of Indian history and tradition, especially prior to the colonial encounter, which held a much more complex and ambivalent attitude toward prostitution than exists in mainstream Indian discourses today, and that reintroducing this complexity into contemporary discussions of prostitution would avoid the British mistake of assuming that all understandings of prostitution different from theirs were to be rejected.[20]

Implications for US anti-trafficking policy

While recognizing that there is no "cultural purity" or neat and tidy separation between one culture and another, especially in a postcolonial and globalized context, it is nevertheless evident that US anti-prostitution policy is particularly problematic when applied to such non-western contexts as Thailand and India.

(1) First, US policy only recognizes one culturally and religiously specific view of normative sexuality and gender (i.e., Western, conservative Christian) which silences and represses alternative indigenous religious and cultural understandings of sexual behaviors, including those of sex workers themselves. Among the most problematic of US funded anti-trafficking activities are so-called "raid and rescue" missions. Often led by Western faith-based NGOs, these missions typically involve alliances with local law enforcement to raid brothels and other establishments where commercial sex is being conducted. All the sex workers discovered are rounded up, taken into police custody, and either arrested, deported, or sent to temporary shelters or rehabilitation homes regardless of whether they are willing or forced, consenting adults or underage minors. Since the raids often involve "manhandling," beating, sexual coercion, and extortion, an fail to protect women in prostitution from physical or sexual violence perpetrated by police themselves (Amin 2004: 12), it is evident that such strategies are more about regulating prostitutes for purposes of social control rather than protecting them from harm.

In addition, raid and rescue activities often leave women in worse situations than before. For example, described as "one of George W. Bush's favorite U.S.

programs" (McKelvey 2004: 3), the International Justice Mission (IJM) was awarded over $2 million dollars by the US Government (IJM website; Wilson 2005). Founder Gary Haugen describes the theological underpinnings of his work with IJM as including the belief that Evangelical Christians have a duty, grounded in biblical exhortations from Jesus, to rescue people not only from poverty and from ignorance of the Christian word of God, but also from "injustice" (Haugen 2002: 1–2).

Given this orientation, it is not surprising to find that one of IJM's main anti-trafficking activities has been "rescue missions" such as one that Dateline NBC featured in its story on IJM's work in Cambodia in 2004 (see MSNBC 2005). Several times in 2001, IJM investigators paid undercover visits to a bar in Bangkok called the Pink Lady. As a result, in a raid conducted a week later with Thai police, forty-three women and girls were rounded up at brothels and other establishments where prostitution was being conducted. In IJM's view, this was another successful "rescue" mission, like many others it has conducted in Thailand, India, Cambodia, and other countries. Within one month following the raid, however, a total of twenty-four girls and women had run away from their "rescuers" (Jones 2003: 3).

IJM advertises these rescues as effective ways to help trafficked girls and women, assuming that all of the sex workers want to be rescued. Such moral reform activities disrespect alternative cultural and religious understandings of the "harms" associated with prostitution and deny moral agency to women, especially those who do not wish to be "rescued" from sex work. Ben Svasti, the coordinator of TRAFCORD, a joint task force formed with US support to attack sex trafficking in northern Thailand, admits that "it's hard to figure out who are the victims" and that he's heard "of the same migrant sex workers being rescued from brothels two or three times" (Montlake 2003). Similarly, many women in Thailand who have been offered factory work or sewing jobs as an alternative to sex work have rejected it in favor of the better money they are able to make in the commercial sex industry, since they do not necessarily share the morality that guided the government's and NGO's efforts (Balakrishnan 2001: 53).

In a second example, in a controversial raid on a red-light area in Sangli, India, with local police in May 2005, Restore International was accused by the Indian NGO Sangram of "rescuing" mostly adult women without their consent (Indian law makes only child prostitution illegal). The FBO retaliated by accusing Sangram of promoting prostitution (VAMP 2005). Sangram (which received a Human Rights Watch Defender award in 2003 for its human rights-based response to HIV/AIDS) lost its USAID funding and had to fight to restore its reputation by obtaining a letter from USAID (which was issued on October 6, 2005) that its funding had been terminated "by mutual consent" after the policy pledge was enacted and not because it had been promoting "trafficking in persons" (see VAMP 2005; CHANGE 2006; Kaplan 2006: 2–3). This case indicates how FBOs are using the loyalty oath and pledge as a weapon against NGOs that promote the rights of sex workers. Such inconsistent cultural understandings have led to conflicts in both Thailand and India.

(2) Second, US anti-prostitution policies harm women who earn their livelihood through commercial sex work. While the prescriptions of US anti-trafficking policy infringe upon the autonomy of all women, it is especially inappropriate as applied to women in non-US, especially culturally non-Western, contexts, where more entrenched systems of sexism and patriarchy may leave women with little to no alternative sources of livelihood. Punishing women for their occupations in prostitution by denying US funding to organizations which refuse to sign the policy pledge exposes these women to further stigmatization, marginalization, and deprives them of resources to services such as HIV/AIDS prevention and other health care facilities.

In India, for example, some of the most successful HIV/AIDS prevention efforts have used sex workers as peer educators. Similarly, in Thailand, the organization EMPOWER has made great strides in protecting sex workers from HIV/AIDS. These and other examples are illustrated in a powerful video called *Taking the Pledge*, which documents the harms that the US-imposed policy pledge has had on sex worker rights and well-being around the world. Organizations that work with sex workers are no longer able to receive US funding, either because their work does in fact or is perceived to contravene the requirements of the policy pledge. Similarly, local government support for such programs risks being identified in the *TIPS Report* as support for prostitution, which puts such governments at risk of receiving a lower tier TIPS ranking.

(3) US anti-prostitution policies bolster patriarchal norms and repressive and gender discriminatory policies of foreign governments and religious establishments. This is evident in both Thailand and India where current prostitution laws discriminate against women. In Thailand, the Thai Prostitution Prevention and Suppression Act passed in 1996 (Thai Prostitution Act 1996), which decriminalized prostitution, continues to make sex workers subject to fines of up to 1,000 Baht (US $50.00) for soliciting in a public place, "behaving" like a prostitute, or causing a nuisance to the public. Due to rampant corruption in law enforcement, moreover, it is still generally the sex workers themselves, rather than the traffickers, pimps, or brothel owners, who are arrested, prosecuted, and treated as the criminals (Pearson 2002).

In the 1980s, the Thai government made special arrangements with foreign governments to prevent trafficking, which effectively "curtailed women's self-determination and freedom of movement, making them, 'for their own good,' objects of state control" (Jeffrey 2002: 88). Raids on brothels by law enforcement officers had resulted in arrests of prostitute women, but not of owners and procurers. As Jeffrey observes: "whenever stronger measures against prostitution were enforced, it usually resulted in harsher realities for prostitute women" (2002: 90). The law has maintained an ambivalent, even hypocritical stance, which enables the government to profit from women's sex work at the same time that it continues to criminalize it and stigmatize the women who work in the sex industry. US anti-prostitution policies only strengthen such repressive and discriminatory provisions.

Indian government and law enforcement today reflect a similarly complex attitude towards prostitution. Even the title of the governing law—the *Immoral*

Trafficking Prevention Act (ITPA)—passed in 1986, reflects this ambivalence since it makes prostitution itself only immoral, not criminal. Solicitation or engaging in sex acts in or near a public place, however, is criminalized. These latter provisions authorize police to conduct searches and to remove, evict, and detain sex workers from brothels and other establishments, which, the Lawyers' Collective notes, leads to the severest forms of human rights violations against individual sex workers and the community as a whole. US anti-prostitution policies reinforce the harms of such national laws by pressuring foreign governments to maintain or even strengthen provisions which criminalize prostitution and contribute to abuse of women by law enforcement.

Both Thailand and India have been the recipients of "Tier 2 Watch List" ratings in the last few *TIPS Reports*, signaling that they may be close to falling to a "Tier 3 rating," and thus facing the threat of sanctions for failing to conform their policies closely enough to those of the US.

(4) A fourth and final problem I would like to mention is the damage to US foreign policy that results from the kind of heavy-handed and culturally insensitive imposition of the US's moral agenda that is evidenced in its anti-prostitution policies. Just as British colonialism and intervention into societies deemed primitive and backward were justified by the view of a "singular future for the masses of the world in which justice and modernity are equated with being European" (Kapur 2005: 22), so the universal application of US anti-trafficking policy, with its hegemonic conservative Christian moralistic views about women and prostitution, is premised on a similar view of "enlightened" American values (see Kapur 2005: 7). Such attitudes can only contribute to resentment and ill-will, rather than promoting international alliances and cooperation on issues of common concern.

In conclusion, the alternative and heterogeneous religious and cultural understandings of prostitution in Thailand and India traced in this chapter indicate that the hegemonic "one size fits all" anti-prostitution policy of the US is misplaced, especially in contexts where the meanings of prostitution vary sharply from those of a conservative Christian worldview, and especially where some of these alternative understandings of prostitution may better serve the needs and interests of women than moralistic US policy.

Notes

1   This chapter was one of the last works of Professor Peach, who did not live to see it in print. The editors are grateful to Shelley Harshe, Senior Administrative Assistant for the Department of Philosophy and Religion at American University, for her invaluable assistance in researching and editing the final version of this chapter.

2   The definition of trafficking in the United Nations' *Protocol to Prevent, Suppress and Punish Trafficking in Persons* requires *both* "the recruitment, transportation, transfer, harbouring or receipt of persons," *as well as* "the threat or use of force, or other forms of coercion, or abduction, or fraud, or deception," etc. (UN 2000, Art. 3 (a)). The Trafficking Victims Protection Act of 2000 (TVPA) *requires* "force, fraud, or coercion" to be present *only* for what it terms "Severe forms of trafficking in persons." Other forms of sex trafficking are defined simply as "the recruitment, harboring, transportation, provision, or obtaining of a person for the purpose of a commercial sex act" (US Congress 2000:

Sec. 103 (9)). In essence, then, prostitution and other forms of commercial sex constitute "trafficking" under US law, regardless of consent or coercion.

3 For example, the Global AIDS Act misrepresents "prostitution, the sex trade, rape, sexual assault and sexual exploitation of women and children" (id. at section 7611(a) (4)) as all equivalently harmful when in fact prostitution and sex work may not involve either trafficking or violence. Whereas the TVPRA contains language explicitly banning advocacy of legalization, the Global AIDS Act is silent on this matter. These policies are also incorporated into the provisions determining distribution of funds under the $15 billion President's Emergency Provision for AIDS Relief (PEPFAR) as well as US State Department anti-trafficking policy.

4 The 2006 *Trafficking in Persons Report (TIPS Report)* states: "The US government opposes prostitution and related activities . . . as contributing to the phenomenon of human trafficking. These activities are inherently harmful and dehumanizing" (US Department of State 2006: 189).

5 The Gospel of Luke (7:36–50), which tells the story of "a sinful woman who bathed Jesus' feet with her tears, dried them with her hair, kissed them, and then anointed them with an ointment that she had brought with her" (Collins 2000: 10–11) may also refer to a prostitute, although the term "sinful" is not further elaborated. While the Gospels have very little to say about Jesus's attitudes towards prostitution, L. William Countryman speculates that since Jesus "does not seem to have been anxious about unattached women and since he even held up contemporary prostitutes as a religious example at one point, we may guess that, insofar as he took prostitution to be ethically wrong, he followed the example of Proverbs in apportioning blame to the man who visited the prostitute more than to the prostitute herself. Jesus still allowed a marriage to be annulled on the grounds of *porneia*, but this, as we have seen, was probably limited to the situation where a bride who was claimed to be a virgin turned out not to be" (Countryman 1988: 189).

6 This was achieved by carrying out their roles impeccably, such as the story of Bindumati, in the *Milandapanha*, who has the ability to make the Ganges River flow backwards through the power of her Truth Act (Srinivasan 2006: 170). The story of the courtesan Ambapali in the *Therigatha* reveals her spiritual power in the Buddha's accepting an invitation to take a meal at her house.

7 The large number of erotic paintings and the openly erotic sculptures adorning Hindu temples suggest that sex and especially female sexuality were far more accepted and respected in ancient Indian culture than they are today. Hindu temples, such as those still extant at Kujaraho, were decorated with images of *apsara*—variously, "prostitutes of the Gods," "dancing ladies of the night," "fairies," or "sex angels," who were considered to be more beautiful than any women on earth (see Orr 2000: 195 n.7; Ringdal 2004: 77).

8 In fact, Vern and Bonnie Bullough contend that there are more than 330 words for prostitution in late Sanskrit (last centuries BCE) (Bullough and Bullough 1987: 86), reflecting the variety of different types and roles. The status of prostitutes appears to have been determined primarily on the basis of caste, with upper caste prostitutes being held in much higher regard than those from lower castes and classes. Regarding the status of prostitutes, Kautilya "stated that a middle- or lower-class woman did not lose status by being a prostitute, unless she took clients from castes lower than her own, but a Brahmin woman who prostituted herself might be killed" (Ringdal 2004: 72). The *Laws of Manu* (X, 47) specify that prostitution belongs to Vaidehakas, one of the lower castes (Henriques 1963: 159) and that Brahmins had to undergo a purification ritual after visiting a prostitute (Meyer 1953: 274; see Henriques 1963: 162; Bullough and Bullough 1987: 98).

9 For example, in his study of British colonial regulation of prostitution in India, Kenneth Ballhatchet notes that: "there is no condemnation of prostitutes on moral grounds, nor

is there any attempt to persuade them to change their occupation. It was generally recognized that religious attitudes were less rigid in India than in England, though social structures were more rigid: prostitutes were not denounced as sinners, but society permitted them no alternative occupation" (Ballhatchet 1980: 20).

10 An entire section of the *Arthasastra*, written by the political philosopher Kautilya (who lived sometime around 290BCE and AD300), is devoted to the *ganikas* (courtesans) and their supervision by *ganikadhyksa* (official courtesan "managers"). Kautilya viewed prostitution as a well-established institution, approved and organized by the state. He felt that prostitutes had certain rights, regardless of how closely regulated they were.

11 These include courtesans who accompanied the expeditions of princes and aristocrats and prostitute women who followed the armies as "camp followers," not only providing sexual service, but also cooking and cleaning for the soldiers (see Henriques 1963: 160). Vedic texts show that people were acquainted with prostitution through references to "loose" women, female "vagabonds," and sexually active unmarried girls (Ringdal 2004: 69–70).

12 Fifteenth-century accounts of India describe prostitutes being provided to the soldiers of the King of Vijanagar, a Hindu state (see Henriques 1963: 174–175).

13 Despite this campaign against prostitution in India, however, British courts and legislatures in India apparently did not accede to Hindu reformers' requests to have *devadasis* legally declared prostitutes for decades, even though their requests were supported by British missionaries (Orr 2000: 15).

14 Orr points to the political expediency of the notion that the traditional role of the *devadasi* was chaste and non-sexual but had degenerated over the centuries for reformers bent on outlawing the tradition and divesting *devadasis* of their roles as specialists in Indian classical dance (Orr 2000: 12). British reformers also objected to *devadasis* being dedicated to temples at such a young age, especially as their roles related to sexual activity, and without their consent. However, as Orr points out, the situation of girls dedicated as *devadasis* was, in these respects, identical to that of every girl in India who would be given in marriage at a similar age (Orr 2000: 13). Yet, it was easier for the reformers to take on the *devadasi* issue than that of marriage customs in India more generally.

15 In opposition to colonial reform efforts, Indian nationalists constructed Indian womanhood as the embodiment of nationalism, especially "their roles as wives and mothers, as chaste and sexually pure" (Kapur 2005: 31). Thus, Indian reformers generally supported the British campaign to abolish *devadasis*, but for very different reasons (Orr 2000: 14–15; *see* Srinivasan 2006: 176). Hindu reformers were more concerned about the threat that prostitution posed to family life, particularly the possibility that a high-caste woman would become a prostitute. In addition, male kin of *devadasis* were keen to have these women thrust into models of respectable Indian womanhood, which precluded them being economically independent (such women being assumed to be prostitutes, and thereby accruing more economic control to males) (Orr 2000: 227 n.21). Orr notes the irony that the view that the only way a respectable woman can have property is through a (sexual) relationship with a man is persistent, even among those "who are aware that the branding of *devadasis* as prostitutes was a politically motivated gesture" (Orr 2000: 227 n.21). Indian reformers also opposed the *devadasi* system as a Hindu reform measure to eliminate any religious sanction for prostitution, which they considered to be public immorality (Orr 2000: 15).

16 One interviewed *devadasi* told the researcher that "*Jogtis* are almost without exception prostitutes. But they are not as Malli says 'professional prostitutes'. 'Our main vocation is serving Yellamma and we live by *jogwa* (begging)'" (Kersenboom-Story 1987: 196).

17 Until they were abolished in 1952, *tawa'if* performances were *the* "quintessential courtly display of high-culture-cum-entertainment in the Princely states" (Qureshi 2006: 315).

Part II

Interrogating practices of representation

5 How not to give rape political significance

Louise du Toit

Introduction

This chapter[1] makes the claim that the meanings of rape should be interpreted in context, especially if we want to make sense of rape as politically significant, which I also claim is an important aim. I believe that feminists should simultaneously investigate the ways in which rape fulfills a variety of political functions *and* should insist on bringing rape into the public domain as an always politically significant phenomenon.[2] This is needed because the usual systematic exclusion of rape from the considerations of the public–political realm is thoroughly intertwined with the exclusion of women as women[3] from that realm, i.e., through the systematic privatization and parochialization of women's interests and concerns as opposed to the ideological universalization of men's. I have argued elsewhere (Du Toit 2007) that such exclusion of women from the foundation of the state is typical of western state formation, and it is globalized to the extent that the state itself is globalized (Pateman 1988; Irigaray 1985). Moreover, I see the invisibility or "impossibility" of rape as a symptom of this blind-spot or distortion (Irigaray's "matricide") at the basis of the state.[4]

While this chapter investigates the particular context of rape in post-apartheid South Africa and offers a reading of these rapes as a symptom of South Africa's political transition, the relevance of the analysis itself exceeds its South African context or transitional societies generally. It serves as a case study that illustrates some of the philosophical issues at stake in drawing out the political significance of rape. The first section of the chapter is devoted to a general discussion of these issues. The second section is an interpretation of rape as a transitional phenomenon in South Africa's case.

Some preliminary considerations

Before embarking on the analysis of the South African situation, I want to ensure that my main claims are not misunderstood, and so I will make a few general points clear. The first point that I want to make is that a focus on rape's political significance may create unease in feminist theorists who epistemologically prioritize the plight of rape victims. I share this unease and understand it to emerge from an intuition that resists a shift in focus away from the meaning of the rape for the victim and towards the meaning of the rape for the wider society, which is often permeated with misogyny. My response to this unease is that, viewed structurally, the lived experience, the damage, and therefore the meaning of rape for the victims is indeed relatively stable across contexts, and it finally matters relatively little to the victims themselves whether they are raped for instance during peacetime or wartime. At least, this variable pales into insignificance in comparison with the structural similarities in rape experiences that have to do with the loss of a world (and its constituting relations), voice, agency, and sexual and bodily integrity—a kind of total loss.[5]

In highlighting and interpreting the political dimension and meanings of rape, we should take great care to simultaneously acknowledge the meaning and damage of rape to the victims (do epistemic justice to them, as Lorraine Code would say (Code 2009)) *and* interpret the socio-symbolic and political contexts within which such rapes take place. This is a delicate task, because the contexts within which rape becomes possible, easy, or trivial are often overtly misogynist even as they often explicitly reject the political significance of rape. Thus the contextual forces typically actively oppose the meaning that the rape has for the victims, as well as their interests that justice should be done to its damage. This task is also tricky, and this is my second point, because when we critically analyze contexts that justify or trivialize rape in order to understand how it happens that rapes occur with impunity or on a large scale, we are not logically engaging in a justification of rape, although such an attempt at understanding may come dangerously close to rationalization or it might create that impression in the reader. The question becomes how to avoid collaborating in the justification of rape in the process of trying to understand it as a political phenomenon. To further illustrate this point, it might be helpful to cast this problematic in the terms of analysis that I employed in an earlier text (Du Toit 2009).

Following Elaine Scarry's careful analysis of torture (Scarry 1985), I have argued there that in rape, like torture, there is, phenomenologically speaking, a collision of two worlds—that of the rapist with that of the victim. I have pointed to an abyss which structurally opens up between the world of the rapist and the world of the victim: for the duration of the rape they inhabit two diametrically opposed universes, with that of the rapist threatening to fully eclipse the world of the victim. Moreover, through feminist analysis we know that a woman's world is traditionally more fragile (see the "wound of femininity" (Cornell 1995) and the notion of "the other of the other" (Irigaray 1992) to understand why her world is always fragile under patriarchal conditions), and the rapist activates and violently drives home to the victim many reminders about precisely how fragile and tentative her contestatory world is within a thoroughly misogynist world (Du Toit 2009). Although the victim's world or frame of reference is systematically dismantled and appropriated by the actions of the rapist which aim at convincing the victim that she matters not, it is important to recognize that *there are two worlds* to start off with and that the target of the rapist's destructive work is the world of the victim, however inadequately that world may be construed or imagined by the perpetrator.

Debra Bergoffen's demonstration of how the meaning-making power of the rape victim's body is not simply destroyed but rather usurped by the rapist and turned into his instrument (Bergoffen 2009), in the context of war rape, might be usefully enlisted here. She shows that rape used as a war weapon is so effective mainly because it sends a message about control to the enemy men: you are no longer real men, because we and not you, control the sexuality of "your" women. Unable to protect "their" women, the enemy men lose their gendered identities as protectors of the vulnerable, as protectors of the nation (typically symbolically equated with the sexualized bodies of the women, especially in contexts where such equation produced shame caused by violation). The effectiveness of war rape is thus parasitical upon a pre-existing social symbolic in which women's sexual integrity is already problematically appropriated by the men and equated with the fragile integrity or honor of the nation.[6]

It should be clear from this example that if we were to subsequently insist that the *real* or only valid meaning of war rape is contained within the rapist's intention, which is conceivably to undo the masculinity of the enemy men, we might very plausibly be colluding with the rapists in validating their aims and further occluding the meanings targeted in the process—those held by their direct victims, both before and after the rape. Put differently, if the only way of giving political significance to the rapes that Bergoffen discusses (those condemned by the International Criminal Tribunal for the former Yugoslavia) is by reinscribing the meanings intended by the rapists, and further obliterating the meanings the rapes might have (had) for the victims themselves, then it is clear on which side of the "war of the worlds" or the "war of meanings" we enlist our services. More to the point, individual women who were rape victims within this context may have already resisted in their personal lives the equation of their own sexuality with the integrity or honor of the nation to which they belong—an equation both assumed and violently reinforced by the motives and behavior of the rapists. Their resistance to such an interpretation—and therefore their "world" or meaningful universe in which they were imaginably autonomous sexual agents and desiring subjects[7]—would be triply erased: first, by the everyday discourse that equated these things symbolically even before the war; second, by the rapists' intended message through the rapes themselves; and third, by our narrow interpretation of the political significance of those events.

My third point in this section is thus that, by insisting that these dismantled or damaged worlds of hidden resistance and repressed contestation are politically significant in themselves, as is the attack on them, I refuse to conflate the rapists' intended meaning-shifting ("we are the sexual masters of 'your' women, not you") with the only true or valid political sense to be made out of such rapes, because the assumption on which it is based is itself likely to be contested by the rape victims. Moreover, if we retain a focus on the contestatory world of the victim and refuse to collaborate with the rapist in erasing that from view, we also refuse the masculine bias of the political as such: we refuse to regard rapes as politically significant only to the extent that they can be translated into typical male-biased political concerns or into indirect male-on-male violation (obtaining political gravity by proxy). By treating the violation of rape as structurally similar in most cases and by insisting on the political significance of rape *as such*, as an act of exclusion of women from the human and political community, we target the systemic blind spot of western state politics and simultaneously challenge the male-biased and/or misogynist contextual discourses that facilitate and justify rape, whether in war or in peacetime. Rape has political significance, not simply because and when it sometimes forms a deliberate part of a war strategy or because it can be construed as a weapon of genocide, but because it is a concrete way in which an extreme form of power is exerted, mostly by a man or men over women or children, more rarely over other men.

My fourth point is thus that rape is politically significant in itself, because it is probably the most effective mechanism available for the most intimate and complete control of another person. As Don Berkich puts it: "the rapist exercises an extraordinary level of control over his victim, one which reaches beyond the victim's will to violate the very grounds by which she guides her own will, her personhood" (Berkich 2009). This is why the rapist manages to cause a shift in the world of the victim, and why the rapist's actions always have meanings beyond his intentions: whatever shift of meaning he aims at through this act of extra-ordinary control over another's personhood, the *effect* of rape is always to severely damage or dismantle the actual, inhabited, and lived world of the victim, together with her personhood, comprised of her agency, voice, and bodily integrity. Whatever the contents of the respective symbolic worlds initially, in rape they clash, and the world of the rapist threatens to engulf and usurp or appropriate the world of the victim. This is the very stuff of politics, playing out on the most intimate level of world and meaning creation, deconstruction, and contestation.

So far in this section I have mainly cautioned against the kind of contextual-ization of rape's political significance that tends to obscure the reality of the victim and argued that a narrow focus on the rapists' motivations may unjustifiably reduce the political meaning of rape to the intended meaning of the rapists—a focus that would reinscribe the rapist's worldview and further dismantle that of the victim. Now I need to make clear why an investigation of the context is nevertheless important for a clearer understanding of rape's political significance, in spite of the many cautionary noises made so far. My fifth point is thus that we should seek the political significance precisely in the clash between two meaningful "universes," if we agree that rape is an event in which one universe is asserted against another in a particularly pernicious and intimately violent way, with the aim to destroy the latter. This implies for me that neither the initial world of the victim nor of the rapist should logically be used in isolation to determine what the meaning and political significance of rape is. The political significance is the fact that these worlds are brought into violent engagement or conflict and that one world is forcefully and violently asserted over the other, with the effect that the status of both change in the process.

It is important to view rape as such a dynamic clash and as a violent assertion of one (usually deeply misogynist, but context-specific) worldview over another, because without this *political* perspective we can all too easily reify rape as a natural phenomenon. There is in this for me a lurking danger of ontologizing the victim status of the victim and the perpetrator status of the perpetrator, which fundamentally dehumanizes, de-historicizes, and depoliticizes both of them, limiting our insight. If we are to resist all fatalistic insinuations of "rape is just what (those kinds of) men do and what some women suffer," we must frame every rape as a political event and carefully analyze it as such.

The following potential problems with emphasizing the political significance of rape have so far been identified in the above: (i) the possible prioritization of the rapists' viewpoint over that of the victims; (ii) the pitfall of reinscribing the public–political realm as essentially masculine; (iii) the danger of reducing the political meaning of rape to the intended meanings of the rapists; (iv) the danger of inadvertently justifying or rationalizing rape in one's attempt to understand its facilitating context; and (v) the danger of losing rape's damage from view.

But there are even more potential pitfalls: (vi) lurking in the recognition by the UN Security Council of war rape (but not rape in general) as a crime against humanity, is the danger of creating a hierarchy of rape victims, which I think can be successfully resisted through an insistence on what I earlier called the relative stability in the kind of damage sustained by rape victims, and which can be explained through my structural analysis of the eclipse of one's world. A further danger is (vii) what I want to call the tendency to "other" rape, which is closely related to the tendency to ontologize rapists and victims. Lorraine Code has an apt description of what this "othering" entails. With regard to the reception in the "white, affluent world of the west" of the decision of the International Criminal Court in the Hague she says:

> "general interest" in it and other war crimes and harms is relatively thin on the ground, deflected again, paradoxically, by the very ordinariness and extraordinariness together in which violent acts in such "other" places tend, for white western folk, to be shrouded ("ordinary" because that is just how people in those places act; "extraordinary" because it is so outrageous that "we" cannot imagine anything like that happening here, so we need not think about it).
>
> (Code 2009)

"Othering" rape in this way and condemning its (natural or ordinary) occurrence in far-off places where it can be safely contained in "extraordinary" contexts with ostensibly "problematic" cultures, allows for both a political selectivity and expediency in the choice of rapes to be politically highlighted and condemned, and a concomitant further entrenchment of the practice of depoliticizing "ordinary" and "domestic" rape.

Related to the tendency to "other" politically significant rapes, is the tendency to dehumanize rapists—this feeds into a further depoliticization of their actions on the home front. If I argue here for the humanization of rapists, this should be clearly distinguished from any attempt at excusing their actions. The humanization of rapists and their aims with raping will to my mind reinforce the political, expedient, power-related and non-necessary nature of what they do and their rationalizations of it. This deliberate humanization is important for a variety of reasons: (i) it is philosophically and morally important to understand how all humans are capable of inflicting great evil upon others; (ii) rape is above all an act of dehumanization; in resisting rape one should work hard not to repeat rape's logic and thereby enact a vicious circle; (iii) by humanizing, historicizing, and contextualizing socio-cultural meanings that facilitate rape, we give it political significance, and simultaneously insist that it is contingent upon such meanings, that it is therefore deeply unnecessary and not a natural feature of human existence; (iv) we help prevent the dangerous political game of "othering" that happens between western and non-western and between supposedly peaceful and conflict contexts (but also within countries, as is the case with South Africa), with all the usual racist and self-congratulatory undertones accompanying such "othering"; (v) we also blur the problematic distinction between war-time and other rapes and become better equipped to notice the political significance of socio-cultural meanings that facilitate, promote, or sustain so-called "rape-prone" societies (Sanday 1996), whether they are in situations of formally acknowledged conflict at any particular point in time or not; (vi) we take more collective responsibility for rape because we address pervasive cultural meanings reinforced by ordinary men and women that render extreme violence against and sexual control over women ultimately normal, trivial, or natural; (vii) by humanizing the perpetrators we acknowledge that rapists and potential rapists are none other than our brothers, fathers, husbands, and sons within the human community, and that we cannot finally build a rape-free society without them. This final point, (vii), echoes some of the sentiments of the African moral emphasis on restorative rather than retributive justice, complete with all the strong points and potential problems this approach entails (Bell 2002).

Rape and transition in South Africa

I have for a number of years been preoccupied with trying to understand why in South Africa we have retained, throughout our ostensibly successful political transition and reconciliation process over fifteen years, such high (one could even say "war") levels of rape in our new, democratic dispensation. In particular, I have wondered about the political significance of this: did this imply that women had been and still are being perceived as a political enemy in the construction of the new dispensation? If so, why? I was very critical of the fact that, on my reading (Du Toit 2007), rape did not feature as a politically significant phenomenon in the work of the Truth and Reconciliation Commission. I suggested that this might be the reason for the ongoing violence against women—the reconciliation between the black and white brothers still excluded the women, and violently so. The rapes that had taken place during the height of the liberation struggle had by the time of the political transition been subsumed under the general violence of that time as politically motivated (and thus sanitized), while the constantly high prevalence of rape since 1994 has been termed by the government as at most a "social" problem, and largely trivialized and privatized.

It is often said in our context that South African men generally have a sense of sexual entitlement which is culturally rooted, and this is offered as the full explanation for these high levels of rape and other forms of sexual violence against women and children. Another (almost contrary) narrative goes that black men[8] have been systematically "emasculated" by apartheid and possibly even further by the democratic dispensation in which women have become equal citizens,[9] and they thus need an affirmation of their manhood which they try to (re-)gain through the violent sexual control of women and children.[10] Long-standing cultural traditions, apartheid, and the shock of the new liberal dispensation, past, present, and future thus blur and blend into multiple explanations offered for the high levels of sexual violence perpetrated by South African men. But, as in many or most other countries, these narratives seldom manage to bestow *political* significance on these "peacetime" rapes. They rather serve to depoliticize the phenomenon through "othering" it in racial or ethnic terms (as just something "they" do), or they serve to rationalize it away by portraying the perpetrators as sexual victims of symbolic castration ("emasculation") in their own right—a kind of psychological explanation. Whatever the explanations offered for our high levels of rape, it is seldom acknowledged as a significant political problem or regarded as a barometer for our political reconciliation process.

My reading of Leonhard Praeg's *The Geometry of Violence* (2007) helped me to think more clearly about the South African transitional and postcolonial situation and especially about the place of violence within it. Praeg draws strongly on a Girardian frame for his understanding of the "extreme," collective violence that often accompanies political transitions. In the limited space available I cannot follow either Praeg or Girard too closely, but will simply highlight what I regard as salient for my purposes. Praeg reads such phenomena as the genocide in Rwanda and necklace and family murders in South Africa during the high point of the liberation struggle as instances of founding violence. He draws on Derrida's insight into "the force of law," to remind us that:

> We are all heir, at least, to persons or events marked, in an essential, interior, ineffaceable fashion, by crimes against humanity. Sometimes these events, these massive, organized cruel murders, which may have been revolutions, great canonic and "legitimate" Revolutions, were the very ones which permitted the emergence of concepts like those of human rights, or the crime against humanity.
>
> (Derrida 2002: 29, quoted in Praeg 2007: 13)

Reading the high levels of rape experienced in South Africa since the struggle (at least)[11] as a similar type of founding violence (as might be suggested by Praeg), in conjunction with my suggestion above that it should be understood as a war of worlds, might help us to better illuminate its political significance within our context. Praeg thus helps me to read this violence with a postcolonial lens, which means in the first place that I try to make sense of it in terms of where our society finds itself and how it sees itself. Second, a postcolonial lens means that I turn my gaze from where I stand towards the western world, and in the process I can better critique the dominant lens through which rape's political significance is often constructed in "exotic and far-off places" like South Africa.

Using just such a postcolonial lens, Praeg makes the important point that the human rights culture and human rights discourse most often used to interpret and condemn violence in transitional contexts are themselves contingent, historical phenomena, with a recent and fragile history, especially in terms of international recognition and enforcement. In other words, when African intellectuals try to interpret for instance rape in contemporary South Africa, we may easily revert to a human rights discourse in which to do so. We may adopt the perspective of western democratic societies. Praeg's point is not that it is completely invalid to do so, but he does caution against a simplistic reliance on human rights discourse, especially when the aim is to understand, explain, or make sense of such violent occurrences, instead of merely condemning them. One of the reasons for caution is that in fact, an international human rights culture is itself in a foundational or transitional stage, contested in many places, and only very selectively or one-sidedly enforced, with many biases favoring the most powerful states (look for instance at the way in which the permanent membership structure of the UN Security Council ensures that human rights sanctions will never be brought against states like the USA or China, irrespective of their recent and ongoing imperialistic behaviors). Moreover, this young movement was itself born directly out of "excessive, collective" violence in the heart of the west: events like the Holocaust and the Armenian genocide. Living after these violent revolutions and the resolutions formed in response, we are all heir to the new human rights dispensation that was born out of those horrors. Even the human rights culture or social order, which is now often used to condemn foundational violence, was founded by violence, Praeg argues.

And furthermore, the particularity of this human rights tradition should in all fairness be recognized: in spite of its universal pretentions and aspirations, it is historically securely rooted in the (globalized and globalizing) Abrahamic traditions with their specific interpretation of the human and the good, whereas these central building blocks are fundamentally alien to many other cultures around the globe.[12] State formation was artificially and violently imposed upon Africa, along with capitalism, Christianity, and a human rights frame. This colonial package sits uneasily upon the traditional cultures and indigenous value systems of Africa, and most Africans today live in an in-between world: the old order is no longer, has been effectively dismantled and discredited, and the new (human rights, democratic state) order has not yet taken root. As Praeg puts it: "Between the passing of a hierarchical, traditional order and the birth of a new democratic order of equality there is a crisis of degree in which neither system functions and the currency used to construct them—age/seniority or equality/rights—has either *no longer* or *not yet* any legitimacy" (emphasis in original) (Praeg 2007: 82). There is moreover much skepticism in Africa and elsewhere about the universalist pretensions of the international human rights community, contrasting sharply with its selective application of enforcement and its collusion with many other injustices perpetrated by the west against Africans and others.

Following Praeg's interpretation of Girard's idea of foundational violence, one could conceivably read these excessively violent phenomena in Africa (like the Rwanda genocide) as collective and largely subconscious attempts at founding order within chaos, founding an intact world and coherent moral universe where there has been none for hundreds of years. But this explanation, which should not slip into a justification, seems problematic. It is important to understand Praeg's assumptions here: by claiming that no new social order is ever established without some form of founding violence, Praeg adopts a bleak perspective on human nature, which is essentially critical of the Enlightenment view of humans as naturally rational beings. In addition, Praeg discusses the predominantly pre-modern psychological function of scapegoats for the cleansing and unification of the divided and fragmented social "group" to construct his explanation of the meaning of transitional violence, and this notion of the scapegoat also needs some clarification.

As I read him, the scapegoat in Girard's theory is the first point of order to emerge in a complex and chaotic situation: the scapegoat as a fairly arbitrarily chosen but always politically and socially powerless victim acts as the target of collectively pent-up fears, frustrations, and desires which are then all conveniently projected onto the scapegoat who comes to symbolically stand for the chaos, fears, and unmet needs of the crowd or collective. The crowd knows that the scapegoat is neither guilty nor innocent, and that it is, more than anything else, their actions of targeting, accusing, attacking, and eventually expelling or killing the scapegoat that bestow upon it its metaphysical (certain) guilt. There is thus a level at which they understand that they are creating the scapegoat to serve the psychological needs of the collective. It is this double consciousness of the crowd that marks the ancient scapegoat ritual as a *pharmakon*—a drug that could both kill and save. It is also this that accounts for the curious double status of the scapegoat itself: it is both punished as somehow being the origin or cause of metaphysical evil and often after its death venerated as a god and savior. The first point of order which crystallizes around the scapegoat thus expands to structure the whole, to unify the crowd in an act that itself necessarily lies outside of the law but which serves to found a new law or community, or to reaffirm an existing but fragmented one.

Transposed onto the issue of the high levels of rape during the South African transition (still ongoing), one might want to venture (following Praeg's logic) that women or female sexuality act as some kind of scapegoat, even as a scapegoat in more than one sense. Reading our rape epidemic as a form of transitional violence like these other phenomena discussed by Praeg, we can interpret female sexuality as functioning as a kind of scapegoat in the collective subconscious for the lingering social and moral chaos in our country which is still in transition. The required complete restructuring of our identities as South Africans, which makes heavy demands reaching right into our deepest desires and fears, means that the transition is still exacting its price and is not over yet. It is quite possible that the repressed strain of transforming society and ourselves and all our relationships and habits of interaction into something new finds an outlet in sexual violence against women and children. The tension involved in redistributing chances and wealth in the most unequal society in the world, and in reshuffling the ingrained hierarchies of all previous dispensations, leads to a sense of world-lessness and loss of orientation. During the struggle and immediately afterwards, the "new South Africa" was clearly defined in terms of what it was *not*: new South Africans are against racism and sexism. Now, that is no longer enough, and we need to know what we are transforming *into*. Very few contemporary leaders betray any clue about what we are transforming into, what a viable, vibrant, and egalitarian South African community or society will ideally look like. In a sense, our future is up for grabs, and different worlds are competing for dominance.

This moral, ideological and metaphysical confusion cannot often be acknow-ledged for fear that the transition will look like a failure and reflect negatively on the abilities of the new black leadership. A certain political amnesia is probably attendant upon every major social transition or revolution. There is a sense in which everyone must believe or pretend to believe in the possibility of a kind of total rebirth, cleansing, metamorphosis, or renaissance. To sustain the façade/ dream of a successful transition to (post)modernity and liberal democracy, South Africans of all races have had to deny and/or flee from their own past. Black South Africans had to forget, eradicate, and deny a deeply humiliating past in which they had been systematically de- and under-developed and dehumanized over centuries, and white South Africans had to try to deny or actively forget their involvement in enforcing and benefiting from that same system. Maintaining the façade of a successful transformation in the face of a daily struggle to create (or resist the creation of) a shared moral universe means that a great deal of psy-chological repression takes place. Within the chaotic and fragmented moral space after the power transfer, where different paradigms and metaphysical orders compete viciously, sometimes violently, women occupy an ambivalent position: they are both relatively vulnerable and marginal, and the single largest group threatening to usurp the powers traditionally concentrated in the hands of elite men. This renders them perfect scapegoats in Girard's interpretive frame.

The different ethnic groups have competed since time immemorial for space, land, rights, and power, but never before have women featured significantly in the equation. In so far as the new democratic dispensation thus threatens male psyches, it seems to evoke sexual violence against women as a way to found a new political order based on the effective political exclusion of women, through a symbolic reduction of their lives to a sexual dimension and function. The high levels of rape against women can thus be interpreted as ways of both founding the new order as a (purified) masculine order, and resisting its founding (as a truly democratic and egalitarian state). Already during the liberation struggle, women's contribution was often reduced to that of sexual service, and the "freedom fighter" has indeed cultivated a sense of sexual entitlement, partly also through the age-old symbolic conflation of the land with women's bodies, with a logic of: "if I risk my life to liberate this country, it [and you] belongs to me."

What Praeg thus helps us with, is not to judge violence in Africa a-historically, or outside its context (against the backdrop of stabilized human rights societies) but to realize that we are witnessing social orders under construction, and we witness a collective, almost subconscious attempt at giving birth to an order which may in future become believable and may eventually even be legitimate, but which is not so yet. Under such a stable, largely uncontested and legitimized order, as one finds within the western liberal democracies, the difference between legitimate and illegitimate forms of violence is fairly clear, and the state possesses a monopoly on legitimate violence. Praeg thus shows to the shocked observer that every social order is born from violence, and he encourages us to look back in history (often recent history) to see how what now pose as naturalized, a-historically existing, stable democratic states, have also been born out of acts of extreme violence, often in the form of genocide unleashed against indigenous peoples, for example in the United States, Australia, etc. Understanding the occurrence of rape in this way in context and in terms of process, does not however mean that we excuse the rapists or try to mitigate their guilt. We are instead trying to grasp better what kind of situation we live in which seems to facilitate rape, to make it easy, likely, trivial, and everyday. Understanding South African rape in context can also assist our activism, prevention, and resistance to it, and should never be used to defend it.

From Praeg's analysis I thus draw the understanding that the high levels of sexual violence against women and children in contemporary South Africa may plausibly be read as an indication of the extent to which the struggle for a political transition to a modern, democratic, and liberal state with one of the most progressive constitutions in the world is still ongoing. In other words, he helps me to understand that violence against these groups is not only going on *in spite of* the transition, but also to a large extent *because of* the transition and its disruptive effect on traditional community structures and individual psyches. Women and children still function as scapegoats: they are seen as the most vulnerable or least powerful members of a threatening force, whether that force is modernity threatening traditional masculine power structures or whether it is tradition threatening the dawn of modernity. It is probably unwise to try and choose between the claims that women are being raped because men resist modernity and that women are being raped because men try to establish a modern, masculine state and autonomous masculine selves. Both these claims are probably true; women are being raped for two contradictory but equally valid (but of course immoral) reasons, but they ultimately pay the steep price for men's attempt to come to terms with and/or resist the full implications of our society's transition into modernity.

It is thus quite possible to read the high levels of violence against women in South Africa as a kind of founding, cleansing, and scapegoating violence similar in logic to the Rwandan genocide, using the combined insights of Praeg and Girard. But in terms of my earlier analysis in the first section, it would be a mistake, I believe, to see this political *function* of rape as the main or only political sig-nificance of these rapes, because it would reduce their political significance to the intentions of the rapists, even if these are largely subconscious. As explained, it is necessary to view the many rapes in South Africa in transition also in terms of a political clash of worlds or worldviews. In other words, it is not only that the rapist tries to assert, affirm, and embed ("make up and make real" in Scarry's terms) his worldview (his ordered world, cleansed of women as political agents and populated only by sexually subservient women) by destroying the projected victim's world (seen as claiming her equal political status which in his view necessarily diminishes his power and masculinity). Rather, we must, as feminist theorists, point out that there is, apart from the projected and contested male-biased worldviews in which rape becomes a political strategy, *also* an actually existing, contestatory women's world that the rapist inadvertently destroys, without knowing (of) it. It is the destruction of the actually existing but fragile women's worlds in their multiplicity and their lived reality that is the deeper or fuller picture of rape's political significance here in South Africa. In these worlds, South African women know themselves to be fully human, to be sexual beings and desiring agents, rooted in caring relationships, and to also be political creatures. It is this hidden and repressed self-knowledge that is willfully or accidentally destroyed through high levels of rape.

It is thus imperative for a proper understanding of the political significance of rape in contemporary South Africa that we both read it within context (in terms of both time and place) and never let go of our feminist insights into rape as a total or world loss to the victim. Making sense of rape and understanding it within context is necessary to combat and prevent it, and to address the mindset of South African boys and men, but this can never be the full story, because such a reduction would lend support to the world-destroying logic employed by the rapist against his victim. The most important political significance of rape in South Africa today is that it fundamentally and almost systematically disempowers women and girls at the center of their personhood; it violently wrings control over their sexuality away from themselves, with permanent psychological damage resulting from this devastating violation of sexual, bodily, and psychic integrity. Never does Cornell's abstract notion of "the wound of femininity" obtain more dramatic concrete manifestation than in the torn genitals and intestines of girls and babies gang-raped by adult men (Cornell 1995). In my opinion, what we experience in South Africa at the moment serves as a clear example of how the apparently clear-cut or easy distinction between war rape and other rapes for the sake of ranking our moral condemnation of these acts is finally untenable.

Notes

1 I wish to thank Debra Bergoffen and Paula Gilbert for very helpful comments on draft versions of this chapter.
2 The formulation of this sentence suggests that these two aims stand in tension with each other, which some readers may find confusing—this tension will be illuminated in what follows.
3 I mean by the expression "women as women" that women as sexually different from men and as differently gendered and socio-symbolically positioned and as having more or less systematically different lived experiences from men, are often not tolerated within the public sphere. The phenomenon that women are expected to leave behind as far as possible their sexual difference upon entering the public space is well documented in feminist literature.

4 For the fuller analysis, see my chapter "Feminism and the Ethics of Reconciliation" in *Law and the Politics of Reconciliation*, (ed.) S. Veitch, Aldershot: Ashgate, 2007.
5 Don Berkich (2009) sees the meaning of rape as contingent only upon the centrality of our sexuality to our personhood, which he seems to think is a given and part of the human condition. The implication is that the meaning of rape will not be easily shifted. In my book (Du Toit 2009) I suggested that the particularly devastating meaning of rape is instead closely tied to the patriarchal nature of the socio-symbolic worlds that we inhabit and as such not a given with the human condition. This implies a more contingent view and suggests ways of actively resisting the dominant meanings that rape normally obtains. This is an interesting debate in itself and there is not enough space to address it here. But even if we go with the more contingent view, we should not be under any illusion that rape's damage is something that can ever simply be "snapped out of" or that the potential shift in meaning should become the victim's political burden (although it might become her therapeutic task).
6 I find it very problematic that the war rape of women has the function of sending a message about sexual control over women between men, and am critical of the socio-symbolic construct that makes such a form of communication effective in the first place. Moreover, I find the wartime construct of (masculine) protector versus (feminine) protected bodies highly idealized, if not contrived, if we take into account how prevalent man on woman rape and other sexual violence is in most countries during peacetime and within communities. Debra Bergoffen (2009) has nevertheless opened my eyes to the ways in which such gender codes are often *also* existentially lived. She writes thoughtfully about the suffering of men who are forced to witness the rapes of their daughters, sisters, and wives, and become undone as gendered men as a result.
7 Drucilla Cornell (1995) may formulate the same point in terms of the protection or violation of one's "imaginary domain."
8 This argument is often broadly related to the apartheid violation of black family life through forced removals, the homeland policies, and migrant labor. There is however no evidence to suggest that black men rape more than white men in South Africa, which, if true, seems to militate against the apartheid victim explanation.
9 Leonard Praeg, whose work is discussed in more detail below, argues that the peak of familicide among Afrikaners during the political transition is indicative of much the same phenomenon: these Afrikaner fathers felt threatened in their patriarchal identities by the new democratic order, and responded to this threat with extreme violence aimed at their wives and children (Praeg 2007). The patriarchal nature of all the traditional cultures in South Africa seems to me to largely overshadow other differences often associated with the racial divide.
10 As Paula Gilbert rightly pointed out to me, both these arguments which I present here as typical of the South African rape discourse are used to explain the violence of men in many other cultures as well. They are nevertheless also very prevalent in our context, and, interestingly, presented as unique to our situation!
11 We do not have reliable rape statistics from pre-1994.
12 As South African philosopher Thad Metz (2007) has convincingly shown, sub-Saharan Africa has an alternative moral tradition and vocabularies to those of the west that pose a challenge to the dominant western ones.

Bibliography

Bell, R. H. (2002) *Understanding African Philosophy: a cross-cultural approach to classical and contemporary issues*, New York and London: Routledge.

Bergoffen, D. (2009) "Exploiting the Dignity of the Vulnerable Body: rape as a weapon of war," *Philosophical Papers*, 38(3): 307–325.

Berkich, D. (2009) "A Heinous Act," *Philosophical Papers*, 38(3): 381–399.

Code, L. (2009) "A New Epistemology of Rape?" *Philosophical Papers*, 38(3): 327–345.

Cornell, D. (1995) *The Imaginary Domain: abortion, pornography and sexual harassment*, New York and London: Routledge.

Derrida, J. (1992) "Force of Law: the 'mystical foundation of authority,'" in D. Cornell, M. Rosenfeld and D.G. Carlson (eds) *Deconstruction and the Possibility of Justice*, New York and London: Routledge.

— (2002) *On Cosmopolitanism and Forgiveness*, New York and London: Routledge.

Du Toit, L. (2005) "A Phenomenology of Rape: forging a new vocabulary for action," in A. Gouws (ed.) *(Un)thinking Citizenship: feminist debates in contemporary South Africa*, Aldershot: Ashgate.

— (2007) "Feminism and the Ethics of Reconciliation," in S. Veitch (ed.) *Law and the Politics of Reconciliation*, Aldershot: Ashgate.

— (2009) *A Philosophical Investigation of Rape: the making and unmaking of the feminine self*, New York and London: Routledge.

Girard, R. (1986) *The Scapegoat*, Baltimore, MD: The Johns Hopkins University Press.

Irigaray, L. (1985) *Speculum of the Other Woman*, trans. G. C. Gill, Ithaca, NY: Cornell University Press.

— (1992) *An Ethics of Sexual Difference*, trans. C. Burke and G. C. Gill, Ithaca, NY: Cornell University Press.

Metz, T. (2007) "Towards an African Moral Theory," *Journal of Political Philosophy*, 15(3): 321–341.

Pateman, C. (1988) *The Sexual Contract*, Cambridge and Oxford: Polity Press.

Praeg, L. (2007) *The Geometry of Violence: Africa, Girard, modernity*, Stellenbosch: SUN Press.

Sanday, P. R. (1996) "Rape-Prone Versus Rape-Free Campus Cultures," *Violence Against Women*, 2(2): 191–208.

Scarry, E. (1985) *The Body in Pain: the making and unmaking of the world*, Oxford and New York: Oxford University Press.

6   Human trafficking

A photographic essay

Kay Chernush

"54 Illegal Migrants Suffocate in Truck in Thailand." Most of us read headlines like this and move on. For most of us human trafficking is a distant and foreign affair. The headlines, though tragic, do not seem to concern us. This was once true for me. That changed a few years ago when I undertook a photography assignment for the State Department and came face to face with the human misery and the heartbreaking stories that lie behind the headlines. It is hard to believe that slavery could exist in our modern twenty-first-century world. Sadly it does.

Since that first assignment, I have worked with survivors of sex trafficking and other forms of labor exploitation in many countries. I have learned that human trafficking exists in every country including my own (the United States). Wherever we are, it flourishes right under our noses.

Trafficking takes different forms in different countries and different circumstances: young girls and boys are sold as prostitutes, become targets for the sex tourist industry, or are pressed into other forms of exploitive labor; domestic workers are physically imprisoned and sexually abused; children are impressed into armies; whole generations of families are trapped in debt bondage, are owned as chattel slaves, lead lives of indentured servitude; migrants are trafficked into sweatshops or ships or fields far from home.

This photo gallery is dedicated to the courageous and resilient survivors of trafficking, and to those who have died, including those 54 human beings—illegal Burmese migrants as it happened, most of them women and children—who died in the back of an unventilated truck that was taking them to the booming tourist resort of Phuket, in southern Thailand.

If the women had made it, their faces would look like the faces here, and their plight would be similar. These are the faces of modern-day slaves.

Sex tourism

In Pattaya, Thailand, girls are arrayed like slaves on an auction block, waiting for customers. It is all out in the open.

The men come from wealthy countries and arrive by the planeload to have sex with an exotic "other." Seeking what they apparently cannot find in their own cultures and socio-economic milieux, they are indifferent to the hardships and coercion that underpin this trade.

The girls, for their part, often see the men as their way out of their impoverished and constricted circumstances.

Girls from rural, impoverished areas dance and give massages in bars and clubs in cities throughout Thailand, where they are expected to entice customers to buy drinks—and more. They must meet monthly quotas or face a reduction in their pay, beatings, or other violence. Customers wanting sex pay the bar owner an "absentee" fee and take the girl off the premises.

Patpong Road, Bangkok, is the center of Thailand's sex entertainment industry. An estimated 4,000 women work here every night as go-go dancers, masseuses, and bar girls. They all owe their Mama-Sans a monthly quota and everyone from agents, landlords, shills, and taxi-drivers get their cut.

Sex trafficking

Mumbai is estimated to have as many as 10,000 brothels. Each brothel is estimated to keep between 20 and 50 women on average. The system is sustained by violence, corruption, and a criminal network of interlocking profit centers, not to mention endless supply and endless demand.

Young women ensnared in prostitution face daily violence from their pimps and their customers. They are particularly vulnerable to HIV/AIDS and other sexually transmitted diseases. Since men will pay more to have sex without a condom, the girls will often have unprotected sex if they are short what they owe at the end of each month.

As girls age and begin to lose their looks, they are forced out of the brothels and onto the streets. Typically a girl will have between 10 to 40 clients a day, sometimes charging as little as $2. After paying off her pimp and paying for her bed, she may keep less than 50 cents.

A Nepalese mother desperately searches for her teenage daughter who was trafficked into a Mumbai brothel two years before this photo was taken. Being displaced to another country is an important part of the trafficking equation, making victims more helpless and vulnerable.

Western Europe's affluent cities are magnets for girls from the poorer countries of Eastern Europe, Russia, and Ukraine. In places like Turin, Italy, they are usually trafficked and controlled by vicious mafias, sold and re-sold until they are simply used up—or somehow manage to escape.

Trafficked women from Africa, particularly from south central Nigeria, are able to buy their way out of their enslaved situation by paying off a bogus debt of 50,000 Euros ($75,000). Frequently they are obliged to pay their Madam an additional 200–400 Euros per month as "rent" for the piece of public sidewalk they work. All this is enforced with fake voodoo rites and violence. If they fail to pay, the women are beaten, threatened with exposure to the police, or their families back home are threatened and attacked.

Rescue is not enough. In order to heal and rebuild their lives, survivors of trafficking generally require legal interventions, housing, social services, psychological counseling, real economic opportunity, and job training.

Slave labor

Near Varanasi, Uttar Pradesh, India, a 9-year-old girl toils under the hot sun making bricks from morning to night, seven days a week. She is typical of many "Dalits," India's lowest caste, whose families become ensnared in debt bondage. They rarely protest, believing this is simply their lot in life.

Young runaways and orphans frequently end up begging on the street in large cities like Mumbai, India, and have to hand over their earnings to criminal syndicates, or face beatings, rape, or maiming.

Since human traffickers prey on the most vulnerable among us, it is not surprising that children are prime targets. In India children are particularly prized in the carpet industry, sari factories, and Mumbai sweatshops for their small nimble fingers and submissiveness.

Meeting the challenge

It is heartening and inspiring to see the heroic efforts of individuals and organizations that are fighting this scourge. But clearly raids and rescue are not enough. The problem is too widespread and too complex. What happens to people once they are rescued?

Ghanaian fishermen near Yeji, Lake Volta, learn about exploitive child labor practices and are urged to voluntarily release young slaves. There are no raids. The work is a painstaking grassroots effort by APPLE, a local organization affiliated with Free the Slaves. The aim is to educate and establish best practices in the entire fishing community and to raise awareness in the impoverished "sending" villages.

In India, social workers from the Catholic charity Balprafulta go daily to Mumbai's central train station to keep tabs on runaways and encourage them to go to a shelter, where they receive clean clothes, food, counseling, and schooling.

On the Thai–Burmese border, where many Burmese and Thai hilltribes live in the shadows of a society that disdains them, DEPDC (Development and Education Programme for Daughters and Communities), a local NGO, devotes itself to community-based prevention programs for children at risk of being trafficked into the sex industry or forced into other exploitive labor.

There is a day school, a boarding school, and an emergency shelter. The organization works closely with teachers, village leaders, and monks to identify impoverished and desperate families who are easily deceived by the networks of traffickers offering to buy their young daughters and sons.

The leafy campus of the day school rings with laughter as children play, free from the predations of the traffickers, free to be children.

Although trafficking has always been with us, it is probably safe to say that today's ease of travel, Internet connectivity, and globalization have made it far easier and more widespread than ever before. With rising awareness and the will to act, perhaps we can use these very elements of modern life to combat it more effectively. My hope is that these photographs will put a face on the headlines, and that instead of averting our eyes we will help in whatever way we can.

7 Marjorie Agosín's poetics of memory

Human rights, feminism, and literary forms

Ricardo F. Vivancos Pérez

Jewish Chilean writer, activist, and scholar Marjorie Agosín reclaims the primacy of poetic discourse as a powerful tool for remembering, accountability, and social justice. Her numerous and varied publications—as of 2009 over twenty poetry collections, five autobiographical works, three books of short fiction, ten volumes of scholarly work and personal essays, and eighteen edited anthologies—not only show a commitment to literature and human rights, but also a constant reflection about the merging of the two. She conceives her poetry as a "poetry of witness" (Agosín 1998a: 13), and defines her writings as "maps of memory" (Agosín 2006: ix). However, she is not restricted to literary writing. Although her emphasis on creativity and imagination comes from her being primarily a poet, her under-standing of the merging of literature and human rights also informs her work as an editor—by promoting women writers and Latin American literature in the U.S., her activism—by collaborating with the relatives of the disappeared in Chile and Argentina, and her dedication to collecting *arpilleras*—the tapestries made by the relatives of the disappeared in Chile. Working as a multifaceted intellectual who has been displaced in the U.S., Agosín has become a spokesperson for those who suffered the violation of human rights in Chile and Latin America. In this sense, her poetry of witness is part of what I will call an overall poetics of memory that enlightens her writings, her work as an intellectual, and even her life as a whole.

Recent scholarship has started to analyze the intersection of human rights and literature. It is now generally acknowledged that both discourses provide "mutually enabling fictions" (Slaughter 2007). Examples of this are studies about the influence of the epistolary novel on the birth of modern human rights in the eighteenth century (Hunt 2007), as well as Joseph Slaughter's comprehensive analysis of the *bildungsroman* as a genre that is crucial to the early development of human rights throughout the nineteenth century (Slaughter 2007). In contem-porary literature, life narratives and the so-called "memory boom" of the last two decades of the twentieth century also illustrate the intersection of human rights and literary forms in a new context in which the vocabulary of human rights is no longer limited to the legal domain (Schaffer and Smith 2004). The study of literature today may offer "unofficial truths" that are necessary for accountability and social justice (Gready 2009). It also raises issues about methodology, ethics, and positionality (McClennen and Slaughter 2009).

In this context, Agosín's writings and her prominent position as an intellectual are worth studying as examples of humanitarian intervention through literature and artistic creation. Her works and her activism highlight a number of important and urgent questions in today's global scene. Can we conceive of poetry as human rights discourse? How does the complicity between feminism and literature work in a poetics of memory and human rights? How can we, as cultural critics, read this "literature of human rights"? These are the challenges that Agosín raises in her works and that I address in this chapter by looking into her writings as the coherent, integrative work of a feminist intellectual and human rights defender.

Sophia A. McClennen and Joseph R. Slaughter discuss how recent literary scholarship on human rights usually treats literary texts and art objects as "humanitarian interventionist narratives," and how "they often end up being either overly celebratory or overly skeptical of the roles that literature and culture play in the struggle for human rights" (McClennen and Slaughter 2009: 9). My purpose here is neither to be laudatory nor skeptical, but rather to expose how the specificity of Agosín's position may create a contemporary poetics of human rights that is humanistic, humanitarian, and full of liberatory potential.

On the occasion of the fiftieth anniversary of the ratification of the U.N. Declaration of Human Rights in 1998, Agosín decided to publish two of her previous poetry collections, one about women who have been unjustly imprisoned, tortured, and/or disappeared, *Zones of Pain* (1988b), and one meant as a tribute to the Mothers of the Plaza de Mayo in Argentina, *Circles of Madness* (1992), together with a new one, *An Absence of Shadows*. The title, which is also the title of the entire volume, refers to Agosín's "obsession," in her own words, with bringing to light, denouncing, and reflecting upon human rights violations, especially those that affect women in Latin America, and the traumas caused by gender violence worldwide (Agosín 1996: 58). Her defense of poetry as human rights discourse in her introduction to this volume is in every way challenging for activists, writers, and scholars working on the intersection of human rights and literary forms:

> Fifty years after its ratification, the U.N. Declaration of Human Rights continues to be our most important legacy. Yet poetry, too, has its place: it demands accountability and truth. It is my hope that readers will share with me a sea of hope, a poetry of witness that honors the U.N. Declaration of Human Rights, a poetry that believes that memory, courage and the right to remember and give voice are also human rights.
>
> (Agosín 1998a: 13)

Agosín's intentional use of the term, "witness," is revelatory. She is alluding here to the poetization of the act of witnessing, or conceiving poetry as another possible register to verbalize acts of witnessing in the wake of studies about the testimonies of the Holocaust. As Dori Laub explains, when the narrative of the traumatized emerges in contact with the witness, the latter immediately becomes an active part in the process: "The listener, therefore, is a party to the creation of knowledge *de novo*. The testimony of the trauma thus includes its hearer, who is, so to speak, the blank screen on which the event comes to be inscribed for the first time" (Laub 1991a: 57). Agosín's "poetry of witness" is reclaiming the validity of her position as a participant-observant regarding human rights violations, and her right to express her own experience through images and metaphors, that is, the validity of a poetization of the experience of witnessing trauma.

In her apparently circumstantial definition of a poetry of witness, Agosín is in fact drawing attention to the elements that are crucial to understanding her writings as a whole: witnessing, memory, courage, and her right to remember and to give voice from her own position as a displaced intellectual in the U.S. Since she herself takes poetry and poetical discourse as a point of entry into humanitarian issues, these are the ingredients that I first propose to explore in the pages that follow, before expanding my analysis onto a more general poetics of memory that inform her overall mission as an intellectual.

Witnessing and exile

Reflecting upon his own experience as a child survivor from Romania, as well as upon his job as a psychoanalyst, as a witness to other Holocaust survivors' accounts, and as a co-founder in 1981 of the Fortunoff Video Archive for Holocaust Testimonies at Yale University, Dori Laub mentions three levels of witnessing: "the level of being a witness to oneself within the experience; the level of being a witness to the testimonies of others; and the level of being a witness to the process of witnessing itself" (Laub 1991b: 75).[1]

For Agosín, the first level, that of being a witness to oneself, comes from her autobiographical awareness as an exile of the Pinochet dictatorship (1973–89) and the trauma of having been a lucky survivor among the many Chileans of her generation who were tortured, executed, or disappeared. In her writings, she returns over and over again to her position and positioning as a writer in exile. Agosín belongs to what other displaced Hispanic writers in the Americas have defined as the "one and a half" generation or "children of exile," that is, those exiles or immigrants who arrived in the U.S. with their families when they were children or teenagers (Pérez Firmat 1994; Blanco Aguinaga 2002–3). For her, exile was a traumatic experience that split her life in half at a crucial age, with memories of a Chilean childhood space that was forever lost. Nevertheless, her Chilean childhood was not completely idealized, since she had already experienced discrimination as a Jewish girl growing up in a traditionally Catholic Chilean society. When she arrived in the U.S. in 1973, she suffered this discrimination again, but this time accentuated by her being not only Jewish, but also a speaker of a foreign language. In addition, she was also identified as a Latina and a "woman of color" according to the labels of the post-sixties U.S., even though she is neither black nor brown (Agosín 2000: 122). Her education in the U.S. led her to a position as mediator between her parents' generation and U.S. culture, and most importantly, to a bilingual and bicultural experience that eventually gave her a privileged position of power within academia and U.S. culture in order to speak of and rally against human rights violations. In this sense, Agosín's exile and displacement signal her position as a mediator and provide her with the tools for becoming a spokesperson for human rights in the Americas.

The second level of Agosín's involvement in the process of witnessing is her participation in the accounts given by survivors and relatives of the victims in Chile and Argentina through her role as an activist and as a collector of testimonies (Agosín 2008: 119–164). As I will explain in more detail later, Agosín has been actively involved in the *Arpillera* Movement in Chile since the first years of the dictatorship, supporting the relatives of the disappeared, and collecting their testimonies and their art.

Agosín recreates both her witnessing of the Pinochet dictatorship and her witnessing of her own family stories of displacement and persecution in her fictionalized memoirs and collections of poetic pieces about her mother, *A Cross and a Star* (1995); her father, *Always from Somewhere Else* (1998a); and her great-grandmother, *Among the Angels of Memory* (2006).

This witnessing also occurs in her fictional autobiography, *The Alphabet in My Hands* (2000); her personal essays published in journals such as *Human Rights Quarterly*—some of them collected in *Ashes of Revolt* (1996); and in her poetry collections. In these texts, she frequently complains about one of the consequences of being a foreigner and an exile: to have to answer repeatedly questions such as where she is from, and why her family came to the U.S. These questions, which she will constantly address in her writings, are ironically those that will empower her as a leading intellectual.

Finally, following Laub's categorization, Agosín is also a witness to the process of witnessing whenever she distances herself from her experience and listens to other victims. In this regard, she reflects upon the inevitable "distortion and subversion of reality" that occurs in this process, according to Laub (Laub 1991b: 76), and puts emphasis on the role of creativity and the imagination. Clear examples of this are those poems in *Among the Angels of Memory* in which the authorial voice and the voice of the great-grandmother, Helena Broder, merge in meditations about the act of witnessing and the function of memory. In this book, as Agosín herself explains, she recovers "many voices, the poet recreating her great-grandmother's steps, but also my own in the process of sensing the memories of others and participating in the post-memory of them" (Agosín 2006: x–xi). As the voice of Helena states in some of the poems, her great-granddaughter's poetic voice provides her with the only discourse available to verbalize her experience of fleeing Nazi Germany (Agosín 2006: 44). For the authorial voice, poetry is also the adequate discourse to recover "the persistent tenacity of remembrance" (Agosín 2006: 66–67). When their voices merge, the verbalization of trauma is a shared act of remembering that involves the poet and her grandmother—both witnesses and victims—and that occurs primarily in the creative domain of poetry:

I am your abode,
the heart of
the forest
the liquid sea
of your eyes,
your tongue,
mine.
I want to embrace
your memory,
to seek out your lineage.
Let me laugh with you.
Let me be a crystal tone
on the walls of
your lips.
(from "Las Odiseas de Helena/
Helena's Odysseys," Agosín 2006: 94–97)

Adapting the language of love poetry—mostly Pablo Neruda's and Gabriela Mistral's—to the experience of witnessing, similar reflections reoccur in many of Agosín's writings. Poetic discourse and the language of poetry become powerful tools to remember and account for women's traumas of persecution, torture, and assassination. And as a witness, the poet is a legitimate and useful voice in the process. Here, Agosín's message is clear: poetry may be part of human rights discourse because it is sometimes the only means by which trauma may be verbalized. In those cases, poets may be the only mediators who can witness and recreate the accounts of victims of human rights violations. Thus, poetic human rights discourse opens the legalistic domain of human rights to the realms of creativity and the imagination.

Agosín and the "memory boom"

To understand Agosín's poetry of witness and her emphasis on creativity, we need to situate her work within the so-called "memory boom" of the last three decades, especially during the 1990s (Schaffer and Smith 2004). This proliferation of life narratives, motivated by important sociosymbolic moments in contemporary history—dictatorships and political repression in Latin America, the fall of the Berlin wall, the Gulf War, the wars in the former Yugoslavia, the 9/11 Attacks, etc.—developed simultaneously with the increasing presence of the discourse and vocabularies of human rights in the public sphere (Ignatieff et al. 2001; McClennen and Slaughter 2009). Commenting on this new situation, human rights scholars Kay Schaffer and Sidonie Smith argue that, in our analysis of this parallel profusion of life narratives and human rights discourses, we need to treat "life narratives and human rights campaigns as multidimensional domains that merge and intersect at critical points, unfolding within and enfolding one another in an ethical relationship that is simultaneously productive of claims for social justice and problematic for the furtherance of this goal" (Schaffer and Smith 2004: 2).

In this context, Agosín's writings are dealing with at least two important issues about the current expansion of human rights discourse: the intersection of multidimensional domains, and the issue of ethics. As to the first issue, problems arise, in my opinion, when we look into the intersection of human rights and literary forms unilaterally from the standpoint of either human rights discourse or literary criticism. On the one hand, human rights documents are unclear about whether to include literature and the arts as tools to combat and prevent human rights violations. When they offer recommendations for the areas and issues analyzed, commissions' reports address the importance of the media, including creativity and the imagination only vaguely and confusingly.[2] On the other hand, literary critics and authors have permanent doubts about the aesthetic value of literary works that are commited to social justice. For example, Agosín herself has to explain, in a position essay entitled "How to Speak with the Dead? A Poet's Notebook," that her writings would better be considered "fast literature" if we followed consecrated Mexican writer Carlos Fuentes's terminology (Agosín 1996: 58). Why does she, as a creative writer, have to explicitly "acknowledge" this? Who is she to "lessen" the aesthetic value of her own works? Is this really an honest statement, or is this a forced response to critics who doubt the literary value of her work and, in general, the aesthetic value of the literature of human rights? No matter what answers we have, Agosín's words are indicative of the presence of the same old tension—aesthetics vs. commitment—that remains in the background of any one-dimensional approach to the intersection of literature and politics. This tension is related to a second and more general one: the tension between aesthetics and truth. In what way is the commitment to truth antithetical to the invocation of literary devices? This question may be answered by looking into Agosín's consideration of ethics and understanding of truths.

Agosín's courage: an ethics of truths

By mentioning courage as one of the essential ingredients of her poetry of witness, Agosín touches on the ethical dimension of literary discourse in relation to human rights. First, her ethics includes an emphasis on the creative side of memory. As we have seen, Agosín claims that poetic discourse is one way, sometimes even the only way, to recover historical memory and verbalize trauma. In addition, using poetry as human rights discourse reveals the validity of creativity in testimonial accounts of trauma. As trauma specialists such as Laub have corroborated, Holocaust survivors are frequently inaccurate and make mistakes about some facts. Does this invalidate their testimonies? Why do they have to remember every detail with precision so that they can be credible? Again, Laub defends the very act of bearing witness and verbalizing traumas as the most important issue at stake. He writes: "what is important is the situation of *discovery of knowledge*—its evolution and its very happenings. Knowledge in the testimony is, in other words, not simply a factual given that is reproduced and replicated by the testifier, but a genuine advent, an event in its own right" (Laub 1991a: 62; emphasis in the original).[3] By considering a poetry of witness as human rights discourse, Agosín suggests an expansion of the discourse of humanitarian intervention in at least two ways: (1) she exposes the fictional side of life narratives, trauma accounts, and their constructive quality; and (2) she emphasizes the aesthetic dimension, and even aesthetic pleasure that may come with a literature that is committed to social justice.

Second, Agosín's ethics, by arguing that the acts of verbalizing trauma and witnessing come from many voices instead of one, defend the existence of many truths instead of one, truths that may come from different perspectives and in specific performances throughout time. Quantitatively, Agosín's ethics point toward multivocality as an antidote to a one-dimensional truth. This is expressed in poems where her voice merges with the fictional voices of relatives and victims who courageously demand accountability and truth:

Find her,
uncover her,
hold her
even though her body be
a mutilated fable,
an equinox of
wounds like legends.
(from "La desaparecida III/Disappeared Women III,"
Agosín 1998a: 168–169)

Both aspects of Agosín's ethics are close to French philosopher Alain Badiou's theorization of an "ethics of truths"—with "truths" in the plural—in order to understand and better eradicate evil. For Badiou, an ethics of truths must be based on three essential resources: courage—"do not give up," discernment—"do not fall for simulacra," and moderation—"do not get carried away to the extremes of totality" (Badiou 2001: 91). For Agosín, courage is the central element of the equation. The motto of Badiou's ethics of truths—"Keep Going!"—is the force that leads the authorial voice throughout Agosín's writings and the essential element that enables identification, empathy, and involvement from a position of participant-observer.

Both Agosín and Badiou come from the same initial position of suspiciousness about the construction of human rights discourse from a one-dimensional imperialistic point of view. This is what Badiou calls "ethical ideology," and rejects as the "final imperative of a conquering civilization: 'become like me and I will respect your difference'" (Badiou 2001: 24–25). Suspiciousness leads both Agosín and Badiou to emphasize the multidimensional, multivocal, and performative qualities that are needed in a more flexible human rights discourse based on an ethics of truths.[4] In this regard, according to them, writers and intellectuals need to bring together multiple dimensions and points of view. Their work as leaders and spokespersons has to be done on a variety of fronts within and outside academia.[5]

Towards a poetics of memory: Agosín's *arpillera* writing

At the intersection of literature and human rights, Agosín's writings offer a mixture of genres and a merging of voices. The hybrid and collective nature of her work is best explained with the metaphor of knitting and weaving. This metaphor is central to her poetics of memory, since it connects the processes of writing and artistic creation with the processes of witnessing and building a community of activists against human rights violations. The knitting of an *arpillera*, a kind of tapestry made out of small pieces of cloth sewn together by the relatives of the disappeared in Chile, is similar to Agosín's writing process in her poetry of witness. In both cases, artists assemble fragments of memory from a mediating position. As in an *arpillera*, Agosín's texts weave different voices and their testimonies. The art of weaving and the art of writing are therefore, in Agosín's view, insisting on the relevant role of artistic creation and the imagination in the building of human rights discourses.

One of Agosín's most important contributions as an activist has been her involvement since the late 1970s with the *Arpillera* Movement in Chile. Agosín has collaborated with this group of mothers—initially fourteen when they started in the 1970s—and has been one of their strongest advocates internationally by publicizing their work and their demands for justice. Her summary of the complex personal and political meaning of the *arpilleras* informs us about her understanding of her own writing process:

> The *arpillera* is an amalgamation of voices and histories appearing in a humble fabric made by the hands of mothers, daughters, sisters, and wives—the living relatives of loved ones who have disappeared. The *arpillera* is made of many things, not just fabric. The process of its creation is similar to composing a poem or planting a tree to commemorate a death. The *arpillera* is born from deep inside of us, in a zone of intimacy, but it embodies the public voice and allows hands, previously used for caressing and loving, to tell their story.
> (Agosín 2008: 15)

The *arpillera* evokes the process of writing a poetry of witness, that is, poetry as human rights discourse. First, it recreates the way memory works when fragments are put together by a trauma survivor or a witness to trauma. In *Among the Angels of Memory*, for example, images of knitting and weaving constantly refer to the process of remembering, which is ultimately an act of love:

> My fingers glide over the words,
> as if each of them
> were a love story,

a fragance among syllables.
I knit words,
luminous waves over the page,
calmly, I take dictation.
And you, on the other side of the
words, in the resonant clarity of light,
smile.

Poetry is the story of love,
eternal flame
to mitigate the solitude of those who love
each other in the dark.
(from "La casa de la memoria/The House of Memory,"
Agosín 2006: 132–133)

Second, the act of knitting an *arpillera* refers metaphorically to the intersection of many voices as a collective act of memory and community-building. We must remember that *arpilleras* are usually anonymous and include embroidered images of victims and activists as well as political messages against the brutal repression of Pinochet's dictatorial regime.

In her poetry of commitment, especially after *Zones of Pain* (1988), Agosín conceives every collection as an "amalgamation of voices."[6] Her technique consists of confusing her authorial voice with the voices of the disappeared, of their mothers, and their living relatives. All of these voices are fictional and meet together in a dream-like space. This space is similar to what Latin American cultural critics have called "magic realism." The "mysterious" world of her poetry unfolds naturally and comfortably to the reader. Each poem becomes a magical space where the communion of voices is not explained by conventional law or logics, but is perceived as natural throughout the collections.[7]

This merging of voices comes from Agosín's strong spiritual connection with victims and their relatives, to the point that she becomes a medium, a channel of communication, through which their voices may be heard. In *Zones of Pain*, she explains how she feels about this spiritual connection:

The zones of pain represent the wandering of buried women and the wandering of searching mothers. The zones of pain are ours, are dark, and at times too easily slip the mind. For those reasons I wrote them down, because I wish to accompany my dead sisters.

(Agosín 1988b: 134)

Agosín's is a poetry of *hermanamiento*, sisterhood. The victims are her sisters, and, as a poet, she is the medium through which they may communicate. Magic sisterhood occurs in her poems to the point that the author herself is surprised by her own obsession to rescue these voices and their stories:

And it is so incredible how I love this dead one, who is not mine,
who is not a cadaver either, but a waterfall, a dialogue,
a shore to be crossed.

(from untitled poem, Agosín 1998a: 92–93)

Agosín applies the feminist idea of sisterhood to the magic and spiritual space of her poetry of witness. In this sense, we can see how her involvement in U.S. Third World feminisms and Latina feminisms has a clear influence in her writings, and in her poetics of memory as a whole. Both her emphasis on "identity-in-difference" in her poetry, and on the importance of writing for feminist activists have been central ideas for feminists of color since the late 1970s, as noted for example by the editors of the landmark anthology *This Bridge Called My Back* (1981), Gloria Anzaldúa and Cherríe Moraga (Alarcón 1990; Moraga and Anzaldúa 2002: 179–213).

As I mentioned above, Agosín herself remembers how in her college years she was considered a "woman of color," even though she was not really a woman "of color." However, she has always acknowledged being indebted to this feminist group. In fact—and this is not very well known—Agosín collaborated in some groundbreaking publications when she was a graduate student at Indiana University. For example, she was the co-editor of the first and only number of *Midwest-East, Midwest-West*, a journal published in 1980 that included some of Chicana writer Sandra Cisneros's earliest poems, as well as writings by Chicana cultural critic Norma Alarcón (Montenegro and Agosín 1980). This publication had a brief life but established networks of collaboration that started the successful journal *Third Woman*, edited by Norma Alarcón, who was also the founder of Third Woman Press. During the 1980s and 1990s, both the press and the journal were pioneer activist vehicles for publishing emerging Latina artists such as Sandra Cisneros, Ana Castillo, and Marjorie Agosín herself.

It is curious how today, after their successful careers, Agosín, Cisneros, and Alarcón share a similar use of the metaphor of weaving at the core of their understanding of literature, activism, and their overall vision of the contemporary world. While pioneer Chicana cultural critic Alarcón talks about "weaving alliances" as a necessary strategy for feminists in the context of multiculturalism (Alarcón 1996), Cisneros explains her ideas about interconnectedness with the metaphor of the *rebozo*, or Mexican shawl in her novel *Caramelo* (2002).

A comparison between the two metaphors—Agosín's *arpillera* and Cisneros's *rebozo*—deserves attention here. In the title, *Caramelo* refers initially to the color of the *rebozo* that Lala inherits as part of the feminine legacy of the Reyes family. Throughout the narrative, the *rebozo* becomes a central metaphor with multiple implications. First, it is a metaphor for the process of construction of the narrative. It refers to the weaving of fragments, footnotes, and citations, or the inter-connections with Cisneros's previous works, accounting for Cisneros's style. Second, it is a metaphor for the worldview constructed by the Chicana girl Lala as a subject-in-process throughout the novel. Life experiences unfold as the weaving of a *rebozo*, as Lala explains several times:

> I look up, and la Virgen looks down at me, and, honest to god, this sounds like a lie, but it's true. The universe a cloth, and all humanity interwoven. Each and every person connected to me, and me connected to them, like the strands of a *rebozo*. Pull one string and the whole thing comes undone. Each person who comes into my life affecting the pattern, and me affecting theirs.
>
> (Cisneros 2002: 389)

In this way, the metaphor of the *rebozo* in *Caramelo* emphasizes interconnectedness from the central vantage point of the Chicana subject. The emphasis on interconnectedness is indicative of the understanding of identity in relational terms. It illustrates the tension between an emphasis on difference and a focus on commonality in the consideration of identity. In the case of Chicana feminism, starting with the individual self allows for the inscription of Chicanas in a set of discourses of history and social life. In this sense, *Caramelo* shows how taking the individual self as a starting point has a liberatory and creative potential that is not in total opposition to a collective ideal.

Agosín's metaphor of the *arpillera* refers to the process of writing and her own style in a way similar to Cisneros's in *Caramelo*. Both crucially suggest that the understanding of identity in relational terms needs the imaginative intervention of literature and the arts. However, Agosín's allusion to a worldview—understanding the world metaphorically as an *arpillera* of voices—has different implications according to our previous analysis. On the one hand, Agosín is emphasizing the fictional creation of a collective voice within the space of poetry and poetic discourse that may account for the voices of victims of human rights violations and their relatives. Her position as mediator or medium, as well as the presence of the fictional authorial voice, also point towards the tension between the individual self and the collective ideal, but in the context of trauma and trauma witnessing. On the other hand, Agosín is interested in the recovery of memory and the verbalization of trauma, while Cisneros focuses on what Chicana historian Emma Pérez calls "memory as history" (Pérez 1999). In other words, Agosín is focusing on human rights issues from a feminist position of displacement—moving across ethnic, religious, and gender markers—while Cisneros is addressing social justice issues by recreating through fiction the history of Chicanos.

Conclusion

I would like to go back to the questions that I raised at the beginning of this chapter, and that I think are essential to an understanding of Agosín's works. Can we conceive of poetry as human rights discourse? How does the complicity between feminism and literature work in a poetics of memory and human rights? How can we, as cultural critics, read this "literature of human rights"? Agosín proposes a specific kind of poetry that may be part of human rights discourses, a poetry of witness, which emphasizes the creative perspective of the poet as a mediator and participant-observer. This poetry, I have argued, is for Agosín part of a global poetics of memory in which courage plays an essential ethical role in both the recovery of memory and the verbalization of trauma through literature and the arts. The ethical dimension of Agosín's writings depends on the complicity between feminism and literature. In the wake of feminists' views on identity and community-building that come from similar positions of displacement, Agosín argues that poetry may sometimes be the only way to remember and to give voice to victims of human rights violations. Overall, she claims that the imaginative intervention of poetry is necessary in our conception of identity in relational terms.

The expansion of human rights discourse and its intersection with literary and artistic forms posits a constant challenge for cultural critics. In this chapter, I have argued that we need to read this "literature of human rights" from a movable, flexible position across traditional disciplines and fields of study. In this regard, to acknowledge the "mutually enabling" relationship between human rights and literary forms is not enough. Now we should look for new approaches that amalgamate different critical standpoints and cultural practices. This new decentered cultural criticism should be self-reflective and inclusive and open to constant revision. Agosín's poetics of memory may be instructive in this regard.

Notes

1 In a more recent study, Kelly Oliver (2001) focuses on two "meanings" of witnessing: "*eyewitness* testimony based on first-hand knowledge on the one hand, and *bearing witness* to something beyond recognition that can't be seen, on the other" (16; emphasis in the original). In her approach to the process of witnessing as central to the formation to subjectivity, Oliver is primarily interested in the tension between address-ability and response-ability: "our experience of our own subjectivity is the result of the productive tension between finite subject position and infinite response-ability of witnessing" (17). In my study of Agosín's works, I prefer to follow Dori Laub's levels of witnessing as more appropriate to analyzing literary texts as discourses that are produced by one author. To analyze the tension pointed out by Oliver would involve a more comprehensive study of the audience and reception of Agosín's works.
2 In their recommendations section, some Human Rights Commissions' reports about Latin America point out the need to improve collaboration between the "media" and government institutions. However, the role of artistic production in publicizing and preventing human rights violations is not acknowledged.
3 This is similar to what Kelly Oliver means when she points out how, in the process of witnessing, the tension between address-ability and response-ability occurs "beyond recognition," that is, beyond a factual given (Oliver 2001).
4 Here Agosín's work is also close to feminist theories that emphasize the performativity of gender, especially to the works of Judith Butler (Butler 1990, 1997).
5 Alain Badiou is also an example of an intellectual who deems it necessary to combine scholarly work, political activism, and creative writing—as a novelist and playwright (Hallward 2003).
6 In her early poetry collections—*Conchalí* (1980), *Brujas y algo más/Witches and Other Things* (1984), *Mujeres de humo/Women of Smoke* (1988), and *Hogueras/Bonfires* (1990)—Agosín deconstructs, from a feminist perspective, the traditional language of love and desire that Latin American poets, and especially Pablo Neruda, popularly codified during the twentieth century.

7   Here I follow Luis Leal's definition of magical realism as an attitude towards a fictional reality with which characters and readers accept its mysteries without trying to explain them by logic or scientific knowledge (Leal 1995; Leal and Fuentes 1998).

Bibliography

Agosín, M. (2008) *Tapestries of Hope, Threads of Love: the Arpillera movement in Chile, 1974–1994*, 2nd edn, Lanham, MD: Rowman & Littlefield.

—— (2006) *Among the Angels of Memory / Entre los ángeles de la memoria*, San Antonio, TX: Wings Press.

—— (2000) *The Alphabet in My Hands: a writing life*, New Brunswick, NJ, and London: Rutgers University Press.

—— (1998b) *Always from Somewhere Else: a memoir of my Chilean Jewish father*, New York: The Feminist Press.

—— (1998a) *An Absence of Shadows*, Fredonia, NY: White Pine Press.

—— (1998c) *Dear Anne Frank: poems*, Hanover and London: Brandeis University Press.

—— (1996) *Ashes of Revolt*, Fredonia, NY: White Pine Press.

—— (1995) *A Cross and a Star: memoirs of a Jewish girl in Chile*, Albuquerque, NM: University of New Mexico Press.

—— (1990) *Hogueras / Bonfires*, Tempe, AZ: Bilingual Press/Editorial Bilingüe.

—— (1988a) *Women of Smoke*, Pittsburgh, PA: Latin American Literary Review Press.

—— (1988b) *Zones of Pain*, Fredonia, NY: White Pine Press.

—— (1984) *Witches and Other Things / Brujas y algo más*, Pittsburgh, PA: Latin American Literary Review Press.

—— (1980) *Conchalí*, Montclair, NJ: Senda Nueva de Ediciones.

Alarcón, N. (1996) "Conjugating subjects in the age of multiculturalism," in A. Gordon and C. Newfield (eds) *Mapping Multiculturalism*, Minneapolis: University of Minnesota Press.

—— (1990) "The theoretical subject(s) of *This Bridge Called My Back* and Anglo-American Feminism," in G.E. Anzaldúa (ed.) *Making Face, Making Soul. Haciendo Caras: creative and critical perspectives by feminists of color*, San Francisco, CA: Aunt Lute Books.

Badiou, A. (2001) *Ethics: an essay on the understanding of evil*, London and New York: Verso.

Blanco Aguinaga, C. (2002–3) "Sobre la especificidad del exilio español de 1939," *Nuevo Texto Crítico* 29(32): 9–16.

Butler, J. (1997) *Excitable Speech: a politics of the performative*, New York: Routledge.

—— (1990) *Gender Trouble*, New York: Routledge.

Cisneros, S. (2002) *Caramelo*, New York: Knopf.

Gready, P. (2009) "Novel truths: literature and truth commissions," *Comparative Literary Studies* 46(1): 156–176.

Hallward, P. (2003) *Badiou: a subject to truth*, Minneapolis: University of Minnesota Press.

Hunt, L. (2007) *Inventing Human Rights: a history*, New York: Norton.

Ignatieff, M. (2001) *Human Rights as Politics and Idolatry*, Princeton, NJ: Princeton University Press.

Laub, D. (1991a) "Bearing witness or the vicissitudes of listening," in S. Felman and D. Laub (eds) *Testimony: cases of witnessing in literature, psychoanalysis and history*, London and New York: Routledge.

—— (1991b) "An event without a witness: truth, testimony and survival," in S. Felman and D. Laub (eds) *Testimony: cases of witnessing in literature, psychoanalysis and history*, London and New York: Routledge.

Leal, L. (1995) "Magic realism in Latin American literature," in L. Parkinson Zamora and
W.B. Faris (eds) *Magic Realism: history, community*, Durham, NC: Duke University Press.

Leal, L. and Fuentes, V. (1998) *Don Luis Leal: Una vida y dos culturas. conversaciones con Víctor Fuentes*, Tempe, AZ: Bilingual Review/Press.

McClennen, S. and Slaughter, J. (2009) "Introducing human rights and literary forms; or, the vehicles and vocabularies of human rights," *Comparative Literary Studies* 46(1): 1–19.

Montenegro, P. and Agosín, M. (eds) (1980) *Midwest-East, Midwest-West*, 1(1), Bloomington: A Chicano-Riqueño Studies Publication, Indiana University.

Moraga, C. and Anzaldúa, G. (2002) *This Bridge Called My Back: writings by radical women of color*, 3rd edn, Berkeley, CA: Third Woman Press.

Oliver, K. (2001) *Witnessing: beyond recognition*, Minneapolis: University of Minnesota Press.

Pérez, E. (1999) *The Decolonial Imaginary: writing Chicanas into history*, Bloomington, IN: Indiana University Press.

Pérez Firmat, G. (1994) *Life on the Hyphen: the Cuban American way*, Austin, TX: University of Texas Press.

Schaffer, K. and Smith, S. (eds) (2004) *Human Rights and Narrated Lives: the ethics of recognition*, New York: Palgrave Macmillan.

Slaughter, J. (2007) *Human Rights Inc.: the world novel, narrative form, and international law*, New York: Fordham University Press.

8 Digital storytelling for gender justice

Exploring the challenges of participation and the limits of polyvocality

Amy L. Hill

Over the past fifteen years, the emerging participatory media production method known as digital storytelling[1] has been taken up in a wide variety of community, health, educational, and academic settings. Drawing from well-established traditions in popular education, participatory communications, oral history, and, most recently, what has been called "citizen journalism," practitioners of digital storytelling in localized contexts around the world are working with small groups of people to facilitate the production of short, first-person digital videos that document a wide range of culturally and historically embedded lived experiences (Lambert 2002; Burgess 2006).

Silence Speaks is an international digital storytelling initiative that endeavors to provide survivors and witnesses of physical and sexual violence and other human rights violations with a safe, supportive environment in which to tell their stories.[2] Workshop participants share and bear witness to each other's testimony; record voiceover narration; collect and generate photos and video clips; and learn, typically through hands-on computer tutorials, how to combine these materials into short digital videos. The resulting media pieces aim to challenge journalistic and anthropological legacies of voyeurism and naturalized representation by placing primary control over what stories get told directly in the hands of the storytellers.

To date, *Silence Speaks* has led more than forty workshops in the United States, South Africa, Australia, Uganda, Canada, Brazil, Congo-Brazzaville, and Guatemala. Participants have shared stories that address, among other topics, child sexual abuse and domestic violence; historical grief and the epidemic of sexual violence against women in the wake of apartheid; and post-conflict issues facing female ex-combatants and youth formerly associated with fighting forces. Specific workshop processes are developed in close partnership with collaborating groups to accommodate the languages, literacies, and technologies of a given setting. Finished stories are shared as training tools, at community organizing events, and in policy advocacy arenas, to promote learning and dialogue and support justice and human rights both locally and globally.

As co-founder of *Silence Speaks*, I come to the work first and foremost not as a filmmaker or artist, but as a survivor and activist. Like so many children raised in complacent, white, middle-class U.S. suburbs in the 1970s and 1980s, I grew up in a family plagued by abuse and dysfunction. I found my political voice as a young woman through queer organizing in San Francisco. The emergence of third world and post-modern feminisms was in full swing, and I became committed to community and cultural practices that understand knowledge as perspectival and power-laden. Such practices acknowledge the ways in which deeply rooted structures of inequality, fed by a complex interplay of race, gender, class, and other categories of "marginalization," inform how individuals and groups make sense of the world and play a key role in determining what knowledge is privileged and what is devalued. Then and now, I choose to ground my own political action in a location that "does not intend to speak about, just nearby" (Haraway 1988) the voices of the oppressed. Rather than assuming commonalities among some amorphous "community" of trauma survivors, I try to attend to the ways that all "experience" is mediated and lived through race, gender, and class subject positions. I approach my work with the understanding that "identities are never unified and, in late modern times, are increasingly fragmented and fractured; never singular but multiply constructed across suffering, often intersecting and antagonistic, discourses, practices and positions" (Hall and Du Gay 1996: 4).

The guiding vision of *Silence Speaks* is reflected by the notion that "Feminists must seek to transform 'the inner world' of bodily experience, psychological colonization, and cultural silencing, as well as the outer world of material social conditions" (Thornham 2000: 8). Over the past ten years, I have seen how the autobiographical storytelling that occurs within the project can, with careful facilitation, serve as a means through which individuals are able to reflect on the extent to which material circumstances (structures) and interior processes and motivations (agency) have jointly shaped their lives. *Silence Speaks* allows for this inner, transformational work by inviting the storyteller to step into a position of power and authority in order to articulate a story that "talks back" to or resists dominant discourses about violence even as it may inevitably also reflect them. Depending on geography and historic moment, these discourses tend to shift back and forth between narratives that are either problem-saturated and oppressive ("once a victim, always a victim") or relentlessly upbeat ("healing and forgiveness pave a sure route from 'victim' to 'survivor'"), thus eliding the complexities of people's lives.

Because *Silence Speaks* stories, like other cultural forms, are shaped by and contribute to broader social and political understandings about violence and trauma, the project raises crucial questions about how stories become media texts and in what circumstances they are viewed. In this chapter, I explore how "participation," power, and authorship play out within *Silence Speaks*. Using a case study of work done in South Africa, I also critically examine the practice of publicly sharing digital stories. I do so to both deepen my own understanding of digital storytelling as a research method, a form of media production, and a strategy for supporting social and economic justice, and to provide an example of methodological transparency that I hope others involved in similar forms of digital storytelling will echo in describing their work.

Exploring "participation"

Digital storytelling has arisen in tandem with an explosion of participatory approaches to new media production, made possible by the increasing availability of (relatively) cheap and user-friendly digital video technologies. Today's participatory video has its roots in radical approaches to facilitative documentary film methods developed in the late 1960s, when pioneering filmmakers in Australia recorded the lives of aboriginal groups and taught them to use cameras and editing equipment in order to represent themselves and their struggles to achieve sovereignty and basic human rights (Barnouw 1993). In the 1970s and 1980s, as analog video replaced film as the medium of choice in broadcast and community media environments, increasing numbers of producers and scholars in the United States began to employ and write about participatory production processes as a way to point to the supposed democratization of the field and address imbalances in mainstream media "misrepresentations" of marginalized communities—youth, people of color, immigrants, working class labor activists, etc. At the international level, development communications specialists adopted participatory video strategies that sought to engage local peoples in script development processes and bring their voices into conversations about how to best address the health and economic crises wrought by the continuing legacies of colonialism (Servaes 1996).

Few who have claimed to be doing "participatory" video work in either the analog or digital era, however, are clear in their articulation of what that participation really means on the ground. In much of the literature on participatory media in an international development context, for example, participants themselves are rarely portrayed as taking active roles in *production* (i.e., through learning camera or editing skills) or as having a stake in how media products are used and distributed (Richards 2001; Servaes 1996, 1999; White 2003). Additionally, much of the writing about participatory media and digital storytelling from within the disciplines of communications or media studies tends to frame production as a neutral activity rather than as a process through which economic structures and ideological meanings are reflected, reproduced, or transcended.[3]

In order to address these oversights, I choose to situate the participatory video method known as digital storytelling as a media-making process onto which the range of ethical issues raised by ethnographic practice can be closely mapped. Like many forms of ethnography, digital storytelling involves the production of a text (in this case, a media text). Just as many ethnographers working in the interdisciplinary field of cultural studies are ever-alert to the need to explore how power dynamics, social, cultural, and historical contexts, and dimensions of difference play out in their fieldwork and writing, so too am I, as a digital storytelling facilitator, committed to resisting assumptions that "participatory" processes eliminate the need for careful reflection about the subtleties of how some voices are privileged and others are silenced, as a given project unfolds.

This reflection must begin by looking at the circumstances through which storytellers become involved in *Silence Speaks* in the first place. While a lengthy exploration of the literature on the psychological risks and benefits of testimony and storytelling is beyond the scope of this chapter, I take very seriously the notion that asking someone who is currently "in" his or her story (i.e., someone in crisis or suffering from flashbacks, anxiety, etc.) to narrate that story can (but won't always) be problematic. I emphasize to project partners that the recruitment of storytellers must involve careful screening,[4] and I require that staff who are trained in crisis counseling be available at workshops, should someone need extra support. This is not to ignore the fact that in much of the world, narratives of suffering are expressed quite organically, without the urging of trained mental health "experts." Psychologists or trauma specialists might disagree, but I believe that most people choose to tell their stories, even if doing so is quite challenging, when they intuit that they have the strength and internal resources necessary for doing so and when they sense that someone capable of truly listening is available to hear them.

To ease these challenges, a space of openness and trust must be established. Like the ethnographer doing fieldwork, I am called on in *Silence Speaks* workshops to practice a deep form of listening. Study and mentoring in Buddhist teachings and meditation practice have been essential to the development of my capacity to carry out this kind of storytelling work. My practice stresses inner awareness rather than superficial "relatedness" to an exterior other and relies on a belief that the key to intersubjectivity is listening not with the mind, with its tendency to categorize, judge, assume, and diagnose, but with an open heart that can sit with the vulnerability and deep feelings that arise when bearing witness to another person's pain and be present in an unconditional way (Welwood 2000).[5]

In recruiting workshop participants, the question of audiences for their stories also arises. When I first conceived of *Silence Speaks* in 1999, I was committed to leaving the decision about when, where, and whether stories would be shared entirely up to the storytellers. As the project has evolved, I have struggled to protect their needs to feel safe, to feel heard, and to take ownership over their work, amidst the desires of partner organizations and funders to develop collections of stories that can be screened publicly. This balancing act has required informed consent as a process rather than a one-time event involving the signing of a form. I ask that project partners make it extremely clear to people *before* they decide to create a story whether or not the story is intended for various kinds of distribution and that they talk with potential storytellers about what some of the risks and benefits of participating might be.

Once they have chosen to attend a workshop, I am confronted with the challenge of guiding participants in a responsible way through the process of making a story that may be shown in a number of different public settings. The focus on first-person narrative and hands-on production suggests that workshop participants can claim full authorship of their stories as they are introduced to skills for recording, collecting and preparing images, and digital editing. In practice, however, other storytellers in the group—during a Story Circle[6]—and workshop facilitators—through one-on-one feedback—very often have significant influences on the content and narrative structure of the final scripts that are recorded and on how these voiceovers are illustrated. Varied learning curves, traditional teacher–student dynamics, and the need to complete the process in a timely way also contribute to what is ultimately a form of *co-authorship*.

How does this co-authorship happen in the moment, in a *Silence Speaks* workshop? In her well-known critique of the notion that stories of experience can be accepted at face value as "truth," Joan Scott writes that "the evidence of experience, whether conceived through a metaphor of visibility or in any other way that takes meaning as transparent, reproduces rather than contests given ideological systems—those that assume that the facts of history 'speak for themselves'" (Scott 1992: 25). I have found that engaging workshop participants in conversations that encourage them to critically analyze and contextualize their own memories can lead to nuanced stories that don't take "experience" at face value but rather historicize its unfolding within specific social, ideological, and political contexts.

The hoped-for result of these conversations is an openness on the part of *Silence Speaks* workshop participants to suggestions about story content, images, and editing decisions. And just as the ethnographer must make decisions about how to "re-present" people, situations, and inner experience within a written text, I, as a digital storytelling facilitator, must think through how to provide assistance, what to offer, and why I'm making the choices I make. This requires a constant ability to attend not only to history (my own and the participant's, both of which I can only ever imperfectly perceive), but also to concerns about emotional and physical safety, confidentiality, and disclosure (in terms of what to say, who to name or not name, what level of detail to go into about certain incidents, and who/what to show or not show [many storytellers choose to remain anonymous and/or to blur faces in photographs]). Perhaps most importantly, it requires a willingness to let go when assistance is *not* desired (which can be challenging for those facilitators who view themselves as "better" artists than the storyteller or assume uncritically that they "know" what someone else is trying to express).

When all is said and done, groups of stories created in a *Silence Speaks* workshop can weave together a collective social story of injustice or struggle. These stories are examples of the counter narratives so widely admired in critical race theory or, more simply, the personal testimonies that have proliferated in discourses about international human rights. James Clifford has written about the shift in ethnography from one to many voices:

> Polyvocality was restrained and orchestrated by giving to one voice a pervasive authorial function and to others the role of sources, "informants," to be quoted or paraphrased. Once polyphony is recognized as a mode of textual production, monophonic authority is questioned, revealed to be characteristic of a science that has claimed to represent cultures.
>
> (Clifford and Marcus 1986)

Polyvocal forms of textual and media production seem to hold much potential for enabling people to participate in authoring their own stories as members of a collective. Yet questions remain about who benefits from the authorship of digital stories and what happens when they are heard (or not heard) in various contexts. I turn next to these issues, by looking at some of the work of *Silence Speaks* in South Africa.

Setting the stage: "traumatic storytelling" and gender justice work in South Africa

Nearly fifteen years have passed since the Republic of South Africa held its first multiracial election in the wake of the apartheid era and seated Nelson Mandela as president. In a marked departure from the Marxist origins of the African National Congress (ANC), Mandela and his predecessors have supported economic and social policies that have arguably done little to address the deeply entrenched poverty and income disparities that continue to plague the country. While the racial demographics of those holding civil service positions and serving in government have shifted dramatically, the radical politics of change that dominated during the years of struggle against apartheid have been largely subsumed by the uncritical adoption of a "Rainbow Nation" ethic, a neoliberal development paradigm, and South Africa's rapid entrée into the constantly shifting field of global capitalism.

In 1997, the South African Truth and Reconciliation Commission (TRC) began hearings on human rights violations that took place between 1960 and 1993. The Commission promised amnesty to those who confessed their crimes under the apartheid system, and many former apartheid and ANC leaders appeared before it. This painful and divisive process designed to encourage "recovery" at the national level gave rise to competing discourses about what has been called "traumatic storytelling"—the sharing of individual narratives that detail the atrocities of apartheid. Anthropologist Christopher James Colvin has written of the imposition of western theories about trauma on both the TRC process and the subsequent establishment of support programs for those who lived through the violence of the apartheid years. He points out that definitions of trauma which locate symptoms within individuals and attempt to apply cookie-cutter approaches to "treatment" (based on western models of psychotherapy) have often been uncritically applied in South Africa. The result, according to Colvin, has been the widespread adoption of particular mental health discourses that continue to shape the subjectivities of those who lived through apartheid as well as of younger South Africans—often in ways that impede the formation of politicized identities and the pursuit of collective action for reparations or justice (Colvin 2004).

As the TRC was doing its work, crime rates exploded in many parts of South Africa, HIV began to spread rapidly, and violence against women was said to be reaching near-epidemic proportions. Rather than foregrounding the material, economic, or historic dimensions of these interrelated problems, many indigenous and international health and development organizations began to point to a previously overlooked yet very relevant "gender lens" that views gender formations privileging men's power and women's lack of equality in all spheres of society as largely responsible for violence against women and children. As a result, programs and campaigns designed to question these traditional gender norms and put forward new visions of what it means to be "male" or "female" that encourage gender identities supporting equity in families and relationships, as well as in the realm of the public, have proliferated throughout South Africa.

Notably, it is in the frequently repeated and increasingly tendentious practice of personal storytelling—first in the context of the TRC and later in the context of projects to archive memories of the apartheid period and capture stories of grief and survival related to HIV and AIDS and gender-based violence—that the impact of trauma and mental health discourses on subjectivity and politics has perhaps been most apparent. The psychotherapeutic framing of personal narratives and the discourse of gender as an explanation for a host of social ills are two of the main features of the larger context in which *Silence Speaks'* digital storytelling work in South Africa has unfolded.

Counter narratives amidst dominant narratives: what's being said, who benefits, and how are stories being heard?

In 2005, I was asked to adapt *Silence Speaks* methods for use in South Africa, as a way of bringing everyday men's and women's voices to bear on initiatives exploring the connections between violence against women and the spread of HIV in the country. A colleague from the Center for Digital Storytelling and I were invited to teach two *Silence Speaks* workshops for youth and adults associated with the Men As Partners Network (MAP), which coordinates training and advocacy to address gender-based violence and HIV and AIDS. The workshop participants decided unanimously to share and produce their stories in English, a language in which they are all sufficiently literate.[7] Because South Africa's media and technology infrastructure is similar to that of the United States, we were able to offer a "hands-on" transmission of skills for digital imaging and editing and assist participants in editing their own stories. This was especially important to me, given that few "community-based"/alternative media environments exist in South Africa, and few of these have explored concepts of participatory media production.[8] Following the production of a compilation DVD of the stories, the MAP Network began to screen them to great acclaim at numerous trainings, community events, and conferences both within and outside of South Africa. In addition to sharing them in small-scale venues, MAP's lead agency posted the digital stories online.

That same year, YouTube exploded onto the media scene and generated an ongoing wave of support for the widespread online circulation of video narratives about human rights abuses. Much of this activity fits within the emerging arenas of media activism, which aims to harness the potential of new media and the Internet for inspiring democratic civic engagement (Carroll and Hackett 2006), or citizen journalism, which positions people untrained in the ethics and research practices of that field as valid participants in the production and transformation of what is commonly accepted as news media (Rodriguez 2001). Both perspectives have heralded the online display of video as a radical alternative to traditional venues for distribution (such as film festivals or theatrical releases) by attaching broad claims for social justice to the practice of making previously unheard voices and images available. But what happens next, once the act of creating has been carried out? What potential exists for web-based videos on their own to catalyze concerned action, and on what basis are people expected to act?

Jean Burgess, in her exploration of digital storytelling as a form of "vernacular creativity," writes that

> somewhat paradoxically from a critical perspective, it is the very qualities that mark digital stories as uncool, conservative, and ideologically suspect— "stock" tropes, nostalgia, even sentimentality—that give them the power of social connectivity, while the sense of authentic self-expression that they convey lowers the barriers to empathy.
>
> (Burgess 2006: 221)

The question that must be asked, however, is this: What is the relationship between watching stories that make viewers feel empathetic and connected to others and social engagement? Megan Boler's work on the interrogation of "multi-culturalism's gaze" suggests that it is problematic. Boler claims that classic definitions of empathy used by educators to justify the sharing of human rights testimonies as a pedagogical strategy result in viewer passivity rather than action and thus "fall far short of assuring any basis for social change and reinscribe a 'consumptive' mode of identification with the other" (Boler 1997: 253).

And what about the impact of authorship, for storytellers, particularly in the South African context? Just as digital storytelling (with its placement of production tools and skills in the hands of citizens at the community level) challenges professionalism and elitism within the documentary film world, a growing number of photography projects aim to "empower" participants and turn conventional photojournalism on its head by putting cameras in the hands of those usually represented as the *subjects* of documentary photography. Julia Ballerini has pointed out that participants in these projects are often not in a position to reap many of the benefits of authorship and has wondered about the extent to which this form of authorship might merely serve as "a legitimizing device whose conveniently taken-for-granted 'naturalness' compensates for documentary photography's increasing lack of credibility (both in terms of current ideology and technology)" (Ballerini 1995: 95). The same concerns must be raised in relation to digital storytelling. *Silence Speaks* and the organizations in MAP benefit by being able to promote stories to funders, supporters, and donors. But leaving aside the experiences of the many *Silence Speaks* participants who have talked about how the project has transformed their lives,[9] what do participants stand to gain by "owning" the contents of their stories?

In 2007, I returned to South Africa to build upon the work done two years earlier. I had stayed in close touch with a number of the workshop participants from the 2005 MAP sessions, including Thoko, who had told a story of childhood rape, yearnings for a father figure, and her emergence as a champion of women's rights. Thoko disclosed to me that since I had last seen her, she had again been raped. With a good deal of hesitation about whether to do so (and feeling relieved when she said she had already considered the possibility), I suggested that she participate in one of the *Silence Speaks* workshops I had arranged to do during my current stay—this time in association with the Sonke Gender Justice Network. Thoko and I communicated several times via phone and email, and, in the end, she did decide to make a second digital story. Here is the script of that story, which Thoko wrote in the form of a letter to her goddaughter.

Dear little princess, It feels like a long time since I welcomed you into this world. They said you were a big baby, but me, I just saw tiny hands and tiny feet. I'm your godmother. You came just when I needed a reason to breathe. This is my story . . .

It's Wednesday, 1st of March. Jacob Zuma is about to go on trial for rape. I've just returned to South Africa from my first-ever international trip. I am excited. Little did I know in just three days my life would change forever. Thursday, I find out my job is hanging by a thread. Friday, I get robbed of a new cell phone and 700 Rands. On Saturday? Saturday, I get raped.

I see the man when I open my gate, and I feel uncomfortable, but he walks away. Just past midnight, I see him again—this time inside my house. I wake up disoriented and directly facing the sharp edge of the biggest knife I've ever seen. I know exactly what he wants. I have never seen the animalistic look that the man is giving me. After some failed negotiations for condom use, he proceeds to rape me.

I guess the negotiations took some steam out of him. When he fails to get it up completely, he tells me I don't taste nice and leaves with my purse. I reported the case to the police immediately, and I got a medical examination and HIV post exposure prophylaxis. I hate those pills, they made me so sick and so weak, while my rapist went around free. But I finished them, and I tested negative.

Of course, like so many rape cases, mine never even got investigated. Nobody could tell me who the investigating officer was, or whether the sample they took from my vagina held any clues to the rapist's identity. So you see, the day you were born, I was ready to give up on life. Why should I bother to live, only to be preyed upon by sick-minded bastards who took my childhood innocence and now my adult sexuality?

Then I held you in my arms, and I knew I had to continue to stand against gender-based violence. I look at you and hope I can protect you from all the injustices I have experienced at the hands of men. So I continue to march the streets demanding freedom. I continue to use pen and paper to highlight the plight of women and children. When the struggle seems futile and my voice gets hoarse, I still carry on my angel, just for you. I love you princess. From your loving godma.

I turn now to issues I have raised about process, authorship, and distribution—through an exploration of three aspects of Thoko's involvement with *Silence Speaks*: what her second story can be said to "represent"; how she, as an author, has benefited from the production of digital stories; and how both of her stories are (or are not) being shared and listened to.

Because we already had a relationship prior to the workshop and because she had been through the storytelling process two years earlier, Thoko was very open to my input on her script. Before she even began writing, we talked about the circumstances of the rape, and she mentioned that she wanted to dedicate the piece to her goddaughter. She first authored a longer version of the above, and together, we edited it for word length and clarity. Thoko then illustrated the story primarily with her own photos; I contributed a few images I had taken during my stay in the country.

The finished piece can be read as challenging the notion that rape is perpetrated by bitter, angry, violent men, with its reference to Jacob Zuma, current head of the ANC and President of South Africa, who at the time had just been acquitted of sexual assault charges (the suggestion being that if such a public figure could be a rapist, so could anyone). It also disrupts the commonly-held view that rape victims lack agency by describing Thoko's attempts to negotiate condom use and by revealing that she reported the rape, got a medical examination, accessed post-HIV exposure prophylaxis pills, and followed up on the investigation of her case. With the inclusion of these details, the story reflects Shari Stone-Mediatore's important argument for acknowledging the power of stories of experience. She writes that people's daily experiences are only partially determined by ideological processes and that "some stories of experience stimulate and enrich political thought, as well as destabilize the more reductive, obfuscating narratives, precisely by the way the texts are constructed and read" (Stone-Mediatore 2003: 5).

In its visual treatment of the rape scene, the story avoids dramatic images of violence or pain and instead relies on a montage of close-up black and white photographs of security fences, bars, and wires—thus suggesting the futility of individual attempts to protect oneself against the backdrop of a larger culture that condones and is permeated by sexual violence. To me, these aesthetic choices help the piece serve Ballerini's call for media practices that challenge the status quo of documentary work by aiming "to disrupt, rupture, and render visible how power works to promote relations of domination and demonstrate an awareness of the politics of representation and the socio-political operations of photographs" (Ballerini 1995: 91).

The story also reflects prevalent discourses about gender-based violence by setting Thoko up as a victim and resolving her despair by positioning her as a survivor. Yet Thoko portrays herself as much more than a survivor; she is an activist committed to challenging injustice and ending abuse. Her decision to represent multiple phases of her experience within the same narrative heeds Jill Blackmore's recommendation that women's human rights advocates must focus not only on the rights of victims, but on the potentials and possibilities for agency and action that can seriously attend to survivors' capabilities and needs (Blackmore 2005). It is also important to keep in mind that language that emphasizes distinctions among terms like "victims," "survivors," and "activists" is an outgrowth of many years of committed struggle across the globe to legitimize claims for viewing gendered violence as a human rights violation—claims that are having very real consequences for many women and girls whose suffering was previously dismissed as a "private" matter or defended with references to "cultural traditions" bound up in, and therefore justified by, essentialized notions of culture.

Placing Thoko's story within this broader human rights context brings me to the question, "who benefits?" from its production and distribution. Thoko told me that she had deliberately leveraged her first digital story to gain entrée to various higher-level public dialogues about women's health and human rights—an entrée that may not have been available to her had she come to these dialogues with her voice alone rather than with a short video. This example of the benefits of authorship for Thoko echoes Judith Butler's contention that identities are typically constructed not prior to, but through, action: "The foundationalist reasoning of identity politics tends to assume that an identity must first be in place in order for political interests to be elaborated . . . my argument is that there need not be a 'doer behind the deed,' but that the 'doer' is variably constructed in and through the deed" (Butler 1990: 142). Like Thoko, *Silence Speaks* participants tend to enter the digital storytelling process at various stages of "healing," and I have witnessed the transformation of many of them simply through the subversive acts of articulating and sharing stories that do not usually make it into the public sphere.

But Thoko's first story has not always been heard in such a useful way. Knowing that she had repeatedly shared her first story, I emailed her in 2008 to ask whether she would be interested in presenting both of her stories at a conference. This is an excerpt from her reply:

> I keep getting invited to present on digital stories and I feel I have more to offer. I still want to help with digital stories on the ground, but not at this level. In the beginning digital stories really did help with the healing process, but after a while it starts rehashing old wounds. . . . Lately I was getting pissed off by the pity looks after I give a presentation. They made me feel weak and victimized. I knew then that it was time to stop.

Thoko has noted that being involved with the project "really did help with the healing process," but she has also admitted that, somewhere along the way (as she began to share her stories), it started "rehashing old wounds." She has expressed feeling that she has "more to offer"—as though people who see her present her story assume she IS the story rather than a living person with many skills and experiences that both pre-date and follow the events described in the story. Thoko has also written that she knew that it "was time to stop" when she began "getting pissed off by the pity looks after I give a presentation," which made her feel "weak and victimized."

Sadly, these comments reflect the work of Megan Boler (1997) and others on the limits of empathy and the ways in which trauma narratives can become media spectacles (see, for example, Feldman 2004; Schaffer and Smith 2004), by suggesting that at the conference presentations to which she has referred in the email, Thoko-as-victim is being consumed by a passive professional audience incapable of seeing her as anything other than deserving of pity. But rather than rejecting *Silence Speaks* altogether, Thoko has stated that she still "wants to help with digital stories on the ground." So how is that ground—the ground on which stories are being shared—taking shape?

The power circulating at large professional conferences where stories are screened (not to mention the isolation of individual web viewings) does not offer a ready solution to the problems Thoko has raised in her email. Certainly attempts can be made to mediate viewings of *Silence Speaks* stories—for instance, by carefully describing the process through which stories are produced and historicizing their contents. Stories can also be verbally introduced with a statement, or presented online with accompanying text, that describes the ethics of participation and authorship. But more importantly, I believe Boler's work offers a path beyond the helplessness that Thoko has described (recognizing that we do not know what the viewers who saw her story were feeling or thinking; we only know of Thoko's sense that they were looking at her with pity) and thus outlines some of the ways in which *Silence Speaks* stories are being shared as part of thoughtful pedagogies of listening.

In discussing the use of Holocaust survivor texts to educate college students, Boler claims that these texts give rise to a form of passive empathy that relies upon the reader's fearful identification with the other (i.e., the sense that "that could be me"), through the construction of "a binary power relationship of self/other that threatens to consume and annihilate the very differences that permit empathy" (Boler 1997: 258). She argues that instead of establishing a platform on which to build critical consciousness, this kind of empathy "produces no action towards justice but situates the powerful Western eye/I as the judging subject, never called upon to cast her gaze at her own reflection" (259).

Boler advocates instead for the concept of "testimonial reading," which recognizes the power relations that define the interaction between reader and text and invokes a responsibility of listening that relies on a willingness to "excavate the forces that constructed the unspeakable, a painful process for the speaker as well as for the listener, because those forces are about oppression" (264). Rather than allowing the projection of the reader's own experience onto the "other" (i.e., identification with "the other"), testimonial reading demands, on the part of the reader, a willingness to "attend to *oneself* as much as to the other—not in terms of fears for one's own vulnerabilities, but rather in terms of the affective obstacles that prevent one's acute attention to the power relations guiding one's responses and judgments" (265).

Silence Speaks stories are not testimonies, per se, but like all texts they are historically situated in power relationships and can therefore potentially be read testimonially. Boler's analysis reminds me to ask always how opportunities can be created for story viewers to engage questions such as "what crisis of truth does this text speak to, and what mass of contradictions and struggles do I become as a result?" (267). A testimonial reading of stories means that viewers must notice, when listening to/watching stories, what emotions surface for them, and why. Boler notes that in so doing, "the reader is called upon to meet the text with her own testimony, rather than using the other as a catalyst or a substitute for oneself" (268).

Boler also cautions us that, "in a historical epoch of saturated communications, there is every temptation to turn our backs, to maintain the habit of denial, and to keep secrets from ourselves through the numb consumption of another's suffering, grateful for the distances that seem to confirm our safety" (268–269). Fortunately, specific pedagogies and practices that resist this temptation and instead support spaces for testimonial readings of *Silence Speaks* stories are unfolding in South Africa and elsewhere. In localized settings, service provider trainings, and gatherings of institutional and public policymakers, skilled facilitators (sometimes the authors of digital stories, sometimes not) are carefully contextualizing stories, analyzing the conditions and historical moment of their production, and resisting simplistic and passive readings in favor of readings that encourage viewers to reveal their own stories and open themselves to raw vulnerability (comparable to that exercised by the storytellers in sharing their lives in the first place) and a form of emotional distress or confusion which makes simplistic explanations or solutions impossible. The hope is that in doing so, rather than pitying storytellers like Thoko, viewers will gain the capacity to interrogate their own place in the shifting strata of power that perpetuate gender-based violence and human rights abuses and, ultimately, the conviction to act in ways that disrupt them.

Notes

1   The term "digital storytelling" is used to describe a variety of media production practices and media forms. For the purposes of this article, the term refers to practices originated at the U.S.-based Center for Digital Storytelling, www.storycenter.org.
2   For more information about *Silence Speaks* or to view stories, visit www.silencespeaks.org.
3   One important exception is the work of the Finding a Voice project, which makes explicit the ways in which power and economics play out in the context of the growing "information and Communications technologies (ICTs) for development" field and "examined the practicalities of stimulating participation through creative engagement with digital ICTs . . . providing unprecedented opportunities for self-expression and the sharing of culture, hopes, and dreams" (Tacchi and Watkins 2009). It is also important to mention that visual anthropologists like Tim Asch and Terrence Ranger have written at length about these issues.
4   The screening questions, developed in collaboration with a licensed clinical social worker, attempt to assess a person's readiness to share a difficult personal story in a group process and identify what emotional support will be available to this person after

the workshop. The questions also rule out individuals who are active substance users or are struggling to meet their basic needs for food and shelter, as our experience in *Silence Speaks* has been that in these cases, people are generally not able to meet the psychic and practical demands of a digital storytelling workshop process.

5 Ironically, Buddhist teachings encourage us to disconnect from the stories we tell about ourselves rather than identify with them. This suggests that it is not the content of the story but the permission to be vulnerable in telling it that underpins the transformative power of digital storytelling. From the perspective of *Silence Speaks*, therefore, the process is not about telling a story about who one "is" but rather about coming to understand who one is *not* (in keeping with the post-structuralist view that identities are provisional, shifting, performed, etc.).

6 Like the general workshops offered through the Center for Digital Storytelling, *Silence Speaks* sessions involve a Story Circle, which invites participants to share their stories with each another and with facilitators. While the Center's Story Circle process zeroes directly in on how narratives will take shape in digital form, the process for *Silence Speaks* is slightly different. Rather than constraining participants' narratives within the Story Circle, I encourage them to recount their "entire" story. I then work one-on-one with those participants who need and request guidance, to help them craft this longer story into a short piece appropriate for production.

7 While South Africa proudly boasts that it has eleven "official" languages, the legacy of apartheid and a subsequent plunge into global economic realities mean that English is the dominant language in schools and institutions. Had our funding made it possible, we would have produced the stories both in English and in participants' languages of choice.

8 As has been the case in the United States, South Africa's neoliberal approach to technology education and the "digital divide" has focused largely on teaching computer skills for low-wage occupations rather than on analyzing the ways in which technology itself often serves to reproduce the class formations that rely on bodies to fill these occupations (for more on this topic, see Eubanks 2007).

9 I refer here to a combination of informal email disclosures by *Silence Speaks* participants about improved familial and intimate partner relationships, reduced anxiety, and increased confidence, following the creation of stories; workshop surveys that invite participants to share their thoughts about making stories; and an unpublished qualitative study of the impact of *Silence Speaks* on storytellers (Landsbaum 2005).

Bibliography

Ballerini, J. (1995) "'Flip': the homeless child as 'auteur,'" *Yale Journal of Criticism*, 8(2): 87–101.

Barnouw, E. (1993) *Documentary: a history of the nonfiction film*, New York: Oxford University Press.

Blackmore, J. (2005) "Feminist Strategic Rethinking of Human Rights Discourses," in W. Hesford and W. Kozol (eds) *Just Advocacy? women's human rights, transnational feminisms, and the politics of representation*, New Brunswick, NJ: Rutgers University Press.

Boler, M. (1997) "The Risks of Empathy: interrogating multiculturalism's gaze," *Cultural Studies*, 11(2): 253–273.

Burgess, J. (2006) "Hearing Ordinary Voices: cultural studies, vernacular creativity and digital storytelling," *Continuum: journal of media and cultural studies*, 20(2): 201–214.

Butler, J. (1990) *Gender Trouble: feminism and the subversion of identity*, London and New York: Routledge.

Carroll, W. K. and Hackett, R. A. (2006) "Democratic Media Activism Through the Lens of Social Movement Theory," *Media Culture Society*, 28(1): 83–104.

Clifford, J. and Marcus, G. E. (1986) *Writing Culture: the poetics and politics of ethnography*, Berkeley: University of California Press.

Colvin, C. J. (2004) "Ambivalent Narrations: pursuing the political through traumatic storytelling," *PoLAR Political and Legal Anthropology Review*, 27(1): 72–89.

Eubanks, V. (2007) "Popular Technology: exploring inequality in the information economy," *Science and Public Policy*, 34(2): 127–138.

Feldman, A. (2004) "Memory Theaters, Virtual Witnessing, and the Trauma-Aesthetic," *Biography*, 21(1): 163–202.

Hall, S. and Du Gay, P. (1996) *Questions of Cultural Identity*, London; Thousand Oaks, CA: Sage Publications.

Haraway, D. (1988) "Situated Knowledges," *Feminist Studies*, 14(3): 575–599.

Lambert, J. (2002) *Digital Storytelling: capturing lives, creating community*, Berkeley, CA: Digital Diner Press.

Landsbaum, L. (2005) "Digital Storytelling with Survivors and Witnesses of Violence: exploring participants' experiences," unpublished thesis, San Francisco State University.

Richards, M. (2001) *Communication and Development: the Freirean connection*, Cresskill, NJ: Hampton Press.

Rodriguez, C. (2001) *Fissures in the Mediascape: an international study of citizens' media*, Creskill, NJ: Hampton Press.

Schaffer, K. and Smith, S. (2004) "Conjunctions: life narratives in the field of human rights," *Biography*, 27(1): 1–24.

Scott, J. (1992) "Experience," in J. Butler and J. W. Scott (eds) *Feminists Theorize the Political*, New York: Routledge.

Servaes, J. (ed.) (1996) *Participatory Communication for Social Change*, Thousand Oaks, CA: Sage Publications.

— (1999) *Theoretical Approaches to Participatory Communication*, Cresskill, NJ: Hampton Press.

Stone-Mediatore, S. (2003) *Reading Across Boarders: storytelling and knowledges of resistance*, New York: Palgrave Macmillan.

Tacchi, J. and Watkins, J. (eds) (2009) *Participatory Content Creation for Development: principles and practices*, New Delhi: United Nations Educational, Scientific, and Cultural Organization (UNESCO).

Thornham, S. (2000) *Feminist Theory and Cultural Studies: stories of unsettled relations*, London: Hodder Arnold.

Welwood, J. (2000) *Toward a Psychology of Awakening*, Boston and London: Shambhala.

White, S. (ed.) (2003) *Participatory Video: images that transform and empower*, Thousand Oaks, CA: Sage Publications.

Part III
Mobilizing strategies of engagement

9 "Sweet electrical greetings"

Women, HIV, and the evolution of an intervention project in Papua New Guinea

Holly Wardlow with Mary Michael Tamia

My Sweet Heart Sister Holly, sweet electrical greetings all the way from your second homeland, Tari. Sometimes we say maybe you are already lost in the world, but then too many of your memories recall you to me, and it seems like you are closer to me always . . . Concerning AIDS awareness, we managed to reach the National AIDS Council, and one of the trainers finally came to Tari and held a workshop. I think the AIDS awareness you started won't break down and it will still exist when you come back to Papua New Guinea. The latest news is that AIDS is becoming like a bush fire and more people are dying.

(letter from Mary Michael Tamia to Holly Wardlow,
September 2005)

Mary and I planned to write this chapter together. Mary has an idiosyncratic and delicious way with English, and the phrase "sweet electrical greetings" goes a long way in capturing her personality: energetic, warm, generous, and funny. However, Mary has only sporadic access to email through contacts she has cultivated with mining company staff at a small community liaison office in Tari. Therefore, the process of co-authorship, in which there is a regular back-and-forth of text, commentary, emails, and revised text, proved impossible. Given these circumstances I, Holly, became the primary author of this chapter.

The discipline of anthropology has, in the past, been critiqued—and, indeed, critiqued itself—for performing acts of "ventriloquism," that is, speaking for the "indigenous other"—and perhaps even textually using informants to voice the discipline's (or particular authors') own theoretical preoccupations—rather than enabling the participants of ethnographic research to act as the authors of their own narratives (Appadurai 1988; Wolfe 1997). However, the production of dialogical and collaborative texts requires more than authorial intention; it also requires electricity, writing implements, and access to the Internet or a functional post office. Since Mary has none of these things (except, occasionally, paper and pen), I have done my best in this chapter to communicate what she wanted me to convey about her experiences carrying out HIV/AIDS prevention, counseling, and care in the Tari area. I have incorporated portions of letters and emails she has written me over the years so that you can hear her voice as well as mine.

I first met Mary in 1995. I was doing my doctoral fieldwork in anthropology and was living in a small flat on the hospital compound in Tari, Southern Highlands Province, Papua New Guinea. After a physical fight with her husband, Mary had run away to stay with her cousin, who lived in the flat below mine. Every day for a week her husband came to our residence—head hung in shame, food and gifts in hand—and stood outside, hoping that Mary might come out and speak with him. Eventually she agreed, but much of that week she spent upstairs in my flat—sharing stories about her life, drinking tea, and giggling at her husband's forlorn expression when yet again she refused to make an appearance. (Mary belongs to a large and supportive family; many women who seek refuge from their husbands with family members are sent back the next day).

We have been friends since that time, and becoming Mary's friend is probably the best and most serendipitous thing that has happened to me in Papua New Guinea. Therefore, when I initiated an AIDS awareness program in the Tari area, Mary was the person I hoped would keep it going after I returned to Canada. This chapter first discusses the HIV epidemic in Papua New Guinea, with a focus on the factors that make women especially vulnerable to infection. I then describe the volatile and violent environment of Tari in the early and mid 2000s, when many civil servants fled the area because of crime and deteriorating social services. I then discuss the small HIV/AIDS awareness project I started in 2004 and describe the ways in which Mary Michael Tamia, with assistance from a local NGO and the community liaison office of a nearby gold mine, dramatically expanded the project. The final pages of the chapter are devoted to the stories of particular women Mary has encountered through her AIDS-related work and the challenges that she has faced as she has struggled to meet the needs of mothers living with HIV/AIDS.

Women's vulnerability to HIV in Papua New Guinea

With a population of almost six million, Papua New Guinea occupies the eastern half of the island of New Guinea and some surrounding smaller islands. It gained independence from Australia in 1975, and although one of its official national languages is English, it is home to more than 800 indigenous languages. Much of the terrain consists of steep mountains and dense tropical rain forest, making infrastructure development and social service delivery difficult. Indeed, when I first went to Papua New Guinea as a Peace Corps volunteer in the late 1980s, I was told that it held the world record for the highest number of airstrips per capita, which was one way of saying that road networks were minimal and that many rural areas were serviced only by the occasional small plane, usually bringing supplies to Christian missionaries. Not surprisingly, then, indigenous beliefs and practices regarding gender, sexuality, marriage, health, and illness vary remarkably from one region to another.[1] Different regions have also experienced quite different histories of Christian missionary work, different degrees of contact with state institutions, and different chances for economic opportunities offered, for example, by mining companies. These varied experiences have shaped sexual practice, use of health services, and interpretations of and responses to HIV.

Papua New Guinea may not be the first place that comes to mind when thinking about the AIDS pandemic. It is not often in the North American media. However, the Papua New Guinea National AIDS Council (NAC) estimates a 2009 HIV prevalence of 2.56 percent (98,757 cases), with a projected increase to more than 5 percent prevalence by 2012 (UNGASS 2008). Although a prevalence of 2.56 percent may sound small compared with the statistics for some sub-Saharan African countries, it is higher than rates found in most Latin American countries, which tend to range between 0.5 percent and 1 percent (UNAIDS 2008). It is also higher than most of the countries in Asia; Vietnam, for example, has a prevalence of 0.5 percent (UNAIDS 2008). Thus, although the absolute number of HIV-positive cases is relatively low (since the total population is relatively small), the proportion of people infected and affected by HIV is relatively high. Moreover, 85 percent of HIV-positive cases in Papua New Guinea are located in rural areas; in other words, this is a generalized epidemic and is not confined to so-called "high risk groups" in urban areas. Heterosexual sex is the primary mode of transmission, with cases distributed equally between men and women, although women, as in many parts of the world, are infected at younger ages than men (UNGASS 2008; Heimer 2007).

Papua New Guinea shares many characteristics with countries that have experienced very high HIV prevalence: an economy that is extremely dependent on mining and other extractive industries (oil, natural gas, logging); a very young population, with approximately 40 percent under age 15; high rates of gonorrhea, syphilis, and other sexually transmitted infections, with studies showing long delays in treatment-seeking (Passey 1998); the contraction of economic opportunity, particularly in rural areas; and the severe deterioration of basic health and educational services, including the closure of rural aid posts and health centers (Duke 1999).

Women in Papua New Guinea are particularly vulnerable to HIV for a wide range of socio-cultural, economic, and political reasons. Because of Papua New Guinea's extremely diverse indigenous cultural systems and regional histories, it is difficult to generalize about the factors that put women at risk. Nevertheless, it can be said that in much of Papua New Guinea women are economically dependent on their husbands. Women are highly valued—and secure themselves a fair degree of agency and independence—for doing agricultural labor; however, they are extremely disadvantaged when it comes to acquiring money. While women often have control over the products of their labor for domestic consumption, they often do not have control over products that are meant for larger markets (coffee, tea, palm oil, vanilla, etc.). Moreover, women make up only 18 percent of the formal labor force (Seeley and Butcher 2006). Class status, of course, shapes the ways in which economic dependency makes women vulnerable to HIV infection. Poorer women, particularly in times of economic downturn, may turn to sex work as the only viable way to obtain cash (Hammar 1998).

Middle class women, for their part, may have achieved that status by marrying a civil servant or businessman and—especially if they have children—may be extremely reluctant to jeopardize it and to risk a fall back into rural poverty by challenging a husband's sexual privilege (Wardlow 2009a).

Moreover, in many Papua New Guinea societies, marriage results in social isolation for women. For example, among the Huli (the cultural group that lives in the Tari area and to which Mary belongs), once a woman's bridewealth is paid, she is expected to live with her husband's family and is not allowed to visit her own kin without his permission.[2] Because violations of this cultural rule often result in a husband's demand for financial compensation, a woman's parents may be reluctant to take her in. Unless she has been severely beaten, they will likely tell her that since her bridewealth has been paid, she must return to her husband and adapt to his desires and expectations. Most of the women I have interviewed (about 75 since 1995) have added that husbands respond negatively when newly married women try to spend time with their "besties" (best friends), fearing that they may be negatively influenced by their female peers. Consequently, married women are often profoundly socially isolated until they have at least a couple of children. (Having children, it is said, "fences a woman in": a woman is expected either to care for her children at home or to take them with her wherever she goes, which makes it extremely unlikely that she will stray from a marriage, sexually or otherwise. Because men's anxieties about being abandoned or cuckolded tend to decrease in proportion to the number of children a wife has, women who have two or more children typically exercise more freedom of movement than other women.)

In terms of HIV risk, women's social isolation often means they feel helpless in the face of a husband's infidelity: surrounded by a husband's kin and with no easy access to their own (who might refuse to help them in any case), they may silently resign themselves to his adulterous behavior even though they know it puts them at risk. Exacerbating this situation is the fact that many rural men must leave home to find work at mines or in urban areas; ethnographic and other qualitative research indicates that separation from home often results in extramarital sexual liaisons and exposure to HIV, which is then transmitted to wives (Wardlow 2007, 2009b).

The social isolation of married women is enforced by extremely high rates of domestic violence. Surveys and ethnographic data from the 1980s up to the present have consistently shown that in both rural and urban areas most married women are beaten (Bradley 1988; Counts 1992; Macintyre 2006; Toft 1985; Wardlow 2006; Zimmer-Tamakoshi 1997). The proportion of women beaten ranges by survey from about 60 percent to 80 percent, and the frequency and severity of violence is, of course, variable from one marriage to another. Nevertheless, the pervasiveness of domestic violence, the failure of police and courts to enforce the laws against it, and the fact that in many areas of the country it is seen as normal, inevitable, and even legitimate disciplinary behavior on the part of a husband makes it very difficult for most women to challenge a husband's sexual privilege.

Also contributing to women's HIV risk is an extremely high level of sexual violence—including gang rape—and, again, a relatively tolerant attitude towards it (NSRRT and Jenkins 1994; Hammar 2008; Lepani 2008b; Macintyre 2008). As Carol Jenkins notes (see also Jenkins 1996; Borrey 2000),[3]

> Most contemporary rape in Papua New Guinea has a culturally specific pattern in that, unlike some societies, at least half of all rapes are perpetrated by groups of men together. This is variously called *line-up, deep line, single file* and, in older ethnographic literature, plural copulation. . . . Most events take place after attendance at discos, clubs, and video parlors in both urban and rural areas, and both alcohol and marijuana play an important role. Sometimes the woman has agreed to have sex with one of the men involved and does not expect to take on others . . . Men give many reasons for group sex or line-ups, most of which are punitive or misogynist.
>
> (Jenkins 2006: 59–60)

Men who participate in gang rape tend to describe it as a legitimate punishment for women who dress or act too seductively, who are "uppity" and not properly deferential to men, who reject men sexually, or who are simply out alone at night and thus "asking for it." In men's discourses about punitive sexual violence women are represented as the seductive and threatening Other, and male solidarity is privileged and reinforced through men's collective violation, enjoyment, and degradation of the woman who is perceived as threatening that solidarity (Jenkins 1996). Not surprisingly, this form of sexual interaction—in addition to being a terrorizing practice that helps reinforce male dominance—is sexually risky, exposing both the female victims and the male aggressors to multiple men's semen.

Establishing the AIDS awareness program

> It is very good to say that you are going to do something, but when it comes to implementation it is very, very difficult. I have felt this. No transport, people fleeing because of tribal conflicts, and I am just a woman holding a loud speaker and camping out with my small baby. Many times I walked miles and miles to remote areas and slept out. After a few days I would walk home late in the evening, and then early in the morning get up and do the same program in another village. Sometimes my husband got angry, and we fought several times, but I would like to say that out of the dead lion comes sweet honey, which means that a lot of challenges were in front of me, but I struggled through.
>
> (letter from Mary Michael Tamia to Holly Wardlow, November 2008)

The AIDS awareness program described here was established in the town of Tari, Southern Highlands Province. Tari, like many small towns in Papua New Guinea, is basically an airstrip around which stores and government buildings have been built. With a population of approximately 5,000, the town consists of a hospital and community school on one side of the airstrip, and stores, a police station, court house, government buildings, and housing for public servants on the other side. Little wage or salaried labor is available in Tari itself; thus, many households rely on remittances from family members working outside of Tari. Porgera Joint Venture (PJV), a gold mine currently owned by Barrick Gold and located north of Tari, is also an important economic resource. Many Huli make the two-to-three-day hike to Porgera in order to look for work, visit family members who have some connection to the mine, or dig through the mine's waste rock for unprocessed gold, an illegal and dangerous activity. Moreover, PJV is almost completely powered by a natural gas plant located south of Tari and is thus dependent on the 78 kilometer-long electrical line that runs through Huli territory. Families who own the land on which the electrical pylons have been built receive annual "occupation fees" from PJV, and the communities that abut these pylons receive some services from PJV, such as road maintenance and school renovations.

In the spring of 2004, the Tari area, and much of Southern Highlands Province, was at a dismal and often violent nadir (Haley and May 2007). The value of the kina, Papua New Guinea's currency, had experienced a precipitous decline, falling from US$0.85 in the mid 1990s to US$0.30 in 2004. The costs of goods and services had inflated accordingly, but people's wages had not. In the Tari area, crime had increased dramatically: households had to have at least one person home at all times in order to deter the theft of pigs, chickens, or even laundry hanging on a line. The longstanding problem of armed holdups on the road between Tari and Mendi, the provincial capital, had worsened to the point that road travel was almost impossible. The one bank and the one large store had been looted by armed gangs in 2002 and had subsequently closed.

Attempts to remedy this chaotic situation were stymied by the fact that the 2002 elections had been plagued by the intimidation of voters and the theft of ballot boxes, and thus were declared a failure, which meant that the province had no government. Provincial government offices in Mendi were looted and left empty. The increase in violent crime, the political instability, and the fact that the police appeared to be less well armed than local gangs had motivated many civil servants to flee the area, leading to the closure of primary schools, health centers, and the post office. Finally, in a good example of community divestment feeding a vicious cycle that results in further divestment, many development organizations, including the National AIDS Council, declared Tari a "no-go zone," asserting that it was too dangerous to send their employees there.

It was in this context that I arrived in Tari for six months of research on why married women are vulnerable to HIV infection. I was known by many people in Tari from having lived there for two years during my doctoral research in the 1990s, but even so I was afraid that a local gang might break into my guest house to rob me. Eventually I decided that I couldn't safely or ethically carry out research without also providing some kind of service to the community, and so a few weeks into my research I decided to embark on an AIDS education program. I calculated that if I visibly provided a service—particularly in this context where people felt abandoned by their civil servants, missionaries, and political representatives—

people would be less likely to consider me a valid target for crime and more inclined to protect me.

PJV had a small office in Tari whose staff carried out community development projects, such as building schools and maintaining roads. In 2002, some Huli—angry that they were not receiving more benefits from PJV—had sabotaged the electrical line leading to the mine, closing it for more than two months and losing PJV millions of dollars. Perhaps not surprisingly, therefore, the staff at the Tari office were happy to support community outreach projects that might improve people's perception of PJV. They generously supplied transportation, a generator, a TV, and a VCR so that I could give informational talks and show AIDS-related videos at local schools, churches, and health centers. Huli society tends to be fairly conservative about sexual matters, and I was told quite bluntly by most of the people who invited me (pastors, nurses, teachers, women's group leaders, etc.) that I couldn't discuss condoms. Promoting condoms, many said, would send the message that illicit sexual behavior was acceptable. Not only would this encourage sinful behavior, it might also jeopardize my own and their reputations; we could all be accused of corrupting people's morals (Wardlow 2008b). I needed to proceed with care, they said. Because my research was showing that most men were familiar with condoms anyway, I decided to take a more socio-cultural and less behavioral approach in my educational talks. In practice this meant that I never publicly told people that they should use condoms. Instead, I would say things like:

> Everyone here knows that many Huli men have to leave Tari to find work and that they are often away from home for months or even years. And everyone here knows that all kinds of things happen in mining towns and in big cities. We humans aren't God: we aren't perfect, and we can't see what other people are doing if they are not in front of our eyes. A husband can't know what his wife is doing when he is away, and she can't know what he is doing. But we all want to protect our families. No man wants to infect his wife with HIV; and no woman wants to give birth to a baby that dies of AIDS.

Implication—and acknowledgement of the socio-economic situations that often lead to extramarital sexuality—seemed to suffice: privately a number of men came to me to ask for condoms, and my Huli male research assistants distributed hundreds of them to their peers. As long as I respected public moral sensibilities and refrained from making condoms an overt issue about which people would then feel compelled to take sides, I was able to make them available.

The films, of course, were what drew people in; they came for the films and stayed for the educational talks. It quickly became clear that men preferred the film, *Born in Africa*, which tells the story of Ugandan pop star Philly Lutaya, his courage in publicly revealing his HIV-positive status, and his eventual death. Women, for their part, tended to prefer *A Kid Called Troy*, which is about the stigma faced by an HIV-positive Australian boy and his family. Both films are quite moving; audiences, male and female, always wept, even if they'd seen the films before. More important, I think, was that they told the stories of people living with AIDS elsewhere in the world. People in Tari felt so isolated and abandoned at that time that I think these films were helpful for conceptualizing AIDS as a globally shared problem, rather than another demoralizing indication of Tari's decline.

Mary's expansion of the project

> I feel a strong desire to help orphans whose parents died of AIDS because my parents died when I was a child. My father died when I was in fifth grade, and my mother died when I was in tenth grade. I have always wondered whether I would have passed all the tests and met all the requirements for further studies if my parents had lived. But they died, and I had to drop out of school because no one would pay for my school fees. Maybe I would be somebody now, but they left me behind and I have had to struggle my whole life.
>
> (letter from Mary Michael Tamia to Holly Wardlow, November 2008)

The Tari AIDS education project was quite small when it came time for me to return to Canada. With sustainability in mind, I integrated Mary into the program so that by the time I left she was giving the talks, showing the videos, and answering people's questions afterwards. Equally important, I was able to convince PJV to (1) pay her each time she gave a talk and (2) enroll her in an official course offered by the NAC in order to increase her knowledge and ensure her credibility.

According to the letters (and, more recently, emails) I have received from Mary since 2004, the frustrations of sustaining this program have been myriad. The pay has never been adequate—more a gesture of appreciation than an actual wage. Transportation has been a continual problem: PJV is a mining company, after all, and so when vehicles have been needed for mine-related work, Mary has been stranded in villages far from her home for hours at a time. Mary has four children of her own and has adopted two AIDS orphans, so being able to get home at a reasonable hour is important. She is also a dedicated leader of her church's women's group, and has had to make difficult choices about which work she is going to prioritize. And she, like most women, wants to be able to put all of her children through school and thus has tried to maintain a small business of selling second-hand clothes. Finally, her HIV/AIDS-related work put an enormous strain on her marriage. The fact that she had a job (however low-paying) and that she was becoming well known and valued in the community led to violent altercations with her husband. He wanted her to give up her job and spend more time on child care and agricultural labor (that is, traditional female activities). She refused. The fact that local male leaders took her side, criticized him for not supporting her work, and mandated that he pay her financial compensation for physically injuring her only made him angrier.[4] (I should note that I employed her husband as a research assistant, that I consider him a friend, and that I have always found him to be a thoughtful, hard-working, gentle, and affectionate man. But, of course, marriage is a different beast, and he, like most Huli men, was raised with the expectation of being the dominant spouse.)

In 2007, in part because of transportation problems, but also in an attempt to cultivate community ownership of the program, PJV turned Mary's program over to a small NGO called Community-Based Health Care (CBHC). PJV continued to pay her wages but wanted CBHC to be responsible for trans-portation, coordination, and monitoring. Run by the Nazarene Church, CBHC uses low-cost, simple, and readily available technologies to strive for community development. As John Vail, its initial founder, explains, the basic aims of the program are "to improve family health, particularly through preventive means, and to stimulate small-scale rural enterprise" (Vail 2007: 113). More concretely, CBHC helps families to build household rain-catchment water supplies and to grow "nutrition gardens" with protein-rich crops, such as soy beans; it provides families with chickens, ducks, and rabbits at subsidized prices and teaches them how to care for them; it trains individuals selected by local communities in first aid and provides them with basic supplies; and it operates a small micro-finance and community-banking project. Mary's transportation issues have not been solved by her integration into CBHC because CBHC has so many programs of its own to sustain; however, she has found herself surrounded by like-minded people, and she has learned the various skills that CBHC has to offer.

Despite the challenges described above, Mary not only continued the AIDS education program but expanded it. Indeed, the tiny awareness program that I initiated has expanded to include AIDS education in a number of local schools; a small hospice for AIDS patients who have been rejected by their families; a support group, micro-credit, and income-generation project for mothers living with HIV/AIDS; and ongoing community courses in basic AIDS awareness and in home-based care for AIDS patients. That she was being paid, was selected to participate in a number of courses offered by the NAC, and quickly garnered local recognition for her work were, of course, highly motivating factors. Equally important, Mary says, is how her own understanding of AIDS—and its impact on the lives of women and their families—changed over time. When she began the work, she was uncertain about how to assess AIDS as a social problem. Church leaders and dominant local discourse tended to explain AIDS as a consequence of moral decline in the community and individual sinful behavior (Wardlow 2008b). However, after having completed her basic training in HIV/AIDS, she took courses on "care and counseling" for people living with HIV/AIDS, and putting this training into practice brought her into people's homes, where she witnessed the fear and stigma they experienced, as well as the difficulties that women in particular face in bearing the burden of caring for orphaned children or dying husbands. She came to realize that the face of AIDS is increasingly a monogamous, female face. She has sent me stories (in their own voices) about some of the women she has assisted and befriended, which I share below.

Woman A

I am 40 years old and have six children, but the last-born boy died at the age of three because of AIDS. My husband worked as a highway driver and had sex with many different women. He was infected with HIV, but he was too ashamed to tell me or anyone in his family. Before he died he told me that he was afraid that people would say, "Oh, he thought he was such a big man. He was a driver. He drove around in his sunglasses and decided who he would give a ride to and who he would leave in the road. But now look at him. His life is meaningless. He was a big driver for nothing." And I think some people did say that.

It was during my pregnancy with my last-born boy that I felt that my body was malfunctioning. So I underwent many tests, and they found that I was HIV positive. With an upset heart full of worries I went back home and told my relatives. They said, "It is a problem between you and your husband. If you had only one or two children, then maybe we could help you leave him, but you have been married for a long time and have many children together, and so now this is your problem." When they found out, my husband's relatives blamed me and said that I had given this virus to their son, but my husband himself came out and said that they shouldn't blame me. He said, "Whatever happens to me is because of my own life." I took care of him when he became very sick. Then he died, and my son died too.

One day one of my neighbors came and told me about how PJV had partnered with CBHC to help people living with HIV. I went to see Mary, and she welcomed me and I did not feel ashamed when I spoke with her. She had started a group for mothers living with HIV, and the women were learning ways to make money. They sewed clothes, they planted seedlings, they were able to get loans so that they could raise and sell chickens. When I spoke with those women I thought I was among a new big family. Now I am making money and I can pay for my children to go to school.

Woman B

I am 30 years old and have three children—two with my first husband and one with my second. I left both husbands and married a third one, but I divorced him too. Now I am living on my own. My first husband was a teacher and he beat me, and so I left him. The second husband was an uneducated village man, but he also beat me, and so I left him. My family has not supported me in leaving my husbands. They say I am a slut.

While I was with my third husband, we went together for HIV testing and we were both positive. We agreed not to tell any of our relatives. We were ashamed. Instead we committed ourselves to be spiritually and physically clean. The church we joined has a lot of laws and regulations to guide Christians. In this church there are some people living with HIV/AIDS too. But after some months, my husband became a back-slider. He left the church. I knew that if I stayed with him that I would leave the church too. We would both start smoking and playing cards again. So I left him. I have never told any of this to my own family. They just know that I have left yet another husband, so they still think I am a slut. I believe that even if I told them the whole story, they would blame me for my illness and wouldn't help me.

I heard that CBHC was helping people infected with HIV, so I went to see Mary. She invited me into her private office and I felt I could tell her my story. She told me first to get treatment for STIs, which did reduce some of my symptoms. Then she gave me counseling and included me in her program. She has helped me establish a nutrition garden, she helped me build a toilet and a clean water supply, and she has welcomed me into the group of HIV-positive mothers.

Important to note in these narratives, I think, are the experiences of stigma and blame, and the happy relief to be welcomed not only into a community of women with similar experiences, but also into a program that tries to meet the needs of mothers living with HIV/AIDS. Mary has found that although having support and solidarity is important to these mothers, more important is being able to prepare their children, as best they can, for lives without them (antiretroviral drugs are not yet available in Tari).[5] The priority, therefore, is to stay healthy long enough to make sufficient money to send their children to school. Many women tell stories, Mary says, of children whose land was seized by relatives after their parents died of AIDS-related illnesses. The stigma of AIDS, she says, not only manifests itself through the shunning of people while they are alive, but also seems to justify behavior towards AIDS orphans—such as the appropriation of their land—that is not permitted when parents die of other causes. Women, in particular, are often helpless to prevent this kind of seizure. Thus, before they are too sick, women want to get their children into school and equip them with some skills. The programs that Mary has initiated with CBHC are helping women to afford their children's school fees and even to bank some money for their children's futures.

Conclusion

> While I have been involved in AIDS intervention programs two of my cousins died of AIDS and left their wives and children behind. They never told me, their own cousin who has been taking the lead on HIV/AIDS knowledge! They were too ashamed to tell me. These experiences with my cousins and their families really strengthened my determination to move forward with my work even though I had problems in my own family.
> (letter from Mary Michael Tamia to Holly Wardlow, November 2008)

The integration of Mary's AIDS prevention and care activities with CBHC's community development programs has been quite serendipitous. CBHC's philosophy has long stressed self-reliance and the integration of health, community development, and household entrepreneurial activities. The services that CBHC makes available—water supply systems, small livestock, preventive health care, micro-credit, and community banking—are precisely what Tari mothers living with HIV/AIDS want, but CBHC was not targeting them until Mary's work made visible the fact that these mothers and their children were the most in need and the most likely to be marginalized and excluded.

It appears that these programs may have an impact on AIDS-related programming elsewhere in Papua New Guinea. During one recent course that Mary attended, participants from around the country were asked to give presentations on the kinds of AIDS intervention activities that were taking place in their communities. According to Mary, very few sites had implemented programs that so effectively addressed the needs of mothers living with HIV/AIDS and that integrated prevention, care, community education about the legal rights of people living with HIV/AIDS, income-generation, and micro-credit. The course leaders were so impressed that they selected Mary to become a national trainer.

Mary herself is once again torn about how to allocate her energy and time. She wants to use her national trainer status to teach others about the programs that she and the CBHC staff have established. However, the programs in Tari are still so new that she worries about what will happen if she neglects them. She also has some ideas for a new program she would like to start in Tari with teen and pre-teen girls who have been orphaned by AIDS and are not in school. Her own observations have made her conclude that these girls are the ones most likely to find themselves channeled into high risk settings and practices. How to keep all these programs going in the absence of adequate funding is also a continual source of distress. CBHC would like to train and hire other people in Southern Highlands Province in order to make their micro-credit and other services more widely available, but there is little money available to pay the salaries of the additional staff needed to implement and monitor any expansion. Mary, for her part, has spent some of her own small salary building a house that serves as a kind of hospice for people living with AIDS who have been ostracized by their families and have nowhere else to go. Her inability to get adequate funding for such projects, let alone a salary that will enable her to support her family (she and her husband have divorced), makes her want to quit sometimes. So far, however, her optimism, resourcefulness, sense of obligation, and vision of what can be accomplished have motivated her to soldier on.

Notes

1   For example, compare Wardlow 2008a and Lepani 2008a for profoundly different social constructions of healthy sexuality among the highlands Huli and the island Trobrianders.

2   Bridewealth, sometimes called bride price, is the anthropological term for the goods given by a groom's family to the bride's family to formalize a marriage. It is often described as a kind of compensation to the bride's family for the loss of her labor and fertility. Many anthropologists prefer the term bride*wealth*, rather than bride*price*, because the former term suggests that marriage-related exchanges are embedded in a larger system of ongoing social reciprocity, while the latter term suggests contractual,

and even venal, motivations and outcomes in which women are commoditized by and alienated from their families. The issue of which term to use continues to be debated by anthropologists of Melanesia (Wardlow 2006)

3 "Plural copulation" was probably a rarity in most pre-colonial Papua New Guinea societies, and the justifications for it in the contemporary context differ from reasons given in the past. In some pre-colonial societies, plural copulation was a ritual practice underpinned by belief systems that attributed cosmological power to both male and female sexual substances; they were thought to make the earth fertile and to increase the spiritual potency of the group. In these cases, plural copulation is thought to have been a consensual act that took place in the context of ritual (Knauft 1993). In other pre-colonial Papua New Guinea societies, "plural copulation" took the form of gang rape, and although it was not a religious practice per se, it was connected to religion in the sense that it was used to punish women for violating taboos or witnessing secret male rites (Knauft 1993).

4 Paying financial compensation to people for injuring them is common practice among the Huli, and men often have to pay compensation for injuring their wives during marital fights. So it is not surprising that Mary's husband had to do so. However, local leaders usually aim to restore some degree of harmony so that each person in a dispute feels that they have won something of what they wanted and so that the source of discord is removed or reduced. So it is somewhat surprising that the local leaders didn't support Mary's husband by strongly urging her to return to her wifely duties. That they supported her work in AIDS education shows, I think, how highly this work was valued.

5 Since this article was first written, antiretroviral drugs (ART) have become available in Tari through the Clinton Foundation and the Catholic Church. Interestingly, the number of women on ART is double that of men, a discrepancy that in part reflects mothers' strong motivation to stay alive for their children. Unfortunately, CBHC has folded due to a lack of funding, which means that this much-valued micro-credit project for HIV positive mothers is no longer available. Oxfam is considering funding a new NGO which would carry out similar work.

Bibliography

Appadurai, A. (1988) "Introduction: place and voice in anthropological theory," *Cultural Anthropology*, 3(1): 16–20.

Borrey, A. (2000) "Sexual Violence in Perspective: the case of Papua New Guinea," in S. Dinnen and A. Ley (eds) *Reflections of Violence in Melanesia*, Canberra, ACT: Asia Pacific Press, 105–118.

Bradley, C. (1988) "Wife-Beating in Papua New Guinea—Is it a Problem?" *Papua New Guinea Medical Journal*, 31: 257–268.

Counts, D. (1992) "'All Men Do it': wife-beating in Kaliai, Papua New Guinea," in D. Counts, J. Brown, and J. Campbell (eds) *Sanctions and Sanctuary: cultural perspectives on the beating of wives*, Boulder, CO: Westview Press, 63–76.

Duke, T. (1999) "Decline in Child Health in Rural Papua New Guinea," *Lancet*, 354: 1291–1294.

Haley, N. and May, R. (2007) "Introduction: roots of conflict in the Southern Highlands," in N. Haley and R. May (eds) *Conflict and Resource Development in the Southern Highlands of Papua New Guinea*, Australian National University E-Press. Online. <http://epress.anu.edu.au/ssgm/conflict/pdf/ch01.pdf>

Hammar, L. (1998) "AIDS, STDs, and Sex Work in Papua New Guinea," in L. Zimmer-Tamakoshi (ed.) *Modern Papua New Guinea*, Kirksville, MO: Thomas Jefferson University Press, 257–296.

—— (2008) "Fear and Loathing in Papua New Guinea: sexual health in a nation under siege," in L. Butt and R. Eves (eds) *Making Sense of AIDS: culture, sexuality and power in Melanesia*, Honolulu: University of Hawai'i Press, 60–79.

Heimer, C. (2007) "Old Inequalities, New Disease: HIV/AIDS in Sub-Saharan Africa," *Annual Review of Sociology*, 33: 551–577.

Jenkins, C. (1996) "The Homosexual Context of Heterosexual Practice in Papua New Guinea," in P. Aggleton (ed.) *Bisexualities and AIDS: international perspectives*, London: Taylor & Francis, 191–206.

—— (2006) "HIV/AIDS, Culture, and Sexuality in Papua New Guinea," Report Commissioned by the Asian Development Bank. Online. <http://www.adb.org/Documents/Books/Cultures-Contexts-Matter/HIV-PNG.pdf>

Knauft, B. (1993) *South Coast New Guinea Cultures: history, comparison, dialectic*, Cambridge: Cambridge University Press.

Lepani, K. (2008a) "Fitting Condoms on Culture: rethinking approaches to HIV prevention in the Trobriand Islands, Papua New Guinea," in L. Butt and R. Eves (eds) *Making Sense of AIDS: culture, sexuality, and power in Melanesia*, Honolulu: University of Hawai'i Press, 246–266.

—— (2008b) "Mobility, Violence and the Gendering of HIV in Papua New Guinea," *Australian Journal of Anthropology*, 19(2): 150–164.

Macintyre, M. (2006) "Indicators of Violence against Women," *Development Bulletin*, 71: 61–63.

—— (2008) "Police and Thieves, Gunmen and Drunks: problems with men and problems with society in Papua New Guinea," *Australian Journal of Anthropology*, 19(2): 179–193.

National Sex and Reproduction Research Team (NSRRT) and Jenkins, C. (1994) *National Study of Sexual and Reproductive Knowledge and Behavior in Papua New Guinea*, Papua New Guinea Institute of Medical Research Monograph no. 10, Goroka: Institute of Medical Research.

Passey, M. (1998) "Community Based Study of Sexually Transmitted Diseases in Rural Women in the Highlands of Papua New Guinea: prevalence and risk factors," *Sexually Transmitted Disease*, 74: 120–127.

Seeley, J. and Butcher, K. (2006) "'Mainstreaming' HIV in Papua New Guinea: putting gender equity first," *Gender and Development*, 14(1): 105–114.

Toft, S. (1985) *Domestic Violence in Papua New Guinea*, Papua New Guinea Law Reform Commission Monograph no. 3, Boroko, Papua New Guinea.

UNAIDS (2008) "2008 Report on the Global AIDS Epidemic," Online. <http://data.unaids.org/pub/GlobalReport/2008.asp>

UNGASS (2008) "United Nations General Assembly Special Session on HIV and AIDS Country Progress Report," Papua New Guinea National AIDS Council Secretariat and Partners.

Vail, J. (2007) "Community-Based Development in Tari—present and prospects," in N. Haley and R. May (eds) *Conflict and Resource Development in the Southern Highlands of Papua New Guinea*, Australian National University E-Press. Online. <http://epress.anu.edu.au/ssgm/conflict/pdf/ch09.pdf>

Wardlow, H. (2006) *Wayward Women: sexuality and agency in a New Guinea society*, Berkeley: University of California Press.

—— (2007) "Men's Extramarital Sexuality in Rural Papua New Guinea," *American Journal of Public Health*, 97(6): 1006–1014.

—— (2008a) "'She liked it best when she was on top': intimacies and estrangements in Huli men's marital and extramarital relationships," in W. Jankowiak (ed.) *Intimacies: love and sex across cultures*, New York: Columbia University Press, 194–223.

—— (2008b) "'You have to understand: some of us are glad AIDS has arrived': Christianity and condoms among the Huli of Papua New Guinea," in L. Butt and R. Eves (eds) *Making Sense of AIDS: culture, sexuality and power in Melanesia*, Honolulu: University of Hawai'i Press, 187–205.

—— (2009a) "'Whip him in the head with a stick!': marriage, male infidelity, and female confrontation among the Huli," in J. Hirsch, H. Wardlow, D. Smith, H. Phinney, S. Parikh, and C. Nathanson, *The Secret: love, marriage and HIV*, Nashville, TN: Vanderbilt University Press, 136–167.

—— (2009b) "Labour Migration and HIV Risk in Papua New Guinea," in M. Haour-Knipe, P. Aggleton, and F. Thomas (eds) *Mobility, Sexuality and AIDS*, London: Routledge, 176–186.

Wolfe, P. (1997) "Should the Subaltern Dream? 'Australian Aborigines' and the problem of ethnographic ventriloquism," in S. Humphreys (ed.) *Cultures of Scholarship*, Ann Arbor: University of Michigan Press, 57–96.

Zimmer-Tamakoshi, L. (1997) "Wild Pigs and Dog Men: rape and domestic violence as women's issues in Papua New Guinea," in C. B. Brettell and C. F. Sargent (eds) *Gender in Cross-Cultural Perspective*, Upper Saddle River, NJ: Prentice-Hall, 538–553.

10 Economic empowerment of women as a global project

Economic rights in the neo-liberal era

Nitza Berkovitch and Adriana Kemp

"If a social evangelist had a choice of picking one tool, one movement with the goal of emancipating the poorest women on earth, the microcredit phenomenon wins without serious competition."[1]

"The function of the social economy is to turn needs into markets."[2]

During the past two decades we have witnessed a proliferation of projects geared to the empowerment of women. Though heterogeneous in their scope and techniques, "women empowerment" projects have become shorthand for social undertakings that seek to overcome structural and individual barriers that prevent women from becoming self-reliant and viable economic actors. Typically, "empowerment" initiatives promote a wide range of income-generating activities based on the belief that enhancing women's spirit of entrepreneurship is a precondition for their social and political emancipation.

Empowerment projects constitute an important part of a refashioned field of social economy. Known also as "solidarity" or "alternative" economy, its main thrust lies in the rejection of the idea that profit is the ultimate goal of economic activity and instead it aims at the "(re)introduction of social justice into production and allocation systems" (Moulaert and Oana 2005). Empowerment projects also represent a renewed belief in the restorative power of civil society amidst neo-liberal globalization and the retrenchment of welfare policies. In its present form, social economy is carried out by a growing number of local and international nongovernmental organizations (NGOs) involved in community development strategies and a broad range of activities directed at, among others, the social inclusion of disadvantaged social groups (Bryn and Meehan 1987; Borzaga and Santuari 2000; Leyshon et al. 2003; Livingstone and Chagnon 2004).[3] Distinctively, the main idea lying behind the current version of "social economy" is that "third sector" or "nonprofit" organizations have the potential to provide opportunities and cater to individual and community needs that neither the state nor the market are likely to meet or be capable of meeting.

Among the most promising and innovative sectors of the social economy of empowerment are microfinance projects, and in particular microcredit schemes on which this chapter focuses, that vie for the social inclusion and emancipation of women through financial systems. Emphasizing access to credit as a key factor in economic independence, and as one of the stumbling blocks that perpetuate the social exclusion of the poor and women, these projects grant micro loans for the purposes of promoting small-scale enterprise.[4] While not novel in the world of development, microcredit has more recently gained increasing recognition not only as a viable mode of economic action, but also as an important and progressive policy tool. Indeed, what started in the 1970s as a collection of banking practices that allowed for the provision of small loans and the deposit of tiny savings and grew out of experiments in low-income countries like Bolivia and Bangladesh, has effectively mainstreamed into major development programs in the developing world, and lately in developed countries as well. Embraced by diverse global institutions such as the World Bank and the United Nations (UN), supported by powerful international donors, sanctioned by national governments, and implemented by NGOs and grassroots organizations, the world of microfinance is designated as *the* means for overcoming world-scale problems through poverty alleviation (if not eradication), gender equality, jobs creation, community building, AIDS eradication, and democratization, to name but a few. In the more developed countries it also serves as an alternative to welfare (Paxton 1995; Raheim 1996, 1997; Rankin 2001, 2002; Viganò et al. 2004; Sanders 2004; Sa'ar 2006).[5] Underlying these varied social goals are gendered assumptions regarding the viability of market-embedded social change. As we will discuss shortly, women not only form the majority of microfinance programs' clientele but they are also depicted as a "better investment" for achieving social and economic goals. Moreover, as we shall argue, the dual position accorded to women in the microfinance world—both as agents and objects of social change—plays a crucial role in mobilizing material and ideological support for the microfinance global project.

This chapter addresses the social processes that allowed for the transformation of microfinance into a "global movement" that managed to mobilize the support, faith, and active participation of powerful global actors, professionals, bankers, consultants, and grassroots activists all over the world.[6] We ask, what made it possible for a movement that aims at the social inclusion of women via financial markets to become one of the most ambitious and overarching social reforms of our times? Or paraphrasing 1998 Nobel Laureate in Economics and Harvard Professor Amartya Sen, what makes microcredit a movement that aims at "bringing hope, prosperity, and progress to many of the poorest people in the world"?[7]

To be sure, microcredit has not only been eulogized by enthusiastic advocates. Alongside its growing popularity, there is also a considerable body of research that points to the adverse effects of microcredit regarding the social inclusion of the poorest populations (Hulme and Mosley 1996); the chances for women's empowerment in general (Mayoux 2001, 2003; Haase 2007) and at the household

(Goetz and Sen Gupta 1996) and community level in particular (Karim 2008); criteria for measuring the impact of the programs (Copestake 2001); and the shortcomings of mainstreaming and scale policies (Rogaly 1996; Johnson 1998), among others. Many of these critiques have been formulated by practitioners and researchers who come from *within* the world of development and microfinance. Thus, while disapproving of specific results on the ground or wary of emergent trends in the field, they do not cast doubt on the philosophy of microcredit as a worthy social endeavor but on the particulars of its implementation.

A different line of research takes issue with the ideological underpinnings of the microcredit industry and attendant gender ideologies as epitome of larger socio-economic and political transformations (Silliman 1999; Rankin 2001). According to this line of critique, the recent prominence of microfinance as a substitute for social policies and its increasing reliance on donors and inter-mediating NGOs that function as "shadow" institutions are all integral elements of a neo-liberal matrix of power. Moreover, the emphases on individual notions of empowerment, self-reliance, and "responsibilising the self" (Peters 2001) that underlie much of the microfinance endeavor are perceived as disciplinary techniques that deliberately partake in the engineering of new liberal subjectivities (Karim 2008).

Notwithstanding the above-mentioned critiques from "within" and "without" the universe of social economy, microfinance programs, in particular those target-ing women, are thriving worldwide. As the continuous growth in the volume of microfinance and its enthusiastic endorsement by unlikely partners and extremely asymmetric stakeholders seem to indicate, critiques have not prevented it from becoming a movement embraced globally and across sectors. Thus, while acknowledging the respective contributions of both lines of critical research, in the present chapter we are less interested in the effects of microcredit programs or their ideological premises than in their institutionalization as global phenomena.

As a global movement, microcredit involves the creation of networks of groups and individuals that have as common purpose the goal to achieve social change; they do so by mobilizing resources, framing issues of public concern, and launch-ing orchestrated campaigns. Therefore, in analyzing the institutionalization of microfinance as a global project or "movement," we highlight two interlinked dimensions, both in which the notion of women is featured prominently. The first relates to the global purchase of the institutions and networks that design, promote, and implement the microcredit programs and practices striving for wider constituencies and new spheres of influence. The second examines the normative claims and ideological justification that account for what has been repeatedly called the microcredit crusade or evangelism (see e.g. Rogaly 1996; Karim 2008).

We argue that the same conditions that allow for microcredit to become global are those that are leading to its recent increasing commodification. As will be shown, the support of microfinance by powerful institutions has been critical in the globalization of microcredit and its expansion so as to involve larger numbers of target members/clients and new contexts of action. Yet, one of the interesting aspects of the institutionalization of microcredit is that it has not only expanded existing markets (that of financial services) into new territories, attracting new consumers for existing goods, but in its latest "stage of development," the micro-credit movement is actually pushing for the creation of new markets through the commodification of socially valued services and of hitherto non-commodified intermediation processes. In that sense, the enthusiastic endorsement of micro-credit by powerful actors and its incorporation in the global agenda have yielded two main effects: first, it reproduces the basic tenets of neo-liberal markets that it is supposedly meant to offset; second, its rendering as "global" subdues divergent interests and tensions that make the heterogeneous world of social economy. Moreover, as we shall discuss in our concluding comments, we argue that it is the gendered assumptions of the microfinance movement and the placing of women as the main target and goal of the global project of microfinance which, unintendedly, ushered its way into the markets and facilitated its growing reliance on principles of sustainability and profitability.

The construction and implementation of microfinance as an all-embracing global project draw on the construction of particular notions of women as the "poorest of the poor" and as thriving self-entrepreneurs. Since the 1990s, micro-finance programs targeting women have become a major plank of donor poverty and gender strategies. Women comprise 60 to 90 percent of microcredit scheme clients, depending on the country and the locale (Mayoux 2005). In a recent study that included 350 microfinance institutions (MFIs) from 70 countries, it was found that women represented 73 percent of microfinance customers on average, a figure that is consistent with findings in previous research literature (D'Espallier et al. 2009). The strong emphasis that microfinance programs put on women as their target is not surprising if we bear in mind that women constitute the majority of the poor and, historically, microfinance experiments emerged around the "discovery" that women face greater difficulties in getting access to credit and financial services.

However, it is not only the fact that women are among the neediest groups that counts. Equally important is the belief among practitioners and advocates that increasing economic self-sufficiency of women is expected to set off a series of "virtuous spirals" for their families and their immediate communities, as well as the whole society (Woodworth 2000; Livingstone and Chagnon 2004; Mayoux 2005). Studies show that women are prone to allocate their resources differently than their spouses, and that women's increased income is likely to increase the level of household consumption and the overall wellbeing and standard of living of all household members more than men's (Morduch 1999; Goetz and Sen Gupta 1996).

Thus, one key element of the microcredit movement is the core frame of women as both objects of social change empowered via their insertion in markets, but also subjects engaged in achieving a long list of desirable global transforma-tions. Economically empowered women are to become agents of social change and facilitators of modernization in their families, communities, and society at large. Thus, improving the situation of women is conceived not only as a socially valuable goal in itself but also as the preferred, widely agreed-upon means to attain higher goals.

The desirability of targeting women was buttressed by ample evidence of women's higher credit repayment (Morduch 1999). Indeed, a recent study that drew on a systematic analysis of a large global dataset confirmed that "women in general are indeed a better credit risk for the MFI" (D'Espallier et al. 2009: 6). This factor became even more important once the new paradigm that emphasized the significance of institutional sustainability and profitability of microlenders was put in place in the 1990s, the same period when women were officially declared in world fora the main target of the global project of microfinance.

The microcredit movement goes global

The origins of microcredit as a development aid device date back to the 1950s, when governments and international donors subsidized the delivery of cheap credit to small farmers in developing countries (Rogaly 1996). During the 1970s and especially in the 1980s, microcredit programs re-emerged in different parts of the developing world, taking a new shape. There were two novelties in the 1970s schemes. The first was their increasing reliance on NGOs as financial intermediary agents substituting subsidized targeted credit provided by governmental institutions. The second was the fact that they were increasingly directed to women as symbols of the most destitute among the poorest populations. The new emphasis on women given in the credit schemes seems to have been informed both by localized concern with women's lack of access to capital and by the increasing incorporation of gender issues and women's rights on the agenda of world organizations (Berkovitch 1999). The events of the 1976–1985 United Nations Decade of Women provided the opportunity to put the issue on the world society's agenda, as indicated by the numerous documents produced following the 1975 United Nations International Women's Conference in Mexico and references made in the widely ratified UN Convention on the Elimination of All Forms of Discrimination Against Women (Mayoux 2005). In both cases, access to credit was defined as a human right currently denied women in many countries of the world. These efforts resulted in, among others, the establishment of the Women's World Banking network by ten women from five continents, which spanned across more than thirty countries and became one of the largest microfinance networks in the world. Other women's organizations worldwide set up credit and savings components both as a way of increasing women's incomes and bringing women together to address wider gender issues. Chief among them, and providing a model for many similar movements around the world, is the Indian organization Self-Employed Women's Association (SEWA), with origins and affiliations in the Indian labor and women's movements. SEWA was one of the first to identify credit as a major constraint faced by women working in the informal sector (Rose 1992).

In other parts of the world, other microcredit-focused NGOs have started to emerge. One notable example is ACCION, which originated in Caracas,

Venezuela, and now has become one of the largest microfinance organizations in the world.[8] Concurrently, major innovations in the microcredit technique were introduced by Dr. Mohammed Yunus, the Nobel Prize laureate credited as being the world pioneer of microcredit and to a great extent associated with its "popularization" across the world. Yunus established his first microcredit program in Bangladesh in 1976, which became the famous Grameen Bank. Originally designed as a pilot lending scheme for landless people, by 2007 Grameen had 7.27 million borrowers, provided services to 79,539 villages, and covered more than 95 percent of the total villages in Bangladesh. It is worth noting that Grameen serves mainly women not only in practice but also as part of its ideology of social change (Woodworth 2000; Yunus 2007a, 2007b).

The method of group lending, in which instead of collateral the borrowers as a group are jointly liable for paying back the loan, has been promoted also by the World Bank and other development agencies and become an integral part of many microfinance schemes around the developing countries (Rankin 2002). In the following decades, microfinance programs gained the open support of powerful international governmental organizations (IGOs), such as the World Bank, and national agencies, such as the United States Agency for International Development (USAID), as an integral part of development aid. The United Nations Capital Development Fund (UNCDF), founded in 1966 with the aim of initiating and supporting development projects, began channeling larger parts of its funding for local development to various forms of microfinance programs and projects. The increasing amounts of funding coming from these organizations as well as from private foundations (e.g., Oikocredit and Ford), donors, and governments, flowing mainly to NGOs, local and global, led to mushrooming of microcredit programs. They also led to the further expansion of existing poverty-targeted microfinance institutions and networks like the above-mentioned Grameen Bank and ACCION and to the creation of new ones, such as the prominent FINCA International.[9]

In these organizations and others, evidence of significantly higher female repayment rates led to increasing emphasis on targeting women as an efficiency strategy to increase credit recovery (Mayoux 2005). For example, in 1980–1983, 34 percent and 39 percent of the members in BRAC and Grameen Bank—the two major Bangladeshi credit programs—were women. In 1991–1992 these figures rose to 74 percent and 94 percent respectively (Goetz and Sen Gupta 1996). Yet, while models of microcredit were already traveling across different continents, at times yielding to innovative practices and adaptations, it was not until the launching of the Microcredit Summit Campaign in 1997 that microcredit was officially declared a "global movement" (Rogaly 1996; Morduch 1999; Bushell 2008). Initiated by RESULTS, a US nonprofit grassroots advocacy organization and held in Washington, DC, the Summit brought together for the first time nearly 3,000 microcredit practitioners, advocates, educational institutions, donor agencies, international financial institutions, NGOs, and others involved with microcredit.[10] Providing a meeting place in which a common agenda could be formulated and a shared language could be devised, the conference gave a major boost to the crystallization of the movement at the global level and to its "global" message. As the organizers stated in the draft declaration announcing the summit, a major objective of the campaign was to send a clear signal worldwide about the enormous potential of microcredit as a means for promoting pro-poor policies and addressing central concerns of donor agencies.

In addition to launching the "global microfinance movement," the 1997 campaign represented a turning point in two additional and interrelated respects: first, it hinted at the new paradigm that would promote scaling up the outreach of microcredit programs together with an emphasis on the financial sustainability of the MCIs; second, though these program have always targeted mainly women, now the campaign placed women unequivocally and officially at the center of the microcredit social endeavor, challenging gendered assumptions that reinforced women's traditional roles outside waged work while simultaneously nurturing their image as "budding entrepreneurs" (Silliman 1999).

Establishing the "empowerment of women" as its second key goal after poverty reduction, the participants in the Summit declared that they were embarking on a "bold campaign to reach 100 million of the world's poorest families, especially the women of those families, with credit for self-employment and other financial and business services by the end of 2005" (Daley-Harris 2006). According to Mayoux (2005), this has resulted in a shift in development projects and government policies in many developing countries in which an extra emphasis has been put on women's entrepreneurship designated as a key strategy for both poverty reduction and empowerment.

Two years earlier, the Consultative Group to Assist the Poorest (CGAP) was formally constituted. As a major international collaborative initiative of states,[11] international development agencies, and donors affiliated with the World Bank, the CGAP has become a major source of mainstreaming donors' funding requirements and a central standardizing agency in the field.

The globalization of microcredit seems to have reached its apex in December 2003 when the UN General Assembly passed a resolution that designated the year 2005 as the International Year of Microcredit. The resolution gave clear evidence as to the official upgrading of microfinance from its original role as a subsidized aid device into an internationally endorsed "magic bullet" for many of the problems afflicting the socially excluded, most prominently women, in the developing world and elsewhere. "Microfinance is much more than simply an income generation tool," explained Mark Malloch Brown, high executive at the United Nations Development Programme (UNDP). "[B]y directly empowering poor people, particularly women, it has become one of the key driving mechanisms towards meeting the Millennium Development Goals, specifically the overarching target of halving extreme poverty and hunger by 2015."[12] Three years later the UNCDF launched MicroLead—a $26-million fund that aims at reaching more than half a million poor clients by the end of 2013 through a combination of grants and loans to microfinance institutions and financial service providers.[13]

In the same year, the Nobel Committee went a step further in bolstering the standing of microcredit as a panacea for many of the problems afflicting socially excluded populations. In 2006, Mohammed Yunus and his creation, Grameen Bank, were awarded the Nobel Peace Prize, thereby recognizing microcredit's contribution not only to poverty reduction but also to world peace. Ever since, microcredit and the idea of "giving the poor the means so they themselves could pull themselves out of poverty" were to become the epitome of a globally perceived win-win solution, acceptable to socially minded reformers and to business elites, to the "development industry" and to grassroots movements alike.

Supersizing microcredit

Given the mobilization of powerful actors, the creation and subsequent expansion of a local and transnational infrastructure of donors, service providers, and microfinance institutions (MFIs), and the symbolic support it garnered, it is hardly surprising that in the last two decades the microfinance field has grown substantially in terms of the volume of transactions and the number of lending institutions and credit recipients.

Table 10.1 shows the results of a survey conducted by the Microcredit Summit Campaign. By the end of 2002, the campaign reported on 67.6 million microfinance clients served worldwide by over 2,500 MFIs. Of these clients, 41.6 million were in the bottom half of those living under their countries' poverty line (defined as the "poorest," Armendariz and Morduch 2005). Between 1997 and 2002, the numbers grew on average by about 40 percent per year and the movement's leaders expect to continue expanding as credit unions, commercial banks, and others enter the market. The increase in the share of women among microcredit borrowers has been exponential as well in this period. As shown in Figure 10.1, the absolute number of poorest women reached by microfinance institutions around the world grew from 10 to 70 million in the 1999–2005 period. By the end of 2007, 3,552 microcredit institutions reported reaching 154,825,825 clients; 71 percent (109,898,894) of them were women. A total of 106,584,679 were among the poorest when they took their first loan. Of these poorest clients, 83.2 percent, or 88,726,893, were women. Assuming five persons per family, the

Table 10.1 Growth of microfinance xoverage as reported to the Microcredit Summit Campaign, 1997–2001

End of year	Number of institutions	Number of clients reached (millions)	Number of "poorest" clients reported (million)
1997	618	13.5	7.6
1998	925	20.9	12.2
1999	1,065	23.6	13.8
2000	1,567	30.7	19.3
2001	2,186	54.9	26.8
2002	2,572	67.6	41.6

Source: Armendariz and Morduch 2005: 2.

Reaching poorest women

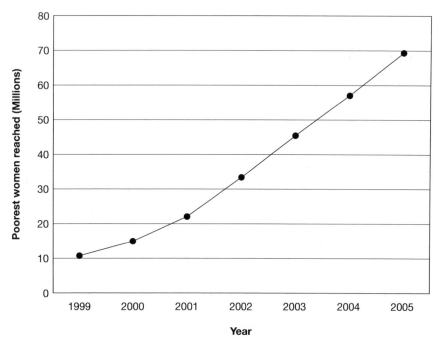

Figure 10.1 Poorest women reached by MFIs, 1999–2005

Source: Daley-Harris 2006: figure 2.

106.6 million poorest clients reached by the end of 2007 affected some 533 million family members (Daley-Harris 2009).[14]

Nowadays, microfinance projects, programs, and institutions are to be found operating almost everywhere around the globe, from large cities in developed countries to the most remote rural areas of developing countries. Many governments, especially in the developing world, have created national commissions, formulated and adopted Action Plans, set up units and designated positions to promote and coordinate microcredit programs. In some countries, for example in Senegal and South Africa, a full-blown special ministry responsible for microfinance has been established.

This massive expansion of socially minded banking services taking place both at the global and local levels has to be understood in light of the fact that the effectiveness of foreign aid to programs that aim at alleviating poverty has been for a long while facing criticism and fundamental questions regarding corruption, paternalism, and lack of institutional viability. In contrast, microfinance institutions are seen as offering innovative, cost-effective paths to poverty reduction and social change (Armendariz and Morduch 2005). Indeed, the phenomenon of NGOs "scaling up" as the reactive flipside of governments "scaling down" is a well-recognized hallmark of neo-liberal configurations (Silliman 1999). Yet, while we concur with this argument, we are also trying to show that the dramatic increase in the size of the microfinance industry and its worldwide purchase has been largely the result of a "supply market" whose creation has involved a great deal of resource mobilization, active endorsement by influential players, and framing as a new progressive policy paradigm that caters to major globally conceived challenges. Furthermore, constituting microcredit as a "global move-ment" allows the downplay of tensions between top-down inducted "microcredit industry" and bottom-up social economy initiatives, glossing over their changing nature.

In the next section, we point to the different logics that converge between socially minded NGOs and profit-minded mainstream banks within an enlarged microfinance industry that draws on the increasing commodification of social services and on the creation of new commodities such as the financial inter-mediation process itself. As will be shown, what was largely, until this point, part of social economy directed by social considerations and operated by third sector or nonprofit organizations guided by the urge to tame either the fallacies of unfettered capitalism or the paternalism of state bureaucracies, is currently undergoing an increasing process of commercialization. Adopting market principles aimed at maximizing profit, microfinance is gradually (and in some parts of the world, very rapidly) becoming a sub-sector of the banking industry, but one which is heralded as a panacea for the ills and problems of the world. Jonathan Morduch (1999) argues that one of the main reasons for the success of microfinance in the public eye lies in its strategic targeting of women. In concluding, we further develop this point, emphasizing the ways in which placing women at the center of the project and branding them as attractive "clients" to profit-seekers and good-doers, to policy makers and grassroots activists alike, were instrumental in the recent transformation of microfinance while facilitating the seeming convergence between the potentially conflicting interests of market and society.

The institutional apparatus enters the market—or a story about the poor, profit making, and neo-liberal drive

During the International Year of Microcredit in 2005, the second Microcredit Summit convened. In its report, it openly advocated a shift from poverty alleviation to wealth creation that reiterated the campaign's commitment to scale—widening the outreach of the microfinance programs—and achieving financial sustainability of microfinance institutions.[15]

The idea was not novel. The emphasis on scale and institutional viability has been around for a while in the microfinance world and it lies at the center of what has been called the "new wave" of financial services for the poor (Rogaly 1996), "counter revolution" (Johnson 1998), or "new world" thinking (Otero and Rhyne

1994) in development, all of which emerged as a critique of subsidized schemes that prevailed in the past. The "new wave" consists of the following beliefs turned dogma: subsidized credit undermines development; poor people can pay interest rates high enough to cover transaction costs and the consequences of the imperfect information markets in which lenders operate; the goal of sustainability (cost recovery and eventually profit) is the key not only to institutional resilience but also to making MFIs more focused and efficient; because loan sizes to poor people are small, MFIs must achieve sufficient scale if they are to become sustainable; finally, while measurable enterprise growth, as well as impacts on poverty, cannot be demonstrated easily or accurately, outreach and repayment rates can and are efficient proxies for impact measurement (Ledgerwood 1999).

This "counter-revolution" in the world of development was actually more of a gradual "evolution" that signaled the emergence of a new cultural understanding, to borrow Taylor's (1999) expression, of what microfinance is, how it should operate, and what should be its underlying logic and ultimate goal, seemingly shared by grassroots organizations as well as by the major institutions in the field. Yet the 2005 Summit provided a world stage on which high level representatives from major banking institutions and the financial sector met with officials from world financial institutions (e.g., World Bank) and aid agencies (USAID), NGOs, and other activists and delegates involved in the field with the purpose of publicly enacting and globally voicing these ways of thinking and doing microfinance. And, indeed, the closing event dedicated to the International Forum on Building Inclusive Financial Sectors made amply clear that within this new "cultural understanding" the spotlight had shifted from sustainability to the profitability of MFIs, focusing on the potential of microfinance as a successful business investment and emerging market.[16]

As noted before, the field of microfinance had been transforming "on the ground" already in the early 1990s from what used to be an exclusive field of action by aid agencies, NGOs, and, at times, the state into one in which private sector and commercial bodies became increasingly key actors. This process took effect in one of two ways: microfinance NGOs transforming into commercial entities (non-bank financial intermediaries or commercial banks) or, conversely, traditional, regulated financial institutions, such as retail banks, including state-owned banks, entering and becoming part of the microfinance sector (Hishigsuren 2006).

The major drive for NGOs to convert to regulated financial institutions (e.g., commercial banks) was to gain access to private sources of capital and the ability to mobilize public deposits, denied to nonprofits, thus enabling organizations to increase their scale of operation substantially. Growth in size and in sources of capital helps them achieve independence from donors and aid agencies (Campion and White 2001) while at the same time allowing self-sustainability and profitability (Hishigsuren 2006). The main idea underlying NGOs' move towards profitability is then to cut the Gordian knot that tied the continued supply of funds, and therefore their outreach to underserved groups, to the donors' agendas and dictates.

As for the banks, deregulation and stiff banking competition in many countries drove them to look for new profitable markets, and apparently microfinance was one of them (Baydas et.al. 1997). Indeed, banks that enter the microfinance market in Latin America, for example, are not only more profitable than their peers in other developing regions, in some instances they are even more profitable than traditional commercial banks in the areas where they operate. Moreover, even microfinance institutions that cater to poorer clients are generally improving their financial performance more rapidly than those that serve a broader client base (Christen 2001).

The trend towards commercialization originated in Latin America with the transformation of PRODEM (a highly successful microlending NGO, founded in 1984, and a member of the ACCION network in Latin America) into BancoSol in 1992 in Bolivia (more than 70 percent of its clients are women).[17] Though still pronounced there, nowadays it is not confined to one region as more NGOs that vary by their methods, outreach, and size experience similar processes worldwide (Campion and White 2001).[18] Evidence of the predominance of the phenomenon and its apparent desirability is to be found in numerous publications reporting that widening segments of the NGO population seek to become regulated MFIs and embark on microcredit activities (e.g., Campion and White 2001; Hishigsuren 2006).[19] Already in 1996 it was observed that in some countries banks were becoming larger providers of loans to microentrepreneurs than NGOs (Almeyda 1996). On a global scale, excluding Bangladesh, as of 2004 NGOs served only 26 percent of total clients, while the formal banking system and finance companies perform as the main microlenders for the greatest share. The prediction of practitioners and researchers alike in a survey conducted in 2006 was that this trend will continue through the next decade and that eventually most services will be delivered by formal financial institutions (Rhyne and Otero 2006: 30).

"Maturation, "natural progression," "graduation," and "natural evolution" were some of the terms employed in reports, how-to manuals, and toolkits, either by the authors themselves or quoting practitioners and policy makers, when referring to the transformation of the field. Semantics aside, all these convey rather explicitly two main ideas: first, the idea that the process is guided by "natural laws" and therefore is inevitable, irresistible, and irreversible, just like forces of nature are; second, the idea of evolutionary progress, as if the marketization of microcredit schemes and infrastructure meant the "end of history," at least as far as the history of microfinance is concerned. Telling in this respect is the following statement that appeared in a CGAP/World Bank report on the transformation of microfinance in Latin America: "For some, this shift signals the entry of microfinance into its *final stage*: the provision of financial services to the poor on a massive scale by commercial enterprises" (Christen 2001: 5; emphasis added).

Even though the transformation of microfinance is constructed as a product of laws of nature rather than being socially made, clearly such a move involves a great deal of ideological work, material support, and technical and bureaucratic help. A whole network of powerful actors, such as multilateral organizations, foundations, and NGOs, backed, financed, and promoted the entrance of banks and the transformation of NGOs into banks or similar financial institutions. Chief among the latter are ACCION and FINCA, two of the world leaders in microfinance. FINCA, which also focuses primarily on women, established FINCA Capital Fund, FINCA Kyrgyzstan, FINCA Ecuador, and FINCA Uganda, all commercial financial services institutions for low-income entrepreneurs. ACCION was instrumental in the creation of BancoSol in Bolivia and in the transformation of Compartamos into Banco Compartamos in 2006 (99 percent of the borrowers in the latter are women).[20] It also provided consulting services for bank regulators on how to make it easier for other private finance companies to enter the microlending market (Gross 2006). The Microfinance Network (MFN), created in the early 1990s as an association of the elite microfinance institutions, serves as an important arena for promoting the idea of commercialization and exchanging information on "how-to" and "best practices." Big foundations play their role as well. For example, Rockefeller Foundation helped start Acumen Fund and the Bill and Melinda Gates Foundation funded some ACCION transformation projects. At times, it was the state that was instrumental in the process, as when the Chilean government directly subsidized the entry of commercial banks into the microcredit market (Christen 2001).

But nothing exceeded the impact of USAID and the World Bank. Both provided the necessary material, technical, informational, and ideological resources needed to set the trend on a steady, unchallenged, and uninterrupted course.[21] Both have commissioned studies, published reports, and held widely attended workshops and conferences that facilitate the forming of a consensus regarding the desirability, necessity, and positive advantages of the process, if only done right, i.e., by following "best practices" devised by CGAP; USAID provides generous funding to microenterprises around the world. Its growing support (both in relative and absolute terms) to the business section operating in the field was no doubt an indispensible facilitator. In 1997 it allocated about 32 percent of all its funding (about $52 million) to for-profit institutions (USAID 1998)[22] whereas in 2007 the share of for-profit organizations grew to 56 percent, totaling $161 million.[23]

It is also interesting to note the large and increasing share that consulting firms get. In 2007 they received $149 million compared to $7 million received only ten years ago. This increase is much larger than the total increase of funding by USAID of all microfinance institutions. Note also that nonprofits received in 2007 only $98.6 million.

The publications of the World Bank (both in print and on-line) outline clearly and loudly the ideological foundations for this growing trend. One important pillar is the role that the private sector should play in helping to eradicate poverty, empower women, and bring about gender equality. If, given the opportunity to operate according to its internal logic of competition free of externally imposed constraints, it will bring about the "gender dividend"—gender equality *and* smart economy—that will benefit all.[24] Note that this claim constitutes an interesting reversal from the opposite argument, familiar to those engaged with gender-equality research and policy, that maintains that it is harder to achieve equality in the private sector than in the public sector and that gender equality requires massive state intervention in the form of laws, regulations, and enforcement (Steinberg and Cook 1988; Franzway et al. 1989; Burstein 1994; Rai 2003). Michael Klein and Bita Hadjimichael, in their book on the role of the private sector in development published by the World Bank in 2003, establish plainly that since competition and market mechanisms transmit best practices to create effective poverty-eliminating delivery systems, the private sector (never before considered a friend of the poor) eradicates poverty and increases the quality of life of the poor.

In this process of expanding markets, capacitation and training are becoming commodities too. Since the aim of microlending is to improve people's ability to generate income of their own and, at times, it provides them the first opportunity to do so, training and technical assistance are usually regarded as an essential component that should complement the loan. Training includes topics that vary from literacy, communication through print and electronic media, using the Internet, marketing, and legal aspects of running a business to women's empowerment and rights. The courses were usually provided by the NGO that granted the loans or by NGOs that specialized in training. In any case, training was provided free of charge or for a minimal fee. In some cases, even, completing courses such as financial literacy was a precondition for getting credit.

Changes have been occurring in this respect too. Business training in the microcredit sector, as microcredit itself, is turning gradually into a profit-making activity. Note the following example: Diálogo de Gestiones (DdG), a microenterprise training program in Colombia, was designed to help microentrepreneurs manage their small businesses more effectively. Apparently, they manage to teach business basics in a way that is accessible and practical and their classes are in wide demand. They developed training modules that have been sold to seventeen institutions, including MFIs, commercial banks, chambers of commerce, and private firms, in fourteen countries (USAID 2003). In doing so, a new market has been created that encompasses services and activities that previously had been carried out outside its borders.

Many analysts and "stakeholders" are debating whether commercialization drives microfinance institutions to deviate from their original missions, that of eradication of poverty and empowerment of women, or as it has been dubbed in the literature: Do we witness a "mission drift"? (see: e.g., Morduch 2000; Christen 2001; Hishigsuren 2007; Copestake 2007). In the present context we will not delve into this debate. We are, rather, interested in its wider implication regarding neoliberal discourse and practice. In its basic form, microfinance and its correlate, microenterprise, endeavor to draw individuals to the market, turning them into productive members as they become producers who generate their own income, which in turn enables them to become also consumers of goods and services. Economic empowerment of women, as one of the avowed main goals of the "microcredit movement," was at times construed as a means to achieve eradication of poverty and at times as a goal of its own. In any case, the whole project of microenterprise funded by microfinance, operated by NGOs, and funded by various types of donors and aid agencies was part and parcel of social economy and not market economy. It did insert individuals into the market and made them into proper neo-liberal subjects, i.e., self-reliant entrepreneurs, but its institutional apparatus operated according to extra-market rules and an alternative ideology.

With the transformation of the sector, the organizational infrastructure has been commodified as well. In other words, this transformation led to the creation of new markets disciplined by competition and ruled by the goals of self-reliance and profit-making. If before only the objects of this global project (women, the poor) were supposed to become self-reliant individuals, now the instruments also were to be self-reliant, economically independent units.

In summary, a project originating in the social economy that aimed at operating according to an alternative logic and practice in order to subordinate the market to social logic has been dissolved into the market, leading to its further expansion and consolidation.

Conclusions

In this chapter we aimed to trace the double transformation undergone by the world of microfinance: first, its transformation from highly localized and grass-roots initiatives into a global movement launched by potent global actors and reaching wider regions of influence; second, its shift from an epitome of progressive social economy wielding local knowledge with cutting-edge international expertise into an engine of mainstream new liberalism that seeks not only to expand existing markets into uncharted populations or territories but also to create new ones. As shown, the creation of new markets by the microfinance movement entails producing new commodities, subjecting the MFIs to the rules of market competition, and finally, reintroducing market-profitability as a major steering mechanism of microfinance activity. In that sense, microcredit and NGOs that have typically been entrusted with fulfilling its emancipatory promises are, whether knowingly or not, becoming the harbingers of the new international economic order and its means of legitimacy at one and the same time (Feldman 1997). Women, being placed at center stage, function in two ways. First, they help mobilize legitimacy and support insofar as the notion of women is portrayed as a symbol of the poorest population and women are portrayed as agents of social change. Second, as reliable, disciplined clients with high repayment records, women contribute to the sustainability and, more recently, also to the profitability of the lending institutions as well as to the attractiveness of new financial markets.

The increasing globalization cum commodification of microcredit is undermining the distinction between social and market economy and between NGOs' and the market's respective theories of practice. But perhaps more importantly, this process points at an interesting reversal in the moral economy of neo-liberalism: NGOs becoming market sustainable as a condition for becoming socially responsible. While much has been written on the modes whereby corporations develop self-regulation practices that render them "socially responsible" while offsetting social critiques and protest (e.g., Shamir 2004a, 2004b), i.e., by construing social responsibility as a condition for market profitability, the "counter-movement" taking place in the microcredit world points in a different direction. The emphasis of the microcredit global movement nowadays is gradually shifting its logic of action and discourse by claiming that the more market-like MFIs become, the more "social" they are. The more they abide by profitability principles and competition laws, the more socially effective they can be, and therefore the more just and "do-gooder." Thus, while large corporations are expected to perform well in "social responsibility" indexes, MFIs are increasingly evaluated according to "financial viability" and "profitability" standards.

Pointing at the problematic of the "social" and the "economic" helps understand better the role women, or more accurately, the role the notion of women has played in the expansion and institutionalization of microfinance. The two main criteria according to which microfinance programs are being evaluated are outreach and sustainability. Outreach, in terms of scale and depth, measures the extent to which programs are able to reach large numbers of poor, otherwise underserved population. Sustainable programs are those that are financially autonomous and are in no need of subsidies and donations. While often thought of as contradictory, both criteria are rendered compatible through women and on their behalf. "Women," repeatedly constructed as the emblem of the most excluded population, symbolize in development, and especially in microfinance discourse, the "social." Moreover, since the effects of empowering women "spill over" to their families and communities, the social good that can be gained by focusing on women is even larger. In this sense women are depicted as a "transmitting belt" of social change. But, it is not only the case that women satisfy the "social" criteria. They also help achieve the "economic" one. Women's higher rates of repayment reduce financial risks and contribute to the financial viability and therefore to the sustainability of microfinance programs. And indeed, programs with higher shares of women clients have had better economic performance than other programs.

But why is that so? Women are considered to be a better investment, both in social and financial terms, exactly because of their attributed gendered characters. Women, though the main object of the transformative financial neo-liberal project, are not expected to become the classical economic actor who acts to promote his own interests and to maximize his own profit, i.e., "man." They are expected to become economically active entrepreneurial subjects, but to remain "brokers of the health, nutritional, and educational status of other household members" (Goetz and Sen Gupta 1996: 46). Or in other words, to keep their "woman" character as nurturers who have the primary responsibility to care for their family. It is only then, that they yield higher returns in social terms.

And why are women better borrowers? As it turns out, women are more likely than men to comply with repayment schedules, so that they could continue the program, because they have fewer alternative borrowing possibilities and economic options. Another reason that is also part and parcel of the patriarchal character of their societies is their lower mobility that stems largely from restrictions on their free movement. Women, therefore, pose less of a "moral hazard problem," i.e., they are less likely to "take the money and run" (Morduch 1999: 1584). Ironically then, it is the discrimination and oppression of women and, as a result, their lack of power and alternatives, which makes them the perfect profit-making clients for microfinance.

To conclude, many have discussed the question of "Why women?" We argue that the answer that is often given, namely that women are a better "investment" in social and economic terms, helps to account also for the two processes on which this chapter focused: the globalization of microfinance and its commercialization. While surely not the main factor, the emphasis on women helped in mobilizing material and ideological support that are indispensible for the project, especially in its latter stage. Moreover, it is the gendered character of the project that enabled the realignment between the logic of the "social" and the "economic" in a way that strengthens the profitability of commercial microfinance institutions and their role as legitimate players in the field of social change. However, does microfinance challenge existing gender power structures in a way that benefits and really empowers women? On this question, the evidence still remains inconclusive.

Notes

1　Quoted from Klobuchar and Cornell Wilkes in Naresh 2004: 128.
2　Grimes (1997) quoted in Amin et al. 2002: 6.
3　Other activities take the form of the creation of cooperatives (of producers and of consumers) and small communally owned businesses; the promotion of microcredit and income-generating programs; the enactment of skill training programs designed for disadvantaged populations or populations with special needs; and the creation of jobs that are protected from overt market competition for vulnerable populations as well as practices such as fair trade, creating local markets of barters, etc. (Ilani 2005; Sa'ar 2006). Writing about Europe, Amin et al. (2002) emphasize credit unions, housing associations, and consumer associations as central to an expanding social economy sector.
4　Other financial services include micro savings, micro payments, remittance, etc. The whole system of financial services for the poor is called microfinance. In this chapter we use the terms microcredit and microfinance interchangeably.
5　See, for example, former UN Secretary-General Kofi Annan's words when announcing the UN-sponsored International Year of Microcredit: "Sustainable access to microfinance helps alleviate poverty by generating income, creating jobs, allowing children to go to school, enabling families to obtain health care, and empowering people to make the choices that best serve their needs" (http://www.mcenterprises. org/studycenter/microfinance).
6　On the notion of microfinance as a "global movement" for poverty eradication see, Microcredit Summit Draft Declaration, 2 November 1995 quoted in Rogaly 1996: 100.
7　Quoted in Armendariz and Morduch 2005, back cover blurb.
8　ACCION began as a student-run volunteer effort in Caracas, Venezuela, supporting the development of solidarity groups lending to urban vendors, and it gradually expanded its services to include business training and other financial services.

9   Founded in the mid 1980s, FINCA established an innovative program known as "Village Banking" that focused on micro loans to low-income women involved in commerce and petty trade. Its success led to its expansion in other countries in Latin America and in the 1990s a similar model was emulated in Africa and Eurasia, starting in Kyrgyzstan, later in Georgia, Azerbaijan, Russia, and Armenia and also Kosovo, Afghanistan, and Tajikistan.

10 http://www.microcreditsummit.org/index.php?/en/about/about_the_microcredit_summit_campaign/ (accessed 4 March 2009).

11 The nine founding members are Canada, France, the Netherlands, the United States, the African Development Bank, the Asian Development Bank, the International Fund for Agricultural Development, the United Nations Development Programme/United Nations Capital Development Fund, and the World Bank, later followed by Australia, Finland, Norway, Sweden, the United Kingdom, and Inter-American Development Bank (Mayoux 2005).

12 UN Press Release, "General Assembly Greenlights Programme for the International Year of Microcredit 2005, Observance will Promote Access to Financial Services and Empowerment of the Poor, Especially Women," New York, 29 December 2003, *Micro Finance Matter* (UNCDF Newsletter). http://web.worldbank.org/WBSITE/EXTERNAL/TOPICS/EXTGENDER/0,contentMDK:20643650~menuPK:2643809~pagePK:64020865~piPK:149114~theSitePK:336868,00.html

13 http://www.us.undp.org/BulletinPDFs/Jan%2009/UN%20Capital%20Development%20Fund%20Launches%20MicroLead.pdf (accessed 3 March 2009).

14 For a breakdown of poorest women clients by region for 2006 and 2007, see table 7 in Daley-Harris (2009). Note, however, that Rhyne and Otero (2006) comment that there are different ways of measuring microfinance figures that result in contradictory estimates.

15 For a detailed discussion on both approaches, see Mayoux (2003).

16 See "International Year of Microcredit Hosts Panel for Wall Street: Discussion Highlights Microfinance as a Successful Business Investment," Maura E. McGill, Robert F. Wagner School of Public Service, New York University; "United Nations to Host International Forum on Building Inclusive Financial Sectors in November: Event to Draw Financial Sector Leaders from All Over the World" http://www.uncdf.org/english/microfinance/pubs/newsletter/pages/2005_07/year_update.php Issue 14 / July 2005 (accessed 3 March 2009).

17 For more on BancoSol, see Gonzalez-Vega et.al. (1997). This bank became the first microfinance institution to be listed on a national stock exchange in 1997 (Campion and White 2001). On women and BancoSol see Christabell (2009).

18 Note for example, K-Rep in Kenya, CARD Bank in the Philippines, BRAC in Bangladesh, Mibanco in Peru, Finsol in Honduras, and Compartamos in Mexico.

19 See series of papers commissioned for the Workshop "Transformation of Micro-finance Operations from NGO to a Regulated MFI" at Microcredit Summit in 2006. All attest to the extent of the phenomenon and its desirability. http://www.microcreditsummit.org/commissioned_papers/ (accessed 3 March 2009).

20 Banco Compartamos's official mission is to meet "the microlending needs of small business run by *women* in rural areas" http://www.ifc.org/ifcext/publications.nsf/AttachmentsByTitle/Making_a_Difference_Financial_Mkts/$FILE/Making_a_Difference_Financial_Markets.pdf

21 For information on recent aid provided to specific institutions for that purpose by World Bank (through International Financial Corporation) and figures of the share of women clients of these institutions see: http://www.ifc.org/ifcext/media.nsf/AttachmentsByTitle/Microfinane_factsheet_Jul08/$FILE/Microfinance_factsheet_Jul08.pdf

22 For-profits include: banks, consulting firms, non-bank financial institutions, finance companies. Not-for profits include mainly private voluntary organizations (such as

churches) and NGOs. Small amounts are allocated to cooperatives, credit unions, and UN-affiliated organizations as well.
23 It includes direct and indirect funding. Calculated from USAID 2008: table 4.
24 http://go.worldbank.org/B6MIYW0P50 (accessed 1 February 2009). For a critique on the win-win proposition see Morduch (2000).

Bibliography

Almeyda, G. (1996) *Money Matters: reaching women entrepreneurs with financial services*. Washington, DC: Inter-American Development Bank.

Amin, A., Cameron, A., and Hudson, R. (2002) *Placing the Social Economy*. London and New York: Routledge.

Armendariz, B. and Morduch, J. (2005) *The Economics of Microfinance*. Cambridge, MA: The MIT Press.

Baydas, M. M., Graham, D. H., and Valenzuela, L. (1997) "Commercial Banks in Microfinance: new actors in the microfinance world," *Economics and Sociology*, Occasional Paper No. 2372. Department of Agricultural Economics, Ohio State University.

Berkovitch, N. (1999) *From Motherhood to Citizenship: women's rights and international organizations*. Baltimore, MD: Johns Hopkins University Press.

Borzaga, C. and Santuari, A. (2000) *The Innovative Trends in the Non-Profit Sector in Europe: the emergence of social entrepreneurship*. OECD/Leed Forum on Social Innovations.

Bryn, S. T. and Meehan, J. (1987) *Beyond the Market and the State: new directions in community development*. Philadelphia, PA: Temple University Press.

Burstein, P. (1994) *Equal Employment Opportunity: labor market discrimination and public policy*. New York: Aldine de Gruyter.

Bushell, B. (2008) "Women Entrepreneurs in Nepal: what prevents them from leading the sector?" *Gender and Development*, 16(3): 549–564.

Campion, A. and White, V. (2001) *NGO Transformation*. Bethesda, MD: Microenterprise Best Practices, USAID.

Christabell, P. J. (2009) *Women Empowerment Through Capacity Building: the role of microfinance*. New Delhi: Ashok Kumar Mittal.

Christen, R. P. (2001) "Commercialization and Mission Drift: the transformation of microfinance in Latin America," Occasional Paper No. 5, January. Washington, DC: Consultative Group to Assist the Poorest (CGAP).

Copestake, J. (2001) "Assessing the Impact of Microcredit: a Zambian case study," *Journal of Development Studies*, 37(4): 81–101.

—— (2007) "Mainstreaming Microfinance: social performance management or mission drift?" *World Development*, 35(10): 1721–1738.

Daley-Harris, S. (2006) *State of Microcredit Summit Campaign Report*. Online. http://www.microcreditsummit.org/pubs/reports/socr/2006/SOCR06.pdf.

—— (2009) *State of Microcredit Summit Campaign Report*. Online. http://www.microcreditsummit.org/uploads/socrs/SOCR2009_English.pdf.

D'Espallier, B., Guérin, I., and Mersland, R. (2009) "Women and Repayment in Microfinance," Working Paper 2009–2. Rural Microfinance and Employment Project, Université de Provence, France. Online. http://www.rumerural microfinance.org/IMG/pdf_WP_200902.pdf

Feldman, S. (1997) "NGOs and Civil Society: (un)stated contradictions," *Annals AAPSS*, 554: 46–65.

Franzway, S., Court, D., and Connel., R. W. (1989) *Staking a Claim: feminism, bureaucracy and the state*. Cambridge: Polity Press.

Goetz, A. and Sen Gupta, R. (1996) "Who Takes the Credit? Gender, power and control over loan use in rural credit programmes in Bangladesh," *World Development*, 24: 45–63.

Gonzalez-Vega, C., Schreiner, M., Meyer, R. L., Rodriguez, J., and Navajas, S. (1997) "The Challenge of Growth for Microfinance Organizations: the case of the Banco Solidario in Bolivia." In Schneider, H. (ed.) *Microfinance for the Poor?* Paris: Development Center, IFAD-OECD: 129–167.

Gross, D. (2006) "Fighting Poverty with $2-a-Day Jobs," *New York Times*, 16 July. Online. http://www.nytimes.com/2006/07/16/business/yourmoney/16view.html (accessed 20 February 2009).

Haase, D. (2007) "Closing the Gender Gap," *ESR Review*, 9(2): 4–11.

Hishigsuren, G. (2006) *Transformation of Micro-finance Operations from NGO to Regulated MFI*. Decatur, GA: IDEAS, Institute for Development, Evaluation, Assistance and Solutions.

—— (2007) "Evaluating Mission Drift in Microfinance: lessons for programs with social mission," *Evaluation Review*, 31(3): 203–260.

Hulme, D. and Mosley, P. (1996) *Finance against Poverty: effective institutions for lending to small farmers and micro-enterprises in developing countries*. London: Routledge.

Ilani, A. (May 2005) *Growth from Another Direction: mapping strategies for community and economic development and observing the process of the growth of Israel's social economy*. Research Report submitted to the New Israel Fund and Shatil. (Hebrew).

Johnson, S. (1998) "Microfinance North and South: contrasting current debates," *Journal of International Development*, 10: 799–809.

Karim, L. (2008) "Demystifying Micro-Credit: The Grameen Bank, NGOs, and neoliberalism in Bangladesh," *Cultural Dynamics*, 20: 5–29.

Klein, M. U. and Hadjimichael, B. (2003) *The Private Sector in Development: entrepreneurship, regulation, and competitive disciplines*. New York: World Bank.

Ledgerwood, J. (1999) *Microfinance Handbook: an institutional and financial perspective (sustainable banking with the poor)*. Washington, DC: International Bank for Reconstruction.

Leyshon, A., Lee, R., and Williams, C. C. (eds) (2003) *Alternative Economic Spaces*. London: Sage.

Livingstone, A. and Chagnon, L. (March 2004) *From Poverty to Empowerment: a research report on women and community economic development (CED) in Canada*. Canadian Women's Foundation and Canadian Women's Community Economic Development Council.

Mayoux, L. (2001) "Jobs, Gender and Small Enterprises: getting the policy environment right," SEED Working Paper No. 15. International Labour Organization: Series on Women's Entrepreneurship Development and Gender in Enterprises (WEDGE).

—— (2003) "From Marginalisation to Empowerment: towards a new approach in small enterprise development." Paper presented to SDC Employment and Income Division Workshop, Small Enterprise Development and Empowerment, 9–10 January, Study Center Gerzensee, Switzerland.

—— (2005) "Women's Empowerment through Sustainable Micro-finance: rethinking 'Best Practice,'" Discussion draft, February 2006.

Morduch, J. (1999) "The Microfinance Promise," *Journal of Economic Literature*, 37(4): 1569–1614.

—— (2000) "The Microfinance Schism," *World Development*, 28(4): 617–629.

Moulaert, F. and Oana, A. (2005) "Social Economy, Third Sector and Solidarity Relations: a conceptual synthesis from history to present," *Urban Studies*, 42(11): 2037–2354.

Naresh, S. (2004) "Book Review of: *The Miracles of Barefoot Capitalism*: a compelling case for microcredit by Jim Klobuchar and Susan Cornell Wilkes," *Journal of Microfinance*, 6(1): 127–130.

Otero, M. and Rhyne, E. (1994) *The New World of Microenterprise Finance: building healthy financial institutions for the poor*, West Hartford, CT: Kumarian Press.

Paxton, J. (1995) *Sustainable Banking with the Poor: a worldwide inventory of microfinance institutions*. Washington, DC: World Bank.

Peters, M. (2001) "Education, Enterprise Culture and the Entrepreneurial Self: a Foucauldian perspective," *Journal of Educational Enquiry*, 2(2): 58–71.

Raheim, S. (1996) "Micro-enterprise as an Approach for Promoting Economic Development in Social Work: lessons from the Self-Employment Investment Demonstration," *International Social Work*, 39: 69–82.

—— (1997) "Problems and Prospects of Self-Employment as an Economic Independence Option for Welfare Recipients," *Social Work*, 42(1): 44–54.

Rai, S. M. (ed.) (2003) *Mainstreaming Gender, Democratizing the State?: Institutional mechanisms for the advancement of women*. Manchester: Manchester University Press.

Rankin, K. N. (2001) "Governing Development: neoliberalism, microcredit, and rational economic woman," *Economy and Society*, 30(1): 18–37.

—— (2002) "Social Capital, Micro Finance and the Politics of Development," *Feminist Economics*, 8(1): 1–24.

Rhyne, E. and Otero, M. (2006) "Microfinance through the Next Decade: visioning the who, what, where, when, and how," ACCION International. Paper commissioned for the workshop Transformation of Micro-finance Operations from NGO to a Regulated MFI, at Microcredit Summit.

Rogaly, B. (1996) "Micro-Finance Evangelism, 'Destitute Women', and the Hard Selling of a New Anti-Poverty Formula," *Development in Practice*, 6(2): 100–112.

Rose, K. (1992) *Where Women Are Leaders: the SEWA movement in India*. London and Atlantic Highlands: Zed Press.

Sa'ar, A. (2006) "'A Business of Your Own': evaluation research of a micro-enterprise project by Economic Empowerment for Women," submitted to the National Security Institute Research & Planning Administration, Division for Service Development. (Hebrew).

Sanders, C. K. (2004) "Employment Options for Low-Income Women: microenterprise versus the labor market," *Social Work Research*, 28(2): 83–92.

Shamir, R. (2004a) "The De-Radicalization of Corporate Social Responsibility," *Critical Sociology*, 30(3): 669–689.

—— (2004b) "Between Self-Regulation and the Alien Tort Claims Act: on the contested concept of corporate social responsibility," *Law and Society Review*, 38(4): 635–664.

Silliman, J. (1999) "Expanding Civil Society: shrinking political spaces—the case of women's nongovernmental organizations," *Social Politics*, 6(1): 23–53.

Steinberg, B. and Cook, A. (1988) "Policies Affecting Women's Employment in Industrial Societies." In Stromberg, A. and Harkess, S. (eds) *Women Working: theories and facts in perspective*. Mountain View, CA: Mayfield, 307–347.

Taylor, L. (1999) "Globalization and Civil Society: continuities, ambiguities and realities in Latin America," *Indiana Journal of Global Legal Issues*, 7(1): 269–275.

United States Agency for International Development (USAID) (1998) *Reaching Down and Scaling Up: meeting the microenterprise development challenge*. Washington, DC: U.S. Agency for International Development Microenterprise Results Reporting for 1997.

—— (2003) *Linking the Poor to Opportunity: the Microenterprise Development Initiative*. Washington, DC: U.S. Agency for International Development Microenterprise Results Reporting for 2001.

—— (2008) *Microenterprise Results Reporting, Annual Report to Congress, Fiscal Year 2007.* Washington, DC: U.S. Agency for International Development Microenterprise Results Reporting for 2007.

Viganò, L., Bonomo, L., and Vitali, P. (2004) "MicroFinance in Europe," Working paper. Milan, Italy: Giordano Dell' Amore Foundation and European Foundation Guido Venosta. Online. http://www.fgda.org/docs/MFEurope.pdf (accessed 1 March 2009).

Woodworth, W. P. (2000) "Third World Economic Empowerment in the New Millennium: microenterprise, microentrepreneurship, and microfinance," *SAM Advanced Management Journal*, 65: 19–28.

Yunus, M. (2007a) *Creating a World without Poverty: social business and the future of capitalism,* New York: Public Affairs.

—— (2007b) *Is Grameen Bank Different From Conventional Banks?* http://www.grameen-info.org/bank/GBdifferent.htm (accessed 20 March 2009).

11 Algerian women in movement

Three waves of feminist activism

Valentine M. Moghadam

The Middle East and North Africa region is better known for its authoritarian forms of governance and for Islamist movements than it is for women's movements. Yet the region is rife with women's organizations, from development-oriented nongovernmental and service organizations to policy institutes and women's rights groups. This chapter examines three waves of Algerian women's collective action since the 1980s: against the new family code in the immediate post-Boumédienne period; against the Islamist movement and *le terrorisme* of the 1990s; and for gender justice in the new millennium. Little known outside a relatively restricted francophone community of scholar-activists, the Algerian women's movement not only undermines continued stereotypes about the absence of independent mobilizations in the Arab region but also confirms the main postulates of social movement theories. The chapter elucidates the links among demographic changes, the "political opportunity structure," the articulation of grievances, and the emergence of women's mobilizations. Characteristics of the Algerian women's movement include a propensity to build and sustain organizations and networks; effective coalition-building, both within Algeria and transnationally (especially within the Maghreb); engagement with government, domestic policies and laws, and the global women's rights agenda; and a rather remarkable fearlessness.

Conceptual framework: structures, grievances, and mobilizations

In their cross-national and comparative study of women's movements during the twentieth century, Chafetz and Dworkin (1986) situate the impetus for "female revolt" and opportunities for gender-based mobilization within broad socio-demographic changes. Especially important is female educational attainment and participation in the urban work force, which provide women with increasing expectations, an emergent gender consciousness, and a clearer understanding of societal constraints, injustices, and opportunities. Education, employment, and smaller households give "modernizing women" more time for other public activities and the capacity to make demands on governments for equality, autonomy, and empowerment. Research has found that the observation of gaps and disparities among women's legal status, social positions, and aspirations leads to the articulation of grievances and collective action of various types. (Margolis 1993: Moghadam 1998: ch. 8)

Social movement theorizing has given rise to the concept of the "political opportunity structure," which pertains to the broad political (but also economic and social) environment in which grievances emerge, collective action is possible, and movements and organizations can take shape. The concept revolves primarily around the nature of the state and its relations to society, and key questions pertain to the open versus closed nature of the state; unity versus cracks within the political elite; and the presence or absence of elite allies for emerging movements.[1] At the same time, the reality of globalization has compelled theorists to examine global or transnational opportunities for social movement organizing, including norm diffusion by international organizations and the proliferation of all manner of nongovernmental organizations (Edwards and Hulme 1992; Smith et al 1997; Keck and Sikkink 1998; Boli and Thomas 1997).

Of particular relevance here is the global women's rights agenda, the product of advocacy sponsored by the United Nations since the Decade for Women (1976–1985) and advanced by the four World Conferences on Women that took place between 1975 and 1995. In that context, governments have adopted international conventions on women's equality, human rights, and empowerment—including the 1979 Convention on the Elimination of All Forms of Discrimination against Women and the 1995 Beijing Declaration and Platform for Women. Creating a global opportunity structure conducive to transnational advocacy of all kinds, including cross-border women's organizing and networking, the international agreements and conferences have provided space, legitimacy, and funding for women's rights and human rights organizations, as well as other types of NGOs (Moghadam 2005). Thus, when the *Collectif 95 Maghreb Egalité* was formed by feminists in Algeria, Morocco, and Tunisia in the run-up to the Beijing conference, the group was able to draw on the emerging global women's rights agenda, as well as funding from German foundations, to advance its case for an egalitarian family code. Moreover, the *Collectif* relied on the support of other transnational feminist networks, notably Women Living under Muslim Laws (WLUML), which had formed in 1984 in opposition to Islamic fundamentalism and discriminatory family laws.

The formation of the *Collectif* took place in the regional context of the emergence of an array of women's organizations. In previous work I have identified seven types of organizing and mobilizing that took place by women in countries of the Middle East and North Africa: service or charitable organization; professional associations; women's auxiliaries of political parties; women's auxiliaries of trade unions; women-in-development NGOs; development research centers and women's studies institutes; women's rights or feminist organizations (Moghadam 1998: ch. 8). These types of organizations may be intersecting; some women-in-development NGOs, for example, exhibit strong feminist objectives.

In understanding the emergence of the Algerian feminist movement and its various waves since the early 1980s, therefore, we note the relevance of the political opportunity structure at both national and global levels, the existence of the global women's rights agenda, and the capacity for collective action on the part of a population of educated and employed women. Also important in shaping the contours of that movement are the evolution of Algeria's political culture and the legal status of Algerian women, to which we now turn.

Historical background: national liberation, patriarchy, and women

In order to provide a historical background to our examination of the three waves of women's activism in Algeria, we begin with the French seizure of Algeria in 1830. In contrast to their colonial policy in Morocco after 1912 and Tunisia after 1882, the French in Algeria sought to dismantle Islamic institutions, including the economic infrastructure and the Islamic cultural network of lodges and schools. By the turn of the century, there were upwards of half a million French-speaking settlers in Algeria, and by 1930 European competition had ruined most of the old artisan class. Small shopkeepers such as grocers and spice merchants survived, but others suffered severely from the competition of the *petits colons*. Industrialization in Algeria was given a low priority by Paris during the interwar period. Local development and employment-generation were severely hampered, and there was considerable unemployment and male migration of the native population. Fierce economic competition, cultural disrespect, and residential segregation characterized the French administration (Metz 1994).

In this context, many Algerians regarded Islam and the Muslim family as sanctuaries from French cultural imperialism. The popular reaction to the *mission civilisatrice* was a return to the foundations of the old community. To many Algerian men in particular, the unveiled woman represented a capitulation to the European and his culture; she was a person who had opened herself up to the prurient stares of the foreigners, a person more vulnerable to (symbolic) rape. The protection and seclusion of women were seen by Algerians as necessary defenses against the French cultural onslaught (Knauss 1987).

The anti-colonial movement and its political and military organizations absorbed some of this thinking. When the Front de Liberation Nationale (FLN) and the Armée de Liberation Nationale (ALN) were formed, military exigencies forced the officers of the ALN to use some women combatants. Upwards of 10,000 women participated in the Algerian revolution. The overwhelming majority of those who served in the war were nurses, cooks, and laundresses. But many women played an indispensable role as couriers and, because the French rarely searched them, women were often used to carry bombs. Among the heroines of the Algerian revolution were Djamila Bouhired (the first woman sentenced to death in the revolution), Djamila Bouazza, Jacqueline Gerroudj, Zahia Khalfallah, Baya Hocine, and Dkoher Akrour; 20-year-old Hassiba Ben Bouali was killed in the Casbah and 17-year-old Djennet Hamidou was shot and killed as she tried to escape arrest; Yamina Abed, who was wounded in battle, suffered amputation of both legs (Cherifati-Merabtine 1994).

One emancipatory development during the national liberation struggle was the admittance of unmarried women into the ranks of the FLN and ALN and the emergence by default of voluntary unions unencumbered by family arrangements, presided over by an FLN officer.[2] After independence, the September 1962 constitution made Islam the official state religion but also guaranteed equality between the sexes and granted women the right to vote. Ten women were elected deputies of the new National Assembly and one of them, Fatima Khemisti, drafted the only significant legislation to affect the status of women passed after independence. Intended to encourage more education for girls, the Khemisti law raised the minimum age of marriage for girls to 16.[3] In this optimistic time, when heroines of the revolution were being hailed throughout the country, the Union Nationale des Femmes Algeriennes (UNFA) was formed. Indeed, one consequence of the Algerian revolution and of women's role in it was the emergence of what Cherifa Bouatta and Doria Cherifati-Merabtine call the "*moudjahidate* model of womanhood." The heroic woman fighter was an inspiration to the 1960s and 1970s generation of Algerians, particularly Algerian university women (Bouatta 1994; Cherifati-Merabtine 1994).

But another, more patriarchal tendency was at work during and after the revolution. One expression of this tendency was the pressure on women fighters during the liberation struggle to marry and thus prevent gossip about their behavior. Moreover, despite the sacrifices of Algerian women, and although the female militants "acceded to the ranks of subjects of history," the Algerian revolution was subsequently cast in terms of male exploits, and the heroic female feats received relatively little attention (Bouatta 1994).

Following independence and in a display of authoritarianism, President Ben Bella proceeded to ban all political parties. The Federation of the FLN in France, which had advocated a secular state, was dissolved; the new FLN general secretary, Mohammed Khider, purged the radicals—who had insisted on the right of workers to strike—from the union's leadership. And of women, Khider said: "The way of life of European women is incompatible with our traditions and our culture . . . We can only live by the Islamic morality. European women have no other preoccupations than the twist and Hollywood stars, and don't even know the name of the president of their republic" (Knauss 1987: 99). In a reversal of the political and cultural atmosphere of the national liberation struggle, patriarchal values became hegemonic in independent Algeria. In this context, the marriage of another Algerian, Dalila, to a foreigner was deemed unacceptable. Dalila's brother abducted and confined her "with the approving and silent consent of the enlightened élite and the politically powerful" (Baffoun 1982: 234).

Patriarchal "socialism"

Thus, notwithstanding the participation of upwards of 10,000 women in the Algerian revolution, their future status under the long rule of Colonel Houari Boumédienne was already shaped by "the imperative needs of the male revolutionaries to restore Arabic as the primary language, Islam as the religion of the state, Algeria as a fully free and independent nation, and themselves as sovereigns of the family" (Knauss 1987: xiii). In the 1960s, marriage rates soared for teenage girls; in 1967 some 10 percent of Algerian girls were married at age 15; at age 20, 73 percent were married. The crude fertility rate was 6.5 children per woman. The Boumédienne government's policy on demographic growth was based on the belief that a large population was necessary for national power. It was, therefore, opposed to all forms of birth control unless the mother had already produced at least four children (Knauss 1987: 111). The government also was confident in the capacity of its oil-based economy to support a large population. By the end of the Boumédienne era in 1979, Algeria was home to a huge population of young people. Some 97 percent of Algerian women were without paid work, officially regarded as homemakers. While Algeria's gender ideology favored domestic roles for women, patriarchal gender relations were reinforced by the economic situation of high male unemployment and underemployment, and the absence of a diversified economy or of labor-intensive industries. By this time, too, the UNFA had become the women's auxiliary of the FLN, devoid of feminist objectives.

In the 1970s and the 1980s, some women candidates were elected to provincial and local assemblies and a few were appointed to ministerial and sub-ministerial positions, but the Algerian political class was overwhelmingly male, and women were greatly under-represented in political decision-making positions.[4] The Algerian professional class included women in such occupations as doctor, nurse, teacher, university professor, and—significantly—judge. But most Algerian women were classified as homemakers, did not take part in gainful employment, and had no access to economic resources or income. By the 1990s, women aged 15–65 were only 8 percent of the labor force. Even accounting for undercounting of women in the rural sector and in the urban informal sector, this figure was not only extremely small by international standards, but it also was small by regional standards, and far below the female share of the labor force in neighboring Tunisia and Morocco (Moghadam 1998: ch. 3). Algeria's economic concentration in the oil and gas sector—which favored capital-intensive tech-nologies deployed by men—was a principal reason for the under-representation of women in the labor force. The very high birth rate in Algeria tended to reduce the size of the employed population—male and female alike—while increasing the size of the dependent population. Finally, as noted, the leaders of post-colonial Algeria saw "the liberation of women from work" and the expansion of the "Muslim family" as a symbol of Algeria's new national identity.

At the same time, state-sponsored education produced a generation of Algerian women who would become a restive force for progressive social change in Algeria and create the new women's movement. In 1990, 20 percent of the university teaching staff and about half the teaching force at lower levels were women.[5] These were the women who loudly and visibly challenged the Chadli Bendjedid government's conservative family code in 1981, who confronted the Islamist movement in the 1990s, and who went on to lead new mobilizations for gender justice at the start of the twenty-first century.

The new women's movement: 1980s and 1990s

The Algerian women's movement emerged in its first wave in the period following President Boumédienne's death in December 1978. This period was marked by a conservative move at women's expense, in line with a shift away from Algerian socialism and toward a market economy, and in response to the growth of political Islam and fundamentalism (*intégrisme*) in the region, with movements either overtly challenging the authority of governments or calling for the return of Islamic law. Just two months after Boumédienne's death, the Ministry of Justice announced the creation of a commission to draft a family code. On 8 March 1979 some 200 university women convened an open meeting at the industrial workers' union headquarters in Algiers to demand the disclosure of the identity of the members of the commission, and to express their concerns and demands. Significantly, they called themselves "the commission of *women who work* at the university" and defined themselves as workers rather than as professionals, partly as an homage to the waning socialist heritage and partly to underscore their identity as employed women (Knauss 1987: 130). In January 1980 the government of Chadli Bendjedid handed the embryonic feminist movement a new issue to protest against when it abruptly prohibited Algerian women from leaving the country without male guardian permission. According to Khalida Messaoudi, a mathematics teacher and one of the organizers of the women's protests, on 8 March 1980: "We organized a huge general assembly and decided to demonstrate in the streets, demanding that the order which hampered women's freedom of movement be definitively lifted. The government retreated: the ministerial order was cancelled" (Messaoudi and Schemla 1995: 49). Messaoudi adds that at this time, when it became clear that the UNFA could or would do nothing to protest the government, the first independent women's collective was formed, consisting of about 50 women.

The draft family code alarmed many middle-class Algerian women, who saw it as an attempt to placate a growing Islamist tendency by institutionalizing second-class citizenship for women. The 1981 proposal offered six grounds for divorce on the part of the wife, allowed a woman to work outside the home after marriage only if specified in the marriage contract or at the consent of her husband, and imposed some restrictions on polygyny and the conditions in which the wives of a polygynous husband were kept. Algerian feminists responded quickly: "They gathered in front of the parliament building to reject the process of drawing up and adopting laws without a preliminary consultation of the most concerned" (Bouatta 1997: 5). The feminists joined with the *moudjahidates*—women veterans of the war of liberation—and demonstrated together on 3 December 1981. On 21 January 1982, the group issued a six-point demand, calling for monogamy; the unconditional right of women to seek employment; the equal division of family property; the same age of majority for women and men; identical conditions of divorce for men and women; and effective protection of abandoned children (Bouatta 1997; Messaoudi and Schemla 1995: 50).

The debate over the family code and the presence of the *moudjahidates* forced the government to withdraw its proposal, but an even more conservative revision was presented in 1984 and quickly passed by the National Assembly before much opposition could resurface.[6] In the revised code, Algerian women lost their right to contract marriage—they now had to be given in marriage by a *wali* (guardian). Provisions for divorce initiated by women were sharply curtailed, as were the restrictions on polygyny; fathers became the sole guardians of children; and women were given an unequal share in inheritance. The only positive aspect of the new family code was that the minimum marriage age was raised for both women and men (to 18 and 21, respectively). Feminists objected that the family code contravened the equality clauses of the Constitution, the Labor Code, and international conventions to which Algeria was a signatory (Cherifati-Merabtine 1994; Bouatta 1997). Protests were again organized, but given the fact that the bill had already passed, they had little impact.

This first wave of the Algerian feminist movement was preoccupied with the family code. Despite the Islamic Revolution in Iran and the growing influence of Islamism in Algeria, the new feminist movement did not focus its energies on fundamentalism until the late 1980s and into the 1990s. Still, the significance of this first cycle of women's protests was clear. As Khalida Messaoudi puts it:

> Apart from the Berber cultural movement, it has been women—yes, women, and they alone—who have been publicly questioning the F.L.N. since 1980–81 and demanding that universal principles be enforced. Do you realize what holding four demonstrations in quick succession to demand freedom, equality, and citizenship represents in a country where no one talks about the Algerian personality except as something forged by Islam and Arabism?
>
> (Messaoudi and Schemla 1995: 57)

Among the new organizations created during the period of the struggle around the family code, *l'Association pour l'Egalité des Droits entre les Femmes et les Hommes* (known as *Egalité*) was established in May 1985, with Khalida Messaoudi as its first president. Also prominent in the group was Louisa Hannoun, a Trotskyist and women's rights activist. Cherifa Bouatta, a participant in the movement, succinctly summarizes the origins of Algerian feminism:

> Under the shadow of the one-party system, the political monolith [*le pouvoir*] some women attempted to create spaces of independent expression through cultural and trade union groups. Psychology students created a working group and a cine-club. In Oran, study and reflection workshops on Algerian women were organized in early 1980, with contributions from historians, economists, sociologists and psychiatrists. The proceedings of these work-shops were published and the organizers created a women's journal, ISIS. Other groups were then created, such as the *moudjahidates* collective and groups that studied and criticized official proposals for a new Family Code. This latter effort gave life to the women's movement, and is indeed regarded

as the spark that led to the emergence, the objective and the strategies of Algeria's feminist movement.

(Bouatta 1997: 4)

Against Intégrisme

The Bendjedid government was pursuing market reforms in addition to its adoption of a conservative family law.[7] Austerity measures combined with political frustration directed at the FLN led to riots in October 1988. The riots in turn ushered in a brief period of political liberalization, which saw the increasing popularity of the Algerian Islamist movement that later called itself the Islamic Salvation Front (*Front Islamique du Salut*). Algerian feminists were alarmed by statements from Islamist leaders such as Ali Belhadj, who declared that "the natural place for a woman is at home" and that "the woman is the reproducer of men. She does not produce material goods, but this essential thing that is a Muslim" (Mahl 1995). The new feminist groups were opposed to the electoral reforms that legalized religious-based parties, such as the FIS, contravening the constitution. The FIS proceeded to condemn the anti-fundamentalist women as "one of the greatest dangers threatening the destiny of Algeria" and brand them "the avant-garde of colonialism and cultural aggression" (Bennoune 1995: 197).

As it happened, the fundamentalist agenda of the FIS was supported by a segment of the female population, and in April 1989 a demonstration of 100,000 women in favor of Islamism and sex-segregation shocked the anti-fundamentalist women. But this display also spawned a network of anti-fundamentalist feminist groups. When *Egalité* seemed to equivocate over the nature of the fundamentalist uprising, Khalida Messaoudi left to form another organization, *l'Association pour le Triomphe des Droits des Femmes*. In this second wave of the Algerian feminist movement, the struggle against fundamentalism took center stage.

The FIS was committed to introducing Sharia law, which it claimed was superior to Western-style civil codes. Hijab would be introduced, ostensibly to free women from the prying eyes of men. According to one FIS leaflet: "The hijab is a divine obligation for the Muslim woman: It is a simple and modest way to dress, which she has freely chosen." How something can be an obligation and freely chosen is not explained. Other leaflets claimed that women are under attack from "pernicious Westernization" and that "a woman is above all a mother, a sister, a wife or a daughter" (Moghadam 2003: 169). Even the participation of women in sports was seen as immoral and corrupting. When Hassiba Boulmerka won the 1,500 meters at the World Athletics Championships in Tokyo in August 1991, becoming only the second Arab woman ever to receive a major sporting title, she was hailed by the Algerian sports minister, Leila Aslaouni, by other government officials, and by many of her compatriots. However, fundamentalist imams affiliated with the FIS united to pronounce *kofr*, a public disapproval of her from the nation's mosques. The object of their disapproval was the fact that Boulmerka had run before the world's eyes "half-naked"—that is, in regulation running shorts and vest (Moghadam 2003: 170).

To the government's consternation the FIS made major electoral gains during the December 1991 parliamentary elections, and the government moved to annul the elections and ban the FIS. Bendjedid—now reviled by feminists and leftists— was removed in January 1992 and replaced by Mohamed Boudiaf, who opposed not only the fundamentalists but also corruption within the FLN. He was assassinated just five months later. In March of that year, when an Algerian court decided to ban the FIS, the court ruling was read by Judge Ziani, a woman judge who could not have held her position under a FIS government. The banning of the FIS was supported by many Algerian feminists, despite their distaste for the authoritarian government. Launching a second cycle of protests, Algerian feminists held demonstrations against the FIS and the establishment of an Islamic state. They had been alarmed when during the latter part of the 1980s the fundamentalists began to bully and attack women who lived alone or were unveiled. It was as if they were anticipating the terrorism (*le terrorisme*) that was to be carried out by the FIS and the GIA in the 1990s.

The cancellation of the election results was met with extreme violence, with much of the terror carried out by the Armed Islamic Group (GIA). At the height of the political turmoil in the early 1990s pitting the government and military against Islamist extremists, Algeria's economic and political transition appeared uncertain, and the state seemed on the verge of collapse. Algeria's feminists were caught between "the devil and the deep blue sea"—*le pouvoir* and *intégrisme*. While highly critical of the patriarchal and authoritarian state that had introduced the family code, they focused their political energies against misogynist and violent *intégrisme*, which they regarded as the harbinger of a fascistic theocracy. As Messaoudi put it, feminists and democrats reject "a state based on divine law" and desire "a state based on rights" (Messaoudi and Schemla 1995: 142).[8]

Islamist terror

After shooting to death one young woman in April 1993 and decapitating a mother and a grandmother in separate incidents early the next year, the GIA issued a statement in March 1994 classifying all unveiled women who appeared in public as potential military targets—and promptly gunned down three teenage girls (Bennoune 1995). The violence against women escalated during that year, and included kidnappings and rapes. Women were denounced in mosques by imams and fatwas were pronounced against them, condemning women to death. Lists of women to be killed were pinned up at the entrance to mosques (Mahl 1995). March 1995 saw an escalating number of deaths of women and girls. Khalida Messaoudi was officially condemned to death by the fundamentalists and forced to live underground. Zazi Sadou, who had founded the *Rassemblement Algérien des Femmes Démocrates* (RAFD) in 1993 and took public positions against theocracy and authoritarianism, was similarly put on an Islamist death list. Nabila Diahnine, an architect and president of the feminist group *Cri de Femmes*, was assassinated in February 1996 while on her way to work (Shirkat Gah 1997). Women took to the streets to protest the sexual violence and the threats against unveiled women, as well as the military government's inability to protect women. After one public protest in the spring of 1994, the independent newspaper *Al Watan* wrote: "Tens of thousands of women were out to give an authoritative lesson on bravery and spirit to men paralyzed by fear, reduced to silence. . . . The so-called weaker sex . . . refused to be intimidated by the threats advanced by 'the sect of assassins' [Islamists]" (*World Press Review* 1994: 34).

General Liamine Zeroual, the country's new president, committed himself to working with the opposition. Berber organizations and new democratic associations similarly condemned the terror while also protesting the government's incapacity. The outcome of the November 1995 and June 1997 elections showed that the government retained popular support.[9] Throughout, Algerian feminists remained active and staunch opponents of Islamism and of terrorism. In a 1995 interview, while still living underground after her death sentence, Khalida Messaoudi's courage and political acumen were in full display:

> More than 80 people a day are being killed by Islamic fundamentalists. . . . Intellectuals, teachers, writers, thinkers—these are the people killed because it is they who defend traditional notions of liberty. But sometimes simple citizens are killed, too, randomly, just for the purpose of terror. . . . They kill women who oppose their views of how we should behave. They cannot allow difference. That is why they insist on veils to cover the difference. They are fascists who claim Allah is on their side and that they are marching under the banner of righteousness. . . . That is not to say that the fundamentalists don't have a popular base. After years of one-party rule people are desperate and many feel the FIS will make a difference. They [the FIS] just want to be the new dictatorship. If necessary they will compromise and absorb members of the FLN Government into their ranks. But it will simply be the old one-party state with a new face.
>
> (Swift 1995)

Mobilizing women and building feminist organizations

The 1989–1994 period saw the formation of several feminist organizations, including *l'Association Indépendante pour le Triomphe des Droits de la Femme* (*Triomphe*); *l'Association pour l'Emancipation des Femmes* (*Emancipation*); *l'Association pour la Défense et Promotion des Femmes* (*Defense et Promotion*); *Rassemblement Algérien des Femmes Démocrates*; *Cri de Femmes*; *Voix des Femmes*; *El Aurassia*; *SOS Femmes en Détresse*. They called for the abolition of the family code; full citizenship for women; enactment of civil laws guaranteeing equality between men and women in areas such as employment, marriage, and divorce; abolition of polygyny and unilateral male divorce; and equality in division of marital property.

Throughout the 1990s, these and other organizations participated in a variety of national and international independent initiatives on violence against women, including a March 1994 tribunal in Algeria "to judge symbolically the responsible

Islamists and the former president of the Algeria Republic for their crimes against humanity." All the women's groups built coalitions to organize street demonstrations in Algeria to defend democracy and the citizenship of women (*Women, Law and Development International Bulletin* 1998: 4). The RAFD became active in documenting human rights violations, particularly those by Islamists against women, and in collecting women's testimonies. It produced a publication entitled *Algérie réveille-toi, c'est l'an 2000!*, a compilation of news articles about the atrocities, and filed a civil action suit in Washington, DC, against the FIS and its U.S. representative, Anwar Haddam. The RAFD was part of the network Women Living Under Muslim Laws and, after the onset of *le terrorisme*, this and other feminist groups advanced the slogan "No dialogue with the fundamentalists" (Mahl 1995: 4).

Like other organizing women in the Middle East, North Africa, and elsewhere in the Global South, Algerian feminists are products of the country's social development: they are urban employed women, mostly with higher education, although some working-class women have participated in the feminist organizations. Many Middle Eastern feminists (e.g., Iranian, Turkish, Palestinian) began as members of left-wing organizations, but what is distinctive about the Algerian women's movement is the extent to which the feminist movement was dominated by left-wing women—which may account for its audacity and organizational capability. When *Egalité* was formed in 1985, many of its officers and members were associated with the Socialist Organization of Workers (OST). Many members of *Emancipation* belonged to the PST (Socialist Workers Party), and those of *Défense et Promotion* belonged largely to the PAGS (*Parti de l'Avant-Garde Socialiste*, or the Communist Party). As Bouatta explains:

> The founding members of the women's movement are, in their majority, influenced by the ideology of the Left. . . . They are mostly academics, students, workers, and union representatives. They convey a message of an emancipatory project based on the equality of the sexes, employment and education, which are considered as the main criteria of women's promotion and socialization. . . . They are women of the post-independence who were fortunate to have access to education and training. They do not consider the day of liberation as very distant.
>
> (Bouatta 1997: 15)

Algerian women activists became known for their trenchant critiques of both the state and fundamentalism. At the height of the Islamist terror, Saida Ben Habylas, a teacher and official Algerian representative to a UN-sponsored regional meeting that took place in Amman in November 1994, gave an impassioned speech denouncing the violence against women.[10] In a newspaper interview, she boldly emphasized the complicity of both the state and the FIS:

> The history of the FIS and other terrorist groups is a series of alliances with a corrupt "politico-financial mafia" that helped bring about the economic

and social inequalities in Algeria during the 1970s and 1980s . . . Political pluralism and democracy could have meant exposure of corruption of the old order. This old order allied themselves with the FIS in the 1980s and agreed to "share power." There was a deal.

(Bennoune 1995: 194)

Notwithstanding its disruptive nature, Algeria's political crisis, along with the constitutional reforms of 1989, opened the gateways to an incipient civil society and saw a large number of independent interest groups emerging as political parties (Entelis and Arone 1994: 211). Henceforth the government would have to tolerate, respond to, and interact with nongovernmental organizations. The conciliatory stance of the state and cracks in the unity of the political elite favored the proliferation of nongovernmental organizations. Often overlooked in accounts of this development, however, is the array of women's organizations that emerged in Algeria during the 1980s and 1990s.[11] According to Bouatta, 20 women's associations were represented at the first national meeting of the women in late 1989 and in 1993 perhaps as many as 24, according to a document published by the United Nations Fund for Population Activities that year. These included women's studies and research associations such as *Aicha, Dafatir Nissaiya,* and *Fondation Nyssa;* feminist organizations such as those mentioned above; women-in-development organizations such as *Femmes, Environnement, Développement;* social-professional associations such as SEVE which sought to promote and assist women in business; and a number of service and delivery organizations.

Not only was the new women's movement among the principal social movements of 1990s Algeria, but Algerian feminists became more visible and more prominent in the established political structures. One outcome of the 1997 municipal and parliamentary elections was the election of 11 women to the National Assembly, among them several well-known activists and feminists. The emergence of a feminist politics—critical of both fundamentalism and the state—shaped the composition and orientation of the newly elected women.[12]

During its first and second waves, Algeria's new feminist movement was unified in its condemnation of the family code and of fundamentalists, and effective links were developed with international feminists, transnational feminist networks, and European foundations. The movement was active within the *Collectif,* and took part in the research that led to the publication of books on the legal status of women in North Africa, issued by the Morocco-based Editions le Fennec. WLUML and the Center for Women's Global Leadership, a feminist think tank at Rutgers University in the United States, sponsored the participation of Khalida Messaoudi at the UN's World Conference on Human Rights, which took place in Vienna in June 1993, where she testified on Islamist terrorism before the Women's Tribunal. Two years later, the *Collectif* was the major organizer behind the "Muslim Women's Parliament" at the NGO Forum that preceded the Beijing Conference.[13] Their participation at the Beijing conference, as well as the preparation and translation of several books, were made possible by funding from German foundations.[14] In 1997, Rhonda Copelon, director of the

International Human Rights Law Clinic at the City University of New York and a well-known international women's rights activist lawyer, filed a suit in the U.S. on behalf of RAFD and Algerian women victims of terror, with the participation of WLUML. The defendants were the FIS and Anwar Haddam, the "representative-in-exile" of the FIS in the United States.[15] These are but some examples of how Algerian feminists collaborated with other North African feminists and with international feminist groups, demonstrating effective use of the global women's rights agenda to oppose patriarchal laws and political Islam.

Toward gender justice: third wave priorities

The new century brought with it a certain normalization of the political scene in Algeria, along with efforts by the political authorities to end the intense political and ideological schisms that had developed in the 1980s and 1990s. President Abdelazziz Bouteflika made several moves to change directions in Algeria: in addition to seeking greater integration in the world economy and—after 11 September 2001—participation in the global "war on terror," he promised to reward women for their sacrifices and collective action in the previous decade, and he sought to "close the chapter" on Algeria's violent past through a peace charter, an amnesty, and a referendum. Thus in the summer of 2002, he appointed an unprecedented five women to his cabinet, including Khalida Messaoudi and put in place mechanisms for an evaluation of the family code with a view toward reform.

The new century, however, also saw cracks in the feminist movement. As leader of the Workers' Party, Louisa Hannoun's tendency to placate the Islamic opposition irked many Algerian feminists, as did Khalida Messaoudi's assumption to the position first of advisor to the president and then of cabinet minister, which was seen as compromising her independence.[16] Whereas feminists had fervently demanded "no dialogue with the terrorists," the Bouteflika government desired national reconciliation, even if it meant an amnesty for the armed militants of the past. These developments brought with them new priorities for the women's movement. The third wave of the Algerian feminist movement has been characterized by a demand for gender justice in the form of (1) opposition to the referendum and amnesty, (2) a new mobilization for an egalitarian family code, and (3) attention toward ending violence against women and sexual harassment at the workplace. I consider each in turn.

In addition to the continuing work of the *Collectif*, new organizations have become prominent, such as CIDDEF (*Centre d'Information et de Documentation sur les Droits de l'Enfant et de la Femme*). The Wassila network began in 2000 and consists of women's NGOs (including *SOS Femmes en Détresse*) and individual professionals, many of whom are psychologists addressing post-conflict traumas (such as Cherifa Bouatta and her *Societé pour l'Aide Psychologique, la Recherche et la Formation*). *Le Centre d'Ecoute et d'Assistance aux Femmes Victimes d'Harcèlement Sexuel* is a counseling service hosted by the country's main trade union, the UGTA. The network and campaign *20 Ans Barakat* (20 Years Is Enough) is a coalition of Algerian women's organizations calling for the abrogation of the old family code and its replacement with an egalitarian law. Most of these organizations also are opposed to the terrorism of the 1990s and to the way the government handled it.

President Bouteflika's civil harmony law in July 1999 offered immunity or reduced sentences to members of armed groups who gave up their arms and disclosed their actions, but it soon became a blanket amnesty for crimes by all who declared they had repented. This came to be opposed by feminist groups and families of the disappeared. While most of the 200,000 dead and 8,000 disappeared of Algeria's civil war were men, women suffered sexual violence. Thus, it was women who formed new organizations dedicated to opposing the blanket amnesty. In his 2005 charter for peace and reconciliation, President Abdelaziz Bouteflika sought to "close the chapter" on Algeria's violent past. The referendum of 29 September 2005 was based on a simple proposition: were people for or against peace? (Kristianasen 2006). Many Algerians within the country and in the diaspora found the wording deceptive enough to boycott the referendum, but it won the majority of votes cast.[17]

Many Algerians remain embittered by the referendum experience and perhaps none more so than feminists who were on death lists or forced to live underground in the 1990s. Some called for a South Africa-like Truth and Reconciliation process; others felt it would amount to impunity for murderers. One published account includes the following sentiments: "Truth and reconciliation on the South African model wouldn't work here: we Algerians aren't made like that." And: "I want peace, but not this peace with impunity that the charter is forcing on us. In South Africa it wasn't like this" (Kristianasen 2006).[18]

Turning now to the campaign for the family law reform, which feminists have referred to as *un text infamant et dégradant,* recall that President Bouteflika promised its reform. In order to accelerate the reform, the coalition *20 Ans Barakat* was formed on 8 March 2003, almost 20 years after the passing into law of the family code. One of the founders is Akila Ouared, a well-known *moudjahidate,* who has called the family code "Algeria's dishonor, an insult to women." Some of the coalition members have been present on the political scene since 1984, such as *Triomphe, SOS Femmes en Détresse, Défense et Promotion,* and *Pluri-elles Algeria.* Framed in the language of international women's rights and secular feminism, the coalition's petition asserts that "the issue of women's equality in Algeria and their recognition as full citizens is the essential and urgent Algerian question of today and tomorrow" and notes that Tunisia and Morocco have introduced reforms for gender equality.[19] The coalition helped effect amendments to the family code in February 2005, and included a change to the nationality law to allow Algerian women married to foreigners to pass on their nationality to their children. With the amendments, marriage is now consensual and relations between spouses are equal. In a divorce whichever parent has care and control becomes the guardian, and the father must provide a decent home for the mother and child.

At this writing, however, activists object to the retention of guardianship (*wali*) over women, polygyny, and unequal family inheritance, which remains two-thirds to sons and one-third to daughters. One argument is that such clauses are insulting to women's dignity. Another is that they are irrelevant and at odds with the social reality, given that women are increasingly helping to support their families. Polygyny, moreover, is rare—although at 5.5 percent of the population, it is more prevalent than it is in, for example, Morocco (Collectif 2005). Nadia Aït-Zaï, a lawyer and professor of law at Algiers University and a director at CIDDEF, is quoted as saying of the family code: "It could have been abolished. . . . Parliament was supposed to vote on the amendment. Instead, Bouteflika had it quietly passed as a presidential decree. As a jurist, I find the reform incoherent: it's got one foot in modernity, the other in the past" (Kristianasen 2006).

Another set of priorities for the women's movement in its third wave pertains to domestic violence, family abuse, and workplace harassment. Early in the new century, the *Collectif* conducted a survey on violence against women, and publicized its disturbing findings on the extent of the problem and the persistence of anachronistic ideas concerning husbands' privileges. President Bouteflika referred to the survey in his International Women's Day address of 2002. Shortly thereafter, work began on establishing the country's first counseling center, and several others were subsequently set up. *Le Centre d'Ecoute et d'Assistance aux Femmes Victimes d'Harcèlement Sexuel* is housed at the UGTA and financed by the trade union. The Centre was born following a consciousness-raising campaign of the National Commission of Women Workers and of human rights groups, and in December 2003 the Center's director Soumia Salhi also started a hot-line for women victims of sexual harassment.[20] At the same time, Algeria passed a law against workplace sexual harassment. Since the Center's opening, there have been thousands of calls from women victims and supporters, though critics say that the majority of calls from victims have no follow-up: "The bravest women register a complaint but don't follow through. They prefer a change of work."[21]

CIDDEF, *SOS Femmes en Détresse*, and other women's NGOs that are part of the Wassila network address an array of issues related to women's rights to dignity and a life free of sexual and family violence. Incest, the problems of unwed mothers, and illegal abortions are also taken up. The Wassila network holds workshops on the above topics, convenes a weekly clinic for children, and publishes papers. In an interview with *Le Monde Diplomatique*, Louisa Aït Hamou, a lecturer at Algiers University, explains that the network provides professional help, engages in reflection about the country and its future, and takes action:

> We are breaking the silence on taboo subjects: sexual aggression against women and children, family violence, rape, battered women, economic violence. Take Hassi Messaoud, a new oil-rich city: 30 women went to work there, where working women are unusual. The local imams accused them of being prostitutes and, in 2001, they were raped and knifed. One was buried alive. Wassila, with other NGOs, ended the long silence over this and

supported the women in their search for justice, though only three of the 30 dared attend the appeal court on 3 January 2005.

(Kristianasen 2006)

In October 2004, the National Popular Assembly adopted an amendment to the Algerian penal code; it condemns men guilty of sexual harassment to a prison sentence. Sexual harassment is now an offence; it is defined as abusing the authority conferred by one's function or profession in order to give orders to, threaten, impose constraints, or exercise pressure on another person for the purpose of obtaining sexual favors. A person convicted of this offence is subject to imprisonment of two months to one year and a hefty fine. But, according to the chairperson of the Algerian League of the Human Rights, "attitudes remain the main obstacle preventing complaints by sexual harassment victims."[22] Thus a challenge is to encourage women to break the wall of silence as well as to ensure enforcement of the law. This is the new phase of the campaign by the UGTA's Women's Commission, the Wassila network, and other advocates for women's rights and gender justice.

Conclusions

Among the countries of the Middle East and North Africa, Algeria is one of the most instructive case studies of feminist activism. Although women played prominent roles in the national liberation movement of the late 1950s and early 1960s, the rise of a radical women's movement and of feminist organizations was a feature of the 1980s and 1990s. Whereas Algerian women were once intimately connected to the project of national liberation and post-colonial state-building through a version of Arab socialism, the new women's movement extricated itself from those projects to demand rights, equality, and security—and all in the language of secular feminism. Though they never separated themselves from the project of building a modern and progressive Algerian polity, feminists have insisted that women's rights are necessary for the achievement of democracy and modernity.

The new women's movement in Algeria emerged in the context of a growing international women's movement, economic crisis and restructuring, the rise of Islamic fundamentalism, and the weakness of the state. It has been sustained by a population of educated and employed Algerian women with social and gender consciousness. The attack on women's legal status in the immediate post-Boumédienne period triggered the initial mobilizations, which have been sustained over time in the form of various organizations, coalitions, and campaigns. Coalition-building with other progressive civil society organizations, as well as alliances with political elites, helped the women's movement grow and achieve policy successes. The global women's rights agenda has provided additional legitimacy, while transnational feminist networks and European foundations have offered resources necessary for the movement's wider reach.

In examining the evolution of the Algerian feminist movement, this chapter has identified three waves: the struggle against the new family code in the early 1980s; the struggle against fundamentalism and Islamist terror in the 1990s; and a multi-pronged struggle for gender justice in the new century. In all three waves, feminists have advanced powerful critiques of patriarchy and authoritarianism, whether of the state or of Islamic fundamentalism, and have drawn attention to the importance of rights and equality to democratization and national advancement. As such, Algerian feminism and the new women's organizations can only be regarded as key players in the country's democratic transition. They constitute a significant part of the emergent civil society, and give new meaning to concepts of citizenship, human rights, and political participation

Notes

1 Other key elements within social movement theorizing are mobilizing structures (the capacity to mobilize financial and human resources and build organizations), and framing processes (the interpretive, cultural, discursive, and symbolic aspects of movement-building). See McAdam, McCarthy, and Zald, (1996).
2 This was poignantly depicted in a scene in Gillo Pontecorvo's brilliant film *Battle of Algiers*. Also, Alya Baffoun notes that during this "rather exceptional period of struggle for national liberation," the marriage of Djamila Bouhired to an "infidel" non-Muslim foreigner was accepted by her community. See Baffoun (1982); 234. Djamila Bouhired married Jacques Vergès, the French lawyer who specializes in political trials.
3 Although the draft bill had originally stipulated age 19.
4 In 1987, women were only 3.3 percent of those at the ministerial level of government, and 0.0 percent at the sub-ministerial level. At the national assembly they constituted only 2 percent. These figures increased in 1994 but were still low: 7 percent of parliamentarians, 7.7 percent of those at the sub-ministerial level of government, and 3.6 percent of ministerial level positions. Data from *The World's Women 1995: trends and statistics*, New York, UN (1995), table 14, p. 172.
5 Even so, Algerian women's educational attainment was not significant, given the country's wealth. In 1990, nearly 80 percent of women above the age of 25 were illiterate (compared with 50 percent of the men 25 years and older). At lower age groups the figures were better, but even so, fully 37.8 percent of young women aged 15–24 were illiterate in 1990 (compared with only 13.8 for men). See *The World's Women 1995: trends and statistics*, table 7, p. 100. Khalida Messaoudi, the Algerian feminist activist and government official, has noted that in post-colonial Algeria, education was free but not compulsory. See Messaoudi, and Schemla (1995); 30. The same book contains a fascinating description of the travails of education in Algeria during the 1970s, when the program of Arabization was first implemented through the importation of teachers from Egypt, Syria, and Iraq—not all of whom were competent in their subject-areas. See the discussions in chapters 4 and 7 in Messaoudi and Schemla.
6 See the description of these events in Messaoudi and Schemla, pp. 51–52. See also Entelis and Arone (1994).
7 The Bendjedid government also encouraged—or at least, turned a blind eye to—the participation of young Algerian men in the Mujahideen movement in Afghanistan, where Islamists were waging a war against the Soviet-backed government in the 1980s. Many came back to join the Islamist's assault on the Algerian state in the 1990s.
8 There is no doubt that the Algerian government carried out its own killings of suspects, real or imagined. But the available evidence suggests that the terror was initially launched by the FIS. Indeed, the roots of Islamist terror may be traced back to Mustafa

Bouyali's Armed Islamic Algerian Movement, which for five years led violent attacks on the representatives of the state in the first half of the 1980s. See Malley (1996): 245. For details on the misogyny, anti-semitism, and anti-democratic statements of the FIS, see Messaoudi, chapters 9–11. On the killings, kidnappings, and rapes of women during the 1990s, see also Flanders (1998): 24–27. Finally, as to whether the FIS was "forced" into the position it took because its victory had been stolen, it is well to compare its response to that of Turkey's Islamist Refah Party years later. When the Refah Party was declared dissolved by the Turkish military in 1998, the leadership chose a non-violent and political response: to regroup under another name. In any event, the vicious verbal and physical attacks on women and girls carried out by the FIS and GIA—as well as the killings of journalists, foreigners, and priests and nuns—cannot be justified.

9 Although fewer people participated in the 1997 elections and there were claims of electoral rigging and criticism of government authoritarianism.

10 My observation at the pre-Beijing Amman meeting, November 1994.

11 For instance, Azzedine Layachi describes how interaction between the state and elements of the nascent civil society intensified after 1993, and he lists those non-governmental organizations, professional associations, and parties that were represented in meetings with the High State Council, but neglects women's organizations in this effort. See Layachi (1995).

12 Among them were Louisa Hannoun, leader of the Workers Party, Khalida Messaoudi, who joined the Rally for Culture and Democracy, and Dalia Taleb of the Socialist Forces Front. All three women were known for their radicalism. The Workers Party is Trotskyist. The RCD's goals are "secularism, citizenship, a state based on rights, the repeal of the family code, recognition of Algeria's Berber dimension, social justice, educational reform, etc." (Messaoudi and Schemla 1995: 94). Likewise, the Socialist Forces Front stands for democracy and Berber rights.

13 My observations at the NGO Forum in Huairou and discussions with participants. See also their documents: *Women in the Maghreb: change and resistance; One Hundred Measures and Provisions for a Maghrebian Egalitarian Codification of the Personal Statute and Family Law* [*sic*].

14 Personal communication, Emil Lieser of the Friedrich Ebert Stiftung, Cairo, 7 July 2008.

15 Flanders (1998); and Kirshenbaum, G. (1998) "Women's Rights are Human Rights," *Ms.*, 8. 3 March/April: 25. Disclosure: I wrote an affidavit on behalf of the suit. The plaintiffs did not win the case but felt that the experience had been important politically.

16 Personal communications from two Algerian women's rights activists, Limassol, Cyprus, July 2000 and Vienna, Austria, October 2000.

17 While employed at UNESCO in 2005, I spoke with approximately 15 Algerians who were opposed to the referendum.

18 I have also discussed the matter with four Algerian feminist activists, none of whom felt that truth and reconciliation were feasible or desirable.

19 "La question du statut égalitaire des femmes en Algérie, et au delà, celle de leur reconnaissance pleine et entière en tant que citoyennes, est une question essentielle et urgente de l'Algérie d'aujourd'hui et de demain." See http://20ansbarakat.free.fr/petition.htm. See also http://famalgeriennes.free.fr/declarations/APEL_decl_111 203. html and http://20ansbarakat.free.fr/ (accessed 25 July 2008).

20 See her interview on http://www.categorynet.com/v2/index.php/content/view/4518/400/ (last accessed June 2010). See also http://www.afrol.com/articles/ 15853 (accessed June 2010).

21 http://www.algeria-watch.org/fr/article/femmes/harcelement_sexuel.htm (accessed June 2010).

22 "Les mentalités restent le principal obstacle qui continue d'empécher les victimes de harcèlement sexuel de se plaindre" (Boudjemâa Ghechir). http://www.wluml.org/french/newsfulltxt.shtml?cmd%5B157%5D=x-157-347521 (accessed June 2010).

Bibliography

Baffoun, A. (1982) "Women and Social Change in the Muslim Arab World," *Women's Studies International Forum*, 5. 2: 234.

Bennoune, K. (1995) "S.O.S. Algeria: women's human rights under siege," in M. Afkhami (ed.) *Faith and Freedom: women's human rights*, Syracuse, NY: Syracuse University Press, 197.

Boli, J. and Thomas, G.M., (1997) "World Culture in the World Polity," *American Sociological Review*, 62.2: 171–190.

Bouatta, C. (1994) "Feminine Militancy: *Moudjahidates* during and after the Algerian War," in V. M. Moghadam (ed.) *Gender and National Identity: women and politics in Muslim societies*, London: Zed Books, 18–39.

— (1997) "Evolution of the Women's Movement in Contemporary Algeria: organization, objectives, and prospects," Working Paper No. 124: 5, Helsinki: UNU/WIDER, 1997.

Chafetz, J. and Dworkin, G. (1986) *Female Revolt: women's movements in world and historical perspective*. Totowa, NJ: Rowman and Allenheld.

Cherifati-Merabtine, D. (1994) "Algeria at a Crossroads: national liberation, Islamization, and women," in V.M. Moghadam (ed.) *Gender and National Identity: women and politics in Muslim societies*, London: Zed Books.

Collectif 95 Maghreb-Egalití (2005) *Guide to Equality in the Family and in the Maghreb*, Bethesda, MD: Women's Learning Partnership for Rights, Development, and Peace. This is an authorized translation of *Dalil pour l'égalité dans la famille au Mahgreb* (2003).

Edwards, M. and Hulme, D. (eds) (1992) *Making a Difference: NGOs and development in a changing world*, London: Earthscan Publications.

Entelis, J. and Arone, L. (1994) "Government and Politics," in H. C. Metz (ed.) *Algeria: a country study*, Washington, DC: Federal Research Division, Area Handbook Series, Library of Congress, 173–233.

Flanders, L. (1998) "Algeria Unexamined," *On the Issues*, 7.2, Spring: 27.

Keck, M. and Sikkink, K. (1998) *Activists Beyond Borders: advocacy networks in international politics*, Ithaca, NY: Cornell University Press.

Knauss, P. (1987) *The Persistence of Patriarchy: class, gender and ideology in 20th century Algeria*, Boulder, CO: Westview.

Kristianasen, W. (2006) *"Algeria: the women speak," Le Monde Diplomatique*, 13 April.

Layachi, A. (1995) "Algeria: reinstating the state or instating civil society?" in Zartman, I.W. (ed.) *Collapsed States: the disintegration and restoration of legitimate authority*, Boulder, CO: Lynne Reinner Publishers.

Mahl (pseudonym) (1995) "Women on the Edge of Time," *New Internationalist*, No. 270. http://www.newint.org/issue270/270edge.html

Malley, R. (1996) *The Call from Algeria: third worldism, revolution, and the turn to Islam*, Berkeley: University of California Press.

Margolis, D. (1993) "Women's Movements around the World: cross-cultural comparisons," *Gender and Society*, 7.3: 379–399.

McAdam, D., McCarthy, J., and Zald, M. (eds) (1996) *Comparative Perspectives on Social Movements: political opportunities, mobilizing structures, and cultural framings*, Cambridge: Cambridge University Press.

Messaoudi, K. and Schemla, E. (1995) *Unbowed: an Algerian woman confronts Islamic fundamentalism*, Philadelphia: University of Pennsylvania Press.

Metz, H.C. (ed.) (1994) *Algeria: a country study*, Washington, DC: Federal Research Division, Area Handbook Series, Library of Congress.

Moghadam, V. M. (1998) *Women, Work and Economic Reform in the Middle East and North Africa*, Boulder, CO: Lynne Rienner, ch. 8.

—— (2003) *Modernizing Women: gender and social change in the Middle East*, Boulder, CO: Lynne Rienner, 170.

—— (2005) *Globalizing Women: transnational feminist networks*, Baltimore, MD: Johns Hopkins University Press.

Shirkat Gah (1997) *Women Living Under Muslim Laws Newsheet*, IX. 1&2: 19–23.

Smith, J., Chatfield, C., and Pagnucco, R. (eds) (1997) *Transnational Social Movements and Global Politics: solidarity beyond the state*, Syracuse, NY: Syracuse University Press.

Swift, R. (1995) "An Interview with Khalida Messaoudi, Women's Rights Activist, Algeria," *New Internationalist*, March 1995. Online. http://www.thirdworldtraveler.com/Heroes/Khalida_Messaoudi.html

Women, Law and Development International Bulletin (January 1998) 4.

World Press Review (July 1994) "Algeria: Women's Revolt," 34.

12 Using law and education to make human rights real in women's real lives

Nancy Chi Cantalupo

> That women have voluntarily engaged law at all is a triumph of determination over experience. It has not been an act of faith. . . . Treacherous and uncertain and alien and slow, law has not been women's instrument of choice. Their view seems to be that law should not be let off the hook, is too powerful to be ignored, and is better than violence—if not by much.
>
> (MacKinnon 1991: 1284)

Although the above quotation is excerpted from an article primarily concerned with United States domestic law on women's rights, it is equally applicable to women's rights in a more international "human rights" context. Since the late 1980s at least, international feminist lawyers have been articulating a series of problems with the usefulness of international law in general and international human rights law in particular for improving the real lives of real women. In the nearly two decades since then, women lawyers and activists throughout the world have been slowly chipping away at these problems. They have not only made remarkable progress but they have transformed aspects of human rights law and activism beyond their applicability to women and gender alone.

As the idea of using human rights laws and legal approaches to address women's rights has expanded, however, the dilemma described by MacKinnon continues to affect opinions about whether relying on the law to create beneficial social and political change for women is worthwhile. For instance, at the 2007 annual conference for the National Women's Studies Association (NWSA), the only sessions dealing explicitly with human rights laws and principles in the context of gender questioned the role of human rights law in advancing women's human rights in women's real lives more than they embraced using the law for this purpose (NWSA 2007: 113). Yet, the same sessions also acknowledge implicitly the power of international human rights laws and principles (NWSA 2007: 113).

Student approaches can reflect this dilemma, as well. For instance, in classes that I teach with two different groups of students, undergraduate women's studies and international affairs students, as well as law students, students are often suspicious of the role that law and legal theory, especially international law and legal theory, play in women's everyday lives, or they are hypercritical and overly focused on the obstacles to changing the law so it will better support women's human rights. In addition, students' understanding of these obstacles can be overblown or inaccurate, and they are generally unaware of either the methods that have been created to overcome those obstacles or the transformative effects of those methods. Students are thereby discouraged from seeing the ways in which they also can use the law to promote women's human rights and seek solutions to the problems that prevent women's rights from being fully realized.

From an educational standpoint, these dynamics are problematic because they may give students an unbalanced or incomplete view of women's human rights generally. From an activist perspective, they are downright distressing because they discourage students from joining efforts towards greater actualization of women's human rights in women's everyday lives or, if students do join those efforts, cause them to discount or dismiss a powerful factor in the success of those efforts. In an attempt to address these problematic phenomena, this chapter discusses a series of pedagogical strategies designed to promote students' abilities to view human rights law as an instrument of beneficial change for women, although not the only or a perfect one. Drawing from a group of courses designed to help create lawyers, potential lawyers, activists, and citizens who understand the opportunities and limits of human rights law in the context of gender, this chapter explores ways to encourage students to use the law in effective ways that will improve the everyday lives of real women and to see the opportunities to do this that constantly surround them.

Critical legal thinking and theorizing to identify and address women's human rights problems

Creating change must begin with proper identification of the problems, a process that is always more difficult than anticipated. In my classes, students experience a range of difficulties in identifying and analyzing the problems, many of which are based in myths or misunderstandings about women's human rights law (both domestic and international) and related issues. Among the undergraduates, in particular, there is only a partial understanding of how the law actually structures women's everyday lives and the key role that it plays in patriarchal systems. Among the law students, there is the opposite tendency to limit one's perspective to the law alone and to forget that law is closely linked to and imbued with politics, whether they be electoral, identity, or some other kind. Moreover, both groups share a number of myths and misconceptions, including the idea that human rights is an international, but not a domestic, issue, as well as a lack of awareness of how the law itself is a patriarchal institution, and quite an obstinate one at that.

None of these approaches is accurate and, more importantly, none of them is particularly effective in promoting women's human rights in a way that actualizes those rights in the real lives of women. Therefore, the first pedagogical task is to shift these understandings in a more politically useful direction by making visible the law's traditionally oppressive role in women's lives and demonstrating how women's human rights activists and attorneys have created new legal approaches that seek to dismantle this oppressive role in a manner that will improve women's lives.

In an undergraduate course that I developed and teach with Meredith Rathbone, an attorney colleague, virtually the entire course is built around encouraging students to view the law itself from a critical viewpoint. Entitled "Gender, Oppression, Liberation and Global Laws," "Gender and Global Laws" for short, the course looks at how the law has been used in the context of gender as a tool of oppression and as a tool of liberation and assesses law's effectiveness as a tool for creating social and political change for women. Ultimately, the central lesson and skill we hope our students will learn and develop is how to examine the law critically to see if, in any given situation, it can help or hurt women, and whether it is the best way to achieve beneficial change for women. With an awareness of the fact that many of these students take the course because they are considering or have already decided to go to law school, we have designed the course in the hopes that both the future lawyers and those not intending to become lawyers will see the opportunities and develop some skills to promote women's human rights in and out of the legal profession.

Talking about every method used to encourage students to be critical about the law as a change agent in the context of gender is beyond the scope of this chapter. However, it is possible to use an example or two to give a flavor of how the course seeks to achieve its goals. For instance, one of the earlier topics of the course deals with the institution of marriage and the role the law plays in structuring this key institution. Marriage and family law is one of the areas where the law is most involved in people's, especially women's, everyday lives, yet it is paradoxically also one of the places where the law is most invisible to those who do not think critically about it. Our experience suggests that the undergraduates who take our classes understand that the law is important to women on relatively discreet issues such as domestic violence, but they are completely unaware of the role that legal institutions, particularly of marriage, play and have played in structuring patriarchal societies and insuring women's subjugation to male authority.

For these reasons, we begin by introducing students to legal sources that demonstrate how marriage operates to control women's reproduction and economic status by focusing on what marriage meant for women's legal status under the common law principles inherited by the United States and other common law countries from England. In the U.S., prior to the legal reforms of marriage that began in the mid-1800s, when a woman and a man got married, for legal purposes they became one person, and that person was the man (*Gubernat* 1995: 132). Women lost all ability to own property, to contract, and to engage in other economic activities. In case this extinguishment of their legal personhood gave women incentives to refuse to marry, laws like those dealing with the naming of children made sure marriage seemed a more attractive alternative to, for instance, risking bearing a child "out of wedlock." In light of the sexual vulnerability of women who lived without a man's "protection" and the lack of reliable birth control at the time, naming laws ensuring that children born to unmarried women would be labeled as bastards, denied property, and otherwise stigmatized (*Gubernat* 1995) could be extremely powerful ways to encourage women to marry despite the institution's drawbacks.

This remains an amazingly hidden history and, although it may seem as if a century and a half of legal reform in the U.S. would make it largely irrelevant, traces of this history remain to the present day and make it disturbingly relevant here and now. In addition, in many countries, women are still fighting the battles that U.S. women began in a much earlier period. By drawing attention to the history of marriage in the U.S. and linking it conceptually to current laws, both foreign and domestic, the course demonstrates how marriage and the law are intertwined in such a way as to form a crucial building block of patriarchal oppression.

Not to lose a full half of the picture, however, the course also demonstrates the ways in which marriage as a legal institution has acted and continues to act as a tool of oppression in other contexts. By examining the history of anti-miscegenation laws, the course introduces students to materials that contrast laws made to forbid marriage between blacks and whites (*Roldan* 1933; *Loving* 1967), versus laws that encouraged white men to marry propertied Native American women and Chicanas (Berger 1997). Asking students to think through the reasons behind these different approaches makes visible the role marriage law has played in racial subjugation in the U.S., by adopting and building upon the oppressive tactics used in the context of gender, to insure that property and power were concentrated in the hands of white men.

Although it is surprising how much many law students can benefit from the same type of critical focus on the law that we encourage in "Gender and Global Laws," in general, a different invisibility problem operates among many of the law students I have taught or with whom I've conversed about women's human rights. These students can focus on the law almost exclusively, often ignoring the connections between law and politics, as well as the ways in which the law influences everyday life as much through its silences or failures to act as it does through its pronouncements and affirmative acts (Skwiot 2008).

In fact, silences and failures to act are crucial, especially in the context of gender. Therefore, it is important to find ways to make them as visible as the pronouncements and affirmative acts. Accordingly, in a law school course entitled "International Women's Human Rights," I spend a lot of time focusing on the development of certain legal theories that highlight the law's tendency to be silent or inactive, to the detriment of women's human rights, and the efforts of women's rights attorneys and activists to hold the law and those who make and enforce the law accountable for these failures.

One of the theories that is particularly helpful in making these dynamics visible is what I think of as the feminist theory of state responsibility. This theory and its development can be attributed in large part to women's human rights activists and attorneys and addresses one of the most difficult theoretical and practical problems of invisibility and obstacles to achieving women's human rights. As such, it is an extremely helpful example for making visible two generally invisible phenomena: (1) how the law's silences and failures to act can make it very difficult to use the law to protect and promote women's human rights, and (2) how determined activists can intervene, surface the silences and failures, and create new theories that have truly transformative powers.

In international law, the invisibility of women and gender is more complicated than just that women are rarely heads of state or appointed to international bodies, although these are important factors. In fact, women and gender are marginalized by the very structure of international law (Charlesworth et al. 1991). International law deals with nation-states and their behaviors, relationships, rights, and obligations vis-à-vis each other. Traditionally, private individuals are not included at all in this structure. Granted, this approach has changed somewhat because international human rights law assumes that a state can be obligated to treat its own citizens in a certain way and that private individuals may complain about violations of their rights by states to an international tribunal.

However, protecting women's human rights is still more difficult under this structure. For one thing, there is a relative absence of articulated rights in international human rights treaties that apply to how women experience rights violations. For another, violations of men's human rights are more likely to occur in the public sphere at the hands of the state or state actors. Furthermore, because international law is the law of states, it is public law, and for a state to have violated an individual's human rights, the state itself must be responsible in some way for the violation. Women's rights are most often violated by private actors in the private sphere, making those rights hard, if not impossible, to redress under traditional international legal theories and approaches.

The best example of these phenomena is violence against women. Violence against women is not explicitly named as a violation of women's human rights in any international treaty, including the Convention to Eliminate All Forms of Discrimination Against Women. While this problem has been addressed through interpretation and declarations by international bodies (CEDAW 1992; DEVAW 1993), this occurred relatively recently and largely as a result of activism by the global women's movement. In addition, these declarations, interpretations, and even a few new treaties on violence against women cannot make up for the silence on violence against women in the older, more established treaties such as the International Covenant on Civil and Political Rights, which enjoy more signatories, wider acceptance by the international community, and greater effectiveness as human rights law. Under these older treaties, forms of violence against women such as domestic violence present a stark state responsibility problem. A domestic violence survivor's human rights are most often being violated by her husband, a private individual who is not being violent towards his wife at the urging of the state or to fulfill any state purpose.

As can be seen from this example, the traditional approach to state responsibility presents a multilayered problem of numerous silences and failures to act, and in reality leaves the vast majority of the human rights violations that women experience totally invisible to and unaddressed by international law. Women's human rights activists and attorneys have therefore set about changing this traditional approach by making the state's silences and failures to act themselves violations of international law.

Dorothy Thomas and Michele Beasley were two of the earliest women's human rights activists to articulate this new approach. In an article entitled "Domestic Violence as a Human Rights Issue," they use the *Velasquez Rodriguez* case decided by the Inter-American Court of Human Rights to advance a theory under which a state can be held responsible for human rights violations committed by a private person (Beasley and Thomas 1995).

In the *Velasquez Rodriguez* case, the Inter-American Court on Human Rights held Honduras responsible for violating the American Convention on Human Rights due to disappearances of citizens suspected to be carried out by the Honduras military. With only circumstantial evidence of the military's involvement, the Court held that Honduras was responsible even if it did not directly carry out the disappearances. Because the state was not taking any action to prevent, investigate, or punish whoever was carrying out the disappearances, the Court said, Honduras was condoning and encouraging such violence and was indirectly responsible for it (*Velasquez* 1988).

Thomas and Beasley took the state obligation to prevent, investigate, and punish created by *Velasquez* and applied it to domestic violence. Because domestic violence is overwhelmingly directed at women, they said, states that fail to prevent, investigate, and punish domestic violence commit sex discrimination in violation of human rights treaties. By not preventing, investigating, and punishing private actors who are committing crimes, the state is condoning and encouraging that harm. Furthermore, because the state is condoning and encouraging criminal activity that overwhelmingly harms one sex, its failure to act is discriminatory on the basis of sex. Therefore, domestic violence is a violation of women's human rights for which states are responsible under every treaty that prohibits sex discrimination (Beasley and Thomas 1995).

This theory of state responsibility has been increasingly adopted by international courts and tribunals. Most close to home, the Inter-American Commission applied it in a case called *Maria da Penha v. Brazil* (*Maria da Penha* 2000), and is currently considering a case against the United States. The case against the United States has been brought by Jessica Gonzales, a woman whose abusive husband kidnapped and killed their three young daughters. Ms. Gonzales was separated from her husband and had a civil protection order that directed police to arrest her husband if he violated its terms. On the night of the murders, Mr. Gonzales kidnapped his three daughters, and the police refused to enforce the CPO, despite Ms. Gonzales's frequent and increasingly urgent pleas for their help. Mr. Gonzales was eventually shot and killed by police when he opened fire on the police station. Ms. Gonzales sued the police department for violations of her due process rights under the U.S. Constitution. The U.S. Supreme Court denied her claim, saying that there is no due process right to enforcement of a civil protection order (*Castle Rock* 2005).

Ms. Gonzales has now filed a complaint at the Inter-American Commission and prevailed on part of her claims (*Gonzales* 2007). If she wins her case, which I expect she will, the international approach to state responsibility, applied to U.S. facts, will stand in stark contrast to the prevailing approach used by our own lawmakers.

As such, the *Gonzales* case is a wonderful teaching tool. First, it shows the links between legal theories and women's lives, and not only how theories can be changed and then applied to fix real problems for real women, but also how it is sometimes necessary to deal with the theoretical in order to affect the practical. Second, the state responsibility discussion, and the use of the *Gonzales* case to illustrate it, are helpful in dealing with other persistent myths held by students, and undoubtedly many others, about women's human rights. For instance, there is a persistent attitude among students that human rights are an international, but not a domestic, issue. Inherent in these attitudes are two assumptions: (1) that the United States is far ahead of the rest of the world when it comes to human rights, including women's rights; and (2) that the United States' legal approach to rights is therefore truer or better than those of the rest of the world. The *Gonzales* case debunks both of these ideas, by showing that the United States' is only one legal approach of many and that the United States' approach is in fact one that is damaging to women and actually out of step with the rest of the world's. By contrasting the definitions of state responsibility increasingly used by international tribunals with the definitions of our own Supreme Court, *Gonzales* demonstrates that human rights violations are not something that only happen in other countries and that there is nothing inherently "true" or "right" about the legal choices and theories that have developed in the United States.

Promoting women's human rights through building practical skills for activism

As powerful as the theoretical, critical, and analytical thinking encouraged by such methods as examining the history and purposes behind the legal institution of marriage and the feminist legal theory of state responsibility can be, educating students to promote women's human rights in a way that makes those rights real for real women cannot just stop there. Instead, if we believe in using education to create activists and citizens who not only understand the opportunities and limits of human rights law in the context of gender, but also will use the law in effective ways that will improve the everyday lives of real women, we must incorporate practical training and skill building in women's human rights coursework.

Once again, it is beyond the scope of this chapter to give more than a taste of some of the pedagogical tools that can be used to introduce students to practical issues and skills that are helpful in the world of women's human rights activism. In addition, such strategies vary considerably based on the student population and inter-discipline in which the course is taught, even more so than the afore-mentioned strategies designed to encourage critical thinking. In the undergraduate context, students are often more diverse in terms of educational focus, plans for their lives post-graduation, and certainty about those plans than are law students. In addition, even the ones who are pre-professionally oriented are less focused on skill-acquisition or how their classroom learning and work life (post-graduation) might be linked than students seeking to enter a profession. Therefore, assignments and class activities designed to encourage activism on women's human rights can be unique in students' experiences, be broader in focus and allow for more creativity than some of the strategies used in the law school context. For instance, in "Gender and Global Laws," my co-teacher designed an assignment in which students take a particular issue discussed in the class and construct an "Action Plan" for how they would try to create beneficial social and political changes for women and/or other gender minorities on that issue. The assignment is explicit that the action plan need not choose a legal method to create change, and in the past students have presented plans ranging from improving stalking legislation to creating a blueprint for a federal subsidized housing program for domestic violence survivors to starting an educational program responding to sexual assault on college campuses.

In contrast, as students studying to enter a profession, law students are naturally thinking to some extent about how to translate what they are learning in the classroom to what they hope to do out of the classroom. Nevertheless, their views on what they can do with the knowledge gained in the classroom is often limited to such established lawyering activities as engaging in courtroom litigation or drafting legal documents, so the challenge is to get them to think about myriad options for using the law outside those traditional legal settings, and the connections between the two approaches. A course designed to encourage activism must seek to broaden their views on how to use their knowledge of the law, both as lawyers expanding their skills beyond traditional lawyering skills or adapting and using traditional skills in new settings, and as citizens with unique and powerful skills who want to create positive change in the area of women's human rights.

This dual purpose means designing course assignments and activities that encourage students to think beyond what they will do in paid legal practice or other employment, as well as to develop skills that will be helpful in legal practice related to promoting women's human rights. Both of these goals are related in the sense that legal skills and knowledge can be quite helpful in non-legal activist settings, while women's human rights lawyers must often have a range of skills that include, but are not limited to, traditional legal skills, because so much of the promotion of women's human rights uses the law outside courtrooms, legislatures, and other legal bodies.

Returning to the example of *Gonzales*, for instance, winning the case will only be the first part of the battle for it to mean anything to real women, most specifically domestic violence survivors holding civil protection orders in the United States. Because the Inter-American Commission, like most international tribunals, has little enforcement power, the power of a case like *Gonzales* will primarily be based in its use as a political tool. Used effectively, the case could help lead to changes in U.S. law by building support for a different approach to state responsibility; changes which will have a real effect on women's lives.

For these reasons, use of the *Gonzales* case need not and indeed should not be limited to teaching the legal theory of state responsibility. Instead, a course designed to encourage student activism should also ask students to think about how to maximize the persuasive impact of the case as a political organizing tool. Using examples from organizations like Equality Now (Equality Now 2008), classes can discuss such methods as how to create media campaigns about the case and its usefulness as a lobbying tool.

For example, in my International Women's Human Rights class, I assign a previous U.S. Supreme Court case that presents similar state responsibility issues as *Gonzales* (*United States* 2000), and split the class into two parts. One group is instructed to act as lawyers for the complaining woman in bringing her case before an international tribunal. They are encouraged to think about such traditional lawyering issues as which tribunal to choose (based on factors like the treaties to which the United States is a party and the effectiveness of the remedies the tribunal can provide), which claims they could bring, and how they would argue their case before the tribunal. The other group acts as members of a women's non-profit or NGO using the case as a grassroots organizing tool, and they are expected to think through and create ways to use the case in such non-legal fora as the media, public education campaigns, citizen action (protest marches, letter-writing campaigns, boycotts, etc.), and the formation of non-profit organizations. In this way, students both apply traditional legal skills in the women's human rights arena and get some practice thinking about the kinds of non-legal skills that are useful to both lawyers and activists in the field.

Of course, in traditional classroom-based seminar courses such as both of those discussed thus far, there are limits to the skills-building pedagogical methods that can be used. Therefore, it is important to consider methods that reach beyond the traditional classroom through combined theoretical and practical pedagogies used in various forms of experiential education such as service-learning in the undergraduate context and clinical education in the law school context. These methods generally combine some sort of unpaid work experience in a public interest area (sometimes under the supervision of a person outside the university faculty, sometimes under faculty supervision, and sometimes under a combination of the two) with academic work in a particular subject or practice area and some reflective method to link the classroom and work experience (National Service Learning Clearinghouse 2008; Ogilvy 2006). As such, just by virtue of the experiential aspect of this type of coursework, students are contributing their volunteer labor to the activist work being undertaken by the organization or project where they are working. However, beyond just this work, these courses are generally designed to inspire students to engage in such work even after the course is complete.

From a women's human rights lawyering perspective, experiential education is particularly important. This is true even in a domestic context and when the fight for these rights manifests in the most traditionally legal way (like in the *Gonzales* case), because the promotion of women's human rights requires so much work that is essentially political, involving organizing and coalition-building, as a partner, a preface, or a predicate to the legal work. Common sense and experience recognize that organizing, media campaigns, and other such political methods require specific skills that are more easily taught and more effectively learned through experiential education.

In an international context, this is even more true, since it is extremely difficult, if not impossible, to understand and promote women's human rights ethically and effectively in a particular local setting when sitting in a classroom or working in a location far removed from that setting. Especially if students and teachers are dealing with women's human rights topics and the local manifestations of those topics in a context where the students and teachers are outsiders, the kind of activist role they can take will be and should be limited by their outsider status.

For example, as a law student in the International Women's Human Rights Clinic at Georgetown University Law Center, I participated in a fact-finding mission on domestic violence in Ghana. Students and faculty traveled for one week to Ghana to conduct the trip. The time prior to the trip was spent preparing by conducting preliminary research on the topic, practicing such skills as interviewing in a simulated setting, and learning all the students could about Ghana and its legal system. The time after the trip was spent writing a human rights report with the group's conclusions regarding the human rights violations it investigated (Cantalupo et al. 2006). As the final report demonstrates, the fact that many domestic violence cases in Ghana are "mediated," often without the full agreement of the domestic violence survivor, was an issue of grave concern to the fact-finding team (Cantalupo et al. 2006: 576–578), and one that emerged as a problem as early as the very first day of interviews conducted in Ghana. Yet the team was completely unaware when preparing for the trip in the United States of the mediation phenomenon. Had the students and faculty simply studied the issues from the United States, this crucial insight about how women's human rights in Ghana were being violated would never have been understood.

Similar lessons have emerged from my most recent teaching experience. I have recently begun teaching and supervising American law students in an intensive summer session experiential learning course focused on women's rights in China. In the course, the students conduct international and comparative research projects for women's NGOs in China through a combination of research in the United States and in China.

The semester begins with an intensive seminar, held primarily in the United States, where the students learn as much as possible about Chinese law, the status of women and girls in China, and international and comparative laws on women's human rights. Next, they travel to China for approximately three weeks to interview various experts and to learn about the laws and surrounding circumstances affecting women in China in their project area (such as sex discrimination in employment or domestic violence). Based on the understanding they develop of how that particular women's rights issue manifests in China, the students then research legal approaches used in other countries to address similar women's rights problems. They write a final report including their understanding of the situation in China and the results of their comparative research and give that report to the partner NGO to use in its local work to address women's rights. Along the way, they learn and practice many of the skills needed by human rights and rule of law attorneys.

As I learned as a student in Ghana, learning about the complexities of such a different country and legal system from so far away and almost entirely from an academic, outsider's perspective was insufficient to truly understand the situation in China or to make our project work useful to our partners. The law in particular is so different between the United States and China that it feels nearly unknowable from halfway around the world. While a mere three weeks in China was certainly insufficient to close this gap, the gap was made significantly smaller by the students' having access to both the knowledge and perspectives of experts inside China.

Moreover, the nuanced understanding of how these women's issues manifest in China is absolutely necessary to the comparative stage of the students' research. Without this understanding, students cannot focus on the comparative legal approaches that will be most useful to addressing the issues in China. For instance, one of the issues that emerged in the context of women and employment is that there are significant evidentiary difficulties to women proving that they have been victims of sex discrimination in the workplace, including gaps in Chinese contract law, weak or non-existent subpoena powers on the parts of courts, and a lack of protection for plaintiffs and witnesses against retaliation. Like the situation with mediation of domestic violence cases in Ghana, this issue was not clear to us when we were simply reading about Chinese women's employment issues while in the United States. However, once we understood it, the students could draw from the extensive evidentiary rules that have developed in the United States related to cases involving discrimination in employment.

In addition, the comparative research portion of the course compels students to link and critically assess different legal approaches, not just uncritically to believe their own country's approach is the best. Therefore, a final lesson that emerges from the course is an enhanced ability to reflect on the merits and demerits of our own laws and the approaches taken to these issues in the United States. We have hardly solved all the problems related to these issues in our own country, and China's differences from the United States can cause us to think more critically about the ways we in the U.S. have addressed these same problems, to reflect on the advantages and disadvantages of our approaches, and to create improvements in our own laws.

Ultimately, all of these courses end with the same basic lesson: that law, both domestic and international, is merely one tool among many that can be used to improve the lives of women. Understanding that the law has often operated more to oppress women than to liberate them and learning to critically analyze and assess its advantages and disadvantages as a tool of beneficial social and political change can help one to use it most effectively. Demonstrating how knotty theoretical problems with damaging practical effects for women can be changed through creating transformative legal theories shows the link between theory and actualizing women's human rights. Focusing on a case like *Gonzales* and encouraging students to think about applications of human rights law here in the United

States helps give students ways to make international human rights laws and norms relevant here and encourages them to be activists around these issues even in their own backyards. Finally, providing opportunities not just to study but also to experience working on these issues, both domestically and internationally, gives students varying degrees of practice and builds important skills for activism in a range of contexts. These are just a few strategies for encouraging students not only to "think globally" but also to "act locally" *and* "act globally" to make human rights real in women's real lives.

Bibliography

Beasley, M. and Thomas, D. (1995) "Domestic Violence as a Human Rights Issue," *Albany Law Review*, 58: 1119–1134.

Berger, B.R. (1997) "After Pocahontas: Indian women and the law, 1830 to 1934," *American Indian Law Review*, 21: 1–39.

Cantalupo, N., Vollendorf Martin, L., Pak, K., and Shin, S. (2006) "Domestic Violence in Ghana: the open secret," *Georgetown Journal of Gender & the Law*, 7: 531–597.

Castle Rock v. Gonzales (2005) 545 U.S. 74.

Charlesworth, H., Chinkin, C., and Wright, S. (1991) "Feminist Approaches to International Law," *American Journal of International Law*, 85: 613–645.

Committee on the Elimination of Discrimination Against Women (CEDAW) (1992) *General Recommendation No. 19*. Online. <http://www.un.org/womenwatch/daw/cedaw/recommendations/recomm.htm#recom19> (accessed 1 June 2008).

Declaration on the Elimination of Violence Against Women G.A. (DEVAW) (1993) res. 48/104, 48 U.N. GAOR Supp. (No. 49) at 217, U.N. Doc. A/48/49. Online. <http://www1.umn.edu/humanrts/instree/e4devw.htm> (accessed 1 June 2008).

Equality Now (2008) "About Equality Now." Online. <http://www.equalitynow.org/english/about/about_en.html> (accessed 1 June 2008).

Gonzales v. United States (2007) Petition 1490–05, Report No. 52/07, Inter-Am.C.H.R., OEA/Ser/L/V/II.128 Doc. 19. Online. <https://www.law.columbia.edu/null?&exclusive=filemgr.download&file_id=13526&rtcontentdisposition=filename%3DAdmissibility%20Decision%2010.4.07.pdf> (accessed 1 June 2008).

Gubernat v. Deremer (1995) 140 N.J. 120.

Loving v. Virginia (1967) 388 U.S. 1.

MacKinnon, C. (1991) "Reflections on Sex Equality Under Law," *Yale Law Journal*, 100: 1281–1328.

Maria da Penha v. Brazil (2000) Case 12.051, Report No. 54/01, Inter-Am. C.H.R., OEA/Ser.L/V/II.111 Doc. 20 rev. at 704. Online. <http://www1.umn.edu/humanrts/cases/54–01.html> (accessed 1 June 2008)

National Service Learning Clearinghouse (2008) "What is Service Learning?" Online. <http://www.servicelearning.org/what-service-learning> (accessed 11 July 2010).

National Women's Studies Association (NWSA) (2007) "Paper Session: human rights, public policy, and feminism," *Past Debates, Present Possibilities, Future Feminisms: a women's and gender studies conference program booklet*.

Ogilvy, J. P. (2006) *An Oral History of Clinical Legal Education, Part I: seeds of change* (documentary film) Washington, DC: Living Memories Productions.

Roldan v. Los Angeles County (1993) 129 Cal. App. 267.

Skwiot, Rick (2008) "Faculty Profile: Laura Rosenbury Family Dynamics: how the law interacts with everyday life," *Washington University Law Magazine*, 2(1): 12–13.

United States v. Morrison (2000) 529 U.S. 598.

Velasquez Rodriguez Case (1988) Judgment of 29 July 1988, Inter-Am.Ct.H.R. (Ser. C) No. 4. Online. HTTP: <http://www1.umn.edu/humanrts/iachr/b_11_12d.htm> (accessed 1 June 2008)

Part IV

Crossing legal landscapes

13 Seduced by information, contaminated by power

Women's rights as a global panopticon

Saida Hodžić

Taking seriously the notion that human rights are not disinterested affirmations of humanity but are thickly saturated by politics, this chapter shows how the regime-like character of women's rights monitoring compromises the possibility of supporting what "rights' stand for. I examine how the work of the international institutions established to support women's rights globally is characterized by the imbrications of rights within the global political economy. My specific site of analysis is the process of CEDAW[1] monitoring at the United Nations and its effects on women's rights advocacy in Ghana. I explore the ways in which the mechanism that is supposed to safeguard women's rights instead induces polyvalent effects, some of which compromise those rights. This chapter will show that the monitoring process partakes in a disciplinary regime in which global inequalities are given another run, resulting in a reinforced gridlock of positions that ultimately fails to support Ghanaian women's rights advocacy.

Building on this material, I suggest a shift in scholarship on women's rights by highlighting the linkages between the theoretical critique of women's rights and the practical consequences for realization of rights in particular contexts. This chapter addresses two fields of scholarship that are rarely in conversation with one another—literature that examines human rights critically[2] and literature that advocates for them.[3] As Grewal writes, for those who take on the task of critique, "the concept of human rights becomes . . . an object for analysis *rather than* a goal to endorse" (Grewal 2005: vii; emphasis mine). I see the challenge of critically examining women's rights in a different light: Can we subject women's rights to careful critique that entails an analysis of power and capital without collapsing the voice of critique and the voice of dismissal? In this chapter, I take human rights as an object of analysis while endorsing the goal of realizing women's rights to which Ghanaian activists and nongovernmental organizations (NGOs) are committed. Moreover, I show that these two concerns are interrelated and argue that there is a causal linkage between the problematic, regime-like character of women's rights and the realization of women's rights in practice.

CEDAW monitoring as the women's rights regime

Before I turn to an examination of the regime-like character of CEDAW monitoring, I will offer a brief introduction to the archeology of the monitoring process—its premises, intended purpose, mechanisms, and self-representation. The CEDAW monitoring Committee is the foremost UN institution concerned with protecting and securing women's rights globally. The main premise of the CEDAW monitoring process is that an international body is necessary for overseeing the implementation of the Convention and that governments will make stronger efforts to secure women's rights if subjected to international scrutiny.

The process is meant to "promote change in the government by forcing it to review domestic law, policy, and practice" (Merry 2006: 84). Country reports are the main way in which a state demonstrates its efforts to implement the Convention's provisions. These reports are read and evaluated by the CEDAW Committee—an international body of 23 members, commonly called "experts." Elected by national governments of countries that have signed CEDAW, experts come from different regions of the world and have backgrounds in women's rights work. This equality of representation is central to the self-understanding of the Committee as an international body, rather than a Western one. The "experts" appraise the countries' compliance by examining "the progress made in the implementation of the present Convention."[4]

While the UN would likely disagree with this characterization, CEDAW monitoring, I will argue, is also a disciplinary regime in which the support of women's rights is intimately tied to the exercise of power. In her ethnography of CEDAW monitoring, Merry hints at this dynamic by referring to the monitoring process as "UN surveillance" (Merry 2006: 88). At the more general level, Grewal sees the entire conceptual apparatus of human rights as a "regime of truth" that "mobilizes all kinds of knowledges and practices—disciplinary, sovereign, military, and governmental" and necessitates "particular kinds of language, bureaucratic apparatus, surveys, statistical analysis, photographic evidence, and psychological information" (Grewal 2005: viii–ix). This chapter is an attempt to analyze in more detail what makes the CEDAW monitoring process a surveillance mechanism and a regime. How does the CEDAW monitoring resemble a women's rights panopticon? What are its characteristics and effects?

A state-centric apparatus

Given its commitments to the universality of rights in the age of post-sovereignty, CEDAW monitoring is surprisingly state-centric. In fact, it is often forgotten that the UN is an international system, and that nation-states are main participants in the regime. CEDAW's state-centric structure stands in sharp contrast to the reality of a largely nongovernmental (in the largest sense of this word) struggle for women's rights in much of the world. NGOs, activists, and coalitions are the locally relevant players who are at the forefront of articulating women's rights and advocating for them. Governments often trail behind them, or stand in the way of their advocacy, as we shall see was the case with Ghana.[5] Hence, non-governmental actors are the actual constitutive other to the international women's rights regime.

The apparatus of CEDAW monitoring allows only accredited NGOs to participate in the monitoring, and that to a limited extent. NGOs are invited to write "shadow reports," providing alternative information to the government-issued report. However, the participation of NGOs is also limited by geo-politics in the sense that NGOs that get access to UN meetings are largely from the US and Europe. As Merry writes, "the sharp resource disparities between North and South radically limit the ability of poorer NGOs to participate in the process" (Merry 2006: 52). Only a few Ghanaian NGOs working on women's rights have the requisite "consultative status" with the UN. This is another way in which the global political economy shapes the character of the CEDAW monitoring process.

The contributions of NGOs are also impeded by the structure of the bureaucratic apparatus. NGOs cannot attend the actual country hearing or participate in the ensuing discussion. Their contributions are restricted to a closed meeting with the CEDAW Committee, at which they can suggest questions that the Committee should ask of the country delegations. However, the possibility to do so is constrained by the fact that these meetings last only 10 minutes and that all NGOs that wish to participate must coordinate sharing this time in advance (United Nations undated: 3). In addition, NGO reports and oral remarks must be submitted well ahead of time and in written copy to all experts on the team.

Liberal dialogue vs. surveillance

The second characteristic of the international women's rights regime is the discrepancy between its self-representation as a form of a liberal communication and its actual exercise of power and surveillance mechanisms. The CEDAW Committee understands the monitoring process as a form of a constructive "dialogue," "discussion," and a "sharing of ideas" (Merry 2006: 81, 82, 84).[6] In other words, CEDAW represents itself as grounded in a set of liberal and democratic mechanisms that include a free exchange of information and open communication. Yet, CEDAW monitoring is governed by discursive rules that set limits not only on who can participate in which form, but also on what can be said and what kind of language can be used.

The monitoring process may *look* like a dialogue, in that it entails a back and forth communication. Yet, this characterization belies the unequal positioning of the participants as well as the exercise of power by the UN. The very structure of exchange between countries and CEDAW experts precludes a dialogue in that there is a strict communicative division of labor and authority: the UN experts ask questions and countries are to provide answers. As Ghana's case makes evident, these roles are fixed—the countries cannot ask questions or make inquiries.

Ghana's 2006 hearing was preceded by a year-long set of written questioning by the CEDAW Committee.[7] After receiving Ghana's 74-page report, the

CEDAW Committee demanded more information and a greater level of information, detailing 29 specific inquiries that Ghana should elaborate on. After Ghana provided a response to these queries and participated in the hearing in New York City, the Committee submitted their final comments to Ghana, exercising the right of having the last word. In many ways then, the monitoring process resembles an interrogation, not a dialogue.

The discursive rules foster certain kinds of statements and prohibit others. For example, direct confrontations and conflicts are discouraged. Merry writes that criticisms are "rarely explicit" and that "experts speak of 'concerns' or of the need for more information" (Merry 2006: 85). When NGOs are explicitly critical, they are seen as "irritants" (Merry 2006: 51).

The dialogue at the monitoring process is also constrained by the restrictive parameters on what counts as "information." The monitoring proceeds according to discursive rules about what can be said and discussed. It functions like a court in the sense that outside evidence is not permitted. The main basis for monitoring are the country reports. Other kinds of knowledge are excluded from formal consideration and thus unauthorized. In particular, the rules preclude experts from participating in the monitoring of their own countries. In other words, those with the most intimate and thorough knowledge of the country in question cannot partake in the monitoring in any official capacity. This limitation of "information" to official sources is particularly problematic given that the experts are not expected to have in-depth knowledge about each country, nor allowed to discuss information that is not shared by everyone. Put more provocatively, the monitoring is a court in which the judges have limited knowledge and mainly listen to the defendant.

Fetishizing information: the productive power of the women's rights regime

The third characteristic of the women's rights regime is its reliance on information and the production of a desire for information. The evolution of the international women's rights regime as a form of governance characterized by a focus on information began at the onset of the UN decade for women. Starting in the 1980s, "conferences aimed at producing documents became a dominant genre" (Riles 2000: 32). In addition, fact-finding has become "one of the principal competencies of the UN and other intergovernmental institutions" (Riles 2000: 179).

One of the most vexing effects of CEDAW monitoring is that it has helped foster the fetishization of information. The more information a country gives to the CEDAW Committee, the more detailed and thorough questioning it receives in response. As a result, country reports are never fully sufficient—it is inscribed in the process that the Committee will always demand more information.

Riles's theory of the linkages between networking and governance by fact helps us understand the larger phenomenon of the information-based regime of women's rights. Riles explains that the "precise purpose of information exchange" is considered irrelevant in this type of governance (Riles 2000: 50). Information, ranging from reports and manifestos to newsletters, is seen as valuable in its own right. In fact, women's rights advocates have developed a normative framework for evaluating information in terms of aesthetics, not in terms of use-value.

However, while it still holds true that information is seen as valuable in its own right, the criteria for judging the quality of information are in fact in flux. The monitoring is getting sharper by trial and error, and the countries that present most detailed information help guide this shift. Since the Committee receives ever-increasing amounts of information, it recalculates what to ask of the countries with each generation of reports. Countries must learn to navigate this shifting terrain of continually revised criteria. As we shall see later, the Committee is no longer fascinated by information alone, but now demands information about specific achievements in women's rights realization.

Equally important, producing information is not merely a top-down imposition, but a process that elicits commitment and "truly engages participants' collective passions" (Riles 2000: 57). Riles describes activists as being "fascinated by the way in which language convinces" and as devoting "considerable time to the close analysis of language and design" (Riles 2000: 66). Put in less charitable terms, information has become a fetish. CEDAW monitoring is one of the crucial nodes in the international women's rights regime that has contributed to this outcome.

By emphasizing the eliciting of commitment, Riles tries to show that the UN exercises productive power over member states (Riles 2000). This form of international politics of women's rights is not based on outright coercion. Rather, the UN exercises productive power, power to compel countries to comply. In Riles's words, the UN "prompt[s] the member states to action" and "elicit[s] commitment and desire" (Riles 2000: 180, 181).

Building on Riles's theory, I would also like to account for the structures of capital that underlie the productive power she describes. The eliciting of commitment does not occur in a vacuum, but in a structure of global capital in which the failure to perform allegiance to rights may have disastrous consequences. I will show that the commitment of countries to comply with CEDAW needs to be considered within an analysis of political economy and the various forms of capital that circulate within it.

The (symbolic) capital of women's rights: politics of development

The continual effort to embed women's rights within the structures of global capital is the fourth characteristic of the CEDAW regime. The stark inequalities produced by the global political economy are reflected here in the sense that this process has a differential import for countries from the global North and countries from the global South. Some countries may see the CEDAW monitoring process as inconsequential; for Northern countries in particular, the stakes of the monitoring process are low. Northern countries are less invested in comparative evaluations of gender equality since their status as harbingers of women's rights is seldom questioned and since they bear few consequences from the monitoring process. For Southern countries that receive development aid, however, the CEDAW process is a form of accreditation, a symbolic stamp of approval which is directly related to their status in the global public sphere.

Given the alliance between women's rights and capital of development, Southern countries see the stakes of their participation in CEDAW monitoring as high. The stamp of UN approval is seen as bringing economic dividends such as facilitation of "aid, trade relations, and foreign investment" (Merry 2006: 79; see also Cheah 2006: 232). The status of women's rights is particularly important for the politics of development, as countries that seek development assistance are often expected to make efforts to promote gender equality.

Gender equality is even understood as an indicator of "development."[8] The former UN Secretary-General Boutros Boutros-Ghali articulated the logics of this indexing: "To examine the situation of women . . . is to provide both a yardstick, and a measure, of progress. We can see from the situation of women in a society whether power and entitlements are distributed fairly" (quoted in Riles 2000: 180). As a result of this logic, "issues of gender inequality . . . have achieved normative status in development-type programs" (Pigg and Adams 2005: 13).

The CEDAW monitoring process measures the efforts countries are making to achieve gender equality and functions as an important way of evaluating and validating such efforts. Hence, the progress in implementing CEDAW functions as an indicator of the countries' commitment. Put more provocatively, if for the UN, gender equality is an indicator of development, then the attempts to achieve this equality indicate the worthiness of development aid. The pursuit of gender equality signals that a country is approaching development (as well as democracy) in the "right" way, and that it should be supported in its efforts.

The impetus to participate in CEDAW monitoring is also motivated by the vexed assemblage among the notions of development, progress, and modernity. At the symbolic level, invested participation in CEDAW monitoring can rectify notions of "backwardness" associated with "Third world" patriarchy. Like Maussian gifts, country reports are offered to the UN, but bestow value upon the givers (Mauss 1967). CEDAW monitoring thus brings together the contemporary *Realpolitik* of development aid and democracy with the postcolonial legacy of aspirations of modernity and global belonging.

The CEDAW Committee is not a stand-alone regime, but partakes in the larger project of measuring Southern countries' commitments to women's rights and democracy. This measuring is structured according to internal rules of the apparatus and framed by the context of postcolonialism and neoliberal politics of development, in which the recognition and validation by the powerful other have both a symbolic value and ensure access to donor funding.

But so what? I anticipate this question, as the systemic imbrications of women's rights in global political economy may be understood as an irreversible given, or as an abstract problem suitable only for academic debate. In the second part of this chapter, I will argue that the regime-like character of CEDAW monitoring and its imbrications in global capital have practical consequences for women's rights in particular countries. I focus on the case of Ghana, exploring how the fetishization of information shifts the priorities of government agencies working on women's rights, and examining the effects of the monitoring process on the contested case of Ghana's Domestic Violence Bill.[9]

The effects of the CEDAW regime on women's rights in Ghana

The CEDAW process is a part in a larger mosaic of efforts that Ghana makes to maintain its image as what Ghanaians call "gender-progressive."[10] Since Ghana receives (relatively) high levels of development aid, it takes international monitoring processes very seriously. One of its goals in engaging in CEDAW monitoring is to attain the United Nation's approval of its efforts and maintain its position as a donor darling by representing itself as complying with CEDAW and exceeding UN expectations.

Historically speaking, Ghana has placed a lot of emphasis on securing a positive image of the state's women's rights record. Early on, Ghana established new institutions, such as the National Council on Women and Development, passed gender-related laws and policies, ratified CEDAW, and engaged in the CEDAW monitoring process. In the last decade, Ghana has renewed its efforts to brand itself as what Ghanaians call "gender-progressive" by establishing the Ministry of Women and Children's Affairs (MOWAC) in 2001.[11] This move has allowed the government to claim that "gender issues . . . receive attention at the highest level of decision making"[12] and that the Ministry "was a demonstration of political will to address the problem of women's marginalization and raise the issues of women's rights and empowerment to a higher national level" (Mahama 2006: 2).

Ghana's efforts have been largely successful. For example, a UN document from 1999 singles out Ghana as an exemplary country spearheading relevant transformations in order to improve gender equality (see United Nations Economic and Social Council 1999). Furthermore, the UN commended Ghana for not only offering promises, but for providing concrete and "comprehensive time-bound targets and benchmarks or indicators for monitoring" (United Nations Economic and Social Council 1999: 2). In the value scheme of UN information, concrete benchmarks had a high standing, as they pointed to something "measurable."

However, as a result of the shifts in the UN criteria for appraising information that I discuss above, the CEDAW Committee now demands that Ghana provide solid facts about its achievements. While in the past, information about gender-related institutions, laws, and policies was sufficient, the Committee now demands information about their implementation. In the 2006 hearings, the Committee questioned the discrepancy between Ghana's lofty promises and the lack of follow through. While Ghana's report highlighted mechanisms that the government had established, the Committee demanded facts about the outcomes of these mechanisms, asking detailed questions about budget and resources available to MOWAC, law enforcement, and effectiveness of policies and institutions.[13] Ghana has yet to navigate this shift toward more refined information on achievements.

Ghana's inability to provide this new type of information has put pressure on the government to present itself in the best light relying on other kinds of achievements. As we shall later see, Ghana deftly diversified its efforts in presenting itself as a gender-progressive country by appropriating the achievements of NGOs and women's rights activists. Equally troubling is that Ghana may not be able to provide information about measurable achievements because of the gaps between women's rights laws and policies on the one hand and their implementation on the other. While these gaps are usually considered an outcome of "poor governance," I will show that the international evaluative processes are not outside of this equation and argue that CEDAW monitoring contributes to the prioritization of "information" over "implementation."

When reports stand for rights: the practical consequences of the fetish

Given the high stakes of the monitoring process and the symbolic and economic capital attached to it, Ghana is invested in participating in the women's rights regime. For this reason, government officials make the production of information one of their main concerns and foci of activity. As I will explain in more detail, the vexing effect of this orientation is that report writing is not an account of the government's women's rights work, but *the work itself.*

The production of information takes both time and effort. Representatives of the Ghanaian MOWAC were preoccupied with writing the CEDAW report two years before its due date. "We will be very busy next year," Cecilia, a high-ranking representative of MOWAC I interviewed told me in late 2003. "We will be preparing for Beijing+10 and writing reports." The report-writing process comes in the way of other kinds of work on women's rights. As a director of the team charged with implementing MOWAC policies, Cecilia's official task is to oversee the nitty-gritty aspects of implementing government policy. In actuality, however, Cecilia and her colleagues focus on gathering information and writing reports for the UN.

We should reevaluate the significance of labor committed to the monitoring process in light of the high pressure to create an appearance of a gender-progressive state, but low resources committed to this task. As I mentioned above, Cecilia's task is to direct the implementation of gender policies; in other words, her job is to perform the labor that CEDAW is monitoring. However, the labor she dedicates to report-writing comes at the expense of the labor that should be the substantive basis of the reports. In other words, while the information in the country report is supposed to be the mirror of the women's rights situation, the mirror in fact subsumes the "reality" it is meant to reflect on. The CEDAW monitoring process creates a paradoxical situation: one reason why the government of Ghana is hindered from promoting women's rights is because it is compelled to create the appearance that it is doing so. The ever-increasing demand for more information leads to a situation in which production of information takes precedence over programming.[14]

This paradox is evident not only in the work of high-ranking MOWAC officials directly responsible for the reports, but has spectral effects on the micro-level practices of Ghanaian civil servants. One example of interest for this chapter comes from the Ghanaian police work on domestic violence, where gathering information about crimes is seen as a noteworthy achievement while solving them fades in the background. The Ghanaian police's Domestic Violence Victim Support Unit[15] is supposed to "prevent, protect, apprehend and prosecute perpetrators of domestic violence and child abuse."[16] However, while their success with preventing and solving crimes has been elusive,[17] they have been very successful at gathering information. The DOVVSU office in the Upper East region, for example, was adorned with statistics on reported cases of domestic violence, sorted by the category of offence: defilement, indecent assault, child maintenance issues, etc. These numbers were shown on a blackboard displayed proudly at the front of the office, commanding attention of all visitors. Not surprisingly, the blackboard did not contain any information about cases that were resolved successfully.[18]

Why does the Ghanaian police fetishize information? To explain this, I look beyond the spread of international norms and aestheticization of rights to a phenomenon I call the political economy of information. The relationship between the allocation of capital and the gathering of information became apparent in DOVVSU officers' complaints about their dire financial situations. They often bemoaned that they did not even have a police car at their disposal with which they could take women and children to the hospital, a process essential to ensuring care and obtaining medical evidence necessary for successful prosecution. In other words, DOVVSU's ability to follow up on reports of violence hinges on the state's willingness to provide them with necessary capital, which despite its professed commitments, the Ghanaian government does not readily dispense with. In contrast, keeping simple statistics about the numbers of people who filed complaints can be accomplished on a low budget.

Providing statistics is thus an expedient response to a complex situation. The intertwined interests of governments and of the UN make certain kinds of information a fetish. Keeping information limited to statistics about "reported cases" allows the government of Ghana to claim that it pays attention to gendered violence without having to make serious financial investments or reform the structure of social services and law enforcement. At the same time, demanding "information" is an established practice of the women's rights regime that allows the CEDAW experts to systematize their inquiries without having to learn about in-depth problems in each country.

Creative manipulations across scale: negotiating the regime

In my final analysis of the effects of the regime-like character of CEDAW monitoring on women's rights in Ghana, I turn to the struggle over recent domestic violence legislation. We shall see that the monitoring process failed to support the efforts of Ghanaian activists to criminalize marital rape, and that this failure was inscribed in the very structure of the regime.

First, a few words of background information about Ghana's domestic violence legislation. Before the Ghanaian parliament passed the Domestic Violence Act in 2007, the government engaged in a long, protracted, and highly contested battle with women's rights NGOs that had drafted this legislation and lobbied for its passage.[19] The Executive (President Kuffuor and his Cabinet) vehemently opposed this Bill and charged the former Minister of Women and Children's Affairs with the task of campaigning across the country and creating the appearance of popular discontent with this legislation. A sore point for the executive was the clause which explicitly criminalized marital rape, and this clause was eventually erased from the version of the Bill presented to parliament.

Since the very purpose of the CEDAW report was to prove its commitment to promoting women's rights, Ghana found a new and creative way to legitimize its opposition to this legislation. First, Ghana presented itself as supportive of the Domestic Violence Bill, claiming that it wanted the legislation to pass. The CEDAW report says: "In response to the Beijing Platform for Action, the government has put in place certain measures and interventions to create an enabling environment for the advancement of women" and then names "the preparation of a draft bill on Domestic Violence" as one of these measures (Republic of Ghana 2005: 16). The assertion that the Bill was "proposed by the government" is repeated throughout the report, whereby each utterance gives the statement a greater force.[20] The government takes the credit for the work accomplished by women's rights activists, and obliterates the fact that it had stood in the way of the Bill.

Second, Ghana crafted an unusual rhetorical strategy to legitimize the exclusion of the marital rape clause. The *usual* way in which countries oppose aspects of women's rights legislation at CEDAW hearings is by claiming culture clashes and financial problems. In fact, CEDAW Committee is all too familiar with these "excuses for noncompliance" (Merry 2006: 5). Moreover, "culture" and "religion" are the two main grounds that countries have named when reserving the right not to implement specific aspects of the Convention.

Hence, to convince the Committee that criminalizing marital rape was a legitimate problem, the government of Ghana engaged in a more complex rhetorical maneuver. Rather than relying on the usual suspects, Ghana represented itself as having the political will to criminalize marital rape, but as being hindered from doing so due to public opposition:

> If the bill becomes law it will then be possible for a man to be prosecuted for marital rape. This section of the draft bill is generating a lot of controversy *amongst the population*. Public views on the bill are being collated. The Bill has been translated into eight local dialects to ensure wide dissemination and input, which ultimately would ensure that the bill when passed into law, would be owned and appreciated by the majority of Ghanaians.
>
> (Republic of Ghana 2005: 27; emphasis mine)

Ghana's CEDAW report mobilizes a discursive framework of popular democracy. If Ghanaians were truly opposed to the criminalization of marital rape, what was the democratic government to do but to acquiesce to popular sentiment? Next to the very notion that "people" should decide whether or not they want the DVB, the report nods to the importance of respecting the will of "the majority of Ghanaians." Appropriating the concept of "ownership," the government appeals to CEDAW experts who are familiar with its implications of power-sharing and "participation" in women's empowerment programs. Finally, by claiming that the Bill was translated into various Ghanaian languages, the report presents the government as attentive to issues of multi-culturalism and minority rights. As a whole, this discursive framework can hardly be argued against. While "culture" is a weak and familiar excuse, the will of the people is a powerful one.

Given Ghana's rhetorical success at CEDAW monitoring, the Committee had no legitimate reason to demand that the government criminalize marital rape. In the following, I will argue that the characteristics of the CEDAW regime shaped this outcome. The exchange of "information" at Ghana's monitoring was mediated by multiple characteristics of the disciplinary regime.

The manifestations of the regime

One of the main reasons why Ghana was able to maintain control over its self-representation as committed to women's rights was the state-centric structure of CEDAW monitoring. This structure allowed the government of Ghana to represent itself in the best light, to appropriate the work of activists and NGOs, and to manipulate the voices of Ghanaian "people." This outcome was shaped in conjunction with the discursive rules that guide the CEDAW regime. As I discussed above, the regime allows only a particular kind of language that is indirect and polite. The Ghanaian NGOs' shadow report was appropriately indirect, voicing only subtle criticism of the government's women's rights record. The shadow report did not expose the government's role in curtailing the scope of the Domestic Violence Bill. The most critical statement says: "The government's draft domestic violence bill unlike many other legislative bills is being subject to unending nationwide consultations" (Netright 2004: 7–8). NGOs did not question the role of the Ministry of Women and Children's Affairs in this process. Rather than exposing the government's appropriation of the gender agenda of this institution, the shadow report merely bemoans the lack of MOWAC's financial and "human resources" and their "lack of political clout" (Netright 2004: 10).

The UN demands of indirectness go hand in hand here with the Ghanaian cultural logics that stipulate politeness and deference to those in power and preclude NGOs from shifting the terms of the debate. While those immersed in Ghana's politics of women's rights can read the implications of such indirect criticism through the lines, CEDAW Committee members do not have that kind of thick knowledge; they are experts of universals, not of particulars. For these reasons, the discussion of Ghana's domestic violence legislation was limited to "information," which excluded the thorny issues of controversy and struggle.

Ghana's case shows how the bureaucratic apparatus of CEDAW shapes the effects of monitoring. While women with in-depth knowledge about women's rights advocacy in Ghana were present on both the CEDAW Committee and in the Ghanaian delegation, they were not able to alter the course of the hearing. The discursive rules of the regime, which stipulate which knowledge is admitted and what can be said at the hearing, went hand in hand with the surveillance mechanism that compels countries to present themselves in the best light.

A Ghanaian lawyer and women's rights activist, Dorcas Coker-Appiah, has been serving at the CEDAW Committee since 2003. She is the executive director of the Gender and Human Rights Documentation Centre, an NGO which published the largest study on violence against women in the country; she knows everything there is to know about the Domestic Violence Bill. Leading the Ghanaian delegation as the Minister of Women and Children's Affairs was Hajia Alima Mahama, a women's rights activist-turned-politician. She had founded an NGO focused on women's rights and rural development, and worked as a gender consultant on various development and research projects. Like Coker-Appiah, Alima Mahama was also a member of FIDA Ghana, the largest women's rights and legal advocacy NGO in the country.

Given that the monitoring rules excluded Coker-Appiah from participating in her own country's hearing, her knowledge about the controversy over the legislation was not authorized as official and hence, could not be used as a basis for discussion.[21] And given Alima Mahama's role as the representative of a government, she was to present officially sanctioned views, not her personal ones. Moreover, the very structure of the hearing that places governments in position of defendants prevents representatives such as Mahama from voicing criticisms of the government.

Here, the very structure of the regime precluded a discussion about the controversy over the legislation, allowing Ghana to succeed in obtaining the CEDAW praise and stamp of approval. It is important to remember that this success was enabled performatively. Ghana's delegation may not have *actually* persuaded the CEDAW Committee that its opposition was legitimate. However, the government was able to deflect outspoken (and written) criticism by manipulating the discursive rules of the regime itself.

Conclusion

In conclusion, I turn to the implications of this discussion for women's rights scholarship. My analysis straddles the unstable ground of the ethics and politics of critique itself. Considering the discursive articulation of rights and the practices of women's rights advocacy as important, but not sacred, is certainly dangerous in the age in which scholarly critique can be appropriated by nationalist voices. Rights are vulnerable to dismissal by those who are all too happy to appropriate the critical voice and make a spectacle out of shouting "Western politics!" Yet, ignoring the ways in which rights are saturated by politics does not seem to me a viable alternative. As Grewal writes, "feminist analysis teaches us . . . to denaturalize the truth-effect wherever we find or see it" (Grewal 2005: vii). Following this line of thinking, I have tried to show that there are dangers in ignoring the ways in which rights are "contaminated" (Cheah 2006: 266) by capital.

I have argued that CEDAW monitoring has the structure of a global panopticon whose disciplinary effects have consequences across the scale. This realization poses a methodological challenge. If we analyze the binary between countries of the global South and the UN, we might endorse Ghana's performative strategies of compliance with the CEDAW regime. In this reading, we would salute Ghana's maneuvers as resistance to the hegemonic liberalism and sovereignty threats as a strategy of accumulating symbolic capital and attracting development industry's "empowerment money" (Elyachar 2002) necessary for the country's survival. Yet, restricting the site of analysis to the effects of the regime on the nation-state and the resulting creative manipulations of CEDAW demands would render invisible Ghanaian women's rights activists as well as "ordinary" women and men.

This is why I find it crucial to examine the effects of the global women's rights panopticon not only on nation-states, but across the scale. Shifting our lens toward a particular site of women's rights monitoring, Ghana's Domestic Violence Bill, I have tried to show how the very character of CEDAW as a women's rights panopticon is responsible for creating barriers to realizing women's rights in practice. In the case of the Bill, CEDAW's fetishization of information worked in conjunction with the disciplinary and state-centric effects of the regime to limit the productive outcomes of the monitoring process. Ultimately, the regime has had contradictory effects on those Ghanaians who mobilize the discourse of rights and seek redress at institutions charged with protecting them. Ghanaian women and men may have come to understand themselves as subjects entitled to rights, but have few options of seeing these rights enacted. In other words, the inscription of women's rights within the current structures of global capital and (neo)liberalism not only compromises the normativity of rights, but also makes rights less viable.

Notes

1 Convention on the Elimination of all Forms of Discrimination against Women is commonly known by this acronym (in this chapter, I also refer to it as "the Convention").
2 See for example Osanloo 2009, the special issue of *American Anthropologist*, "Anthropology and Human Rights in a New Key" (Volume 108 (1), March 2006); Eisenstein 2007; Cheah 2006; Riles 2000; Hesford and Kozol 2005.
3 The latter scholarship is more copious, and includes volumes edited by Cook (1994); Peters and Wolper (1994); Mamdani (2000); Agosín (2001); Molyneux and Razavi (2002); Ferree and Tripp (2006).
4 http://www2.ohchr.org/english/bodies/cedaw/mandate.htm (accessed 25 March 2009).

5   This is not to say that NGOs should be exempt from analysis and critique, but that task is beyond the purview of this chapter.

6   The final comments to Ghana say: "the Committee appreciates the frank and constructive dialogue that took place between the delegation and the members of the Committee" (United Nations 2006b: 1).

7   See Republic of Ghana 2005, 2006; United Nations 2006a, 2006b, 2006c.

8   The United Nations Human Development Report regularly features "gender-related development" indices; the 1995 Report focused on gender, proclaiming that "human development, if not engendered, is endangered" (United Nations Development Programme 1995: 1).

9   In following also referred to as the DVB or the Bill.

10 The Ghanaian state also presents itself as "progressive" in the larger sense of being committed to "African affairs and new international relations based on equity and social justice" (Manuh 2007: 130).

11 The government of Ghana did not endow MOWAC with significant resources, thereby effectively tying its hands. While MOWAC's budget has increased from less than US$1 million in 2001 to almost US$7 million in 2009, this is still a negligible fraction of over US$1 billion Ghana receives in official development assistance annually. This lack of economic commitment impairs the work of both the national and regional offices. The representative in the Upper East region told me "We cannot do much. My budget is 500,000 cedis a quarter [then US$50]. I can organize one workshop per quarter, nothing else." (For MOWAC budget, see http://www.ghana.gov.gh/files/2009_budget_statement.pdf. For the overview of official development assistance, see http://devdata.worldbank.org/external/CPProfile.asp?CCODE=gha&PTYPE=CP.)

12 http://www.mowac.gov.gh (accessed 16 April 2005).

13 See United Nations 2006a, 2006b, 2006c.

14 This paradox extends to the relationship of many governments and NGOs toward the UN women's rights regime. Riles's ethnography tells a similar story about organizations in the Pacific which "devoted the majority of their time from 1993 to 1995 to preparations for the Beijing Conference and the NGO Forum" (Riles 2000: 13).

15 Commonly known by its original acronym, "WAJU."

16 http://64.226.23.153/waju/home.htm, accessed (25 March 2009).

17 In fact, the gaps between reported incidents, court appearances, and convictions are large. For a complex set of cultural and structural reasons, out of 11,335 cases brought to the Accra DOVVSU office between 1998 and 2004, only 19 percent appeared in court, and only 13 percent of those led to convictions (Adomako-Ampofo et al. 2005: 229). While Ghanaian researchers and activists bemoan the gap between reported cases and court appearances, for the government of Ghana, the very act of assembling and providing the statistics is an achievement in its own right.

18 The cultural logics of "reporting to the police" in Ghana add another dimension to my analysis. Despite their limitations, the statistics DOVVSU gathers serve as an index of locally meaningful practices, as in Ghana the sheer fact of being reported is often seen as a punishment. While legal procedures distinguish between the act of reporting violence and its eventual prosecution, many Ghanaians understand the very process of reporting as a disciplinary measure, irrespective of its final outcome. Hence, men fear "going to WAJU," as being interrogated by the police is seen as an act of punishment. Likewise, "sending a husband to court" is often the last resort for abused women, and one that many are reluctant to turn to. In light of this consideration, the numbers gathered by DOVVSU signal the willingness of Ghanaians to seek redress for domestic violence, and this willingness is something that Ghanaian gender activists have long tried to cultivate.

19 I provide a detailed ethnographic account of this battle in "Unsettling Power" (Hodžić, 2009).

20 The government's representation as a supporter of the Domestic Violence Bill is consistent with Ghana's self-representations to other international bodies. For example, Ghana's *Poverty Reduction Strategy Paper Annual Progress Report*, which the government provides to other African Union members as well as its donors such as the International Monetary Fund, also refers to its activities regarding the Domestic Violence Bill as an important area of achievement (Republic of Ghana, National Development Planning Commission 2005: 121).

21 It is possible that Coker-Appiah was able to influence the course of proceedings unofficially, as evidenced by one CEDAW Committee member's pressing of the Ghana delegation about the criminalization of marital rape and her display of the kind of in-depth knowledge that was not available in reports. The expert Patten "enquired whether Criminal Code section 42 (g), which was in contradiction with article 2 of the Convention, would be repealed once the domestic violence law was enacted" (United Nations 2006c: 7), thus referring to the controversial clause.

Bibliography

Adomako-Ampofo, A., Awotwi, E. and Dwamena-Aboagye, A. (2005) "How the Perpetrators of Violence against Women and Children Escape," *Women and Violence in Africa*, Dakar: Association of African Women in Research and Development.

Agosín, M. (ed.) (2001) *Women, Gender, and Human Rights: a global perspective*, New Brunswick, NJ: Rutgers University Press.

Cheah, P. (2006) *Inhuman Conditions: on cosmopolitanism and human rights*, Cambridge, MA: Harvard University Press.

Cook, R. (ed.) (1994) *Human Rights of Women: national and international perspectives*, Philadelphia: University of Pennsylvania Press.

Eisenstein, Z. (2007) *Sexual Decoys: gender, race and war in imperial democracy*, New York: Palgrave Macmillan.

Elyachar, J. (2002) "Empowerment Money: The World Bank, non-governmental organizations, and the value of culture in Egypt," *Public Culture*, 14(3): 493–513.

Ferree, M. M. and Tripp, A. T. (eds) (2006) *Global Feminism: transnational women's activism, organizing, and women's rights*, New York: New York University Press.

Grewal, I. (2005) Foreword, in Hesford, W. S and Kozol, W. (eds) *Just Advocacy? women's human rights, transnational feminisms, and the politics of representation*, New Brunswick, NJ: Rutgers University Press.

Hesford, W. S. and Kozol, W. (eds) (2005) *Just Advocacy? women's human rights, transnational feminisms, and the politics of representation*, New Brunswick, NJ: Rutgers University Press.

Hodžić, S. (2009) "Unsettling Power: domestic violence, gender politics, and struggles over sovereignty in Ghana," *Ethnos*, 74(3): 331–360.

Mamdani, M. (ed.) (2000) *Beyond Rights Talk and Culture Talk: comparative essays on the politics of rights and culture*, New York: St. Martin's Press.

Manuh, T. (2007) "Doing Gender Work in Ghana," in C. M. Cole, T. Manuh, and S. Miescher (eds) *Africa after Gender?* Bloomington: Indiana University Press, 125–149.

Mauss, M. (1967) *The Gift: forms and functions of exchange in archaic societies*, New York: Norton.

Merry, S. E. (2006) *Human Rights and Gender Violence: translating international law into local justice*, Chicago, IL: University of Chicago Press.

Molyneux, M. and Razavi, S. (eds) (2002) *Gender Justice, Development, and Rights*, Oxford: Oxford University Press.

Osanloo, A. (2009) *The Politics of Women's Rights in Iran*, Princeton, NJ: Princeton University Press.

Peters, J. S. and Wolper, A. (eds) (1994) *Women's Rights, Human Rights: international feminist perspectives*, New York: Routledge.

Pigg, S. and Adams, V. (eds) (2005) 'Introduction: the moral object of sex,' in *Sex in Development: science, sexuality, and morality in global perspective*, Durham, NC: Duke University Press.

Riles, A. (2000) *The Network Inside Out*, Ann Arbor: University of Michigan Press.

Primary Documents

Mahama, H. A. (2006) "Introductory Statement." Online. <http://www.un.org/womenwatch/daw/cedaw/36sess.htm.>

Netright (Network for Women's Rights in Ghana) (2004) Ghana NGO Alternative Report for Beijing + 10. Online. <http://www.wildaf-ao.org/eng/IMG/doc/Ghana_ENG-2.doc>

Republic of Ghana (2005) *Convention on the Elimination of All Forms of Discrimination against Women; Combined Third, Fourth and Fifth Periodic Reports of States Parties: Ghana*. United Nations Document CEDAW/C/GHA/3–5, 1–74.

—— (2006) *Responses to the List of Issues and Questions with Regard to the Consideration of the Combined Third, Fourth and Fifth Periodic Reports: Ghana*. United Nations Document CEDAW/C/GHA/Q/5/Add.1.

Republic of Ghana, National Development Planning Commission (2005) *Poverty Reduction Strategy Paper Annual Progress Report*. IMF Country Report No. 06/226.

United Nations, Committee on the Elimination of Discrimination against Women (2006a) *List of Issues and Questions with Regard to the Consideration of the Combined Third, Fourth and Fifth Period Reports: Ghana*. United Nations Document CEDAW/C/GHA/Q/5.

—— (2006b) *Concluding Comments of the Committee on the Elimination of Discrimination against Women: Ghana*. United Nations Document CEDAW/C/GHA/CO/5.

—— (2006c) Summary record of the 741st meeting (Chamber B). United Nations Document CEDAW/C/SR.741 (B).

—— (2006d) Summary record of the 742nd meeting (Chamber B). United Nations Document CEDAW/C/SR.742 (B).

—— (undated) "Information note prepared by OHCHR for NGO participation," Online. <http://www2.ohchr.org/english/bodies/cedaw/docs/NGO_Participation.final.pdf.>

United Nations Development Programme (1995) Human Development Report 1995: Gender and Human Development, Overview. Online. <http://hdr.undp.org/en/media/hdr_1995_en_overview.pdf.>

United Nations Economic and Social Council (1999) Follow-up to and Implementation of the Beijing Declaration and Platform for Action. Commission on the Status of Women. United Nations Document <E/CN.6/1999/2/Add.1.>

14 Human rights of women and girls with disabilities in developing countries

Amy T. Wilson

Culture, custom, religion, or laws in many countries prohibit women from owning or inheriting land, receiving an education or appropriate health care, being employed or earning a fair wage, receiving information or assistance concerning their sexual and reproductive rights, or generally receiving the same rights as men in their community (Mertens et al. 2007). Women and girls, who differ physically or mentally from other females in their communities, form a subgroup that experiences this same discrimination and more as negative stereotypes about their "different-ness" along with barriers created by inaccessible environments harmfully change their "difference" into a "disability." Deprived of the equal rights and equal status of men because of being born female, women with a physical or mental "disability" are doubly discriminated against because of society's crippling attitudes.

As 80 percent of girls with disabilities are born into poverty, girls with disabilities are less likely to be educated, to find employment, to marry and raise children, to be included in development assistance programs or receive appropriate or adequate health care and services (WHO 2009). They are less likely to participate in family and social events, are excluded from religious or traditional cultural activities, and are at a higher risk of physical, sexual, and emotional abuse. Stigmatization, marginalization, and low expectations fill disabled girls and women with feelings of low self-esteem and low self-worth. Being born female with a disability in some communities can be deadening and deadly.

Two United Nations Conventions specifically include provisions to protect the rights of women with disabilities. First, the General Recommendation 18 to the Convention on the Elimination of Discrimination Against Women (CEDAW) asks that states report on the situation of women with disabilities under each of its rights, on the measures to be taken to enhance the status of women with disabilities, on the progress made toward human rights for women with disabilities, and on the difficulties and obstacles encountered in obtaining those rights. Yet, surveys show that there is minimal reporting on the discrimination experienced by women with disabilities and monitoring reports lack information describing the benefit woman with disabilities obtain because of CEDAW (Quinn et al. 2003).

Therefore, Article 6 of the Convention on the Rights of Persons with Disabilities (CRPWD) holds much promise for women with disabilities as it recognizes "that women and girls with disabilities are subject to multiple discrimination, and in this regard (the CRPWD) shall take measures to ensure the full and equal enjoyment by them of all human rights and fundamental freedoms" (United Nations Enable 2008c). This chapter will examine the situation of women with disabilities, specifically in developing countries, and discuss those measures that these women may make in advocating for their deserved human rights.

Disability in developing countries

Although reliable global disability statistics do not exist, the World Health Organization (WHO) estimates that the number of people with disabilities is between 7 and 10 percent of the world's population or approximately 650 million people. The number of people with disabilities is increasing with the spread of sexually transmitted diseases such as HIV/AIDS, poor maternal health care, drug or alcohol use in mothers, population growth, aging, inherited disabilities, widespread use of poisons and pesticides, and medical advances that preserve and prolong the lives of those who may have died in past years (United Nations Economic and Social Commission for Asia and the Pacific 2003). Higher incidence of injuries due to road accidents, landmines, violence, and war also result in disabilities as does malnutrition, unsanitary living conditions, and inadequate health/medical care for people living in poverty (WHO 2008a, 2008b). It is estimated that 2 billion people, or one-third of our world's population, is affected by disability as families may assist and/or care for a family member with a disability (United Nations Enable 2008a).

Since many people with disabilities lack access to education, health care, employment, and political and legal protections, they often live in chronic poverty, remaining poor for much or all of their lives. Those who live in poverty without a disability are more likely to become disabled as a result of dangerous, unsanitary, and precarious living situations in which they must struggle to survive day to day. Without access to vocational training or employment, people with disabilities raise their families in poverty where their children are also more susceptible to becoming sick or injured resulting in a disability. Poverty and disability create a continuous cycle which must be broken.

Throughout history, and today throughout the world, negative attitudes toward disability have been the greatest barrier for people with disabilities (National Library Service for the Blind and Physically Handicapped, Library of Congress 1992). A number of cultures, religions, and communities believe that a disability is bad luck or that a disability gives a person supernatural powers (Gettleman 2008). Others believe that people are born with or acquire a disability as a punishment from god(s), or as the result of a malicious magical spell. Some families may believe that their disabled child is incapable of learning, walking, caring for themselves, or communicating and will treat them as invalids, which puts the child in the position of becoming an economic burden to the family. Some disabled children are hidden away so that the opportunities for siblings to marry will not be spoiled (UNESCAP 2003). As children in some societies are expected to care for their elders, families may give fewer resources (education, nutrition, or attention, for example) to their disabled child as he/she develops, and focus instead on the able-bodied child who has an assumed improved chance of earning an income and fulfilling their familial responsibility.

Women and girls with disabilities in developing countries

Women and girls with disabilities suffer discrimination worldwide, no matter if they reside in a northern industrialized country such as the United States or in southern unindustrialized countries such as those found in Sub-Saharan Africa. Yet in poorer countries, women and girls are more likely to acquire a disability than men as the result of violence, armed conflict, gender-biased cultural practices, such as female genital mutilation (FGM), and when those in power limit disabled women's and children's access to food, shelter, medical care, and a safe working environment (United Nations Enable 2008b). Human Rights Watch (2006) reports that in low and middle income countries, women make up 75 percent of the disabled population and are less likely to receive medical care and health services compared to disabled males.

Although not well documented, it is believed that in developing countries infanticide may occur more often when a girl is born with a disability than when not (Boyes 2007). If a girl with a disability is allowed to live, there is only a 5 percent chance that she will attend school or job training because, (a) her male siblings will take precedence over the girl for the family's financial resources, (b) the school will be inaccessible to the girl either because of physical barriers, attitudinal barriers, or lack of special materials, or (c) her guardians may believe their disabled daughter is unable to be educated (Human Rights Watch 2006). Many women and girls with disabilities are hidden away in their homes because of the family's shame rooted in cultural bias, or because of the belief that their daughter is not "worth" the same as "normal" girls. Parents may be overprotective, or perhaps unaware of how to access mobility aids or special resources for their daughter (Wilson 2005). The roads may be inaccessible or there may be a lack of transportation so the woman is left alone in the home, isolated and unaware of her rights or of how she can better the quality of her life.

Only about 3 percent of people with disabilities receive rehabilitation services, which are often expensive and more often given to men rather than women (Helander 1999). Estimates report that women and girls with disabilities receive only 20 percent of the small number of available rehabilitation services because of favoritism toward males and because rehabilitation services are usually located in urban areas. Eighty percent of all people with disabilities live in rural areas and many disabled women are not allowed to travel alone outside of their community or to travel at all (United Nations Economic and Social Commission for Asia and the Pacific 1995). A UNESCAP (1995) study done in India showed that women were hesitant and/or unwilling to go for rehabilitation services as most of the specialists who would examine them, fit their prosthetics, or give them services were men.

As the anticipated role for most girls is to be a dutiful wife and daughter and nurturing mother, disabled girls are often considered unmarriageable, as it is thought their disability might be passed on genetically or there may be doubts about whether the disabled woman is able to look after a home and family. Therefore, women with disabilities are not expected to marry and actually are less likely to marry than non-disabled women or disabled men (Groce 2004). A Nepalese survey reported only 20 percent of women with disabilities were married while a Chinese study showed 48 percent over the age of 18 were married (UNESCAP 1995). Disabled women are more likely to have an absent partner who leaves her with their children, thus "facing social stigma, loneliness, and poverty" (Lewis et al. 1997). Since women are largely defined by their roles as wife, daughter, and mother and by the labor they accomplish both in and outside of the home, disabled women are unable to claim either status or a social identity other than often being referred to in their community as the "disabled one."

Women with disabilities find it difficult to achieve economic self-sufficiency as they are often dependent on family members when they are unable to find employment. Research done in the rural areas of the Asia Pacific region reports that more than 80 percent of disabled women had no independent means of earning an income (Porta 1988). Even when disabled people begin to organize themselves into organizations or associations, women are rarely found in leadership positions or even invited to attend meetings. If they do participate, they are often in the role of serving their disabled male peers.

Violence against women with disabilities

A United Nation report discusses "intersectionality" which recognizes that male dominance intersects with "race, ethnicity, age, caste, religion, culture, language, sexual orientation, migrant and refugee status and disability" and that discrimination and forms of violence against a woman will vary according to her personal characteristics (United Nations 2006a: 101). A light-skinned upper-class elderly woman who is the matriarch of a family settled for generations in a rural village may be protected from violence due to her social status, while a dark-skinned, lower-caste girl whose family has fled civil unrest to a neighboring country and lives in poverty amongst other refugees is less protected and more often a target for violence than not. Some perpetrators may prey on disabled females who are highly unlikely to seek assistance or report the incidents as they are unable to report abuse because their disability impedes their ability to communicate easily, such as with deafblind women without language, women with mental illness facing communication issues, or women with cerebral palsy who may physically be unable to speak; or they do not report the abuse because of fear of reprisal, they may be physically unable to travel to a police station, they may be cognitively disabled, or because of disbelieving family members thinking the victim is not sexual or sexually attractive.

Researchers at the University of Minnesota reported that in the United States,

> Women with disabilities experience the highest rate of personal violence—
> violence at the hands of spouses, partners, boyfriends, family members,
> caregivers, and strangers—of any group in our society today. Yet, they are
> often invisible in the crime statistics, frequently find community services such
> as domestic and sexual violence programs inadequately prepared to fully
> understand and meet their needs, face disability service systems that don't
> clearly see and effectively respond to the violence, and are all too commonly
> devalued and unsupported because of societal prejudice.
>
> (IMPACT 2000: 1)

In Europe, North America, and Australia, more than 50 percent of women with
disabilities have experienced physical abuse, compared with one-third of non-
disabled women (Human Rights Watch 2006). No worldwide statistics have
been gathered on violence against women but it can be assumed that in other
countries where negative beliefs and attitudes about disability are common, the
situation for women and girls with disabilities is similar or worse. A United Nations
resolution states, "Girls and women of all ages with any form of disability are
generally among the more vulnerable and marginalized of society" (United
Nations 2000: 20). A United Nations report concerning violence against women
stated that women with disabilities may experience violence in their homes
and institutional settings, perpetrated by family members, caretakers or strangers
(United Nations 2006a). A United Nations Secretary-General's Study on Violence
against Children also showed in a multi-country study that children with
disabilities are particularly vulnerable to violence (United Nations 2006b). Up to
21 percent of women in some countries reported having been sexually abused
before the age of 15 and it is believed that this percentage would be much higher
for girls with disabilities. Since disabled girls are often thought to be nonsexual,
and therefore presumed to be virgins, a global survey of HIV/AIDS and disability
shows a significant number of rapes of disabled children in cultures where it is
believed that HIV-positive individuals can rid themselves of the virus by having
sex with virgins (Groce and Trasi 2004; Wilson and Monaghan 2006). One
African study found that 38 percent of disabled women reported being affected
with a sexually transmitted disease (Mulindwa 2003) and, because of their
disability or their lack of power, were unable to "negotiate" for safer sex practices
(Janssen 2005).

From charity to empowerment

There has been a paradigm shift throughout much of the industrialized world
about how "disability" is viewed and defined. This shift is spreading globally and
impacting the lives of disabled men and women throughout the rest of the world
(Mertens et al. 2007). At one time, "disability" meant that a person had a physical
difference from a "normal" body. Much of society, especially medical personnel,

did not consider a person with a disability as a whole person; rather they thought of people with disabilities as having an "impairment" that needed to be cured, rehabilitated, or protected. For example, children with conditions such as epilepsy, diabetes, or mental illness would endure odd treatments or potions to be cured, or deaf children would undergo stressful speech training to learn to speak (with much failure), or children with cognitive disabilities were shuttered away in institutions to be protected (but often were abused).

As disabled people began to advocate for themselves, the thinking about disability changed as they maintained that "impairment" is an individual limitation such as blindness or a physical disability that makes it difficult to walk or dress themselves or makes it harder for them to understand or learn. Society focused on the impairments and what a woman could *not* do, rather than what she *could* do, thus overlooking her value to her community and limiting her access to programs and social services generally available to those who were not physically or mentally different than the norm. The inability of society to look past the impairment has become an additional limiting factor (other than gender, tribe, caste, economic status, etc.) to women worldwide.

A "disability," then, is caused by society as "the limitations imposed on people with disabilities by attitudes, and social, cultural, economic, and physical barriers to their participation in society. The physical and mental health of women with disabilities will improve when communities improve access, challenge prejudice, and create employment opportunities" (Maxwell et al. 2007: 7). Only when employers are able to see the employable skills a wheelchair rider brings to a job interview, rather than the wheelchair, and a teacher learns a sign language rather than labeling a child "low-functioning," or a technician develops a means to read all forms of text and graphics on a computer monitor, will there be equity for disabled individuals.

Human rights are women's rights are disabled women's rights

As mentioned at the outset, the hardest challenge women with disabilities face is the attitude others hold about disabilities, yet many disabled women have acquired strength from their friends, their family, their faith, and from within their core selves and have courageously included themselves in activities from which they might have normally been barred. At the local level some women have succeeded in income-generating schemes with which they have created means to earn money so as not to be economically dependent on family members (Dixon 2001). Sewing clothing, designing jewelry, or transcribing audio tapes to typed text have been means for disabled women to bring home funds, to interact socially and create a new role for themselves within their community, and to improve their status in their family and society (ILO 2008b). Yet this struggle is one that few disabled women attempt as they may not know their basic human rights or are not physically or intellectually able to challenge the status quo.

Societies will improve access and create employment opportunities more quickly when those who are oppressed organize themselves and their allies, and challenge the prejudice and discrimination they confront daily. Therefore, in some countries, disabled women have joined with disabled men to form Disabled People Organizations (DPOs) in order to advocate for their rights, to establish self-help schemes, and to socialize with one another. Some DPOs are aware of disabled women's issues, such as the Federation Organization of the Disabled People in Swaziland (FODSWA) which promotes gender sensitivity among its members and aims to insure that half their elected and appointed leaders are women (Disability World 2002). When gender sensitivity has not been included in a DPO's mandate, issues related specifically to women with disabilities emerge when women become recognized as leaders in the DPO and bring their concerns forward. DPOs may create subgroups where female members of the parent organization add a "women's wing" to address their needs as did the women in the Zambia Federation of the Disabled (ZAFOD). The female members established the woman's wing, the Zambia Federation of Women in Business, where disabled women could receive training in acquiring and improving their business skills so as to establish small businesses (ILO 2008b).

Another alternative for women, other than surviving day-to-day alone or being a member of a DPO or its woman's wing, is to establish grassroots self-help organizations for women, by women. WWDA is an example of a nongovernmental organization, "initially established by a group of women with disabilities who felt that their needs and concerns were not being acknowledged or addressed within the broader disability sector, or the women's sector in Australia" (WWDA 2009). Disabled women's organizations aim to inform and educate their families, communities, governments, national and international development assistance organizations, women's organizations, and human rights organizations about the discrimination suffered by women with disabilities and how positive steps can be taken to empower rather than oppress them. In some countries women have founded organizations solely for themselves, as did the members of the Zambia National Association of Disabled Women (ZNADWO). Through their organization's efforts, they secured funding to offer seminars, workshops, and training for their members to gain the technical skills to work with computers and to adapt materials about HIV/AIDS and reproductive health to formats accessible to people with disabilities (Communication and Initiative Network 2002).

Since disability laws do exist in many countries, especially in those that have ratified the Convention on the Rights of Persons with Disabilities, disabled women can educate themselves about their civil and human rights and learn processes through which they can advocate for themselves locally, regionally, nationally, and globally. Women can participate in their local disability organizations, through women's groups, or groups specifically established by women with disabilities, and by joining a wider network with groups such as the International Network of Women with Disabilities (INWWD 2009) or the Global Partnership for Disability and Development (GPDD 2009). Armed with knowledge, they can inform organizations how to include people with disabilities within their organizations as well as in the organizations' projects and programs. Motsch-Heinicke and Sygall (2004) describe in their book *Building an Inclusive Development Community* the preferred manner in which women with disabilities can obtain their human rights through the process of inclusion. Instead of creating programs specifically for women with disabilities, organizations facilitate the inclusion of women with disabilities into projects that are offered to all women.

As an example, organizations of women with disabilities worked with the International Labour Organization's Developing Entrepreneurship among Women with Disabilities (DEWD) project which:

> works in partnership with local organizations of and for disabled persons to support the participation of disabled women entrepreneurs in mainstream activities organized by Women Entrepreneurship Development and Gender Equality (WEDGE). It also seeks to sensitize national and local government and women's entrepreneurs' associations to disability issues, so that they too start to focus on the business development needs of persons with disabilities.
>
> (ILO 2008b: 9)

Disabled women in Ethiopia, Tanzania, Uganda, and Zambia have created tailoring businesses and built tanks to distribute water to neighbors with assistance from their DPO, which had partnered with ILO (ILO 2008a).

Many national DPOs are advocating for national constitutions, such as those in South Africa and Uganda, which mandate that parliament must include members with disabilities. As a result many people with disabilities have been appointed to government posts (Shriner 2002). Such legislation made it possible for a woman with a disability, Florence Nayiga Sekabira, who was a leader in the National Union of Disabled Persons of Uganda (NUDIPU) to become the Minister of State for Elderly and Disability Affairs where she worked toward the creation of the National Council for Disability (Walugembe and Peckett 2005). Having women with disabilities in political positions can infuse the perspective of women with disabilities in all pieces of legislation.

Promoting the rights of women with disabilities

Disabled People's Organizations (DPOs) are pressuring their governments to include information about disabled family members when demographic statistics are gathered to reflect the true state of people with disabilities within their countries in order to campaign governments and national and international bodies for appropriate assistance. The resource kit for disabled women (Disability Awareness in Action 1997) also suggests that there should be an increase in (a) participation of disabled women in their communities, within disability organizations, and in the mainstream women's movement, (b) education and training specifically for disabled women along with increased access to services, facilities, and transportation, (c) available resources to support and educate the families and the community about disabilities, and (d) support for disabled women in forming local groups and self-help organizations to increase their self-esteem. All of these suggestions are excellent, but if laws do not support change, change is slow in coming.

The United Nations Convention on the Elimination of All Forms of Discrimination against Women, CEDAW General Recommendation No. 18, "recommends that States parties provide information on disabled women in their periodic reports, and on measures taken to deal with their particular situation, including special measures to ensure that they have equal access to education and employment, health services and social security, and to ensure that they can participate in all areas of social and cultural life" (United Nations 1979). Yet most states still have failed to use CEDAW to protect disabled women from human rights abuses. CEDAW does not address the significant barriers that disability raises for women such as the discrimination she faces solely because she has a disability. Societal barriers caused by attitudes and beliefs are not considered in CEDAW, nor the segregation and isolation families force their disabled daughters to live in throughout their lives. Economic and political marginalization resulting from lack of access to an education or vocational training because of their disability is also not addressed.

Thus, DPOs laud the importance of the United Nations adoption of the Convention on the Rights of Persons with Disabilities, signed on December 13, 2006, as it can be used in conjunction with CEDAW to ensure that women with disabilities secure their human rights. The Convention illustrates a paradigm shift about how "disability" is currently being viewed and defined. Rather than people with disabilities being treated as needing medical treatment, a cure, charity, or protection, the Convention states that persons with disabilities have rights and

> are capable of claiming those rights and making decisions for their lives based on their free and informed consent as well as being active members of society . . . (the Convention) adopts a broad categorization of persons with disabilities and reaffirms that all persons with all types of disabilities must enjoy all human rights and fundamental freedoms. It clarifies and qualifies how all categories of rights apply to persons with disabilities and identifies areas where adaptations have to be made for persons with disabilities to effectively exercise their rights and areas where their rights have been violated, and where protection of rights must be reinforced.
>
> (United Nations Enable 2008c)

Within the Convention there is a specific article on women with disabilities and several references to girls, women, and gender issues. Within the Preamble it is written that the Convention is

> (p) Concerned about the difficult conditions faced by persons with disabilities who are subject to multiple or aggravated forms of discrimination on the basis of race, colour, *sex*, language, religion, political or other opinion, national, ethnic, indigenous or social origin, property, birth, age or other status,

(q) Recognizing that *women and girls with disabilities* are often at greater risk, both within and outside the home of violence, injury or abuse, neglect or negligent treatment, maltreatment or exploitation,

(s) Emphasizing the need to incorporate a *gender perspective* in all efforts to promote the full enjoyment of human rights and fundamental freedoms by persons with disabilities.

(United Nations Enable 2008d)

Further, Article 6 is specifically about women with disabilities and it is written:

1. States Parties recognize that women and girls with disabilities are subject to multiple discriminations, and in this regard shall take measures to ensure the full and equal enjoyment by them of all their human rights and fundamental freedoms.

2. States Parties shall take all appropriate measures to ensure the full development, advancement and empowerment of women, for the purpose of guaranteeing them the exercise and enjoyment of the human rights and fundamental freedoms set out in the present Convention.

(United Nations Enable 2008e)

Other references naming gender as important are also found in (United Nations Enable 2008c):

- Article 8—Awareness-raising (paragraph b);
- Article 16—Freedom from exploitation, violence and abuse (paragraphs 1, 2, 4, 5);
- Article 25—Health (introduction and paragraph a);
- Article 28—Adequate standard of living and social protection (paragraph 2b);
- Article 34—Committee on the Rights of Persons with Disabilities (paragraph 4).

The recognition in the Convention of gender as being an area worth emphasizing is significant as it will assist disabled women's groups in fighting for their human and civil rights internationally, nationally, and regionally. Disabled women's organizations and Disabled People's Organizations (DPOs) can carry human rights education to their individual constituencies but it is also critical to establish effective partnerships with one another, and also with other organizations outside the disability movement (groups concerned with bioethics, human rights, gender and social justice, international development, rights for people who are gay, lesbian, bisexual, and transgendered). Together they can either lobby for their country to sign and ratify the Convention, or develop training programs to learn the skills to monitor the Convention in order to recognize when it is being violated and to identify and provide a legal framework by which the state can be held accountable and pressured to obey and follow the articles of the Convention (Miller 1999).

Flowers et al. (2008) have recently published a manual that can be used in training programs to teach people with disabilities and their allies how to integrate a comprehensive human rights approach in their advocacy work based on the UN Convention on the Rights of Persons with Disabilities. As women fight for their rights, the pernicious link between poverty and disability could begin to dissolve and that could create changes in attitudes and laws. As international, national, regional, and local human rights policies and laws demand the inclusion of women with disabilities in all facets of society, people will become more educated and comfortable with women who are "different" from themselves. As attitudes change, it will be less of a struggle to enforce relevant laws as negative beliefs about disability in families and communities lessen. Attitudes will reinforce laws, and laws reinforce attitudes.

An increasing number of women with disabilities are becoming integrated into society today and their movement toward equality is growing stronger—so much so that you are reading about their efforts in this book. Professionals can educate themselves about the CRPD and become allies by supporting a societal and systemic transformation of attitudes and beliefs about women with disabilities and advocate for their human rights to be recognized.

Bibliography

Boyes, R. (2007) "'Dump Your Children Here' Box to Stop Mothers Killing their Babies." *The Times* (London). Overseas News; 31. Online. <http://www.timesonline.co.uk/tol/news/world/europe/article1572569.ece> (27 March, accessed 16 June 2008).

Communication and Initiative Network (2002) "T-Shirts to Web Links: women connect!" Online. <http://www.comminit.com/en/node/2193> (accessed 23 October 2008).

Disability Awareness in Action (1997) *Disabled Women: disability awareness in action resource kit No. 6.* Online. <http://www.independentliving.org/docs2/daakit61.html> (accessed 18 June 2008).

Disability World (2002) "Swaziland Federation Organization of Disabled People Develops Women's Program," September–October, 15. Online. <http://www.disabilityworld.org/09–11_04/women/fodswa.shtml> (accessed 23 October 2008).

Dixon, H. (2001) *Learning from Experience. Strengthening organizations of women with disabilities: Solidez, Nicaragua.* London: One World Action.

Elwan, A. (1990) *Poverty and Disability: a survey of the literature.* Washington, DC: World Bank. Online. <http://siteresources.worldbank.org/INTPOVERTY/Resources/WDR/Background/elwan.Pdf> (18 December, accessed 16 June 2008).

Flowers, N., Balfe, J., Guernsey, K., Karr, V., and Lord, J. (2008) *Human Rights. YES!: action and advocacy on the rights of persons with disabilities.* Minneapolis, MN: Human Rights Resource Center, University of Minnesota Law School. Online. <http://www1.umn.edu/humanrts/edumat/hreduseries/TB6/index2.html> (accessed 18 June 2008).

Gettleman, J. (2008) "Albinos, Long Shunned, Face Threat in Tanzania," *New York Times.* Online. <http://www.nytimes.com/2008/06/08/world/africa/08albino.html> (8 June, accessed 18 June 2008).

Global Partnership for Disability and Development (GPDD) (2009) Online. <http://www.gpdd-online.org/> (accessed 5 September 2009).

Groce, N. (2004) "HIV/AIDS and Individuals with Disability—The Yale University/ World Bank Global Survey on HIV/AIDS." World Bank Group. Online. <site resources.worldbank.org/DISABILITY/Resources/Health-and-Wellness/ HIVAIDS.doc> (accessed 18 June 2009).

Groce, N. and Trasi, R. (2004) "Rape of Individuals with Disability: AIDS and the folk belief of virgin cleansing," *The Lancet*, 363(9422): 1663–1664.

Healthlink Worldwide (2008) "Creating Spaces—for women with disabilities (WWD) to communicate and advocate for their rights in South Asia," Online. <http://www. healthlink.org.uk/projects/disability/wwd_evolution.html> (accessed 23 October 2008).

Helander, E. (1999) *Prejudice and Dignity*. New York: United Nations Development Programme.

Human Rights Watch (2006) "Women and Girls with Disabilities." Online. <http://hrw. org/women/disabled.html> (accessed on 16 June 20008).

IMPACT (Fall 2000) "Feature Issue on Violence and Women with Developmental or Other Disabilities," Vol. 1(3): 1. Online. <http://ici.umn.edu/products/impact/ 133/133.pdf> (accessed 16 June 2008).

International Labour Organization (ILO) (2008a) "Count us in! How to make sure that women with disabilities can participate effectively in mainstream women's entre-preneurship development activities." Geneva: ILO. Online. <www.ilo.org/public/ english/employment/skills/disability/download/countus.pdf> (accessed 8 October 2008).

— (2008b) "Voices of Women Entrepreneurs in Ethiopia, Tanzania, Uganda and Zambia." Geneva: ILO. Online. <http://www.ilo.org/public/english/employment/skills/ disability/whatsnew.htm> (accessed 8 October 2008).

International Network of Women with Disabilities (INWWD) (2009) Online. <http:// groups.yahoo.com/group/inwwd/> (accessed 5 September 2009).

Janssen, M. (2005) "HIV/AIDS and Disability: the long way from exclusion to inclusion: observations from Southern Africa." *Sexual Health Exchange. Royal Tropical Institute.* Online. <http://www.kit.nl/exchange/html/2005–1_hiv_aids_and_disability.asp> (January, accessed 14 June 2008).

Lewis, C., Sygall, S., and Crawford, J. (eds) (1997) *Loud, Proud, Passionate®: including women with disabilities in international development programs*. Eugene, OR: Mobility International USA.

Maxwell, J., Belser, J., and Darlena, D. (2007) *A Health Handbook for Women with Disabilities*. Berkeley, CA: Hesperian Foundation. Online. <http://www.hesperian.org/ publications_download_wwd.php> (accessed 18 June 2008).

Mertens, D., Wilson, A., and Mounty, J. (2007) "Gender Equity for People with Disabilities," in Klein, S. (ed.) *Handbook for Achieving Gender Equity through Education*. Mahwah, NJ: Lawrence Erlbaum, 583–604.

Miller, A. M. (1999) "Realizing Women's Human Rights: nongovernmental organizations and the United Nations treaty bodies," in Meyer, M., and Prugl, E. (eds) *Gender Politics in Global Governance*. London: Rowman and Littlefield, 161–176.

Mobility International USA (2008) *Women with Disabilities and Development*. <http:// www.miusa.org/idd/women> (accessed 18 June 2008).

Motsch-Heinicke, K. and Sygall, S. (2004) *Building an Inclusive Development Community: a manual on including people with disabilities in international development programs*. Eugene, OR: Mobility International USA.

Mulindwa, I. (2003) "Study on Reproductive Health and HIV/AIDS Among Persons with Disabilities in Kampala, Katakwi and Rakai Districts. Kampala: (knowledge, attitudes, and practice)." Disabled Women's Network and Resource Organization. Online. <http://cira.med.yale.edu/globalsurvey/mulindwa.pdf> (accessed 16 June 2008).

National Library Service for the Blind and Physically Handicapped, Library of Congress (1992) *Bibliography on Disability Awareness and Changing Attitudes*. Online. <http://www.rit.edu/~easi/pubs/ezbib2.htm> (accessed 16 June 2008).

Porta, G. (1988) "The Situation of Disabled Women in Rural Areas: a problem in need of concerted action." Paper presented at the Second DPI Asia Pacific Regional Assembly and Training Seminar on Equalization of Opportunities, 27 August–2 September, Bangkok. In United Nations Economic and Social Commission for Asia and the Pacific (1995) *Hidden Sisters: women and girls with disabilities in the Asian and Pacific Region*. New York: United Nations. Online. <http://www.un.org/Depts/escap/decade/wwd2.htm#discrimination> (accessed 16 June 2008).

Quinn, G., Degener, T., with Bruce, A., Burke, C., Castellino, J., Kenna, P., Kilkelly, U., and Quinlivan, S. (2003) "Human Rights and Disability: the current use and future potential of United Nations human rights instruments in the context of disability." United Nations, Office of the High Commissioner for Human Rights.

Shriner, K. (2002) "Disabled Members of Parliament Wield Influence in Uganda." *Disability World*, 1. Online. <http://www.disabilityworld.org/March2000/English/uganda.htm> (accessed 23 October 2008).

United Nations (1979) *Convention on the Elimination of All Forms of Discrimination Against Women* (CEDAW). Online. <http://daccessdds.un.org/doc/RESOLUTION/GEN/NR0/378/07/IMG/NR037807.pdf?OpenElement> (accessed 18 June 2008).

—— (2000) *Further Actions and Initiatives to Implement the Beijing Declaration and Platform for Action*. General Assembly Resolution S23/3 of 10 June, annex, paragraph 63: 20. <http://www.un.org/womenwatch/daw/followup/ress233e.pdf> (accessed 16 June 2008).

—— (2006a) *In-Depth Study on all Forms of Violence Against Women: Report of the Secretary-General*, 101. Online. <http://www.un.org/womenwatch/daw/vaw/SGstudyvaw.htm> (July, accessed 16 June 2008).

—— (October 2006b) *Secretary-General's Study on Violence against Children*. Online. <http://www.violencestudy.org/a553> (accessed 16 June 2008).

United Nations Economic and Social Commission for Asia and the Pacific (UNESCAP) (1995) *Hidden Sisters: women and girls with disabilities in the Asian and Pacific Region*. New York: United Nations. Online. <http://www.un.org/Depts/escap/decade/wwd2.htm#discrimination> (accessed 16 June 2008).

—— (2003) *Focus on Ability, Celebrate Diversity: highlights of the Asian and Pacific decade of disabled persons, 1993–2002*. Social Policy Paper No. 13, ST/ESCAP/2291. New York: UNESCO. Online. <http://www.unescap.org/esid/psis/publications/spps/13/toc.htm> (accessed 18 June 2008).

United Nations Enable (2008a) *Relationship Between Development and Human Rights*. Online. <http://www.un.org/disabilities/default.asp?id=33> (accessed 15 June 2008).

—— (2008b) *Factsheet on Disability*. Online. <http://www.un.org/disabilities/default.asp?id=18> (accessed 18 June 2008).

—— (2008c) *The Convention of the Rights of Persons with Disabilities*. Online. <http://www.un.org/disabilities/default.asp?id=150 10> (accessed 16 June 2008).

—— (2008d) *Preamble*. Online. <http://www.un.org/disabilities/default.asp?id=260> (accessed 18 June 2008).

—— (2008e) *Article 6—Women and Disabilities*. Online. <http://www.un.org/disabilities/default. asp?id=266> (accessed 18 June 2008).

Walugembe, J. and Peckett, J. (2005) "Power Struggle: Uganda has an impressive array of people with disabilities involved in politics. But do they get to have their say?" *New Internationalist.* N. 384. Online. <http://www.newint.org/issue384/power-struggle.htm> (November, accessed 23 October 2008).

Wilson, A. T. (2005) "Studying the Effectiveness of International Development Assistance from American Organizations to Deaf Communities." *American Annals of the Deaf,* 150: 292–304.

Wilson, A. T. and Monaghan, L. (2006) "HIV/AIDS and Deaf Communities." *Deaf Worlds,* Focused Edition, 22(1).

Women Watch (2008) "Women with Disabilities." Online. <http://www.un.org/womenwatch/enable/> (Summer, accessed 18 June 2008).

Women with Disabilities Australia (WWDA) (2009) *About Women with Disabilities Australia.* Online. <http://www.wwda.org.au/about.htm> (accessed 4 September 2009).

World Health Organization (WHO) (1999) *Note for the Press No 16. 1 December 2000. Is There Equality of Opportunities for People with Disabilities? A Recent WHO Report Sums up the Situation.* Online. <http://www.who.int/inf-pr-2000/en/note2000-2016.html> (accessed 18 June 2008).

—— (2008a) *Concept Note: World Report on Disability and Rehabilitation.* Online. <http://www.who.int/disabilities/publications/dar_world_report_concept_note.pdf> (accessed 18 June 2008).

—— (2008b) *Disability, Including Prevention, Management and Rehabilitation.* Online. <http://www.who.int/ncd/disability/index.htm> (accessed 18 June 2008).

—— (2009) *World Report on Disability and Rehabilitation.* Online. <http://www.who.int/disabilities/publications/concept_note_2009.pdf> (accessed 14 February 2010.

15 Gender and customary mechanisms of justice in Uganda[1]

Joanna R. Quinn

The resolution of conflict and the requisite social rebuilding, in many cases, takes place within a framework of what has come to be known as transitional justice. In many parts of the world, however, this rebuilding takes place within the kinds of mechanisms that are customarily used in Uganda to resolve conflict and to re-order communities after a dispute. At present, these mechanisms are being employed to deal with the circumstances arising from the protracted conflicts which have been present in Uganda since at least 1971. This chapter explores the access that women in Uganda, who shoulder much of the burden of civil conflict, abuse, and abduction, have to these mechanisms, and their agency therein. It is clear that women are often left out of the social rebuilding process. Their attitudes toward, and inclusion in, traditional mechanisms of justice are explored below.

Certainly, there are no easy conclusions to be drawn about gender and customary mechanisms of justice in Uganda. For the most part, it seems that women are involved in such practices only in a limited manner, sometimes only as informal advisors, if at all. Ugandan women themselves do not seem to agree on the value and efficacy of such practices. While this can be explained by a number of factors, including modernization, education, or women's own direct exposure to conflict, what is clear is that women on all sides of the divide continue to respect the traditional practices of their communities, and that women are beginning to demand more of a direct role in the resolution of conflict and the rebuilding of their communities.

Background and history of current conflict

Since the time of Independence in 1962, Uganda has been wracked by conflict. Under both Idi Amin and Milton Obote, many thousands of Ugandans were wounded and killed. It is estimated that between 300,000 (Briggs 1998: 23) and 500,000 (Museveni 1997: 41) Ugandans were killed during the time of Idi Amin, from 1971 to 1979. Under the rule of Obote, between 1980 and 1985, approximately 300,000 (*Uganda* 1998: 53) to 500,000 (Nadduli interview with author) were killed. The current President, Yoweri Museveni, seized power by means of military force in 1986. As with his predecessors, Museveni has faced considerable opposition from many of the 56 different ethnic groups throughout the country. Between 1986 and 2008, Museveni faced more than 27 armed insurgencies.[2]

One of the longest-lasting, and most devastating, is the conflict in northern Uganda. Joseph Kony and his Lord's Resistance Army (LRA) troops have perpetrated brutal abuses on the people of northern Uganda, including widespread child abduction and forced conscription. Women, particularly, have been brutalized, and have faced significant numbers of sexual crimes, whether as sex slaves or as innocent bystanders. Northern Uganda has been devastated by this conflict, which "has over the years spread across the entire northern region and parts of the east" (UNOCHA 2006). At the height of the conflict, it was estimated that 1.8 million (Latim interview with author, 2004; World Vision 2004: 4) people were internally displaced (IDP) within the region and living in ostensibly protected camps for the internally displaced, a figure which represented more than 80 percent of the region's population.

In 2006, peace talks between the government of Uganda and LRA rebels began in Juba, South Sudan, mediated by Riek Machar of the government of South Sudan (Quinn 2009a). In 2008 the peace talks came to an end and Kony walked away. The LRA remains active within the region. It is not known precisely how many rebel soldiers remain "in the bush"—a local colloquialism that refers to the theatre of war—with the LRA; estimates range from 200 to 20,000. In reality, the war is far from over.

Methodology

The inquiry into women's access to, and involvement in, traditional mechanisms of justice in Uganda is part of an ongoing research project that has considered the use and utility of customary approaches to justice in transitional, post-conflict and "pre"-post-conflict Uganda. Since 2004, I have been engaged in a qualitative study that seeks to understand traditional methods of conflict resolution and post-conflict reconciliation. I am specifically interested in the role that these processes play in a society's acknowledgment of past crimes and abuses, and whether or not they are able to succeed where other "Western" approaches, like the truth commission or other judicial mechanisms, have failed.

This chapter focuses on gender differences, and on the gender-specific nature of the application of these mechanisms of justice in Uganda. It is an investigation into the agency and access of women throughout Uganda to traditional practices of justice, recognizing that women have been especially hard-hit by past and current conflicts throughout the country (Isis-WICCE 2004: 5), and that women simultaneously fulfill a number of different roles in society (Ní Aoláin and Rooney 2007: 340). Although this chapter focuses on gender difference and women, it is not analytically oriented either toward or from a feminist perspective (Mohanty 1998: 77; Tsing and Yanagisako 1983: 516). Rather, through the use of "thick description," it seeks to understand the impact of a particular phenomenon—the continued use of traditional mechanisms of justice (Geertz 1973: 7–10).

In total, 47 interviews were conducted, as well as seven focus group meetings, in August and September 2006. Due to security fears, the granting agency had stipulated that the research team must remain in and near Kampala, so all of the interviews and focus groups were conducted there. To avoid selection bias, the interviewees were selected primarily on the basis of ethnicity, but also with regard to age, level of education, and occupation. These individuals represented 17 different ethnic groups, including Acholi, Alur, Baganda, Bafumbira, Bagisu, Banyankole, Banyoro, Baruli, Basamia, Batooro, Iteso, Jopadhola, Lugbara, Sabiny, Langi, Karamojong, and Kumam. Of the 47 individual interviews that were conducted, five men were interviewed, and the balance of interviewees were women. The composition of the focus groups varied, from small groups of three to one with 95. The women interviewed ranged from well-educated women working in professional jobs to conflict-displaced women living in shanties or on the street. There were seven focus groups altogether. In total, the focus groups included more than 152 women.

Traditional mechanisms of justice

Traditional or customary mechanisms of justice have been used in societies including aboriginal communities in North America, across Africa, and elsewhere.[3] They are used to resolve problems and conflicts. Each of Uganda's many ethnic communities traditionally used different forms of customary mechanisms of justice to deal with conflict. And although in some instances these kinds of traditions have disappeared, subsumed by the Western model of retributive justice, in other places they are still regularly used. Rather than pass judgment on whether their decline is either positive or negative, this chapter aims to explore the nuanced understandings of the women who are familiar with them about how they operate, and their opinions about them.

Traditional values and teachings inform such practices. In many instances, these customs look very similar to the kinds of mechanisms that existed in pre-Western societies. In other instances, they are simply modeled on old institutions, with changes made to make them relevant to contemporary circumstances; in this way, they are "neo-traditional" institutions (Brown 2005; Hayner 2001: 192). In many cases, these mechanisms have also been formalized, in that their proceedings are regularized and carried out according to pre-arranged and codified rules. For example, Article 129 of the 1995 Constitution provides for Local Council (LC) Courts to operate at the sub-county, parish, and village levels ("Uganda," 2005).[4] Under the subsequent Children Statute 1996, these courts have the authority to mandate any number of things including reconciliation, compensation, restitution, and apology (GOU 1996). These mechanisms either provide a parallel model of justice, or sometimes they are used in addition to Western mechanisms. Although these mechanisms broadly fit within very different approaches to justice, whether retributive or restorative, and fulfill different roles within their respective societies, from cleansing and welcoming to prosecution and punishment, what they have in common is that they draw upon traditional customs and ideas in the administration of justice in modern times. Little or no attention is paid to women as these practices are carried out.

In Uganda, many of the ethnic groups throughout the country continue to utilize such practices. For example, the Karamojong rely on the *akiriket* councils of elders to adjudicate disputes according to traditional custom (Novelli 1999: 169–172, 333–340), which includes various forms of cultural teaching and ritual cleansing ceremonies (Lokeris interview with author). The Baganda traditionally used *Kitewuliza*, a juridical process with a strong element of reconciliation, to bring about justice (Waliggo 2003: 7; 2005: 1). A system of elder mediation is used in family, clan, and inter-clan conflict by the Lugbara (Ndrua 1988: 42–56).

The Acholi, the group most affected by the current conflict in northern Uganda, utilize a number of different ceremonies (Harlacher et al. 2006). One such ceremony is *mato oput* (drinking the bitter herb), and another is called *nyouo tong gweno lumuku* (a welcoming ceremony in which an egg is stepped on over an *opobo* twig). Through these ceremonies, the Acholi acknowledge that a person has been accepted back into the community, and that the community is pleased to have them back. In many cases, these ceremonies appear to have more cultural relevance than other initiatives (Quinn 2006: 23–27).

> For the Acholi, for one to stay away from his home for a long time, that is never acceptable, that is always something bad, something associated with bitterness. So these words always are part of the ceremony for returnees. *Wa ojoli paco*, these are also words spoken at the ceremony. It means, "we welcome you home." It is to say that, "the people have forgiven you every-thing, the Acholi people welcome you back and they now want you to take responsibilities in the community." Immediately you are welcomed in the community, the community is beginning to extend its services and responsibilities to you. People will come and talk to you. Once a child is born in Acholi culture, that child becomes part and parcel of that particular family, and the clan, and then the community. So the whole community would also expect some responsibility from you.
>
> (Hovil and Quinn 2005: 24)

Both of these ceremonies are being used to welcome ex-combatants, both men and women, boys and girls, home from the current conflict after they have escaped from the rebel army (Finnström 2003: 297–299). In 1985, *gomo tong* (the bending of spears), an inter-tribal reconciliation ceremony, was held to signify that "from that time there would be no war or fighting between [the following ethnic groups:] Acholi and Madi, Kakwa, Lugbara or Alur of West Nile" (Finnström 2003: 299). A similar ceremony, called *amelokwit*, took place between the Iteso and the Karamojong in 2004 (Iteso focus group).

It is my observation that ethnic groups which were traditionally organized hierarchically, such as the Baganda, are less likely now to utilize these mechanisms. Conversely, those ethnic societies that were arranged horizontally, with a system of equal clans, like the Acholi, are more likely to continue to utilize these mechanisms (Quinn 2009b). It seems that the hierarchical stratification of societies with entrenched kingdoms, whose social order was organized from top to bottom, were more likely to coordinate whole formalized political systems, of which justice formed one part. Certainly, this is the case in Buganda, where the *kitawulizi* courts, used mostly at the sub-sub-county level, were headed by the head of that particular political strata; he, in turn, reported to *muluka* chiefs, and so on, up to the *katikkiro*, and ultimately, the *kabakka*, or king, who had the power to reverse the decisions made (Walusimbe interview with author). This pattern seems to repeat itself in Uganda today, in that those ethnic groups with highly stratified kingdoms, including Buganda, Toro, Ankole, and others, use such traditions infrequently.

Certainly, and not surprisingly, the role played by traditional mechanisms of justice has changed. This mirrors what has been shown about social institutions throughout the world: institutions change over time, influenced by current social practice (Weber 1968). Influences including colonialism and the imposition of a central government have altered the way in which justice is administered (British Colonial Office 1961). The war itself has caused tremendous change, and has made it difficult to "teach the children [the] Acholi culture" (Oballim 2006); some feel that the younger generation does not recognize or understand such mechanisms any longer, a complaint that is not uncommon in many societies around the world. As well, the introduction of other religions, and in particular Christianity, appears to have led many to reject the use of traditional mechanisms of justice—although a number of people interviewed referred to the level of compatibility between their religious beliefs and Acholi traditional mechanisms of justice, and saw no contradiction. There is also considerable evidence to show that, in some cases, Christian practices have been incorporated into traditional mechanisms of justice—in Toro, for example, where previously human blood was used in rituals, it has now been replaced by holy water.

There is some evidence of the decline of such practices.[5] "The traditional values, cultural knowledge and social institutions of everyday life are threatened" (Finnström 2003: 201).

> Certain practices and beliefs are still widespread in some areas of Acholi but less common in others. Moreover, some rituals might not have been performed for a long time in a particular area because it has not been possible to put together all the necessary components due to extreme poverty or war-time insecurity, but might still be applicable and sought after by the community.
>
> (Harlacher et al. 2006: 113)

Also, the social meanings of the ceremonies that are still practiced appear, in some cases, to be shifting as people move farther away from their *gemeinschaft* communities (Finnström 2003: 298). Among the Karamojong (Novelli 1999: 201–225) and also among the Acholi (Finnström 2003: 76, 219; Evans-Pritchard 1937: 154) cultural education, through practice and social education, is beginning to decline.

The ongoing conflict is another factor that explains the reduced use of traditional mechanisms of justice amongst the Acholi people. Particularly in the IDP camps, these kinds of traditional practices have been disrupted. Spending such a long time in what were initially perceived as temporary facilities has significantly changed the way of life of those who live there. "[P]eople are no longer able to sit around a campfire in the evenings and talk, as it is too dangerous . . . [T]he essence of their lives ha[s] been destroyed by displacement: the physical structures of the camps have created an artificial environment that has damaged the fabric of the communities" (Hovil and Quinn 2005: 24). Others have noted a "diminishing respect for elders" in the camps (Okello and Hovil 2007: 442), which also contributes to the declining use of such mechanisms.

Yet many Ugandans feel that these traditional mechanisms of justice have a great deal to offer. Many people reported to me that "everyone respects these traditions" (Sabiny man interview with author) and that reconciliation continues to be an "essential and final part of peaceful settlement of conflict" (Waliggo 2003: 9). A common understanding of these symbols, ceremonies, and institutions, and their meanings remains throughout Uganda.

> It would be wrong to imagine that everything traditional has been changed or forgotten so much that no traces of it are to be found. If anything, the changes are generally on the surface, affecting the material side of life, and only beginning to reach the deeper levels of the thinking pattern, language content, mental images, emotions, beliefs and response in situations of need. Traditional concepts still form the essential background of many African peoples, though obviously this differs from individual to individual and from place to place. I believe . . . that the majority of our people with little or no formal education still hold on to their traditional corpus of beliefs.
>
> (Mbiti 2002: xi)

Finnström and others also take this into account: "These practices, far from being dislocated in a past that no longer exists, have always continued to be situated socially. They are called upon to address present concerns. Of course, like any culturally informed practice, with time they shift in meaning and appearance" (Finnström 2003: 299). "Ideas about old models are often used to help shape new ones" (Allen 2005: 84). After the conflict has ended, however, it is "not clear whether the post-colonial state [will] return to a pre-colonial experience" (Kiogora 2003: 25) or whether such institutions will continue to adapt to new experiences and conditions. Whatever the case, Ugandans will attempt to "re-member . . . to put parts back where they matter, to bring about a wholeness" (Kiogora 2003: 25).

Women and conflict

Women are deeply affected by war and armed conflict (Moser and Clark 2001: 4). Women "suffer the impact of conflict disproportionately" (Isis-WICCE 2004:

5). They face gender-specific crimes such as rape, gang rape, and sexual slavery (*Women* 2004). Indeed, during "civil conflicts in Africa . . . rape and forcible abduction [are] systematic, deliberate strategies of the wars" (Turshen 2001: 55). For many women and girls, these crimes occur while they are going about the business of everyday living, collecting firewood or water, for example ("Only Peace" 2006: 26). It is women, predominantly, who carry out these tasks. And, "[w]hile they likely did these tasks before displacement, women now do them with the fear of being raped by the UPDF and its auxiliary forces, or by the LRA and marauding deserters. As one interviewee stated: 'Now we have to go far and it is not safe. But we go because there is no option. We cannot afford to buy firewood or charcoal, so we end up taking risks'" (Okello and Hovil 2007: 439).

> [W]omen are expected to serve as the 'shock absorbers' that take in all the pain and suffering. They nurse the injured and the ill due to rampant 'opportunistic diseases' [*sic*], provide solace to the orphaned; and fill the gap created by their men, who are away at war . . . [W]ar and armed conflict increases women's responsibilities. They are—as well—expected to knit together the ragged social fabric as their husbands, brothers and sons are more often psychologically hit hard by their 'failure' to keep families together and to provide for and protect them.
>
> While—as mentioned above—women fight hard to ensure the survival of others, . . . war and armed conflict reduces women's survival rate overall; as it intensifies all forms of violence against them. 'Women are the first ones to breathe and sleep with the burdens of war, and the last ones to be allowed to fall into depression and despair.'
>
> ("Unhealed Scars" 2003: 9–10)

"[M]any women and girls in northern Uganda are left unprotected in every area of their lives with few alternatives, and the 'protection gap' with respect to girls and women appears to be more serious than other protection issues" ("Only Peace" 2006: 26). There is often a "noticeable shift in the traditional values of men and women; [*sic*] as both groups engage . . . in activities they never would have done under normal circumstances" ("Unhealed Scars" 2003: 57). "Societal practices and norms have been perverted. Distortions in pre-displacement cultural values have hindered appropriate responses in the camps, which have now become sites for contesting norms" (Okello and Hovil 2007: 437). Conflict changes societies.

Contrary to much of what has been reported for a number of years, women are themselves agents of conflict. Women have increasingly participated in armed groups at formal and informal levels (Moser and Clark 2001: 9). Throughout the world, women have been implicated in uprisings such as the Palestinian *intifada* in protest against Israel's occupation of the territory, in the Rwandan genocide, in the Tamil rebellion in Sri Lanka (Cockburn 2001: 21). This is complicated, of course, in the case of northern Uganda, where women and girls are routinely abducted against their will, and forced to perpetrate abuses themselves (Hovil and

Lomo 2005: 9). Similarly, mothers of abducted child soldiers often provide their children with food and supplies—not so much to assist the war effort, as to care for their children.

The agency, and subsequent culpability, of women is deeply affected by this plurality of roles, since women and girls can be identified as both victims and perpetrators in the ongoing conflict (UN Secretary General 2000). The application of intersectionality theory, which provides a framework for analysis of "social categories or 'identities'" (Ní Aoláin and Rooney 2007: 340) is helpful in this regard, as it effectively captures the complex situation created both by and for women in northern Uganda. Women simultaneously have a number of differing identities as wide-ranging as victim and perpetrator—and everything in between. Any analysis must recognize and incorporate this intersectionality.

Women in Uganda

Historically, there were strictly defined gender roles for both men and women in Uganda. In pre-colonial Acholi, for example,

> Being rich for a man . . . meant primarily having many cattle as well as many wives and children (although having many wives and cattle was a consequence as well as a sign of wealth). Prestige for both men and women depended very much on having many children. Without having "produced" one could certainly not be a respected person in the community.
>
> This was especially true for women. And in addition to bearing and raising children, women had to work hard and for long hours to make the household run. It was considered their work to fetch water, collect firewood and cook every day, while simultaneously looking after children and smaller domestic animals. Collecting wild fruits and mushrooms was also regarded as women's work . . . Agricultural work was shared fairly equally between men and women, with men also responsible for looking after cattle, hunting, physical protection, and warfare.
>
> Women had to show high respect towards men. For example, they were expected to kneel down when greeting their husbands and visitors, and usually had to wait until the men had finished with their meal before they ate.
>
> (Harlacher et al. 2006: 40–41)

Certain occupations, such as spirit healer (*ajwaki*) (Harlacher et al. 2006: 57), priestess, healer, and fortune-teller (Kabahoma interview with author), were typically held by women. This is consistent with the history of most African societies, where women have been responsible for the fetching of water and firewood, milking of cattle, and carrying the produce from farms to sell at markets (HRDD 1972: 359). Traditionally, subsistence "tends to dictate certain clearly defined roles . . . [And v]arious beliefs and religions in Africa also provide a basis for status definition, most often to the advantage of the male" (HRDD 1972: 360).

The coming of the colonial British to Uganda in the late nineteenth and early twentieth centuries began a process of social change. Britain formally declared a protectorate over the area which now comprises Uganda in 1894 (Pirouet 1996: 303–306), and introduced foreign systems of taxation and governance (Ngologoza 1998), disrupting the region's "equilibrium" (Novelli 1988: 117–124). Traditional leadership was effectively abolished by the colonial government (Harlacher et al. 2006: 30–32; Ngologoza 1998: 61–64). The coming of missionaries, too, caused misunderstanding, confrontation, and resistance (Behrend 1999: 113–127). "The adaptation of Acholi religious beliefs started right from the beginning of evangelization. This can be interpreted as an expression of the original Acholi attitude towards religion, which reflects a high level of flexibility and ability to incorporate and tolerate" (Harlacher et al. 2006: 51). Similarly, in Karamoja, "the Africans . . . [were not the colonials'] equals, able to enter into dialogue with them. They were simply objects of their work" (Novelli 1988: 148). "The missionaries tried to force everything out" (Sempangi interview with author 2004). At the time, these changes meant little to many of the women of Uganda, who still carried out traditional gender roles, as outlined above. For some women, though, "modernity influenced traditions that used to give a place to women, if indirectly" (Kabahoma interview with author).

Independence in 1962, however, marked a significant change for the status of women in Uganda. During this period, women began to agitate for political rights and power (Tamale 1999). "[I]t is clear that there has been, and continues to be, considerable activity among women to achieve gender equality in formal politics" (Ottemoeller 1999: 92) and in other spheres as well, although "women's groups sometimes avoid political advocacy" (Staudt and Glickman 1989: 5), making their advocacy difficult to see. Uganda instituted the practice of electing a separate slate of Women Members of Parliament in every national election in 1986, which ensures more representation for women at the highest level (Mugyenyi 1998: 38). And a number of laws, including the Constitution (1995), the Penal Code Act, the Trial on Indictment Act, the Succession Act, the Divorce Act, and the Children Statute have been passed for the protection of women's rights. "Collectively [, they] criminalise early and forced marriage, defilement, forced prostitution, rape, indecent assault, and female genital mutilation" (Okello and Hovil 2007: 436).

Conflict, of course, has changed the way that women and men are able to interact in Ugandan society. Since the coming of Independence, conflict has wrecked various regions of the country. And, as outlined above, women have borne the impact of these conflicts disproportionately. But the shifting traditional roles of men and women during conflict have not simply disappeared when various conflicts have ended. Women continue, in many cases, to perform tasks that were once carried out exclusively by men ("Unhealed Scars" 2003: 57). There is now no *one* "everyday gender system, discussed in singular and monolithic terms, since no such 'system' exists" anymore (Sanders 2000: 470).[6]

In Ugandan society today, women continue to be treated unequally (*BBC News* 2007). "Questions of women and gender are new in the discourse" (Allimadi interview with author). Women and girls continue to be targets of increasing numbers of rapes ("Defilement cases" 2007). Ugandan laws have institutionalized this discrimination, making it illegal for a married woman to have an adulterous affair, but not illegal for a husband to do the same (*BBC News* 2007). "Women are not yet empowered" (Kanakulya interview with author). "Moreover, gender inequality is embedded in the local culture and traditions . . . so women have always been powerless and excluded from the public arena" (*Women* 2003: 61).

Women and traditional mechanisms of justice

Traditionally, women were left out of Ugandan traditional practices involving conflict resolution or peacemaking. The male elders of each clan of each ethnic group carried out such ceremonies. "Women had no authority, no agency" (Kabahoma interview with author). "While elderly women would be involved in these rituals, they would play no official role. They would be at the back of the process" (Kigule interview with author). Others told me that "women, in recon-ciliation matters, do not play a very active role. But views are sought by the elders from everyone, including women" (G. Onentho interview with author). "Elderly women would sit behind, and not meet men face-to-face" (Kabahoma interview with author).

Ceremonies differed considerably when women were involved as victims or perpetrators. The treatment of men and women was, and is, simply, different. In Acholi, "the procedure for cleansing someone who has killed a woman differs in a number of ways. First, the ritual lasts four days instead of three. Second, the killer is required to perform all the work a woman is expected to do in society" (Harlacher et al. 2006: 104). In Toro, "if a girl got pregnant too early, her elder brother would spear her and kill her. There is no reconciliation. But there is no punishment for a man unless for incest" (Mutoro woman interview with author). Among the Alur, after household assets like chickens were stolen, "punishment differed for men and for women. If a man has stolen the chicken, he is caned and must repay what was stolen. If a woman has stolen the chicken, the husband is made to pay for the woman's crime" (G.Onentho interview with author). In times of reconciliation, if a woman has done something wrong, "she is demeaned and made to feel worthless" (G. Onentho interview with author).

Women's formal involvement in these ceremonies, traditionally, was relegated to their exchange as little more than chattels. In most areas of the country, for example, after a conflict, intermarriage between formerly conflicting parties was carried out, and girls were exchanged from one party to the other without a say in the matter (Iteso focus group). "Women would rarely take a case to the chief. If a conflict was between a wife and husband, the wife would take her case to her brothers, who would decide the case" (G. Onentho interview with author). "Even in the home, women had no voice. Women don't always want to dig, have cows, that sort of thing. But if your husband wants to sell [livestock or produce], you cannot challenge him. He is not asking, just informing you. And you should not complain, because you are a woman. So also only the men could take the soup [for the mato oput] because they were the ones doing war" (Northern Uganda focus group). This is consistent with the practice, across most of the country, of arranged marriage, wherein a woman has no choice about the man she will marry.

In spite of that, Ugandan women proudly explained their role as private advisors to their husbands. "A man doesn't like a woman out-talking him in public. In private, he would consult her. But he cannot say he is going to consult her. He would be said to be spoiled by a woman" (Iteso focus group). "A woman's role in these ceremonies was behind the scenes" (R.Othieno interview with author). Instead of being angry that they were relegated only to function as a kind of *consiglieri*, all of the women I interviewed were proud of this contribution, and saw nothing strange about the separation of genders in this area. Indeed, this kind of popular African feminism is "based on the vestiges of the matriarchy where women enjoyed a special privileged status" (Touré et al. 2003: 2–3; Dolphyne 1991).

Women, too, played an important role in the counseling of other women. In Karamoja, for example, women have a parallel elders' system, in which they decide a number of things for the community (Karamojong focus group). In all parts of Uganda, women of all ages, but particularly older women, known as "the aunties," played an important role in carrying out the social teaching of girl children. In Sabei, "the aunties taught us how to behave. [Childhood] was a period of education for people to teach about how to raise children and live in harmony and how to behave in society. These teachings were taught before and after cutting [circumcision]" (Sabiny woman interview with author). In Teso, "young girls were mostly handled by the aunties, who taught them digging and cooking and so on" (Iteso man interview with author). In Acholi, if a woman has problems with her husband, or needs advice, "she goes to her auntie, or to her mother. Girls and boys are separated like this" (Acholi focus group). In Toro, "the women met separately to decide sex education for the girls, also domestic concerns like harvest and planting, and things like witch-craft" (Mutoro woman interview with author).

In some circumstances, women are involved to a greater extent. Among the Alur, for example, the participation of women in these ceremonies, which are still carried out today, is determined by how the ceremony is organized. Most commonly, if the ceremony is carried out with the participation of the royal clan, and presided over by the chief, then the participation of women is rare, and almost all of the activity is carried out by men. But if the ceremony is carried out at a lower level, such as between families, then women play a greater role. Women are able to contribute to the overall discussion, but if the victim of the crime in question is a woman, then the women are given substantially less input. The negotiators, in all cases, are men (G. Onentho interview with author).

In Acholi, "[t]he voice of women is traditionally heard in community discussions, although women's status, particularly as controllers of the household economy, has arguably been severely lowered compared with pre-colonial days. The *Rwot mon*, as an older respected 'elder' of the women, carries considerably more respect than the recently elected women's representative on an LC" (Pain 1997: 38). "Women leaders are also respected and their voice listened to. These *Lawii-mon* or, more formally, *Rwodi-mon*, are those who are knowledgeable in all aspects of women's affairs. They are also respected on clan affairs. One of them is traditionally installed at the same time as the *Rwhot-mo*" (Pain 1997: 73). At the present time, female ex-combatants and their children participate equally in ceremonies of *nyouo tong gweno lumuku* and *mato oput* that are organized by the Acholi elders (Harlacher et al. 2006: 64–92).

The women I interviewed were somewhat divided, therefore, about the utility of such ceremonies in modern times. There seemed to be a division of opinion between those women who were from the greater north and those from the south. Indeed, this seems to be due, in part, to the fact that the war in northern Uganda has affected only northerners. But this is also, as discussed above, due to the significance of such customary practices in horizontally or vertically organized ethnic societies; the majority of societies organized vertically are in the south, while more of those in the north are organized horizontally. Northern Ugandans, and particularly those from Acholi and Lango, overwhelmingly saw these ceremonies as useful—although opinion was divided on the further issue of punishment, amnesty, and the International Criminal Court (Hovil and Quinn 2005).

While most of the women had opinions, some "modern" women, living and working in the capital, admitted that they had never before seen even one of these kinds of rituals (Bantebya interview with author). Still, they understand and respect the importance of such ceremonies and practices. "My mother-in-law knows that I am modern and educated. But I respect her traditions and she respects me as a modern woman" (Acholi woman interview with author). "Even those of us who live in the city, and have schooling, everyone respects these traditions" (Sabiny woman interview with author). For these women, there was no conflict between the acceptance of traditional mechanisms of justice and the use of modern means.

Overall, "these days, women can talk" (Northern Uganda focus group). Indeed, women's groups in Uganda recognize that women's "participation is vital to forging the consensus necessary for lasting peace" (*Women* 2003: 61).

> There is a growing recognition that women have a right to participate . . . and women's participation is increasingly supported . . . by positive action programs and other mechanisms. Women in war zones who struggle to get their voices heard offer a different and unique perspective on the purpose of the peace negotiations and the rationale for their participation. They argue that women as victims have a right to voice their concerns at the peace table because they are often the deliberate targets of physical and sexual abuse. They are forced out of their homes and villages. The peace-table provides an opportunity for all stakeholders to foster confidence and initiate the long process of reconciliation and healing. Without the presence and the voices of the stakeholders on all sides this process can never be complete.
>
> (*Women* 2003: 62–63)

A number of peace-focused groups led by women are active all across Uganda. Two of the best-known and most active of these are Isis-Women's International Cross-Cultural Exchange, and the Centre for Conflict Resolution. Focusing almost exclusively on women and women's experiences in conflict, these groups train groups of women as negotiators and mediators, in carrying out psycho-social trauma counseling, and in the process of reconciliation. "It is easy for women to talk to fellow women, and we know we're the ones influencing our husbands and children" (Iteso focus group).

Throughout late 2006, women in Uganda also pushed to become involved in the ongoing peace talks with the LRA in Juba, South Sudan. This is consistent with Security Council Resolution 1325, which encourages the involvement of women in decision-making about peace processes. With the assistance of UNIFEM, a small number of women have been present at the talks, including Hon. Betty Ocan, Gulu District Women MP (Ocan interview with author). Otherwise, however, women have been excluded.

Conclusions

The role of women in Ugandan society is changing, and has been changing over the past 50 years. Women have become educated. They now play a more equal role in all aspects of society—in many cases, even assuming the traditional roles of men as these roles have been abdicated over the years. In part, this process has been speeded up by the many conflicts that have consumed the country in the same period. To be sure, women have suffered the consequences of the conflicts unequally.

It is clear that women play only a small direct role in the traditional mechanisms of justice that are carried out to remedy conflict. Indeed, their role behind the scenes is larger. But even this is so small as to be relatively inconsequential. Yet, I came away with the understanding that the women I talked to were not troubled by this lack of agency. In fact, many of these women still feel protected by the social conventions of their communities—even when those communities have been blown apart by conflict. The women seemed to feel that traditional mechanisms of justice address their needs, to an extent.

But, like others, women want peace. And a return to normalcy. And many of them seem to feel that if these mechanisms can go some way toward getting to peace, their use should continue.

Notes

1   Research for this project was carried out with assistance from the AUCC Canada Corps University Partnership Program (2006) #X2730A20.
2   These include rebellions by Action Restore Peace, Allied Democratic Forces, Apac rebellion, Citizen Army for Multiparty Politics, Force Obote Back, Former Uganda National Army, Holy Spirit Movement, the Lord's Army, Lord's Resistance Army, National Federal Army, National Union for the Liberation of Uganda, Ninth October Movement, People's Redemption Army, Uganda Christian Democratic Army, Uganda Federal Democratic Front, Uganda Freedom Movement, Ugandan National

Democratic Army, Uganda National Federal Army, Ugandan National Liberation Front, Ugandan National Rescue Fronts I and II, Ugandan People's Army, Ugandan People's Democratic Army, Uganda Salvation Army, and the West Nile Bank Front (Hovil and Lomo 2004: 4; Hovil and Lomo 2005: 6).

3   The terms *institution, mechanism, custom, ceremony*, and *ritual* are used to describe those traditional or customary practices used in the social rebuilding process. Different terms are used because the nature and scope of these practices vary across groups.

4   The LC Courts were formerly known as Resistance Council Courts and "were first introduced in Luweero in 1983 during the struggle for liberation. In 1987 they were legally recognized throughout the country" (Waliggo 2003: 7).

5   Allen reports that a study funded by the Belgian government revealed that young people no longer automatically respect the elders (Allen 2005: 76).

6   Although it would be easy to draw grand and overarching conclusions about differing gender roles from the information presented here, this would be inappropriate. It is important to note that the experiences of the women to whom I spoke are very deeply rooted in the particular circumstances of Uganda. And so I am reluctant to do so.

Bibliography

Allen, T. (2005) *War and Justice in Northern Uganda: an assessment of the International Criminal Court's intervention*, London: Crisis States Research Centre, Development Studies Institute, London School of Economics.

Barnes, C. and Lucima, O. (2002) "Introduction," *Accord*, 11.

BBC News "Ugandan adultery law 'too sexist.'" (2007) Online. Available at <http://news.bbc.co.uk/go/pr/fr/-/2/hi/africa/6528869.stm.> (5 April, accessed 23 April 2007).

Behrend, H. (1999) *Alice Lakwena and the Holy Spirits: war in Northern Uganda 1986–1997*, Kampala: Fountain Publishers.

Berg-Schlosser, D. and Siegler, R. (2000) *Political Stability and Development: a comparative analysis of Kenya, Tanzania and Uganda*, Boulder, CO: Lynne Rienner.

Briggs, P. (1998) *Uganda*, Old Saybrook, CT: The Globe Pequot Press.

British Colonial Office (1961) *Report of the Uganda Relationship Committee*.

Brown, S. (2005) "Forging National Unity in Rwanda: government strategies and grassroots responses," paper presented at Reconciliation, a conference held by the Nationalism and Ethnic Conflict Research Centre at the University of Western Ontario, May 14–15. Author's collection.

Cockburn, C. (2001) "The Gendered Dynamics of Armed Conflict and Political Violence," in Moser, C.O.N. and Clark, F.C. (eds) *Victims, Perpetrators or Actors? Gender, armed conflict and political violence*, London: Zed Books.

"Defilement cases increase," (2007) *New Vision*. Online. <http://www.newvision.co.ug/D/8/17/562865> (1 May, accessed 1 May 2007).

Dolphyne, F. A. (1991) *The Emancipation of Women: an African perspective*, Accra: Ghana University Press.

Evans-Pritchard, E.E. (1937) *Witchcraft, Oracles and Magic Among the Azande*, Oxford: Clarendon Press.

Finnström, S. (2003) *Living with Bad Surroundings: war and existential uncertainty in Acholiland in Northern Uganda*, Uppsala Studies in Cultural Anthropology No. 35, Uppsala: Acta Universitatis Upsaliensis.

Geertz, C. (1973) "Thick Description: toward an interpretive theory of culture," in C. Geertz (ed.) *The Interpretation of Cultures*, New York: Basic Books.

Government of Uganda (GOU) (1996) *The Children Statute 1996.*

Harlacher, T., Okot, F. X., Obonyo, C.A., Balthazard, M., and Atkinson, R. (2006) *Traditional Ways of Coping in Acholi: cultural provisions for reconciliation and healing from war*, Kampala: Thomas Harlacher and Caritas Gulu Archdiocese.

Hayner, P. (2001) *Unspeakable Truths*, New York: Routledge.

Hovil, L. and Lomo, Z. (2004) *Behind the Violence: causes, consequences and the search for solutions to the war in northern Uganda*, Working Paper 11, Kampala: Refugee Law Project, Feb.

Hovil, L. and Lomo, Z. (2005) *Whose Justice? Perceptions of Uganda's Amnesty Act 2000: the potential for conflict resolution and long-term reconciliation*, Working Paper 15, Kampala: Refugee Law Project, Feb.

Hovil, L. and Quinn, J. (2005) *Peace First, Justice Later*, Working Paper 17, Kampala: Refugee Law Project.

Human Resources Development Division (HRDD), United Nations Economic Commission for Africa, Addis Ababa (1972) "Women: the neglected human resource for African development," *Canadian Journal of African Studies*, 7.2.

Isis-WICCE (2004) "Important Observations on Armed Conflict and Women," *Documenting the Violations of Women [sic] Rights during Armed Conflict: Proceedings of the Isis-WICCE 2004 Institute*, 23 Aug.–3 Sep., Kampala: Isis-Women's International Cross-Cultural Exchange.

Khiddu-Makubuya, E. (1989) "Paramilitarism and Human Rights," in Rupesinghe, K. (ed.) *Conflict Resolution in Uganda*, Oslo: International Peace Research Institute.

Kiogora, T. G. (2003) "Good Governance for Development: perspectives from the African traditional cultural heritage," in Rupesinghe, K., Assefa, H., and Wachira, G. (eds) *Peacemaking and Democratisation in Africa*, Nairobi: East African Educational Publishers.

Mbiti, J. S. (2002) *African Religions and Philosophy*, Kampala: East African Educational Publishers, 1969.

Mohanty, C. (1998) "Under Western Eyes: feminist scholarship and colonial discourses," *Feminist Review*, 30.

Moser, C. O. N. and Clark, F.C. (eds) (2001) *Victims, Perpetrators or Actors? Gender, Armed Conflict and Political Violence*, London: Zed Books.

Mugyenyi, M. R. (1998) "Towards the Empowerment of Women: a critique of NRM policies and programmes," in Hansen, H.B and Twaddle, M. (eds) *Developing Uganda*, Kampala: Fountain Publishers.

Museveni, Y. K. (1997) *Sowing the Mustard Seed*, London: Macmillan.

Ndrua, J. (1988) "A Christian Study of the African Concept of Authority and the Administration of Justice among the Lugbari of North Western Uganda," M.A. diss., Catholic Higher Institute of East Africa.

Ngologoza, P. (1998) *Kigezi and Its People*, Kampala: Fountain Publishers.

Ní Aoláin, F. and Rooney, E. (2007) "Underenforcement and Intersectionality: gendered aspects of transition for women," *International Journal of Transitional Justice*, 1.3.

Novelli, B. (1988) *Aspects of Karimojong Ethnosociology*, Verona: Museum Combonianum, no. 44.

—— (1999) *Karimojong Traditional Religion*, Kampala: Comboni Missionaries.

Oballim, B. (2006) "Camp Leader, Labuje Camp, Kitgum," cited in *Trapped in Anguish: A call for Acholi reconciliation*. Produced by Northern Uganda Peace Initiative, Eyes on Africa. Videocassette.

Ofcansky, T. P. (1996) *Uganda: tarnished pearl of Africa*, Boulder, CO: Westview.

Okello, M. C. and Hovil, L. (2007) "Confronting the Reality of Gender-Based Violence in Northern Uganda," *International Journal of Transitional Justice*, 1.3.

"*Only Peace Can Restore the Confidence of the Displaced*" (2006) *Update on the Implementation of the Recommendations made by the UN Secretary-General's Representative on Internally Displaced Persons following his visit to Uganda*, 2nd edn, Geneva and Kampala: Internal Displacement Monitoring Centre and Refugee Law Project.

Ottemoeller, D. (1999) "The Politics of Gender in Uganda: symbolism in the service of Pragmatism," *African Studies Review*, 42.2.

Pain, D. (1997) *"The Bending of Spears": producing consensus for peace and development in Northern Uganda*, London: International Alert and Kacoke Madit.

Pirouet, L. M. (1996) "Uganda: history to 1971," in Middleton, J. (ed.) *Encyclopedia of Africa South of the Sahara*, New York: Charles Scribner's Sons.

Quinn, J. R. (2006) "Comparing Formal and Informal Mechanisms of Acknowledgement in Uganda," paper prepared for presentation on the panel, "Africa as a Subject of International Justice," at the International Studies Association Annual Meeting, 23 March.

—— (2009a) "Getting to Peace? Negotiating with the LRA in Northern Uganda," *Human Rights Review*, 10.1 (March): 55–71.

—— (2009b) "Here, Not There? Theorizing about why traditional mechanisms work in some communities, not others," paper presented on the panel, "Lost in Transition? Justice and Traditional Practices in Post-Conflict Societies," International Studies Association, New York, 15 February.

Sanders, T. (2000) "Rains Gone Bad, Women Gone Mad: rethinking gender rituals of rebellion and patriarchy," *Journal of the Royal Anthropological Institute*, 6.

Security Council (2000) Resolution 1325 (S/RES/1325).

Staudt, K. and Glickman, H. (1989) "Beyond Nairobi: women's politics and policies in Africa revisted," *Issue: A Journal of Opinion*, 17.2.

Tamale, S. (1999) *When Hens Begin to Crow: gender and parliamentary politics in Uganda*, Boulder, CO: Westview.

Touré, A., Barry, M. C., and Diallo, P. (2003) "The Two Faces of African Feminism," *CODESIRA Bulletin*, 1.

Tsing, A. L. and Yanagisako, S. J. (1983) "Feminism and Kinship Theory," *Current Anthropology*, 24.4.

Turshen, M. (2001) "The Political Economy of Rape: an analysis of systematic rape and sexual abuse of women during armed conflict in Africa," in Moser, C. O. N. and Clark, F. C. (eds) *Victims, Perpetrators or Actors? Gender, armed conflict and political violence*. London: Zed Books.

Uganda (1998) Brooklyn: Interlink Books.

"Uganda: Constitution, Government and Legislation." (2005) Online. Available at <http://jurist.law.pitt.edu/world/uganda.htm.> (30 April, accessed 30 April 2005).

"Unhealed Scars: experiences of women in the Arua armed conflict," (2003) Kampala: Uganda Women's Network.

UN Office for the Coordination of Humanitarian Affairs (UNOCHA)(2006) "Uganda: war-ravaged north rues Museveni win," IRINnews.org. Online. Available at <www. irinnews.org/print.asp?ReportID=51960.> (1 March, accessed 10 March 2006).

UN Secretary General (2000) "Secretary-General Calls for Council Action to Ensure Women are Involved in Peace and Security Decisions" Press Release SG/SM/7598. 24 October.

Waliggo, J. M. (2003) "The Human Right to Peace for Every Person and Every Society," paper presented at Public Dialogue organized by Faculty of Arts, Makerere University in conjunction with Uganda Human Rights Commission and NORAD, Kampala, Uganda, 4 December. Author's collection.

—— (2005) "On Kitewuliza in Buganda, 3 May 2005," Author's collection.

Weber, M. (1968) *Economy and Society: an outline of interpretive sociology*, New York: Bedminster Press.

"'*When the sun sets, we start to worry . . .*': An Account of life in Northern Uganda (2003) OCHA/IRIN.

Women in Human Rights, Peace Building and Conflict Resolution: a handbook (2003) Kampala: Isis-WICCE.

Women, War and Trauma (2004) Prod. Isis-WICCE. Videocassette.

World Vision (2004) *Pawns of Politics: children, conflict and peace in Northern Uganda*, Kampala: World Vision.

Wright, N. G. (1996) "Uganda: history from 1971," in Middleton, J. (ed.) *Encyclopedia of Africa South of the Sahara*, New York: Charles Scribner's Sons.

Confidential interviews conducted by author

Allimadi, S. A. UNIFEM (15 August 2006) Kampala, Uganda.

Anonymous Acholi woman living in Kampala (23 August 2006) Kampala, Uganda.

Anonymous Iteso man living in Kampala (31 August 2006) Kampala, Uganda.

Anonymous middle-aged Acholi man, in Acholi language with RLP interviewer (5 March 2005) Gulu town. (See Hovil and Quinn 2005: 24.)

Anonymous Mutoro woman living in Kampala (24 August 2006) Kampala, Uganda.

Anonymous Sabiny man studying at Makerere University (7 November 2004) Kampala, Uganda.

Anonymous Sabiny woman living in Kampala (12 November 2004) Kampala, Uganda.

Bantebya, Dr. Grace. Head, Women and Gender Studies Department, Makerere University (29 August 2006) Kampala, Uganda.

Kabahoma, Sister Speciosa. Uganda Catholic Justice and Peace Commission (24 August 2006) Nsambya, Uganda.

Kanakulya, M. Deputy Peace Desk Coordinator, Church of Uganda (23 August 2006) Kampala, Uganda.

Kigule, Dr. Juliet. Institute of Public Health (15 August 2006) Mulago, Uganda.

Latim, G. Secretary to the Paramount Chief of Acholi (22 November 2004) Gulu town, Uganda.

Lokeris, Hon. Peter. Minister of State for Karamoja (18 November 2004) Kampala, Uganda.

Nadduli, A. LC5 District Chairman (17 November 2004) Luweero town, Uganda.

Ocan, Hon. Betty (16 November 2006) Vancouver, British Columbia.

Onentho, G. Uganda Catholic Justice and Peace Commission (24 August 2006) Nsambya, Uganda.

Othieno, R. Centre for Conflict Resolution (29 August 2006) Kampala, Uganda.

Sempangi, Hon. Rev. Dr. Kefa (18 November 2004) Kampala, Uganda.

Walusimbe, Dr. Livingstone. Institute of Languages, Makerere University (16 May 2006) Kampala, Uganda.

Focus groups conducted by author

Acholi focus group (26 August 2006) Kampala, Uganda.
Iteso focus group (31 August 2006) Kampala, Uganda.
Karamojong focus group (18 August 2006) Kampala, Uganda.
Northern Uganda focus group (23 August 2006) Kampala, Uganda.

16 Policing bodies and borders

Women, prostitution, and the differential regulation of U.S. immigration policy

Deirdre M. Moloney

One of the most compelling areas of concern among women's rights activists and scholars during the past decade has been that of global human trafficking, especially the practice of sexual exploitation of girls and young women, who have few educational or economic opportunities in their rural towns and villages in poor regions, including those in Russia, other parts of the former Soviet Union, and in Asia. Those women migrate to wealthier regions in search of employment, often through the influence or coercive actions of recruiters from organized networks who mislead them. But while the details differ, this concern is far from new. Government agencies and nonprofit groups in Europe and in the United States mobilized around global trafficking issues at the beginning of the twentieth century, when migration increased in response to economic shifts in both the countries of origin and destination points. A major contemporary issue that concerns human rights organizations, such as Amnesty International, has been the murder and disappearance of over 400 young Mexican women along the Cuidad Juárez/El Paso border since 1993, where *maquiladoras* bring many women who work for U.S.-based manufacturers. Human rights groups have documented the inadequate response of government officials from the U.S. or Mexico to protect these women and solve these cases. As this chapter details, the lack of adequate response to widespread violence against Mexican women along this vital border region also has parallels to the early twentieth century. My research has found that in the first decade of the twentieth century police and immigration officials in Texas border towns had evidence that young Mexican women were being raped after crossing the border and failed to intervene to investigate or prosecute these crimes.[1]

Beginning in 1909, U.S. immigration officials focused many of their regulation efforts on the transnational "white slave" trade, the practice of importing women from Europe and Russia to serve as prostitutes. Several lengthy investigations were launched, often in conjunction with the local police, to uncover prostitution rings among immigrant women and their usually male "procurers" in New York City, the largest port of entry for immigrants at the time. Marcus Braun, of the Immigration Service, traveled throughout Europe and undertook a major study of prostitution in Paris and other capital cities in order to regulate immigrant women who might come to the United States as prostitutes. Another immigration official, Helen Bullis, led a major investigation of numerous houses of prostitution in New York City. These "white slavery" investigations occurred just prior to the release of the Dillingham Commission's report that influenced 1920s immigration restriction laws that greatly reduced immigration from Europe. Another major case, that of Lumbertine and Albert Bosny, was launched at the behest of William A. Williams, the Commissioner of Immigration, who expended a great deal of effort and resources in both New York and in Belgium, where the proprietors of a brothel had lived previously. Ultimately, Bureau officials viewed these European prostitution rings as highly organized operations run much like other international cartels, but concluded that most women were not coerced or kidnapped by procurers.[2]

A second investigation, the focus of this chapter, examined prostitution at southern border locations, especially in Texas and Arizona. That investigation was not as extensive as those undertaken in New York, but did reveal much about notions of migration from Mexico and how it was viewed differently from trans-atlantic migration. I argue that among immigration officials, Mexican men and women were not seen as permanent immigrants, but rather as contingent labor.

Immigration officials provide the sources for this situation, so the perspectives and voices of the women themselves are virtually impossible to uncover. Newspapers in Mexican border towns did not report on these investigations, nor would the women have likely written about their experiences, assuming they were even literate. Indeed in the years prior to the Mexican Revolution, just 13 percent of Mexican women were able to read and write. Yet, despite these challenges to writing about disadvantaged immigrants, and the biases inherent in government accounts written by officials who were, in the case of the Mexican border investigations, both male and white, these records allow historians to understand some of the women's circumstances, and in a few cases their reactions to deportation, even when mediated by those official government accounts (Sánchez 1993: 27–28).[3]

In this period, Mexican and European women along this liminal border between the U.S. and Mexico who engaged in prostitution did not elicit the same level of concern as European prostitutes in New York City, and to some extent those in San Francisco and Chicago. Today, of course, Mexican immigration to the United States is highly contested and the border heavily patrolled, but early in the twentieth century, immigration concerns about morality and prostitution were focused on those who were considered permanent immigrants and future citizens.

This decentralized investigative effort along the Mexican border occurred in several cities and towns along the border where Mexican and European immigrants were actively engaged in prostitution. The Immigration Service did not launch a special investigation, as was the case with Marcus Braun's and Helen Bullis's studies. Instead, the Bureau relied on officials already working at immigration stations to submit reports on the prevalence of prostitution on the border, thereby expending few resources on white slavery along the southern

border. In addition to Mexican women, French and Eastern European Jewish women were found to have moved to this region in significant numbers to work as prostitutes. The Bureau of Immigration's Braun and Bullis Reports on European and New York prostitution concluded that immigrants from France, Russia, and other points in Eastern Europe were among those engaged in the houses of prostitution they investigated in the urban United States. One immigration official concluded that immigrant women older than 30 tended to relocate from the East Coast to the Mexican border, and were especially prevalent in mining camps.[4]

The Immigration Service dedicated far fewer of its resources and personnel to investigating the causes of prostitution along the Mexican border, and generally seemed less concerned about the threat it posed there. This attitude also markedly contrasted with the Bureau's early emphasis on limiting Chinese prostitution, beginning with the 1875 Page Law that made it virtually impossible for an unmarried Chinese woman to emigrate to the United States, because of the supposition that she was being brought to the United States to work as a prostitute. That prohibition, combined with laws barring racial intermarriage, also made it difficult for Chinese immigrants to form families in the United States and led to a highly skewed gender ratio that reached 27:1 men to women within the Chinese immigrant community in 1890. The 1882 Chinese Exclusion Act virtually eliminated immigration from China, with the exception of merchants, students, and a few other categories. By 1907, most Japanese immigration had been curtailed (Chan 1991: 106). As a result, employers on the West Coast and in the Southwest, increasingly relied on Mexican immigrants as a labor source. Southern and Eastern Europeans' immigration to the East Coast reached its height in the first decade of the twentieth century, but those immigrants remained concentrated in the Northeast or Midwest.

There are several explanations for the discrepancy between regulation of prostitution among Europeans in East Coast cities and along the Mexican border. The focus of immigration regulation remained primarily on Europe because the sheer numbers of immigrants arriving from that continent remained significantly higher than from other regions. Mexicans could migrate on a cyclical basis far more easily than Chinese immigrants, because until the U.S. Border Patrol was established in 1924, the continental border was relatively porous and more difficult to regulate than was immigration by sea.

Another notable contrast between the European investigations and those along the Mexican border is that, in several instances, the male procurers along the Southern border faced deportation or arrest for violation of Section 3 of the immigration law. My research finds that in New York and in other major U.S. cities, male European immigrants engaged in the prostitution trade as procurers were rarely arrested, detained, or deported. As I'll discuss, several such Mexican and European men were apprehended as part of the investigations along the Southern border.

The fact that relatively few federal resources or personnel were appropriated to investigate prostitution on the border further assured the maintenance of a

contingent, productive, and inter-regional agricultural workforce at a time when the Immigration Service was housed within the Department of Commerce and Labor and Southwestern mining and agricultural interests were well represented in Washington. In contrast to Mexican immigrants, who were still viewed as contingent labor and inter-regional migrants rather than permanent immigrants, Europeans were viewed as future citizens. The fact that Mexican laborers were the likely clients of prostitutes along the border concerned immigration officials less than would have been the case if those clients were native-born or European immigrants. Moreover, the presence of prostitutes "serving" predominantly male, migrant mining camps would seem a less troubling phenomenon than having large numbers of Mexican families relocate to the United States and would have been seen as a fair trade off for having an inexpensive labor force readily available in major sectors of the U.S. economy. Mexican men, like Italian immigrants, often came to the U.S. temporarily and without their families to save as much of their wages as possible. In this circular migration pattern, wives or other family members typically remained on their farms in their communities of origin. Wage employment options for women in Southwestern mining communities were limited (Sánchez 1993: 41).

The Southwest, having been acquired as an American territory in the mid-nineteenth century, remained sparsely populated, and had not yet been fully incorporated into the American political system or its discourse. By the 1930s, the region would become a major focus of immigration regulation as the Great Depression led to greater concerns about the economic effects of Mexican immigration. Politicians such as Senator Patrick McCarran of Nevada and Congressman Martin Dies of Texas would become active opponents of immigration following their election in the 1930s, and both would later become well known for their staunch anti-communism in Congress. Therefore, addressing the influx of prostitution from Europe, and the danger it posed to young immigrant women, was viewed as a more compelling project in the years prior to major European immigration restriction legislation in the 1920s and the economic crisis of the 1930s.

Unpacking white slavery

The fact that the moral panic over prostitution was labeled "white slavery" might have been yet another relevant dimension to this differentiation in resource allocation. The choice of the term, "slavery," was most obviously intended to connote the brutal and inhumane treatment of African-Americans and African slaves who were forcibly brought to Europe, many of its colonies, and later, the United States. It also consciously linked the transnational religiously-based movement to that of the abolitionist movement earlier in the nineteenth century, which had now been broadened beyond Quakers and other liberal Protestant denominations to encompass Catholics throughout Europe and in the United States.

But the term also emphasized that the victims of coercion were white. As several scholars have noted, the term, "white slavery," had been used prior to the late nineteenth century to describe the condition of Massachusetts women workers employed in the Lowell textile mills and the Lynn shoe factories. In Europe and in the United States, it was used widely as a metaphor for labor exploitation more generally. As Eric Foner and David Roediger have each detailed, it was used in much the same way as the term "wage slavery." Prior to the Civil War, Southerners, seeking to defend slavery, used the term to argue that Northern abolitionist factory owners were hypocritical in their opposition to slavery because they continued to exploit workers in their mills.[5]

Gradually the term came to be used specifically to refer to prostitution by emphasizing the exploitation and coercion of its young, unsuspecting victims. Historians such as Judith Walkowitz have written about prostitution in Victorian London and the agitation against it. Three decades after the panic took hold in England, Jane Addams and other American reformers began focusing on white slavery in the United States. Addams published *A New Conscience and an Ancient Evil* in 1912, incorporating research from the Juvenile Protective Association of Chicago.[6]

Addams's first chapter establishes a strong parallel between prostitution and racially-based slavery: "Thus the generation before us, our own fathers, uprooted the enormous upas [toxic tree] of slavery" (Addams 1912: 18–19) and deemed modern-day prostitution "a twin of slavery." The first example she discusses is of Marie, an adolescent "convent-bred" Breton girl whose father's age and economic misfortunes led her first to leave school to seek work in Paris. The adolescent then immigrates to Chicago under the guise of performing in an acting troupe. Addams also attributes prostitution among immigrants as an outcome of undue influence by a male lover, a stranger, or acquaintance offering what appears to be genuine help, or strained family relationships. Young women who arrived in Chicago from rural areas were particularly vulnerable to prostitution, whether they migrated from neighboring states or from Europe or Russia. She also noted how jealous partners sometimes used deportation to exact revenge on women (Addams 1912: 28, 33–34).

Addams discusses at length the structural economic inequalities that led women to engage in prostitution, including the narrow range of viable opportunities for young immigrant women in the urban United States. Although she does not discuss it in significant detail, she notes that domestic service rendered women particularly likely to become prostitutes. She also emphasizes how women employed for low wages in department stores and cafes came into contact with male procurers (Addams 1912: 167–172, 64–70).

Though her book is clearly focused on white women, Addams does briefly address African-American women's specific vulnerability. She argues that decreased occupational opportunities and housing discrimination, as compared to poor white women, led to African-American women's high concentration in domestic service, especially in areas and buildings where prostitution was widespread. She notes the irony of the U.S. abolishing slavery as an institution only later to render African-American women vulnerable to this particular form of sexual slavery. She further notes that their court testimony against white men was less likely to be believed because of their race (Addams 1912: 119, 169–170).

Scholars Janet Beer and Katherine Joslin discuss the idea of white slavery as concerned with "poor women adrift in the city [who] became unwitting victims of sexual slavery, a depiction that avoided a more powerful image of urban working women forging neighborhood communities and organizing labor unions, claiming their place in the city and even reshaping the manners and mores of the middle class" (Beer and Joslin 1999: 1–18). It is somewhat ironic, then, that Jane Addams and her friend, Charlotte Perkins Gilman, an early women's rights advocate, who through both their words and their actions challenged traditional expectations about women's roles and the image of women as victims, joined in this campaign. Yet, despite her middle class bias, her traditional views of sexual behavior, and her maternalist perspective, Addams offered a trenchant critique of social inequality that would resonate with activists working on global trafficking issues today (Beer and Joslin 1999: 1–18).

Narratives of "white slavery," which largely reflected middle class anxieties about immigration, "race suicide," women's power, and rapid urbanization, fueled this concern over prostitution and portrayed young women and girls as powerless and gullible. Therefore, neither Mexican women, who were defined as non-white, nor older, European (often French or Jewish) women who worked as prostitutes in mining towns or small cities along the Southern border, fit seamlessly into this narrative of exploitation. As a result, their personal safety was largely ignored by both local police and federal immigration officials.

Investigations in Texas and Arizona

Attitudes toward Mexican women by Anglos along the Texas border at the beginning of the twentieth century are illustrated in an article in the *El Paso Daily Times*, entitled "Wiles of Mexican Girls." The article seems to serve as both a warning and an acknowledgment that Anglo men found Mexican women particularly appealing. A fictive "Mexican girl" was stereotyped as an exotic creature who "loves naturally to dominate and expects man to bow abjectly to the ordeal. She rules him and caresses him into obedience in the same breath. She is haughty with him if the mood strikes her, but flattery is the straw that whisks her off her pedestal" (*El Paso Daily Times* 1908).[7] Mexican women are also portrayed as an antidote to the "drab Anglo-Saxon." Though not specifically about prostitution, this article suggests the ways that Mexican women were objectified and sought after by Anglo men along the border and certainly cast as the "other." It further implies that there was a market for Mexican prostitutes among white men based on stereotypes of Mexican women's perceived differences from staid Anglo-American culture.

Frank R. Stone of the Immigration Service reported on the local investigation of prostitution in Laredo in 1909. He concluded that most houses of prostitution were operated by Mexican women, "*duenas*" (or madams) and housed Mexican "inmates," most of whom had resided in the United States for fewer than three years, and many of whom traveled back and forth across the border. In an ironic twist, one such house, "Casa Blanca," was occupied by "American" women, and was located in the building formerly occupied by the Immigration Service. American railroad workers were also seen as colluding with *duenas* by transporting women across the border posing as family members to work as prostitutes (NARA 25 February 1908a).

Stone's investigation revealed that prostitutes were routinely brought North from Nuevo Laredo. He reported that a constable, Pedro Leas, was responsible for bringing many women into Laredo for prostitution and that he served as the procurer for "some of the most influential and prominent City and County officials" (NARA 25 February 1908a), including Laredo's sheriff, Luis Ortiz, who arranged for Leas to bring a young Mexican woman from a prominent family for his "use." Laredo's district attorney knew this family and he and the mayor returned the woman to Mexico before she was "ruined at that house." In his report, Stone attributed this widespread abuse to the fact that "almost the entire city and County Government are Mexicans. . . . and from the high-handed manner in which they handle State laws here [,] they don't seem to have much respect for the Federal laws" (NARA 25 February 1908a). He went on to conclude that most are "dissolute, with little conception to the laws of morality."

It was also alleged that hackmen or *coacheros*, working for procurers, routinely transported women across the border from Nuevo Laredo to houses of prostitution in Laredo. After taking the women into their rooms in houses of prostitution, they would rape them as a type of brutal induction rite, thereby forcing them into lives of prostitution. Though this practice was reported on as a routine event, there seemed to be no subsequent attempt to launch a criminal investigation or effort to learn the identities of the hackmen or their victims.

Pedro Leas and a *duena*, Ruby Brown, were arrested in an effort to disable the major conduits in the cross-border prostitution trade, but no action was taken to stop the sexual violence perpetrated against women working in the city (NARA 25 February 1908a). The situation reported in Laredo involved a much higher level of force and coercion than suggested by investigations into how European immigrant women came to become prostitutes. In Immigration Service narratives arising from Marcus Braun's investigation and others, European women were seen as entering prostitution as a result of the influence of a lover, frequenting night spots in marginal urban neighborhoods, or disputes within their families. This difference might have simply reflected negative stereotypes about Mexican morality among Immigration Service personnel. But, if some of these Texas scenarios were accurate, the description of unsuspecting girls brought across the border and forcibly coerced into prostitution that embodied the white slavery narrative should have prompted a greater public outcry.

Moreover, in his report Frank Stone seemed to be concerned more with enforcing the letter of the law than its spirit. His interactions with *duenas* led to their assurances that they would seek to employ only those women who had been in the United States for at least three years. Therefore, in these accounts prostitution itself was not viewed as particularly problematic, nor was the exploitation and/or rape of young Mexican women. Rather, the most objectionable aspect was that the houses were operating in violation of federal immigration law, based on immigrant women's engaging in prostitution within three years of arrival.

Charles Cornell, the acting immigration inspector stationed in Douglas, Arizona, was far more zealous than Stone in pursuing the male procurers involved in prostitution. These investigations led to the arrest of several men. Cornell also undertook a more thorough investigation of prostitution in the Mexican cities from which prostitutes emigrated, including Juárez, Chihuahua, Nogales, and Sonora. He compiled a list of 150 prostitutes in those Mexican cities and forwarded them to immigrant inspection stations in El Paso, Tucson, and elsewhere in the Southwest. He reported that he had arrested fourteen immigrants for prostitution-related violations of immigration law. Of the twelve females, eleven were deported and one was imprisoned for violating immigration laws. Both of the male procurers, or pimps, were arrested, one was awaiting trial and the other was imprisoned. Interestingly, while half of the prostitutes were Mexican, neither procurer was: one was Spanish and the other French. Additionally, he reported that two male U.S. citizens of Mexican origin were arrested for violation of Section 3 of the immigration law (NARA 26 December 1909).

Cornell also emphasized that several mining camps in Arizona where many Mexican workers were employed also drew many prostitutes. He asserted that in the mining towns of Clifton and Morenci, many prostitutes first accompanied Mexican male workers to the state as "concubines," or common-law spouses, before being deserted and moving into houses of prostitution. He notes further that the pimps resided in other towns to avoid arrest (NARA 26 December 1909). In fact, these towns are where Linda Gordon situated *The Great Arizona Orphan Abduction*, her study that analyzes how a community controversy revealed the complex dynamics between race, class, religion, and gender in the early twentieth century Southwest (Gordon 2001).

Cornell also mentions the trend of older European women migrating to the Southwest from New York City, and remitting their earnings to their husbands and families who remained in New York. He estimated that over 95 percent of Jewish prostitutes in Arizona and New Mexico were over 30. He also suggests that many French prostitutes first entered the trade with promises of marriage or employment once they arrived in the United States (NARA 26 December 1909).

The Texas investigations also focused to some extent on Jewish and French prostitution in addition to Mexican immigrant prostitution. In San Antonio, Stone discussed the case of Edward Frion, a French "mack" whose wife was practicing prostitution in a "crib," a slang term used to describe a rundown room where prostitutes had sexual relations with customers. He asserted that though the husband was "wealthy and has a fine ranch," his wife "is just a natural born prostitute and can't resist it." He elaborated by noting that this woman makes annual trips to France, which are "not entirely for the good of her health" (NARA June 1909).

The notion that some women were hypersexualized and engaged in prostitution to satisfy their sexual appetites, rather than for economic reasons, was a well-known cultural stereotype in the era. Cesare Lombroso, an Italian criminal anthropologist, published research on female criminals in the late nineteenth century. He argued that women who became prostitutes are biologically predisposed and had physical features that differed from "normal" women. For example, prostitutes were more likely to experience the early onset of menstruation, to become sexually active as children or early adolescents, and "clearly manifest exaggerated and unceasing lustfulness" (Lombroso and Ferraro 2004: 171). He argued that prostitutes were more like men than like "normal" women, whom he characterized as frigid. These stereotypes also arose from the perception among many Americans that Europeans, and the French especially, were more morally corrupt than Americans, a perception that was clearly evident in the Braun Report.[8]

In San Antonio, "the acre," was the section of the city where prostitution was prevalent and "cribs," small wooden shack-like structures, were more prevalent than houses of prostitution. Stone noted that city officials were involved in the prostitution business, and deemed San Antonio, "the rottenest" city he had ever seen. San Antonio's rabbi had worked to end prostitution among Jews in the city, because he saw it as "a disgrace" that reflected poorly on the religious community as a whole. Though Stone acknowledged that "American" women were also working as prostitutes, "their influence is not so concerted and well organized, hence not as efficacious and corrupt as the foreign element" (NARA June 1909).

In an unusually detailed coda to his report, Frank Stone reported that while his investigation was ending in San Antonio, and several women were about to be deported as prostitutes, he spent a great deal of time locating, and finally retrieving, the women's laundry from an African-American woman. He paid for this service out of his own funds.

In one of the few instances where prostitutes' perspectives are heard in these Texas and Arizona investigations, he states that "they refuse to pay the bill, saying the Government is responsible for their leaving before their laundry is finished" (NARA June 1909). Here they found a symbolic way to protest their treatment, however quotidian. Yet, in some cases their laundry, or apparel, probably represented a significant portion of their material assets. Perhaps the garments represented their dignity; this was their sole way to demand that the U.S. government treat them fairly. For some, their garments were essential components of their trade and they would need these items should they continue to practice prostitution once they returned to Mexico. Stone concluded that "I believe we owe it to these women to get their laundry for them inasmuch as they are deported without it" (NARA June 1909).

Some case files reveal interesting details about how women began work as prostitutes and their life circumstances. Rosa Tijerina was brought into custody for a hearing to determine whether she should be deported to Mexico from Brownsville, Texas, in 1908, based on her entry to the United States without passing inspection. At this point, immigration across the border of Mexico was far less regulated than it would be with the passage of literacy tests and the creation of the Border Patrol in 1924. Immigrants crossing into the United States were required to pass through immigration stations, however. Her true transgression was her occupation as a prostitute. Most notable was the fact that she was born in the United States, and therefore under normal circumstances, should have been treated as a U.S. citizen, and thereby not subject to deportation. But as it happened, she had married a Mexican citizen prior to the Cable Act, which allowed women to retain or obtain their citizenship status separately from their husbands. Though she had been separated from him for some years, she, like most non-elites living in Mexico, did not obtain a divorce because it was so costly. Therefore, immigration officials determined that she was eligible for deportation. The mother of five children in a household without her husband's income, she admitted practicing prostitution in Matamoras for three months prior to her arrival in Brownsville. After coming to Brownsville, she returned to Matamoras every few weeks, most likely to see her children.[9]

The case for Tijerina's deportation was made difficult because of the absence of public records in Mexico or in the United States to verify details about her life, as well as the lack of church records documenting some key aspects of her testimony. There was no record of her birth in Cameron County, Texas, no baptism record, no marriage or divorce record, no registration at the American consulate in Mexico, nor other documentation of significant life events. Two witnesses, who were government officials, did testify that she was born on a ranch in Texas.[10]

Tijerina was socially marginalized in a few ways: by working in an occupation that was viewed as morally reprehensible, by having no citizenship rights apart from those of her estranged husband, and by being rendered invisible in the official records of two separate countries. In essence, until she was detained for possible deportation, she did not exist as a citizen or even as a subject. The record does not indicate whether she was ultimately deported or encouraged to repatriate voluntarily, but she was not represented by anyone at her hearing, suggesting that she was probably not allowed to remain in the United States.

A similar case was that of Coka Puiento, a Mexican immigrant who in 1909 was suspected of practicing prostitution in Corpus Christi, having crossed the Rio Grande in a rowboat and eluded immigration inspectors. She stated that she had been earning a living as a prostitute for the previous five years and that she was registered as one in Nuevo Laredo. She stated that she had been born in Spain, a fact that she might have asserted as part of a strategy for claiming whiteness, so that she would receive greater consideration by immigration officials (NARA 25 February 1908a).

Sara Servantes and Simon Chávez were detained at El Paso in 1908. Chávez was charged with seeking to import Servantes for immoral purposes and her two daughters, aged 8 and 10, were held in the county jail on likely to become a public charge (LPC) charges. It was not clear from the charge whether she would earn her living as a prostitute or whether she was, in the Immigration Service phrasing, "a concubine," living with Chávez as a common-law spouse. Ultimately, though immigration officials initially considered using her as a witness against Chávez, she was deported along with her daughters.[11]

Conclusion

In contrast to what my research on European immigrants demonstrates, Mexican men who were connected to prostitution activities, or perhaps simply accompanying a lover or common-law spouse across the border, were far more likely to be detained, arrested, or deported than were European men. Racial bias among members of the U.S. Immigration Service led them to view Mexican men as a greater threat to social stability, even when the practice of prostitution itself was not viewed as problematic along the Mexican border as it was among Europeans in major East Coast cities.

Another significant difference between some of the cases and trends discussed in the prostitution trade among Europeans and Mexicans was that the latter revealed more instances of physical coercion and force. It is certainly troubling to those in the twenty-first century to read accounts that claim that young Mexican women brought into houses of prostitution were routinely raped. It is also disturbing to learn that the immigration inspector who reported on this practice does not seem to have attempted to substantiate them, and if true, to arrest the perpetrators. Indeed violence against young women along the border between Mexico and the United States remains pervasive. Today, neither Mexican nor American officials have effectively intervened to solve the epidemic number of murders or to insure that more Mexican women are protected from murder. While it is possible that the allegations of widespread rape of young Mexican women in San Antonio as a method for forcing them into prostitution were spurious and simply a way to demonize Mexican men as brutal and immoral, the straightforward tone of the report and the fact that this allegation was buried in the narrative rather than emphasized as noteworthy or shocking suggests a second conclusion. In the early twentieth century, there was little outrage in the fact that women, or at least non-white women, began their lives as prostitutes by first being subjected to rape. Indeed, the ongoing violence against Mexican women along the Texas border today, suggests that the indifference and lack of will among both public officials and the general public to address violence against Mexican women brought to the U.S. for prostitution has not dissipated.

By comparing these two investigations—of European immigrant prostitutes in major cities with Mexican and European prostitution along the U.S. border with Mexico—one might conclude that "white slavery" accurately describes the latter situation more than the first. But ultimately, while the inhumane and exploitative conditions they were seeking could be found on the Southern border, immigration officials were less concerned with prostitution and the welfare of women along this border and thus expended fewer resources to address the issue there.

Notes

1 This chapter is based on papers presented at the European Social Science History Conference in Lisbon in February 2008 and at the University of Houston in March 2008. The author wishes to acknowledge the helpful suggestions of her conference co-panelists and members of both audiences, as well as to Debra Bergoffen and Paula Gilbert for their editorial advice. Much of the writing was undertaken during a fellowship at the Woodrow Wilson International Center for Scholars in Washington, DC, in 2007–2008. Amnesty International. Report on Women of Juárez and Chihuahua (2006) http://www.amnestyusa.org/violence-against-women/justice-for-the-women-of-juarez-and-chihuahua/page.do?id=1108394 (accessed 22 February 2009).

2 I discuss the European "white slavery" investigations and moral panic in detail in a *Journal of Women's History* article and in a recent paper. See: "Women, Sexual Morality, and Economic Dependency in Early Deportation Policy," *Journal of Women's History* vol. 18, no. 2 (Summer 2006): 95–122 and "Investigating Female Immigrants, Interrogating European Morality," paper presented at the Social Science History Conference, Chicago, 16 November, 2007.

3 The corresponding figure for men was 33 percent. Literacy rates varied significantly by region and class, but it is unlikely that prostitutes had particularly high literacy rates in this era.

4 On the New York investigation, see File 524841/F. On the Mexican border, see Files 52484/8-A, 52484/8-B, and 52484-C. RG 85. National Archives (NARA).

5 Gunther Peck, "White Slavery and Whiteness: A Transnational View of the Sources of Working-Class Radicalism and Racism," *Labor: Studies in Working Class History of the Americas* vol. 1, no. 2 (2004) 41–63; Christopher Diffee, "Sex and the City: The White Slavery Scare and Social Governance in the Progressive Era," *American Quarterly* vol. 57, no. 2 (2005): 411–437. Eric Foner, *Free Soil, Free Labor, and Free Men: The Ideology of the Republican Party before the Civil War* (New York: Oxford University Press, 1970) and David Roediger, *The Wages of Whiteness: Race and the Making of the American Working Class* (London: Verso, 1991), especially pages 73–87.

6 Judith Walkowitz, *Prostitution and Victorian Society: Women, Class, and the State* (Cambridge: Cambridge University Press, 1982). Also see: Ruth Rosen, *The Lost Sisterhood: Prostitution in America* (Baltimore, MD: Johns Hopkins, 1982). Jane Addams, *A New Conscience and an Ancient Evil* (New York: Macmillan, 1912).

7 The author wishes to acknowledge Jaime Aguila for directing her to this article.

8 I discuss cultural stereotypes of French and other continental Europeans in my 2006 *Journal of Women's History* article and "Investigating Female Immigrants, Interrogating European Morality," paper presented at the Social Science History Conference, Chicago, 16 November, 2007. On Cesare Lombroso's theories of criminality and prostitution, see: Cesare Lombroso and Guglielmo Ferraro, *Criminal Woman, the Prostitute and the Normal Woman* (1893). Translated with a New Introduction by Nicole Hahn Rafter and Mary Gibson (Durham, NC: Duke University, 2004), 171. See chapter 22 in particular.

9 Memo, to F. W. Berkshire, to Charles Earl, Acting Secretary of Commerce and Labor, 23 February, 1908, warrant for Tijerina, 25 February, 1908, testimony of hearing, 29 February, 1908. Memo to Murray from F. H. Sargent, 6 March, 1908. File 51777/56. RG 85, Entry 7. NARA.

10 Ibid.

11 Luther C. Steward, Acting Supervising Inspector, to Daniel Keefe, Commissioner-General of Immigration, letter and reply from Keefe, both 23 April , 1909. Steward to Keefe, 12 and April, 1909 and Keefe's reply, 17 April, 1909. F. H. Larned to Steward, 3 December, 1908. FVB, Supervising Inspector, El Paso, to Keefe, 27 November, 1908. Acting Commissioner General, to Steward, 18 November, 1908.

Steward to Commissioner General of Immigration, 18 November, 1908. File: 52241/20. RG 85. Entry 7. NARA.

Bibliography

Addams, J. (1912) *A New Conscience and an Ancient Evil*, New York: Macmillan.

Amnesty International (2006) "Report on Women of Juárez and Chihuahua." Online. Available at: <http://www.amnestyusa.org/violence-against-women/justice-for-the-women-of-juarez-and-chihuahua/page.do?id=1108394> (accessed 22 February 2009).

Beer, J. and Joslin, K. (1999) "Diseases of the Body Politic: white slavery in Jane Addams' 'A New Conscience and an Ancient Evil' and selected stories by Charlotte Perkins Gilman," *Journal of American Studies*, 33: 1–18.

Chan, S. (1991) *Asian Americans: an interpretive history*, Boston, MA: Twayne Publishers.

Diffee, C. (2005) "Sex and the City: the white slavery scare and social governance in the progressive era," *American Quarterly*, 57(2): 411–437.

El Paso Daily Times (1908) "Wiles of Mexican Girls," 30 January.

Foner, E. (1970) *Free Soil, Free Labor, and Free Men: the ideology of the Republican Party before the Civil War*, New York: Oxford University Press.

Gordon, L. (2001) *The Great Orphan Abduction*, Cambridge: Harvard University Press.

Lombroso, C. and Ferraro, G. (2004) *Criminal Woman, the Prostitute and the Normal Woman*, Durham, NC: Duke University.

Moloney, D. (2006) "Women, Sexual Morality, and Economic Dependency in Early Deportation Policy," *Journal of Women's History*, 18(20): 95–122.

—— (2007) "Investigating Female Immigrants, Interrogating European Morality," paper presented at Social Science History Conference, Chicago, 16 November.

National Archives and Records Administration (NARA). "On the Mexican Border," File 524841/F; File 52484/8-A; File 52484/8-B; File 52484-C. RG 85.

—— (23 February 1908) "Memo, to F.W. Berkshire, to Charles Earl, Acting Secretary of Commerce and Labor," File 51777/56. RG 85, Entry 7.

—— (25 February 1908a) "E.B Holman to F.P Sargent, Deportation Warrant dated July 1, 1907," File 51777/34. RG 85, Entry 7.

—— (25 February 1908b) "Warrant for Tijerina," File 51777/56. RG 85, Entry 7.

—— (29 February 1908) "Testimony of Hearing," File 51777/56. RG 85, Entry 7.

—— (6 March 1908) "Memo to Murray from F. H. Sargent," File 51777/56. RG 85, Entry 7.

—— (18 November 1908) "Acting Commissioner General, to Steward," File: 52241/20. RG 85. Entry 7.

—— (18 November 1908) "Steward to Commissioner General of Immigration," File: 52241/20. RG 85. Entry 7.

—— (27 November 1908) "FVB, Supervising Inspector, El Paso, to Keefe," File: 52241/20. RG 85. Entry 7.

—— (3 December 1908) "F.H. Larned to Steward," File: 52241/20. RG 85. Entry 7.

—— (12, 16 and 17 April 1909) "Steward to Keefe and Keefe's reply," File: 52241/20. RG 85. Entry 7.

—— (23 April 1909) "Inspector, to Daniel Keefe, Commissioner-General of Immigration, letter and reply from Keefe," File: 52241/20. RG 85. Entry 7.

—— (25, 27, and 28 June 1909) "F.R. Stone to Commissioner of Immigration," File: 5248418-A. RG 85. Entry 9.

—— (26 December 1909) "Charles Cornell to Commissioner General of Immigration," File: 524848-C. RG 85, Entry 9.

Peck, G. (2004) "White Slavery and Whiteness: a transnational view of the sources of working-class radicalism and racism," *Labor: studies in working class history of the Americas*, 1(2): 41–63.

Roediger, D. (1991) *The Wages of Whiteness: race and the making of the American working class*, London: Verso.

Rosen, R. (1982) *The Lost Sisterhood: prostitution in America*, Baltimore, MD: Johns Hopkins.

Sánchez, G. (1993) *Becoming Mexican American*, New York: Oxford University Press.

Walkowitz, J. (1982) *Prostitution and Victorian Society: women, class, and the state*, Cambridge: Cambridge University Press.

17 The institutionalization of domestic violence against women in the United States

Julie Walters

"Pandemic" is a word that evokes disturbing images of profound human suffering observable across myriad geographic and political borders. In the early twenty-first century, extensive media coverage concerning the global reach of viruses such as the avian (H5H1) and swine (H1N1) influenzas might lead one to believe that those illnesses are among the most serious and immediate instruments of pain, injury, and death on a global scale. But such a belief would ignore a long-existing pandemic that continues to insidiously devastate individuals, communities, economies, and the social fabric: *domestic violence against women.*

Domestic violence against women, also often referred to as intimate partner violence, is an act of gender-based violence that results in, or is likely to result in, physical, sexual, or mental harm and suffering to women, including associated threats, coercion, and/or arbitrary deprivation of liberty, whether occurring in private or public life (UN 1993; Krug et al. 2002). The term covers violence by current and former spouses and partners. It is not only an epidemic in the United States (U.S.), crossing all demographic categories, but also in countries throughout the world (UN 2006; Garcia-Moreno et al. 2005; AMA 1992). Even with reports documenting its prevalence as epidemic in proportion, known rates of intimate partner violence are likely low as many victims choose not to report their abuse. Though women can be violent toward men in relationships and violence exists in same-sex partnerships, the largest proportion of domestic violence is perpetrated by males against their female partners (Krug et al. 2002; NCVS 2006). Indeed, 85 to 95 percent of victims of such violence are women (AIDV 2001; Rennison and Welchans 2000).

While these statistics provide an initial sobering alert on the severity of the problem, peel them back and the spotlight illuminates myriad related con-sequences that go beyond the tragedy suffered by each individual victim. Domestic violence wreaks havoc on the entire fabric of society, affecting virtually every individual whether directly or indirectly. The costs its perpetrators impose on the U.S. economy, for example, annually reach approximately US$12.6 billion (Waters et al. 2004). The annual cost related to lost productivity alone is estimated to exceed US$700 million, with nearly US$8 million paid workdays lost each year (NCIPC 2003). Though healthcare costs for victims eat away at income, insurance, family and community resources, only occasionally does a related news story receive global attention. One such case is that of Connie Culp. In 2004, Culp survived a murder attempt by her estranged husband, whose shotgun blasts leveled at her from a close distance, tore away most of her face rendering her unable to breathe without a tube, eat solid foods, or smell. She made international news not for the horrendous violence she survived at the hands of an intimate nor the short prison sentence of seven years her husband received, but for the full face transplant she received, among the first in the world. The cost of the surgery, estimated between US$250,000 and US$300,000, as well as subsequent costs for the entire treatment regimen are being absorbed by the hospital providing the surgeries, the Cleveland Clinic.

Media coverage of Culp's case highlighted the costs of face transplant surgery, not those associated with intimate partner violence generally. Also missing in the reporting was an investigation into the enduring nature of associated costs. For example, the social and economic costs a perpetrator forces on others extends beyond the immediate generation as a child observing domestic violence is at risk to repeat the cycle either as a perpetrator or victim in the future (Coker et al. 2000).

The continuing prevalence of domestic violence against women indicates an enduring crisis of public policy; one that simply has not been successfully addressed despite the enormity of the problem. Effective public policy can make positive and dramatic differences in the quality of life for people in every community and effective policies typically reflect knowledge, coordination, education, and careful administration. Nevertheless, when a subject such as intimate partner violence is involved a serious question arises as to why, despite targeted government efforts to address the tragedy, the problem continues across space and time. One possibility is that policymakers and others concerned with the problem have not understood it as an *institution*. Accordingly, this chapter sets forth the characteristics of domestic violence against women that render it an institution.

When institutions are involved, their complex natures often render difficult the formulation of public policy aimed at remedying problems created by them. By understanding domestic violence against women as an institution, policymakers and others may more easily recognize and address weaknesses in their current systems that permit the perpetuation of domestic violence across space and time. Though the context is the United States, the institutionalization of domestic violence in that country reflects a phenomenon pervasive throughout the globe. Hence, the framework provided may serve as a foundation for future research that will better inform policymakers in their attempts to use law and policy to effect change.

An institutional perspective

Expanding upon foundations articulated by Max Weber and Emile Durkheim, contemporary applications of institutional research, particularly those drawing upon sociological considerations, look to formal and informal rules, values, routines, and other aspects of political and cultural life to understand institutional structure and behavior. An *institution* is a multifaceted system incorporating symbolic elements (cognitive constructions and normative rules) and regulative processes carried out through and shaping social behavior (Scott 1995). Meaning systems, monitoring processes, and related actions are all interwoven in an institution and although individual actors construct and maintain it, an institution assumes the guise of an impersonal and objective reality. In short, institutions consist of regulative, normative, and cognitive structures and activities that provide stability to social behavior (Scott 1995: 33). Such structures evoke the image of fundamental supports of the larger institution. These structural supports undergird an institution to varying degrees but, nonetheless, provide stability whether exerting a strong or weak influence.

Regulative structures underlying an institution include formal rules, laws, and sanctions that achieve compliance among the individuals, groups, organizations, and others within the institutional environment. Institutional legitimacy is established through legal dictates while related sanctions are the cultural carriers of regulative institutional elements and governance structures. Protocols and standardized procedures are often evident in the regulative foundations of a particular institution (Scott 1995).

The normative foundational structure of an institution relies upon social obligation as the basis of compliance among those within the institutional environment. Organizational or individual certification and accreditation serve as normative indicators and fulfilling binding obligations provides for institutional legitimacy. Related values and expectations are norms carried by culture within this foundation, while authority systems provide the social structures for transporting normative elements. Conformity and performance of role-defined duties are routines that carry such norms within the institutional environment (Scott 1995).

Cognitive foundational structures reflect subconsciously engrained values and principles which shape behavior. Such mechanisms are repetitive, and mimetic, in nature; they emphasize imitation. Legitimacy for individuals and organizations within the institutional environment is established due to conformance with culturally supported and conceptually correct activity. Scripts, including language, and cultural objects with symbolic meaning serve as carriers of cognitive elements (Scott 1995).

The extent to which regulative, normative, and cognitive foundational structures underpin an institution may vary and that dynamic has served to interest researchers across myriad topics. Whether discovering patterns of behavior and structure in local government organization in American cities (Frederickson and Johnson 2001) or explaining gender inequity in law firm attorney promotions (Beckman and Phillips 2005), an institutionalist perspective provides an approach for understanding the complex dynamics of domestic violence against women and its continuing prevalence.

Accordingly, the following section sets forth the characteristics of domestic violence against women in the United States which render it an institution, and subsequently provides an analytical framework incorporating a number of the primary regulative, normative, and cognitive structures that have served to establish and maintain domestic violence against women as an American institution, often inhibiting policy efforts at reducing and or eliminating the problem. Many of such structures are interwoven, serving to influence each other, such as norms influencing law and law influencing norms and cognitive structures. Hence, a primary benefit of modeling domestic violence against women in the United States as an institution is its ability to embrace these often complex regulative, normative, and cognitive aspects of the problem.

Domestic violence against women as an institution

As previously mentioned, an institution is a multifaceted system incorporating symbolic elements (cognitive constructions and normative rules) and regulative processes carried out through and shaping social behavior (Scott 1995). One of the most prominent examples is the institution of marriage. In common parlance, people of the United States speak of the *sacred institution of marriage,* placing its legitimacy as a core element of individual identity within the realm of myriad social structures including religion, governmental regulation, and culturally defined associated behaviors. More specifically, in the U.S., when two people marry, there are laws that both govern the process of marrying and the aftermath as well as cultural and religious norms governing marital behavior in society as a whole.

Domestic violence against women in the United States is similarly situated and a review of common regulative, normative, and cognitive structures underlying it reveal that, just as with marriage, it is an American institution. Viewing it within an institutional framework can illuminate why efforts over the past several decades have not been successful in eradicating it.

Defining domestic violence

How the legal system, public, religions, and others define domestic violence varies, and this is a source of tremendous difficulty in formulating effective policy. For example, while the United States Department of Health and Human Services (USDHHS 2009) and the World Health Organization (Garcia-Moreno et al. 2005) recognize physical, mental, and sexual abuse by an intimate, including a former intimate, as uncondonable domestic violence, political, judicial, and religious leaders in any individual country may not. Finding a shared definition even within various government structures can be difficult also. This is the case in the United States.

The United States represents a federal model of government in which vertical layers—national, state, and local—are autonomous with regards to certain powers. Investigating, arresting, and prosecuting domestic violence perpetrators falls within the power of each of the fifty states, rather than the national government. Definitions of domestic violence articulated by the USDHHS, the American

Medical Association (AMA), and the World Health Organization (WHO), are not necessarily shared by each state for purposes of arresting and prosecuting a perpetrator. Each state's criminal laws do not include many components of domestic violence recognized by medical and other professionals—patterns of economic coercion, psychological attacks, behaviors aimed at control of the victim (Erskine 1999; CWIG 2008). Nevertheless, these differences are respected by the federal and other state governments as part of the state's jurisdictional authority and each state is not forced to comply with a national regulatory model on domestic violence.

For example, in some states, the process of protecting a victim and pursuing prosecution of a domestic abuser may be the same as if a stranger were involved. Even when a state defines domestic violence within its civil code (the system which often provides for personal protection orders (PPO)), the definition usually does not recognize threatening behavior that is verbally abusive or shows a pattern of economic coercion. Nevertheless, the transition in the states to allowing civil courts to handle requests for PPOs has marked progress for victims-rights advocates and others as typically the evidentiary burden placed on a victim to get a PPO in a civil court against her abuser is lighter than if she sought the PPO in a criminal court (CWIG 2008).

Within the regulative powers of government, how domestic violence is defined is relevant not only to the criminal law and the prosecution of perpetrators, but also to the regulative power of government in providing for funds and other resources that create and sustain victims' support programs, shelters, public education initiatives, etc. Since the 1980s, state and federal laws creating and funding programs to aid domestic violence victims and provide community education have typically used the more expansive clinical definition that recognizes abuse and violence as more than an instance of assault and/or battery creating bruises or other physical harm.

Hence, policymakers and advocates have been, and continue to be, faced with differing definitions across societal sectors, most notably the deep divide between state criminal laws and domestic violence definitions recognized by medical professionals, victims' advocates, and many prosecutors who recognize the problem as more than an isolated case of observable physical violence. The continued disconnect in the perception of what constitutes domestic violence against women has the very real implication of allowing it to continue; in short, of perpetuating the institution that it is.

Domestic violence: institutional regulative structures

Formal and informal legal regulations, including law and enforcement mechanisms, are core regulative structures within domestic violence. Until the late twentieth century, in the United States, regulative tools addressing domestic violence against women were exclusively creatures of each state and in many cases reflected judge-made law—the common law—on how crimes such as assault and/or battery would be applied in the husband/wife relationship, as opposed to assaults among strangers. Laws passed by legislatures came secondarily, and federal involvement only came with the end of the twentieth century (CWIG 2008).

Much of how the courts have viewed domestic violence in the United States has reflected a societal view that wives were a form of property—chattel—of their husbands (Dobash 1979; Eskow 1996; Connerton 1997). For many judges of the eighteenth and nineteenth centuries, simple reference to William Blackstone's seventeenth-century treatise, *Commentaries on the Laws of England,* was sufficient evidence under the common law that wives did not have their own legal status. Of particular interest to the nature of a woman's status in marriage was the concept of *coveture* in which "husband and wife are one person in law: that is, the very being or legal existence of the woman is suspended during the marriage, or at least is incorporated and consolidated into that of the husband: under whose wing, protection, and cover, she performs everything" (Blackstone 1765: 442). *Coveture* legitimized a larger social belief that in marriage, a woman became her husband's property (also that property she owned before marriage became his), purportedly in the name of marital harmony and family relationship (Eisenberg and Micklow1977).

An extension of the "wife as property" legal and social notion has also been reflected in the issue of marital rape. In viewing a woman as her husband's property, both the legal system and society did not consider it possible for him to rape her. She was not deemed as having a voice in the area of consent to sexual relations. It was not until 1976 that the state of Nebraska became the first of all fifty states to abolish the marital rape exemption. Until that point, a husband could negate a wife's charge of rape simply by proving they were married at the time of the assault. The effect of the exemption was that, in the eyes of the law, rape could never occur within a marriage. Further, in the state of New York, marital rape was not prosecuted until 1984 (*People v Liberta*). Similarly, it was not until 1984 that the Commonwealth of Virginia revoked the common law rule concerning the marital rape exemption. Such laws and judicial treatment reflected, and continue to reflect, centuries of precedent—extending in the United States back to English common law, the inherited structure of jurisprudence dominating the American legal system (Anderson 2003). Though no state allows a marital exemption for forcible rape any longer, approximately half still allow for some type of marital immunity in cases where other types of sexual offenses are involved (Anderson 2003, also, see Alaska Stat. § 11.41.425 (2001)). The treatment of wives as owing sexual and other obligations to husbands has reflected a cultural presumption, codified in law, that upon marriage a woman essentially melded into her husband's being. Its consequences not only provided for potential physical and psychological violence but served to leave wives wholly dependent on husbands economically and politically as states typically restricted their rights to own property and make contracts, as well as vote, serve on juries, or hold public office into the twentieth century (Larson 1973).

Federal involvement

Only in the late twentieth century did federal law enter the regulative structure surrounding domestic violence. In the United States, most crimes against individuals are governed by each state's legal system. This reflects recognition by the country's highest court, the U.S. Supreme Court in interpreting the Tenth Amendment to the U.S. Constitution, that each individual state has the power to create and enforce its own laws regarding the health, safety, and morality of its citizens, as previously mentioned. This recognition of individual state jurisdiction extends to the prosecution of violent acts perpetrated by its citizens. The first federal efforts addressing intimate partner violence began in the late twentieth century with such legislation as the Family Violence and Prevention Services Act of 1984 (FVPSA) and the Violence Against Women Act of 1994 (VAWA or Act). The FVPSA is the largest funding source for emergency services for victims of domestic violence, including victim assistance programs and crisis lines, among others. It is administered by the U.S. Department of Health and Human Services and was reauthorized under the Keeping Children and Families Safe Act in 2003. Though authorized to fund at a level of US$175 million, FVPSA appropriations have never been fully funded. Fiscal year 2009 appropriations were US$127 million (McLaughlin 2009).

The Violence Against Women Act coordinates state and federal attempts to fight domestic abuse and other crimes against women by providing funds and programming related to issues such as victim's rights, law enforcement training, and support services. In addition, it provides for federal prosecution of domestic violence perpetrators who cross state lines. Appearing to herald a new era of national government inclusion in the regulative structures underpinning the institution of domestic violence against women, this federal initiative has not been without legal challenge nor has it been fully administered. The Act's constitutionality came into question when the United States Supreme Court curtailed Congress's power to formulate federal legislation that would otherwise be state-created but for federal assertion that the subject matter of the legislation affected interstate commerce under the U.S. Constitution's Commerce Clause (Article I, Section 8, Clause 3). For much of the twentieth century starting in the mid-1930s, Congress used its Commerce Clause power as authority for creating laws regulating a wide range of activities from environmental protection (Clean Air Act, Clean Water Act, Endangered Species Act) to civil rights issues in employment and voting (Civil Rights Act of 1964 and Voting Rights Act). Until 1995 with a challenge to the Gun Free School Zones Act (*United States v. Lopez*) and then again in 2000 with a challenge to the Violence Against Women Act (*United States v Morrison*), no federal legislation had been held unconstitutional by the Supreme Court for violating the Commerce Clause (Tatelman 2004). Nevertheless, in the Morrison case, a close 5–4 decision, the Court found part of VAWA unconstitutional, namely, the section that allowed for a federal civil rights remedy to victims of gender-based violence even when no criminal charges had been filed (*United States v. Morrison*). Speaking for the majority, Chief Justice Rehnquist argued that with this provision, Congress had exceeded its Commerce Clause power because the violent acts VAWA was meant to remedy were local and did not substantially affect interstate commerce (for an analysis of the reasoning of both the majority and dissent see, Russell 2003). Four of nine justices dissented in the Morrison case with a shared argument among them that Congress had assembled a tremendous amount of data showing the effects of violence against women on interstate commerce. They patently disagreed with the majority's contention that a case had not been made on this crucial element. One vote in the other direction, with the dissenters, and the VAWA provision in question would have sustained the challenge. The socio-cultural implications of this close decision are myriad and reflect a continuing perception, despite evidence to the contrary, that the effects of domestic violence against women are quite limited. Such a view, as reflected in the majority opinion, mirrors centuries of belief that because the problem involves intimates it, by nature, is contained within the home.

Enforcement issues

Before the 1980s, courts and law enforcement officials rarely pursued the problem of domestic violence (Colker 2006). This reflected over a century's pattern of willful disregard, as during the nineteenth century most courts were loath to admit that the law permitted domestic abuse and authorities rarely punished abusers, citing the importance of preserving domestic harmony and/or the privacy of the home (Siegel 1996). Many states rejected proposed laws that would prohibit wife-beating and it was not until 1882 that one state, Maryland, moved forward and became the first to pass such a law (U.S. Commission on Civil Rights 1982). Wide-ranging efforts to provide support for victims of domestic violence through the legal system and public initiatives did not emerge until the 1980s, being largely the result of the women's movement during the 1970s to educate the public and policymakers about battered women and the related failure of the legal system (Colker 2006).

In an initial, and what looked to be dramatic, new approach to the problem of correcting for policy indifference to domestic violence, calls involved the creation of new legal requirements for mandatory arrest of the primary physical aggressor. Approximately half of all states have provided for mandatory arrest of abusers in which the police do not have to have a warrant to arrest an abuser (ABA 2007). Mandatory arrest laws require that police arrest an alleged abuser when the officer has probable cause to believe that an act of domestic assault and/or battery has occurred, whether he has a warrant or not, and regardless of a victim's wishes (Han 2003). The practice of adopting mandatory arrest laws began in the late 1980s after a number of court cases in which judges found that local police were failing to properly protect victims of domestic violence (Han 2003). Concerned over the evidence that police officers often treated such calls as purely private and that victims appeared to not want their abusers arrested, some policymakers saw the creation of mandatory arrest laws as a solution that would help punish the abusers and reduce the numbers of women maimed and murdered by their partners. Research has reported mixed results on the success of these laws in changing the incidence of domestic violence in their respective states with much debate over whether one legal initiative is enough to even moderate impact on an enormous problem with roots that include, but go beyond, the legal system (Han 2003; Miller 2000; Garner 1997).

Another late 1980s attempt to use the legal system to reduce domestic violence involved a concept called *no-drop prosecution*, still in use in some jurisdictions. Here policymakers were concerned with the high number of dropped prosecutions in domestic violence cases, many of which were dropped due to victim unwillingness to testify against her abuser and/or unwillingness to come to court (Davis et al. 2001). In a no-drop prosecution the state prosecutor decides whether to prosecute a domestic violence perpetrator, regardless of the victim's wishes. Many no-drop states will pursue a prosecution vigorously and include in their vigor the subpoenaing of a victim to testify against her will. Prosecutors may go so far as to arrest or even imprison victims who fail to comply with their subpoenas (Han 2003). As with mandatory arrest laws, no-drop prosecution policies are equally controversial in that while there is evidence that they increase convictions of domestic violence perpetrators there is no consensus that victims are safer in the long run (Davis et al. 2001).

The core regulative structures underlying the institution of domestic violence are state criminal laws. Unfortunately, even with developments of the late twentieth century, current domestic violence criminal law reflects a deep disconnect with the reality of domestic violence against women. In viewing domestic violence as a crime simply in terms of incidences producing physical harm or death or fear of such, the law misses fundamental elements of the problem reflecting ongoing patterns of control and coercion that involve psychological stress and economic dependency, among others. Federal and state efforts of the late twentieth century that provide funding for domestic violence shelters, public education programs, and related efforts are tremendously helpful in addressing the problem, but also suffer from chronic underfunding.

Nevertheless, perpetrators who use manipulation to isolate their victims from supportive people and organizations, create economic dependency in their victims, and manifest a continual pattern of verbal and emotional abuse typically are beyond the reach of current prosecution standards as their behaviors are short of actual or the threat of actual physical violence. This is an element of the institution of domestic violence that allows its continued perpetuation. Coupled with chronic underfunding of victim support programs, community education initiatives, and other efforts to address the problem, this lack of a legal and regulatory structure that appreciates the nature of intimate partner violence simply aids the perpetuation of the problem.

Institutional normative structures of domestic violence

Values and expectations are norms carried by culture while authority systems provide the social structures for transporting normative elements. Conformity and performance of role-defined duties are routines that carry such norms within the institutional environment

Even when the law, as discussed previously, does not provide for a regulative, coercive influence in perpetuating domestic violence against women as an institution, various social norms have existed to similarly shape the behavior of Americans. Though in the eighteenth century a few judges refused to accept a man's defense for beating his wife that such behavior was recognized as acceptable in the common law, the general view was that such acts were within the norm. This is particularly evident in the *rule of thumb* standard that some within the legal system and society as a whole referenced as originating in English common law. Though some commentators on linguistic origins and the evolution of the common law have argued that this phrase was not observed in the common law tradition, whether in England or the United States, published judicial opinions and commentaries have revealed that at least four jurists from the late seventeenth to the early twentieth centuries recognized it as existing within the common law context (Straton 2002; *State v. Oliver* 1917; Stedman 1917). Hence, it was understood by many authorities within the U.S. legal system as having legitimacy within the common law tradition and within society as a whole.

As mentioned in discussing the U.S. legal system's resistance to eliminating the marital exemption for sexual assault cases, societal norms viewing women in terms of their sexual and labor obligations to husbands were often codified in law. Even when they were not, they served to have the coercive effect of law, as families and communities often acted as enforcers of behaviors that defended abusers and blamed the victims and/or saw domestic violence as purely private and beyond the reach of the law (Feinman 1995).

Religion can serve as a regulative governance structure beyond the state (into the afterlife) as well as a creator and carrier of norms that guide the daily lives of citizens. Notions that wives are akin to property of husbands are well established in much of Jewish, Christian, and Muslim tradition and are often paired with accompanying social norms. With all such religions, different cultural groups, both in historic and modern times, have interpreted core religious documents in ways that often perpetuate not only woman-as-property but also the appropriateness of abusive behavior for male-defined transgressions of gender roles. For example, the Judaeo-Christian command not to covet a neighbor's wife, among his other property, is an early indicator of the wife-as-property cultural and religious tradition among many adherents (Exodus 20:17). In his letter to the Ephesians (5:1–23), Paul of Damascus wrote that women must submit to their husbands in everything, and while some theologians and congregants interpret this within a larger dual responsibility of equal and mutual respect among partners, others do not. As inequality (e.g. in law, opportunity, economics) is strongly related to domestic violence, governance structures that emphasize that inequality keep the door open for its continuation. For many religious adherents, literal interpretation of core religious texts provides for a belief that domestic relationships are naturally or divinely hierarchical, with males possessing the dominant role. For some Muslim adherents, "this belief is both derived from and reinforced by *shari'a*, which tends to be interpreted to give men power over women family members" (Hajjar 2004). Indeed, none of the major religious traditions, including Buddhism and Hinduism, are entirely free of ideologies that posit women's inferiority and justify their subordination (Brooks-Thistlewhite 2009).

Recent research indicates that while religious institutions can provide emotional support for victims, they can also provide for the perpetuation of domestic violence by encouraging an environment of silence on the issue, imposing a duty on wives to maintain a marriage under all circumstances, enforcing a sense among victims of responsibility for their own abuse, and/or recommending solutions that may actually endanger the victims (Clark 2001; Pyles 2007).

Further evidence of continuing perceptions of wife-as-property is the identification in correspondence of a wife as Mrs. John Doe. Similarly, the taking of a husband's surname and rejection of one's birth surname is an artifact reflective of the property construct. The steadfastness of this tradition is seen in the twenty-first century as the vast majority of American women who have married continue the practice (Boxer and Gritsenko 2005). While many modern women argue that they take their husbands' surnames so that their children will have a shared identity and they (the wives) will not be seen as unrelated to them, it is clear that societal pressures continue as an alternative practice of children and/or husbands having hyphenated surnames incorporating both parents' surnames or husbands dropping their surnames in favor of their wives' is rare. Regulative structures aid this social behavior as the majority of states allow women, without fees, to change their surnames at marriage simply by noting their new names on the marriage certificate. For males to change their names at marriage, they must usually file a separate petition for a name change in court and pay associated fees.

Other social assumptions that reflect norms are notions of the domestic sphere being private and dominated by a father/husband—what happens in a man's castle, stays in the man's castle. Continuing notions of abuse as strictly private, rather than as a public problem, serve to dissuade others from offering support, reporting the abuse, and otherwise attempting to stop the status quo.

Institutional cognitive structures of domestic violence

Cognitive foundational structures reflect subconsciously engrained values and principles which shape behavior. Such mechanisms are mimetic in nature, emphasizing imitation. Legitimacy for individuals and organizations within the institutional environment is established due to conformance with culturally supported and legitimated activity. Accepted categories and typifications serve as cultural carriers of cognitive concepts (Scott 1995). In domestic violence, how men, women, girls, and boys think about intimate relationships reveal deeply engrained beliefs that reflect socialization through family, community, religion, and law. This is particularly evidenced in gender-role definitions.

Much of the perpetuation of domestic violence reflects core gender definitions and sex stereotypes that become taken-for-granted ways of thinking when it comes to relationships. From birth, adults begin using language and behaviors that reinforce role expectations on growing female and male infants. In the United States, it is common for parents to dress their baby girls in pink and baby boys in blue, a color patterning encouraged throughout childhood and associated with femininity and masculinity. In addition, parents often reinforce expectations among their children that emphasize nurturing and passive behaviors in girls and competitive and assertive behaviors in boys (Pomerleau et al. 1990). These expectations are observable not only in parent–child interactions but also in the manufacture and marketing of toys to children. For example, play toys emphasizing physical attractiveness, nurturing, and domestic skills are manufactured and accepted in society as appropriate for girls. Conversely, toys linked with competition and violence are seen as more appropriate for boys (Blakemore and Centers 2005).

Indeed, verbal and nonverbal forms of expression such as those above revealing the socialization of children toward appropriate gendered behaviors are a phenomenon which parallels cognitive expectations surrounding domestic violence. In the United States, many see domestic violence as involving a narrow range of perpetrators and victims. In essence, stereotypes that define characteristics of a *typical* victim and a *typical* abuser exist which do not reflect the reality that perpetrators and victims are represented in every demographic category (Harrison and Esqueda 1999). Again, such ignorance, reflected in cognitive constructs, is yet another example of the institutional nature of domestic violence and highlights the necessity of it to be viewed as such.

While interpersonal language also reflects embedded cognitive structures that reinforce the perpetuation of domestic violence against women, so do more formal entities such as media sources. Media reports provide insight into how language and its formal expression reveal embedded expectations about the roles of women and men and perpetrator versus victim, among others. Researchers using discourse analysis within the past few years have documented continuing characterizations in professional journals and media reports that obscure the role of male as abuser and/or indicate shared responsibility for the violence on the part of the male batterer and the female victim (Phillips and Henderson 1999). Other research focusing exclusively on broadcast and print media reports on violence against women produce similar results where the choice of words and their placement in a story create a narrative in which male abusers are seen in a forgiving light and female victims are treated as blameworthy or unimportant. Indeed, researchers have found media coverage of murder/suicide stories tending to omit details about a perpetrator's continual abuse and violence toward his wife and instead focusing on a wife or estranged wife's character flaws in the context of the murderer's love for his wife and job pressures (Meyers 1999). Further, media outlets also remain potent carriers for their lack of language highlighting each perpetrator's responsibility for the economic costs he imposes on society. As previously mentioned, in the Connie Culp case, her story made news not for the short prison sentence her husband received nor the dramatic financial burden his violence laid at each taxpayer's doorstep, but for the pioneering surgery the victim received.

Other media sources such as films and television continue to provide examples of the female as the "fixer" of the bad boy, a notion which encourages young women to stay in abusive relationships. The cognitive stream begins at a young age as fairytales from centuries ago get a professional film industry touch to appeal to millions of cinema patrons. For example, Belle, the lead female character from the Walt Disney Company's 1991 film blockbuster, *Beauty and the Beast,* appears to be an independent, confident, and dutiful young woman who would never let anybody mistreat her. Nevertheless, we see that despite the lead male character's cruel behavior, often driven by rage, Belle senses that she can change him into a kind and loving creature, a feat that no other human or animal has been able to do. Fortunately for fairytale princesses and other imaginary female heroines, the power to change abusive people is quite common. Unfortunately, similar tales, shared with children throughout history in all cultures, are integral in perpetuating domestic abuse and violence, for in reality, even within the context of professionally designed and administered counseling programs, changing an abusive personality into a non-abusive one is rare (Gondolf 1997).

Evidence for another cognitive script shared across society in the United States is a belief that domestic violence against women occurs in other people's communities. For example, in a 2006 poll, a random, national sample of 1,100, respondents were asked the degree to which they thought domestic violence was a problem in their own communities. Forty percent responded that it was either not too serious or not a problem at all (Harvard School of Public Health 2006). In a 1997 survey (national randomized sample of 1,000) that inquired whether domestic violence was a problem nationally, 74 percent of respondents agreed that it was a major problem (Insurance Research Council 1997). Again, this is one of the many elements making up a strong cognitive institutional foundation that aids in the perpetuation of domestic violence.

Putting it all together: a framework for formulating future policy

A policy program that attempts to end or reduce domestic violence against women must recognize the characteristics of the institution that makes it resistant to change. Regulative, normative, and cognitive components provide stability for the status quo—the perpetuation of the problem. Understanding that domestic violence against women is an institution, in the same way as marriage, is an initial step in crafting policy programs to address the problem.

First, although since the 1980s many states have amended their laws to recognize the criminality of physical violence in intimate relationships and provided easier availability of personal protection orders for those living in fear of harm, the legal system has not recognized the underlying nature of domestic violence, namely the control and coercion, that extends to psychological and economical violence. As previously mentioned, current domestic violence laws reflect common law definitions of assault and battery without an appreciation for the continuing pattern of psychological and economic control perpetrated on victims. As an example, Professor Deborah Tuerkheimer of the University of Maine's School of Law and a former prosecutor specializing in domestic violence cases has proposed state adoption of a specific format of criminal law for domestic violence that provides an enhanced definition of battery that includes the control and power, psychological injury, etc. involved in domestic violence. Tuerkheimer's (2007) recommended change to current state law on battery used in domestic violence cases may be the most pragmatic in recognizing difficulties inherent in changing the legal foundations of regulating destructive behavior. Despite its pragmatism in providing a workable recommendation for institutional change it has not been adopted among the states.

Funding for laws such as the VAWA is also integral to a successful policy solution to domestic violence against women because programs and shelters supported under these types of laws and regulations are able to address normative and cognitive structures underlying the institution also. In conjunction with state criminalization of domestic violence via the Tuerkheimer model, enhanced funding of VAWA and other legislation, is further state development of employment laws that allow domestic violence victims job protection through paid or unpaid leave for purposes of attending court and seeking medical and counseling services, among other activities related to domestic violence. Though paid leaves are preferred, so that victims can achieve financial independence, as a base requirement for employers, job protection is a first step.

To eradicate domestic violence against women, effective policy will need to reflect an understanding of elements in three institutional support structures: regulative, normative, and cognitive. This will require extensive coordination between not only lawmakers and professional groups representing victims, prosecutors, and judges, but also religious leaders (national and local), business representatives, teachers, and the medical community. Though a formidable task, it is necessary for breaking down institutional substructures that currently render the problem resistant to change.

Lastly, by reconceptualizing domestic violence against women as an institution, normally unrecognized characteristics are revealed. For example, discourse on domestic violence against women, whether provided by media sources, policymakers, or individuals, reflects a continued refusal to recognize the primary role perpetrators have in imposing excessive economic burdens on society, even for future generations. Dismantling the foundational elements of an institution is not easy, but ignoring or failing to recognize them simply aids in the perpetuation of the problem. As for policymaking, when those in authority, in addition to individual citizens, do not recognize domestic violence as an institution they become part of the problem.

Bibliography

Alaska Stat. (2001) 11.41.425–.427 (Michie 2010).

Alpert, E. J. (2002) "Domestic Violence and Clinical Medicine: learning from our patients and from our fears," *Journal of General Internal Medicine*, 17(2): 162–163.

American Bar Association (ABA) (2007) Domestic Violence Arrest Policies by State. Online.<http://www.abanet.org/domviol/docs/Domestic_Violence_Arrest_Policies_by_State_11_07.pdf.> (accessed 14 February 2010).

American Institute on Domestic Violence (AIDV) (2001) "Domestic Violence in the Workplace Statistics, 2001." Online. <http://www.aidv-usa.com/statistics.htm.> (accessed 24 February 2010).

American Medical Association (AMA) (1992) "American Medical Association Diagnostic and Treatment Guidelines on Domestic Violence," *Archives of Family Medicine*, 1: 39–47. Online. <http://archfami.ama-assn.org/cgi/reprint/1/1/39> (accessed 21 February 2010).

Ammar, N. H. (2009) "Wife Battery in Islam: a comprehensive understanding of interpretations," *Violence Against Women*, 13(5): 516–527.

Anderson, M. J. (2003) "Marital Immunity, Intimate Relationships, and Improper Inferences: a new law on sexual offenses by intimates," *Hastings Law Journal*, 54: 1463–1572.

Beckman, C. M. and Phillips, D. J. (2005) "Interorganizational Determinants of Promotion: client leadership and the attainment of women attorneys," *American Sociological Review*, 70(4): 678–702.

Blackstone, Sir William. (1765) *Commentaries on the Laws of England*. 1: 442–445.

Blakemore, J. E. O. and Centers, R.E. (2005) "Characteristics of Boys' and Girls' Toys," *Sex Roles: A Journal of Research*, 53: 619–634.

Boxer, D. and Gritsenko, E. (2005) "Women and Surnames across Cultures: reconstituting identity in marriage," *Women and Language*, 28(2): 1–11.

Brooks-Thistlewhite, S. (2009) "God's Batterers: when religion subordinates women, violence follows," *On Faith, The Washington Post*. 27 February 2009. Online. <http://newsweek.washingtonpost.com/onfaith/panelists/susan_brooks_thistlethwaite/2009/02/gods_batterers_when_religion_s.html> (accessed 28 January 2010).

Child Welfare Information Gateway (CWIG) (2008) "Definitions of Domestic Violence," Online. <http://www.childwelfare.gov/systemwide/laws_policies/statutes/defdomvio.pdf> (accessed 14 January 2010).

Clark, R. (2001) "The Silence in Dinah's Cry: narrative in Genesis 34 in a context of sexual violence," *Journal of Religion and Abuse*, 2(4): 81–98.

Colker, R. (2006) "Marriage Mimicry: the law of domestic violence," *William and Mary Law Review*, 47: 1841–1882.

Coker, A. L., Smith, P. H., McKeown, R.E., and King, M. J. (2000) "Frequency and Correlates of Intimate Partner Violence by Type: physical, sexual, and psychological battering," *American Journal of Public Health*, 90: 553–559.

Connerton, K. C. (1997) "The Resurgence of the Marital Rape Exemption: the victimization of teens by their statutory rapists," *Albany Law Review*, 61: 237–284.

Davis, R. C., Smith, B. E., and Davies, H. J. (2001) "Effects of No-Drop Prosecution of Domestic Violence Upon Conviction Rates," *Justice Research and Policy*, 3(2): 1–13.

Dobash, R. E. (1979) *Violence Against Wives: a case against the patriarchy*, New York: Free Press.

DiMaggio, P. J. and Helmust, K. H. (1990) "The Sociology of Nonprofit Organizations and Sectors," *Annual Review of Sociology*, 16:137–159.

DiMaggio, P. J. and Powell, W. W. (1991) "Introduction," in DiMaggio, P. J. and Powell, W. W. (eds) *The New Institutionalism in Organizational Analysis*, Chicago, IL: University of Chicago Press: 1–38.

Dutton, D. and Golant, S. (1997) *The Batterer: A Psychological Profile*, New York: Basic Books.

Eisenberg, S. E. and Micklow, P. (1977) "The Assaulted Wife: 'Catch 22' revisited," *Women's Rights Law Reporter*, 3: 138–146.

Erskine, J. (1999) "If It Quacks Like a Duck: recharacterizing domestic violence as criminal coercion," *Brooklyn Law Review*, 65: 1207–1229.

Eskow, L. R. (1996) "The Ultimate Weapon?: demythologizing spousal rape and reconceptualizing its prosecution," *Stanford Law Review*, 48: 677–709.

Feinman, M. A. (1995) *The Neutered Mother, the Sexual Family, and other Twentieth Century Tragedies*, New York: Routledge.

Frederickson, H. G. and Johnson, G. A. (2001) "The Adapted American City, A Study of Institutional Dynamics," *Urban Affairs Review*, 36(6): 872–884.

Garcia-Moreno, C., Jansen, H., Ellsberg, M., Helse, L., and Watts, C. (2005) "Violence Against Women: initial results on prevalence, health outcomes and women's responses," Geneva: World Health Organization.

Garner, J. H. (1997) "Evaluating the Effects of Mandatory Arrest for Domestic Violence in Virginia," *William and Mary Journal of Women and the Law*, 3: 223–239.

Gondolf, E. W. (1997) "Pattern of Re-assault in Batterer Programs," *Violence and Victim*, 12(4): 373–387.

Gun Free School Zones Act (1994) Public Law 101–647.

Hajjar, L. (2004) "Religion, State Power, and Domestic Violence in Muslim Societies: a framework for comparative analysis," *Law and Social Inquir*, 29(1): 1–38.

Han, E. L. (2003) "Mandatory Arrest and No-Drop Policies: victim empowerment in domestic violence cases," *Boston College Third World Law Journal*, 23(1): 159–192.

Harrison, L. A. and Esqueda, C. W. (1999) "Myths and Stereotypes of Actors Involved in Domestic Violence: implications for domestic violence culpability attributions," *Aggression and Violent Behavior*, 4(2): 129–138.

Harvard School of Public Health (2006) Poll. 21 June–26 June.

Insurance Research Council (1997) Survey. 10 June–24 June.

Krug, E. G., Dahlberg, L. L., Mercy, J. A., Zwi, A. B., and Lozano, R. (2002) *World Report on Violence and Health*, Geneva: World Health Organization.

Larson, T. A. (1973) "Montana Women and the Battle for the Ballot," *Montana: The Magazine of Western History*, 23(1): 24–41.

McLaughlin, M. (2009) "State Coalition Talking Points, VAWA, FVPSA and VOCA Appropriations FY 2009," Washington, DC: National Coalition to End Domestic Violence. Online. <http://www.nnedv.org/docs/Policy/talkingpoints_localprograms.pdf> (accessed 28 January 2010).

Meier, H. D. and Rowan, B. (2006) *The New Institutionalism in Education*, Albany, NY: SUNY Press.

Meyers, M. (1999) *News Coverage of Violence against Women*, Thousand Oaks, CA: Sage.

Michigan Domestic Violence Prevention and Treatment Act, MCLA 400.1501.

Miller, S. L. (2000) "Mandatory Arrest and Domestic Violence: continuing questions," in Muraskin, R. and Alleman, T. (eds) *It's a Crime, Women and Justice*, New York: McGraw Hill: 287–310.

Narisi, S. (2008) "States Pass Laws for Domestic Violence Leave," *HRLegal News*. Online. <http://www.hrlegalnews.com/states-pass-laws-for-%E2%80%9Cdomestic-violence-leave%E2%80%9D/> (accessed 9 January 2010).

National Center for Injury Prevention and Control (NCIPC) (2003) *Costs of Intimate Partner Violence against Women in the United States*, Atlanta, GA: Centers for Disease Control and Prevention.

National Crime Victimization Survey (NCVS) (2006) United States Department of Justice, Bureau of Justice Statistics. Online. <http://dx.doi.org/10.3886/ICPSR22560> (accessed 14 February 2010).

O'Leary, D. K. (1988) "Physical Aggression between Spouses: a social learning theory perspective," in Van Hasselt, V. B., Morrison, R. L., Bellack, A. S., and Hersen, M. (eds) *Handbook of Family Violence*, New York: Plenum Press: 31–55.

People v. Liberta, 474 N.E.2d 657 (N.Y. 1984).

Phillips, D. and Henderson, D. (1999) "'Patient Was Hit in the Face by a Fist . . . ' A discourse analysis of male violence against women," *American Journal of Orthopsychiatry*, 69(1): 116–121.

Pomerleau, A., Bolduc, D., Malcuit, G., and Cossette, L. (1990) "Pink or Blue: environmental gender stereotypes in the first two years of life," *Sex Roles: A Journal of Research*, 22: 359–368.

Pyles, L. (2007) "The Complexities of the Religious Response to Domestic Violence: implications for faith based initiatives," *Affilia Journal of Women and Social Work*, 22(3): 281–292.

Rennison, C. M., and Welchans, S. (2000) *Intimate Partner Violence*, Washington, DC: U.S. Government Printing Office.

Russell, S. S. (2003) "Covering Women and Violence: media treatment of VAWA's civil rights remedy," *Michigan Journal of Gender and Law*, 9: 327–414.

Scott, R. W. (1995) *Institutions and Organizations*, 1st edn, Thousand Oaks, CA: Sage.

Scott, R. W. (2007) *Institutions and Organizations*, 3rd edn, Thousand Oaks, CA: Sage.

Sewell, B. D. (1989) "History of Abuse: societal, judicial, and legislative responses to the problem of wife beating," *Suffolk University Law Review*, 23: 983–997.

Siegel, R. G. (1996) "The Rule of Love: wife beating as prerogative and privacy," *Yale Law Journal*, 105: 2117–2207.

State v. Oliver (1917) 70 N.C. 60.

Stedman, B. (1917) "Right of Husband to Chastise Wife," *Virginia Law Register*, 3: 241, 244–248.

Straton, J. (2002) "Rule of Thumb versus Rule of Law," *Men and Masculinities*, 5(1): 101–107.

Tatelman, T. B. (2004) *Congress's Power Under the Commerce Clause: the impact of recent court decisions*, Congressional Research Service Report for Congress: RL32446.

Tjaden, P. and Thoennes, N. (2000) "Extent, Nature, and Consequences of Intimate Partner Violence: findings from the National Violence against Women Survey," National Institute of Justice and the Centers for Disease Control and Prevention. Online. <http://www.ncjrs.gov/pdffiles1/nij/181867.pdf> (accessed 19 February 2010).

Tolbert, P. S. and Zucker, L. (1983) "Institutional Sources of Change in the Formal Structures of Organizations: the diffusion of civil service reform, 1880–1935," *Administrative Science Quarterly*, 28(1): 22–39.

Tuerkheimer, D. (2007) "Renewing the Call to Criminalize Domestic Violence: an assessment three years later," *George Washington Law Review*, 75(3): 613–626.

United Nations (UN) (1993) "Declaration on the Elimination of Violence Against Women," A/RES/48/104. Online. <http://www.un.org/documents/ga/res/48/a48r104.htm> (accessed 24 February 2010).

United Nations (2006) "In-depth Study on all Forms of Violence against Women," A/61/122/Add.1. Online. <http://www.un.org/ga/search/view_doc.asp?symbol= A/61/122/Add.1> (accessed 1 July, 2010).

United States v. Lopez (1995) 514 U.S. 549.

United States v. Morrison (2000) 529. U.S. 598.

U.S. Commission on Civil Rights (1982) *Under the Rule of Thumb: battered women and the administration of justice*, Washington, DC: U.S. Commission on Civil Rights. Online.<http://www.eric.ed.gov/ERICDocs/data/ericdocs2sql/content_storage_01/ 0000019b/80/2f/cd/27.pdf> (accessed 24 February 2010).

United States Constitution. Online. <http://www.archives.gov/exhibits/charters/ charters_downloads.html>.

United States Department of Health and Human Services (USDHHS) (2009) "Domestic Violence against Women, What Is Abuse?" Washington, DC: Office on Women's Health. Online. <http://www.womenshealth.gov/violence/signs/> (accessed 24 February 2010).

United States Violence Against Women Act (1994) Public Law 103–322.

Waters, H., Hyder, A., Rajkotia, Y., Basu, S., Rehwinkel, J. A., and Butchart, A. (2004) *The Economic Dimensions of Interpersonal Violence*, Geneva: Department of Injuries and Violence Prevention, World Health Organization.

Part V

Confronting global gender justice

18 Configuring feminisms, transforming paradigms

Reflections from Kum-Kum Bhavnani—scholar, activist, filmmaker

Kum-Kum Bhavnani and
Connie L. McNeely

Kum-Kum Bhavnani is Professor of Sociology and Chair of the Women, Culture, and Development program at the University of California, Santa Barbara. Highly respected as a researcher and teacher, her work has addressed a wide range of critical issues involving questions on gender and women, the Third World and development, cultural studies, and film. She is widely known for her contributions to the analysis of racism in feminist theory and to developing a new paradigm for development studies. She has been a member of the *Feminist Review* editorial collective, was a founding and then associate editor of *Feminism and Psychology*, has been a guest editor for special issues of *Signs*, and was the inaugural editor of the acclaimed journal *Meridians: Feminism, Race, Transnationalism*. In addition to her numerous books and articles, she has published important collections on race and gender in their complex dimensions and intersections with politics, youth culture, and feminism, and, in 2006, released her award-winning feature documentary, *The Shape of Water*. Recognizing her critical achievements, commitment, and work confronting questions of global gender justice, we take this opportunity to probe her ideas for transforming feminist paradigms as she reflects on her life as a renowned scholar, activist, and filmmaker.

An interview with Kum-Kum Bhavnani by Connie L. McNeely

Please tell us a bit about your background and "formative years." Transnationalism seems to have long been a central feature of your life. Born in India and migrating with your family to the United Kingdom at a young age, would you say that this move was what ultimately put you on the road to your life as an activist, scholar, and artist? How did your family and education affect your direction?

It is always hard to say precisely what affects which part of one's life. I know that when I read Chomsky's critique of B. F. Skinner while I was studying psychology at Bristol University, it showed me a new way to think about human beings.[1] When

I saw *The Home and the World* (*dir.* Satyajit Ray),[2] I started to learn how to see everyday life of people differently; Miriam Makeba and Hugh Masekela led me to better grasp the meaning of apartheid in everyday life for most people in South Africa; my mathematics teacher at school made me determined to do even better because she told my mother I always wanted to finish work quickly, which was why I was so good at mental arithmetic, because I always looked for the shortest route to the answer! These are all one-off events that I remember with great clarity. In other words, my life, like that of many others, is a messy compilation of events, people, histories, travel, and politics.

But, of course, my migrations, my parents, my sisters and their families—my migrations, the two children I have, my partner—have also helped to shape me (not without some reluctance on my part, I have to say) into the person I now am.

We migrated to the UK when I was a very small child, in the late 1950s. I remember my aunt telling me at Delhi airport, as we prepared to step onto the plane, that I must make the hand luggage I was carrying look as light as possible, so no-one would stop and search it, and perhaps make us miss our flight. That injunction was meant to teach me, if I am a little grand about it, that if you look the part, you can fool people. While of course this is true, I started to realize then that I wanted people to know me as who I am—however heavy the luggage— because that way I had no need to cover up my experiences or feelings.

Going to primary school in a working-class area of London meant that I experienced a very different cohort of children to the ones I used to know. My father had been a High Court judge in India, my mother had her own school ("Kum-Kum School" was the name), my sisters had been at a boarding school run by nuns in a hill station, Mussoorie. Now, in the UK with very little money, we were living in Dollis Hill where my mother went to teach in Southall every day (a 45-minute drive to an area that is now the backdrop for films like *Bend it Like Beckham*), and my father had little work, largely because of racism on the part of English people and the British state. However, when I was 11, my school suggested I sit an Entrance Examination for a girls' day school three miles away, South Hampstead High. I was admitted to the school.

South Hampstead had a large effect on me. Going to school only with girls, and studying sciences, meant that I was not seen as (too) weird, and it has also meant that I still have very close friends from that age. We were encouraged to try our hands at many things, including singing—I was dreadful but the teacher still encouraged me, art at which I was useless and the teacher did not encourage me, and writing, where my teacher within my first few months of starting at the school read out my essay to the class—imagine the pride I felt at having my work selected, and she then announced it was one of the worst essays she had ever read, and that I would never be a writer. My other teachers saw me as someone they enjoyed teaching, and encouraged me to study the sciences, history, French, and mathematics. Due to the UK educational system, this was not possible at my school, so I opted for the sciences.

However, I was younger than the other girls in my year. I decided, therefore, on hearing about the American Field Service Scholarships, that I would go to the

US between my penultimate and final year at school. Although I pleaded with the committee to send me to a public high school, so I could see the contrast between a small, semi-private girls' school and a much larger school, I was placed in a private girls' high school in Buffalo, New York—the Buffalo Seminary.

I was not a "typical" AFS student at Sem. Not only could I not sing (but the choirmaster insisted I be in the choir, as all AFS students had been, and he insisted I mime!), but my political awakening happened here. Most of the girls were from wealthy Buffalo families, a number of whom were debutantes and held coming-out parties. Two girls in my class, however, were black—African American—and both were on scholarships. We came to be very close friends. One of them discussed her politics openly (it was in the years after the large Civil Rights marches) and the other came to political awareness as she saw her fiancé drafted to fight in Vietnam while all the wealthy white young men had made the right arrangements so that they would not be drafted. Those two as well as two other women (with whom I am still friends) were a lifeline to me as I learnt to navigate this upper-class society. Ironically, it was at Sem that I was taught about communism, socialism, fascism, and capitalism by our modern history teacher, and, once again, I realized how little I knew about much of the world.

On my return to Britain, I went to the tenth anniversary march of the Sharpeville massacre in South Africa, and discovered my passion for politics lay not just in books. At university I studied psychology, sociology, politics, and philosophy and, again, worked very hard politically. It was there that I learned about trades unions, through supporting a national dustbin workers' strike, explaining to people, soon after I learnt myself, what strike-breaking meant and how it affected workers' everyday lives at the most minute levels. I also studied quite hard, went to the US during one summer to work and travel, and was awarded a good degree. Films were my passion at Bristol, along with theatre. I had done a lot of theatre outside my school: I was never selected to be in any of the school plays. I was one of the three non-white girls in the whole school, and had a drama teacher who was not particularly alert to matters of racism (to put it at its most generous)— and I am delighted I spent so much time watching films, being close with people who did the same, as well as, of course, studying. Although this was a time for a lot of experimentation with drugs, my one or two attempts with marijuana never had any effect on me, so I avoided that pitfall easily. Thank goodness.

After Bristol, I did an MA in child psychology—working with children with developmental difficulties such as autism and clinical issues. I loved that work, which was with parents and children simultaneously, and, again, I learnt a lot about inequality and how class/"race"/gender did not explain every trouble that people experience. Not that I think biology is a determinant; rather, the point is that often our individual personal histories, including family, nationality, and migration, are aspects of our lives about which we can do little and which can have a distinct impact on us.

So, my formative years were shaped deeply by my family: we lived in a small not-so-posh house, with a very hardworking mother whose commitment to her pupils and to us was, I now realize, inspiring; a father who was (rightly) resentful he could not get work at the level he ought to have, which made for much internal tension for him, and quite a few arguments with all of us. And I had two sisters who went to the same high school and who were, to me, rather different. And me—someone who worked alongside her mother to help her with the domestic work from the age of 7, whose family could not go on holiday except for one huge trip round continental Europe in a car when I was 11, who had a paid summer job every summer from the age of 13, and who went to the USA at the age of 16, spending one year away from my parents. I have an independent soul, I think, and perhaps it has been deepened and shaped by my first 18 years?

What were some of the political issues and activities with which you were involved in the past and currently, and how was it that you came to be involved with them as an activist in the first place?

I spent a lot of my time, after I was 18, in the UK being politically active. My initiation into politics following the dustbin workers' strike was intense—and very enjoyable. The 1970s were a period of lively political activity at Bristol (and other UK universities, of course), which meant that I was able to get involved with feminism, left-wing, and Marxist groups, and spent time thinking about racism. If I am honest, a lot of progressive people did not spend much time thinking about racism in terms of daily life. But I had to, being a psychologist in the decade after Arthur Jensen's famous *Harvard Education Review* article that looked at the differences in IQ test scores between African American and white children in the US.[3] He proposed the adoption of different educational strategies for the two groups, so that black children would learn by rote and white children in a more creative way. I had heard about the article a few years after it came out, and asked one of my lecturers if he could offer a lecture on it. I remember he was taken aback (it was very long, very dense, and full of statistics), but he was a good sport: "You want me to read the whole article and tell you all about it, by next week?" He knew my answer.

That lecture was fascinating. Looking back I see that it was at that time that I understood that figures did not always offer only one answer, that the most respectable of academic titles (Jensen is presently Professor Emeritus at UC Berkeley) did not guarantee respectable research, and, finally, that I had to learn how to critique ideas both *from within their premises as well as from outside*. In this instance, not only did I learn how to take apart Arthur Jensen's argument by critiquing his psychological arguments and assumptions, by offering a reinterpretation of his statistics, but, also, by arguing that education was not about only caring for those who had had many opportunities in life—and these are three points I carry with me whenever I critique academic writing, whether I agree with it or not!

Jensen's article allowed me to engage with many of the books and pamphlets on racism in education, including a key document by Bernard Coard (he became a Minister in the revolutionary Grenadian government under Maurice Bishop, only to be imprisoned in connection with Bishop's murder that opened the door to US intervention), *How the West Indian Child is Made Educationally Sub-Normal in the*

British School System: The scandal of the black child in schools in Britain.[4] It was in that piece that he showed how the "antisocial" behaviors of children in schools was often a reaction to overt racialism and institutional racism.

Those two words, racialism and racism, had different meanings for us at that time. Racism referred to the institutional practices by which systematic discrimination occurred against people of color (not a UK phrase). That is, when one saw that fewer black people were headteachers or in management positions in local authorities, or were refused entry to the UK because of immigration legislation, this was referred to as "racism" because no individual could be held responsible for this pattern. Racialism, however, refers to the individual acts of discrimination carried out against people: bus conductors not letting you onto the bus by ringing the bell just as you are about to get on, being served last in a queue even though you were there before everyone else, having racial insults hurled at you—sometimes by teachers—while at school and so on. The argument had been that the two are intimately related, that the racism of the individual immigration officer at the point of entry is what would lead him/her to interpret the regulations such that a South Asian woman entering, if she was about to be married to a UK citizen, had to be subjected to a virginity test on the grounds that South Asian women had to be virgins before marriage. So if someone was not defined as a virgin, then she was, "obviously," trying to enter the country for the wrong reasons. Needless to say, we—a group of women who called ourselves "Awaaz" (*voice* in Hindi—I think the name was thought up by Amrit Wilson)—opposed this vehemently and loudly, wearing saris, at Heathrow airport. As noted by Frances Webber, "Apart from the inevitable echoes of eugenics, Nazis, and apartheid, in Britain, the imposition of virginity testing on wives from the Indian subcontinent in the late 1970s led to picketing of Heathrow airport."[5]

My point is that we distinguished between those terms so that one could talk about state racism and individual racialism. I am not pedantic about words; although I do like to be precise in how I use words, I do consider this distinction as helpful. It has always, for me, pointed a way on how to remedy the situation: is it an individual who is to be taken to account, or the state, which removes the politics out of "race," thinks about it as merely policy issues—if we have quotas, affirmative action, and so on, all will be well: no acknowledgement of the very basic issue that any first year undergraduate sociology student could speak to, namely the power inequalities inherent in such relationships.

The formative issues and politics for me were education and "race," immigration and "race." This was the decade following UK Member of Parliament Enoch Powell's "rivers of blood speech," when dockers marched in support of his argument, when the UK government changed its immigration and citizenship laws so that people who had British passports but had not been in Britain and did not have a grandparent or parent born in Britain were given lesser rights than white people. South Asians living in East Africa are the most well-known group: they were given British passports and told they could enter Britain at any time. However, once Idi Amin started to expel South Asians from Uganda, the British Government passed legislation within a matter of days to ensure that that group, i.e., non-white people with British passports, did not have the same rights as other British citizens.

And women. I realized, around the time of the immigration changes and virginity tests, that white women and black women had different interests at many points in time (this later led to the article I co-wrote with Margaret Coulson, "Transforming Socialist Feminism: The Challenge of Racism," published in *Feminist Review* in 1986). In 1978, Pratibha Parmar (who is now a successful filmmaker, and still holds those politics dear to her) and I wrote a discussion document for the Manchester Socialist Feminist Conference on how white women and black women had different interests and that feminists could not move forward in our politics until we took this into account (one of the early, if slightly naive, UK statements on "difference," as far as I know). It led to lots of terrific discussion. We were pleased: the issue was now out and could be engaged.

We sent our piece to *Spare Rib* (the magazine for Women's Liberation women) as a discussion document to encourage wide discussion of the issues. To our immense surprise, we received a polemic back (I won't say which member of the collective sent it, as it was sent on behalf of the *SR* Collective), against us, saying that we were wrong, that we did not understand feminism and that *SR* would not be publishing the piece. That was quite an eye-opener, and it was then that I realized that white feminists could also harbor the same racist and racialist thinking we encountered elsewhere. That was why, when *All the Women Are White, All the Blacks Are Men, But Some of Us Are Brave* and, a few years later, *This Bridge Called My Back* came out, we were so happy, even though it was from the USA and not in the tradition of socialist feminism, a politics which still informs my life.[6]

I suppose the late 1970s were the period when I came to political adulthood, as it were—I realized I needed to learn more and more, I needed to constantly work with the contradictions of any ideas and practices, and I knew that it was crucial to be public when one did not agree with something (years later, the AIDS slogan "Silence=Death" reminded me of that), and I knew that I was heterosexual, that I loved being a black woman, and that life was for experiencing as much as possible.

During that time I worked as a lecturer (assistant professor) at Leeds Polytechnic (The Clash played there; punk became very important there in the mid-1970s), teaching development/life-span psychology to social workers, and being active in my trades union, as well as in anti-racist and feminist work. These last were, of course, outside of my employment.

In the very late 1970s I worked as an educational psychologist for a local authority for 18 months or so. I was still politically active, determined to try to make my personal life be in line with my politics, understood in a very clear way how the daily life of people, especially poor people, is greatly shaped by racism, gender/sexuality inequalities, as well as discrimination on the ground of *assumed* abilities. Working with an 8-year-old child, for example, who had thrown a pencil at his 3-year-old sister which blinded her, and then did not speak for a year or so afterwards was instructive. The care the school had for him showed me that schools could be compassionate places. The concern of his parents taught me that not having money was not a barrier to being involved with your children's lives and their aspirations (my mother also showed me that), the lack of desire for revenge on the part of his sister allowed me to see that humans are not intrinsically revengeful, and the fact that eventually, after six months of my working with him, with the school, with his parents and his sister, he started to speak, showed me that people can and do change, however unlikely the possibility might appear to be.

The job was exhausting however, and I could not reconcile that, however hard I worked, and however much I followed educational policy, offered strong arguments against segregating children into "different ability" schools, was supported by parents and, sometimes, by the teachers and the mainstream school, children could still be placed in segregated education ("Special Education" as it was called), because of assumptions made about their race and intellectual abilities.

At that time, I was also active with Awaaz, which we later renamed Asian Women's Community Workers' Group (AWCWG). I would travel to London for meetings, and we were successful in receiving a grant from the Greater London Council (before Ken Livingstone became mayor) to set up the first refuge for South Asian women, in South London, seeking an escape from domestic violence. Our argument was that at such a crisis time for women—leaving home to escape violence—South Asian women did not need to be in an atmosphere, with white women, where they might be subjected to racism by the white women in the refuge. We were not in opposition to the other women's refuges, and they understood that—the more refuges we could have, the better.

AWCWG showed that having kitchens and sleeping spaces and workers who were closer in terms of cultural history than were white women from Judeo-Christian traditions allowed the South Asian women more breathing space to work out what they wanted to do. And not making the women speak through translators was critical as well. The grant was huge for those days. I was elected Chairwoman of the group as the GLC insisted we had to have a conventional structure of Chair, Treasurer, Secretary, etc., etc. Again, I had to travel down to London a lot—by this time I was a Senior Lecturer at Preston Polytechnic—but, within three years, due to arguments within the group as well as being physically unable to do the regular traveling that was demanded of me (I had to be at meetings constantly, to act as a mediator), I had to step down—and I did have a full-time, and also meaningful, job that I enjoyed.

After working as an educational psychologist, you went to Cambridge, where you earned your Ph.D. at King's College, doing some path-breaking research on working-class youth in Britain, which resulted in your first book, Talking Politics.[7] *Did this work also speak to your position on social justice and your identity as a feminist? Did it affect your decision to go into academia?*

While I was teaching Developmental Psychology at Preston Polytechnic, I was given resources to set up an observation room so that small children could play with one person and be observed by a psychologist sitting with the parents on the other side of a one-way mirror: the children were always shown what was going to happen—they saw the mirror from both sides and were told we would be sitting watching them play, but that they would not be able to see us. I learned this set of ethics from Elizabeth and John Newson at Nottingham, where I did my MA in Child/Educational Psychology.

While I was at Preston Polytechnic, Margaret Coulson and I were invited to conduct an investigation into sexual harassment at Preston Polytechnic, with a view to suggesting appropriate policies for the institution. We did that research. One instructive aspect was when we asked the director to allow us to have a meeting of all the women staff—including faculty—at one time to discuss the project and to let them know how best they could come and speak with us (this was well before the days of email). He agreed. For that one hour meeting, the whole polytechnic had to be closed down, because although there were few women in positions of power, it was the other women who ran the place. No telephones could be answered, no student queries could be dealt with—I do think that allowed our sympathetic director to see something he had not seen before.

At the same time, I started to think about youth unemployment. This was in the heyday of Thatcherism in the UK, just after the Falklands/Malvinas war with Argentina, and I wanted to know how young people felt about being un-employed, and whether they thought things could be different—namely, how they thought about political issues. I submitted one grant application, but was refused, and was also told that because I did not have a Ph.D., I would be unlikely to ever receive academic grants.

This was the impetus I needed to do a Ph.D. I was intellectually curious about the issues, needed time to think, write, and research, and if I got a book/Ph.D. out of it, so much the better!

I was accepted by the Social and Political Sciences Committee to do the doctorate at Cambridge, and received a quota award from the UK Economics and Social Research Council. I went there as an "older" student (i.e., not directly from my undergraduate work), spent my first year loving my research but hating being in such a privileged place where most of the students had no idea of their privilege or the sense of entitlement they exuded, and finally, realized what a wonderful opportunity I was being handed. I started to enjoy my time there— hearing speakers including C.L.R. James, Noam Chomsky on his linguistic theories, Raymond Williams on culture, and John Bowlby on maternal deprivation. Not too many women.

My *Talking Politics* work is central to my development as an intellectual— namely as someone who insists on, and enjoys, academic rigor *alongside* my politics.

I deliberately drew on feminist approaches to research to conduct my empirical work: single-sex discussion groups with working-class youth to see what the issues might be regarding unemployment and their futures. That is, I tried to develop the interview agenda from their views as well as mine, not only from what I thought they ought to be thinking about. I also drew on grounded theory and feminist theories (and my politics?) to always remind myself that people are not passive dupes but, rather, are thinking beings who have views about the world around them. I relied on my psychology training to ensure that the research, which was qualitative, was scientific in the sense of having a theoretical rationale for every step in the study. In the process, I drew on my politics and love for interdisciplinarity by (re)reading Gramsci, Angela Y. Davis, Benedict Anderson, Rosa Luxemburg, and Stuart Hall—again, not very many women, and not many women of color. Therefore, I tried to keep up with all the writings that were emerging, fast and furious (literally, sometimes) from black women around the world, among many others whose writing have informed and shaped my work at a deep level.

I became interested in youth not only because of the inequalities they experience due to their age, but, also, because the culture of being youthful is so valorized. It is those contradictions, again! But, of course, I was mainly interested in why working-class youth are seen as being either politically apathetic or politically militant, with very little room to be neither or both. The close to 100 percent unemployment for 16-year-olds when they left school in Manchester shocked me, and my love for tables, figures, and statistics led me to work closely with (on) the unemployment statistics, so that I could try to see what was going on, why the figures were so high, were they accurate and so on. It is that idea of critiquing from within, while also critiquing from outside.

Talking Politics was researched and written when I still called myself a psychologist, although it was a cultural studies approach to the issues. I would present findings for my research at youth conferences as well as at psychology conferences. It was at one of the latter when I found myself approached by other graduate students who told me that my determination to conduct qualitative research *as a psychologist* had inspired them to remain in psychology and use qualitative approaches for their own research. I don't know to what extent that holds true (whether it was just the one or two people I spoke with at the time) but I am delighted if my research has led to social psychology shifting its identity, even in a very small way.

While at Cambridge I was heavily involved in the miners' strike—going to picket lines, taking food and clothing to miners in the pit villages two or three hours from Cambridge—and also got to know a number of international students. There were very few black "British" students in the arts or social sciences at that time—especially as graduates: I don't know if I am the first black woman from the UK who got a Ph.D. from King's College Cambridge—in 1988. The politics and research of these students, often on Third World issues, led me to think more deeply. I had always read the newspaper closely, and felt I was up on current affairs, but to think about such Third World issues *as an academic* was a real eye-opener for me. Overall, Cambridge was very good for me—I was intellectually challenged in a deep way, which I enjoyed. I made close friends with many women living in the town, and I also spent a lot of time with undergraduates whose political *nous* was so nuanced, and who were so open to a range of political issues—they were not at all defensive like the white feminists I encountered inside and outside the academy—that I again saw how much I enjoy working with young people: their openness, their interest in many things, and the sense of adventure and surprise—a kind of appropriate wackiness—that they bring to politics.

You are well-known internationally as a feminist scholar and for the significance of your work on gender issues and social justice around the world. You have authored several books in this field and your expertise is widely recognized, especially in regard to women and development. What would you say is your driving motivation for this work? Is there a particular moment of significance in your development as a feminist scholar/activist/artist that you can identify? What have been some of your highest and most memorable moments as a scholar?

I am a universalist—as far as I can see there are universal principles according to which societies ought (*sic*) to be organized, principles that span histories, cultures, geographies, and numbers.

For example, I think violence against women is not acceptable. I also do not think religious leaders ought to be the gatekeepers of what women say, do, or wear, or over women's bodies. Reading about Rwanda led me to those positions very clearly, as did my reading about FGM (female genital mutilation). At the same time, I am mindful that it matters who says what to whom, in terms of what people/groups/nations ought to do—cultural imperialism is something that is real and that is to be avoided all the time. I am not saying that women living in the First World, whether of color or white, ought to prescribe behaviors to women in the Third World. Nor am I saying that white women in the First World ought to tell women of color in the First World how to organize ourselves.

At the same time, I do think it is important to decide for oneself what we think is the right way to do things. And fear of being called a "cultural imperialist" ought not to stop us from thinking about universals and how to implement them in our future societies. If we make a mistake in this regard, someone is sure to put us right: it has happened to me many times.

You were a designated International Observer for the first free and open elections in South Africa in 1994 after official apartheid was dismantled there, at least formally. What was that experience like? What do you think about the current situation there and possibilities for the future?

I was placed in Port Elizabeth, a town in the Eastern Cape Province, a province in which many of the present ANC leaders had been born and educated. I have many vivid memories of that time.

Five days before the election, I went to a voter education session in the men's maximum security building of St. Albans prison. Three weeks earlier, the prisoners had set fire to many parts of the prison—as a protest to demand their right to vote, which was finally granted. So the voter education I witnessed had a particular set of stakes attached to it. When the mechanics of the voting process were explained, the attention of the men was riveted on the speaker. But when he explained why people should have a vote, they seemed to pay less attention. Not, I think, because they did not agree—but because it seemed to me that it was self-evident to all of the black population of South Africa, which included the men in this prison, that the right to vote was fundamental, vital to recognizing them as human beings and part of the polity; they merely wanted to exercise that right.

On election day, four of us, international observers, went around the Port Elizabeth area to monitor the elections in places where there were likely to be few reporters. The key to how fast a polling station could move its line of voters along was dependent on how many private polling booths there were. In Dimbaza, the first polling station we visited, there was only one polling booth, with the result that only 60 people were able to vote per hour, and the queue outside was 1,400 people long. It was beginning to get hot, and people were dressed in their best clothes. There were no vendors, no water, no food, and no chairs. As international observers we were expected to not intervene in such situations, but to merely record them and move on to the next polling station. The four of us agreed, however, that we could not behave in that way. I called a number of District Election Officers to explain the crisis at Dimbaza, and it was an hour before I received a promise that more polling booths and ballot papers would be sent before the end of the day, as well as a mobile voter registration unit which could issue temporary voting cards. People had begun to faint during this hour, and the Red Cross was not present. We left Dimbaza late in the morning, having done as much as we felt we could do. When we returned at dusk, the lines had totally disappeared; the extra equipment had arrived within an hour of our departure that morning. A very happy ending—and we even felt we had contributed to making the day better for some people.

After Dimbaza we went to a very tiny location—Kidikidikana—where voters were sitting down on chairs, were being served bread and tea, were being driven to the local voter registration center, and where, crucially, there was no shortage of equipment or supplies. It was a way for us to see how the elections could have been an important community affair, if enough resources had been distributed.

Later that day, at 4.00 p.m., we arrived at Middledrift polling station. The situation was akin to that which we had witnessed at Dimbaza, but much worse. There were 2,000 people in line, many of whom had been waiting since 6 a.m. to vote. They were ANGRY. None of the lines seemed to be moving. Most places we had been to we had been greeted with enthusiasm for the role of the international observers. Not at Middledrift. No voters responded to our attempts to draw them into conversation. People there insisted we leave as the mood of the crowd was getting increasingly tense, so we did. Later that evening, we heard from the TV news that the election workers at Middledrift had been taken hostage by voters because they had run out of ballots. I wanted to drive straight back, to help mediate—the other three absolutely refused!

The abiding memory of too many black people with no teeth brought home to me the impact of apartheid—as a poverty creating system. I talked with Gareth, who was eating fresh pineapple he had just bought at a market stall: Gareth with no teeth, but pleasure all over his face as he sucked on the fruit. "Is it sweet?" I asked. "So-so," he said, "but I am just thinking about how much sweeter pineapples will taste after the elections."

How long, though, will those pineapples take to ripen, so that they are truly sweet, and not merely sweeter, with the underlying tang of sourness still present? Successive ANC governments have promised much, but they have also had very serious limitations. The elections were fueled by a desire to create a better life for people's children. South Africa has the potential to be one of the most exciting democracies of the twenty-first century, and I hope, so desperately, that that desire is implemented. It is a potential that still needs to be realized. Given the history of struggle, with women as strong participants, and given what I saw and learned while I was there (I returned in 2001 to attend the anti-racism congress in Durban), I retain optimism that this can happen, as history unfolds. If a system as hateful and harmful as apartheid could be undone, so too might the forms of inequality that have outlived it.

A few years ago, the founding editors of the journal Meridians *were asked in an interview to discuss the three terms that constitute the journal's subtitle: feminism, race, and transnationalism. In particular, they were asked to define, for themselves, the power of these terms and also their limitations. As the inaugural editor of* Meridians, *what are your perceptions about the meanings of those concepts and the intersections among them?*

I opened my first editorial for *Meridians* as follows:

> The end of the twentieth century marks a time of realignments in the cultural and political economies of gender throughout the world. Protests in many places against the World Trade Organization, the International Monetary Fund, and the World Bank have brought together a range of constituencies which had been fairly remote from each other in the previous decade. Women's organizations seem to be making links despite ethnic, sexual, and national boundaries, and racial/ethnic difference is much spoken about— and occasionally engaged with—sometimes creating an illusion that racialized inequalities are dissolving.[8]

The work of the journal was, for me, a chance to read work that examined such ideas and allowed readers to reflect on how the twenty-first century was bringing profound changes into our daily lives.

I argued, for example, that transnationalism can be understood both as a way for movements of resistance to link up against the processes of economic globalization, *as well as* the means by which multinational corporations organize their profit-seeking imperatives, thereby creating unprecedented poverty on a global scale. Multinational corporations use the labor of people (including women, men, and children) in the Third World, and of many immigrants in the First World. In setting down this very well-known idea, it is possible to bring into view the instability of the divide between Third and First Worlds (i.e., poor people and people of color in the First World could also be, simultaneously, Third World peoples who have migrated to the First World). However, at the same time, to elide the peoples of the Third and First Worlds could mean a privileging of one at the expense of oversimplifying, or making invisible, the other. In other words, we need both the distinction and the elision so that we are able to constantly hold both aspects simultaneously in our minds. The unstable divides (I used to call them "false distinctions") between race and ethnicity, among academic disciplines, between fiction and nonfiction, and between scholarship and advocacy also deserve this type of sustained exploration.

It is this type of unexpected and unpredictable outcomes of globalization and transnationalism that I sought for pieces published in *Meridians*, and, at the risk of sounding immodest, I like to think the journal achieved that, and continues to do so.

Across your work, you consistently engage issues affecting women of color in particular, and have argued that "identity and experience and culture all articulate with each other, and, simultaneously, with issues of representation, politics, and power." Given that the term "women of color" encompasses a variety of considerations relative to identities, class, location, etc., how do issues of gender entwine with those of race, ethnicity, class, and nation in your work?

Questions have always arisen in my scholarship: Which women's lives are being analyzed, interrogated, and even evaluated? In which parts of the world? Which aspects of their lives? Which voices? Who edits the documentation? And, indeed, are there any continuities in the lived experiences of women across class, region, nation, sexuality, and "race"/ethnicity? Such questions are key of course—difference is central. But how does one theorize difference? I do not know for sure, but my thinking begins as follows.

I know that readers will be familiar with the thesis that "race," ethnicity, class, gender, location, sexuality, and nationality are some of the axes of inequality which intersect and cut across each other. None of us has adequately theorized the ways this happens, although I am very partial to the stricture that as we work theoretically on this issue that we not draw up a "hierarchy of oppression," by which I mean that we not say, for example, that "race" is the most salient axis of inequality *in all circumstances*. Rather, the argument is that the power of each of these inequalities recedes or comes into the foreground at different times, in different situations, and in different locations; and, that it is not just one in the above list that shapes the others at any given moment, for it could be two or three that are in the foreground at the same time.

"Woman" is a category that is commonly used across the academy. And readers of this piece will be familiar with the arguments that the category of woman is not a neutral category, it is a category that is saturated with inequalities. The usual way to move through these discussions is to engage with the intersectionality of the category "woman"; that is, woman is defined as a category that is intersected by axes of inequality other than gender—such as race, sexuality, nationality, wealth—which all cut across woman, and each other at different angles.

I prefer to use the word "configurations" rather than intersectionality. To configure connotes more movement and fluidity than the metaphor of intersection suggests; it is closer to an idea of dancing (viva Emma Goldman!) as we pick our way through this tangle of power and inequalities, without tripping up, and yet being confident in our sure-footedness. "Configuration" also connotes agency, offering a way of thinking about how inequalities such as "race," gender, nation, sexuality, and wealth work with and against each other. For me, the idea of con-figurations suggests agency, activity, and graceful movement, with a consequent attribution of agency to the subjects of the configurations. Intersectionality is too static, too close to losing sight of agency. It is too angular, with very sharp boundaries and edges.

In my thinking on female genital mutilation, for example, I try to keep in mind that, for example, elective plastic surgery has increased dramatically in the USA, Europe, and the Middle East, while governments are banning FGM in many places. How do these two instances of "modern society" shape each other? How do they affect our notion of what is the Third World and the First World? What are the boundaries (and there are many) between culture and coercion? How do they relate to each other?

Your contributions have spanned so many areas in regard to women's lives—women in prison, development, violence, psychological dynamics, culture, etc. Have you a general philosophy in addressing these myriad topics relative to women as object and subject?

Trying to ameliorate inequalities, wherever and whenever I can, through understanding how people actually live and think about their everyday lives has been my driving motivation. I was seven when I asked my father the meaning of communism, as we watched the news. He explained to me that communism was where everyone had an equal share. When I asked him what was wrong with that, he said, "nothing, but it can never work." "We must make it work," was my retort, and still is.

I taught in two men's maximum security prisons in the 1970s, and the memory of that has never gone away. I was teaching about Gender for the Open University and we had to analyze advertisements in women's magazines. I was dreading that session, as I had assumed that the men would flick through the magazines, and drool over women's scantily clad bodies, and I would have to deal with it in the context of knowing that they had not been with women, in any way, for a long time. I had already anticipated this, and had been trying to think through the idea of who was I to judge the men if they wanted to talk about this?

However, the men turned instantly to the pages on which the recipes were photographed—and spent much of the session discussing what food they missed, how revolting the food was in the prison and what their first meal would be when (if?) they left. Needless to say I was staggered, and that incident once again taught me to always reflect on people's everyday lives, and to remember that human beings are not just a complex of social categories—they have agency; they often smash the stereotypes we hold; they can be creative in unpredictable ways.

I am definitely someone who thinks prisons ought to be abolished, somehow, and that societies need to seek other ways to tackle antisocial behavior, even for those whose financial dealings have led to them becoming very rich, and to their investors being robbed of the small amounts of money they had.

Although you were a first-time filmmaker when it was released, your documentary, The Shape of Water, *won you wide acclaim. Did you have a background that helped prepare you for the rigors that come with making such a film? How did you get the idea to make the film? Why did you make it? What were you hoping it would do?*

My personal intellectual passions have shifted in the past 25 years: from critical social and developmental psychology to "race" in the US imaginary, to the lived experiences of women in the Third World, to the Women Culture Development (WCD) paradigm, all inflected by feminist thinking. This move has been one which has ensured that my interdisciplinary passions continue to be realized, because to do Third World/Development Studies I need to understand economics, politics, literature, culture, and the specificity of culture, alongside sociology and psychology. Further, my passion for ethnographic inquiry has never been diluted. In fact, ethnography, a key means of conducting narrative research, has been my most enduring mode of inquiry in these last two to three decades.

In my teaching of women, culture, and development I use ethnographic research and also screen documentaries in my classes, such as *Love, Women, Flowers* (1988), *Something Like a War* (1992), or *Amazon Sisters* (1992). What I have found, however, is that none of the documentaries I screened *quite* did what I wanted to do. All too often, even as the opposite was attempted, viewers ended up seeing the women as victims who need to be rescued or saved by women and men living in the First World. What I was seeking were films that showed the lived realities of women in differing regions of the Third World while documenting their struggles as they create social justice for themselves, their communities, and others. In other words, I was constantly looking for films that presented women's realities as the realities of those who are both experiencing hardship, yes, but are simultaneously active in the creation of a new world. I wanted films that used feminist lenses through which narrative structures are explicated, and which demonstrate how social justice is being realized. And that is what led me to direct *The Shape of Water*.[9]

While I was at *Meridians* I had started a new project looking at four successful examples of women's organizations regarding employment, environment, peace, and sexuality, each in a different region of the Third World, in order to suggest some categories within which to imagine feminist futures and alternative development in the twenty-first century. They are the Self-Employed Women's Association (SEWA) in India, the Xapuri Women's Group in Brazil (women rubber tappers and others), Women in Black in Israel/Palestine, and Tostan in Senegal (a group prominent in achieving the ban on female genital mutilation in that country). These organizations integrate the concepts of gender, sexuality, and culture as lived experiences within their work. My hope was that in analyzing the actions, histories, and future goals of these four organizations, my research might contribute to rethinking economic globalization, and to discussions on how, at the very least, to slow down the alarming rate at which poverty, environmental degradation, and insecurity are becoming increasingly feminized around the globe. Eventually, I decided to make a film from that research, as I felt that was a more effective way to bring into focus what women in the Third World are doing to move towards greater security in everyday lives, and how they are going about it.

Of course, documentary is also different from academic work because it shows the immediacy of people's lives with an intensity that the academic word can seldom, if ever, accomplish. Film also offers the chance to experience the textures and wholeness of those lives which scholarly writing is rarely able to do. Although scholarly work does provide a depth of explicit analysis and context that is often impossible to achieve with documentary film, documentary film allows audiences to witness dialogue and relationships among people, institutions, and cultures in a unique way. That is, film is particularly apt at depicting culture in action and thus offers a set of truths in a form that scholarly writings cannot. This is not to dismiss scholarly, written work, not at all. But I also want to show how documentary film has the potential, not always realized, of course, to show people dealing with grounded, rather than abstract, issues.

I am well aware that filmmaking is an art form. But it is also fieldwork, and the making of a film/documentary demands research which ultimately brings the subject/issue/topic/people much more directly into view.

I turned to documentary filmmaking because, like novels, it has the potential to bring people's stories to life in a very powerful and immediate way. At the same time, however, like the scholarly analyst, the documentary filmmaker integrates her own standpoints into the work. These become integrated not merely through the questions posed, but also through the selection of shots, how interviewees and their words are represented, what stories to tell, and, indeed, many of the techniques essential for filmmaking such as lighting, camera angles, and so on.

Decisions are also made as to what type of context to provide for the stories. Of course, this happens with printed research as well. For example, is it mainly a statistical context that is offered for the story? What intimate details of the key characters' lived experiences should be highlighted? To what extent are "experts" asked to offer analyses of the lived experiences? All of these dimensions can be conveyed in documentary film with a depth and texture different—not necessarily better—to that of academic work.

My desire to make a documentary emerged, therefore, because, like academic feminist ethnographers, I wanted to depict people speaking about their lives, yet always with the understanding that there has been substantial editing and choices made as to what is presented. Film permits those editorial choices to be fairly explicit.

The theoretical underpinning for *Shape* was the Women, Culture, Development paradigm, an approach I helped develop with other close collaborators, including John Foran, Priya Kurian, Debashish Munshi, Peter Chua, Molly Talcott, Light Carruyo, and Krista Bywater.[10] This perspective draws on cultural studies, and feminist and anti-racist scholarship. Our goal has been to reinvigorate discussions about the future of development, because for many people development practice has failed the peoples of the Third World, and development studies have been at an impasse. However, if one thinks of development as a form of planned social transformation (I also prefer to see that specified into development as redistribution of land, wealth, and power), whether by the state, NGOs, or grassroots organizations, it becomes possible to see a way out of the impasse. That is, if the economic is *not* privileged above other frameworks—the cultural, racialized, gendered, and sexual, for example—then there may be ways to initiate movements for social change that ameliorate poverty and improve life for the poor. This is where WCD comes in. This new approach to development studies focuses on the integration of production and reproduction in people's lives, to bring culture, "race," and the economic together, alongside gender.

If we center the relationship between production and reproduction—the social and the biological—both of households and of communities, women's agency becomes visible. WCD suggests that it is *lived experiences and structures of feeling* that are to be the nodal points for scholarly analysis—not simply the "grand narratives" of globalization, transnationalization, and internationalization. We suggest this because those terms can sometimes lead to an acceptance of the present social formations, and thus silence or discourage interdisciplinary analysis that might contribute to an understanding of the present as open to change of a positive kind. The economic remains a key means of grappling with the subordination of poor women in the Third World, yet privileging the economic above other aspects of people's everyday lives obscures as much as it reveals.

What is culture? We do not think of culture as "high" or "low." To our minds, culture emerges from the ways in which people live their lives, in which *we* live our lives. It is not a static property that resides within people or groups, but, rather, it is formed through relationships, often relationships of inequality. Because culture is inherent in all relationships it offers a non-economistic, yet still material, way to produce knowledge and to present different strategies for making struggle and social change. And it is shifting constantly.

While the elements in WCD are not new (one thinks of Gita Sen and Karen Grown's wonderful *Development, Crisis, and Alternative Visions: Third World Women's Perspectives*[11]), what is new is that we have put them all together into one theoretical framework. We do this in a period when development is coming to be a less and less familiar term, with the horrors of globalization and its underlying philosophy of neo-liberalism—both being the very antithesis of the potential of a development that centers on people's needs and lives—taking its place as key terms in this conjuncture. In addition, WCD is self-consciously interdisciplinary and works both in and against development studies, feminist studies, and cultural studies to open new lines of perspective for comprehending the twenty-first century.

In sum, this new paradigm for development studies is one that puts women at the center and culture on a par with political economy, and keeps a focus on critical pedagogies, practices, and movements for justice.

With *The Shape of Water*, I have attempted to realize some of the potential of this paradigm for understanding how social justice comes about. By creating films that help me see how inequalities are shaped and resistances are actively forged, I suggest that there are new forms of ethnography which permit a glimpse into the possibilities of a world in which scholarship and people's lives speak more directly with each other.

How does your activist work compare to your scholarly work, or to your work as a filmmaker for that matter?

I understand your question as being about links. In all of my work, I inevitably ask: What forms of politics can move us towards a more just world? That is the key link amongst all of the ways I live my life.

As a professor, scholar, and filmmaker, you are in the position to influence generations of young women and men. What advice would you give to them regarding possibilities for a global gender justice and the challenges of social change?

I often say that the thing I value most is that I am able to work in order to make the world better for others. It is a little like Pastor Martin Niemöller's dictum:[12] but it is also different because we do this not to protect ourselves in the long run, but because the meaning of life is to make the world better for others.

What remains to be done? What realistically can be done?

In the *Communist Manifesto*, Marx and Engels described capitalists as "stoop[ing] to pick up the golden apples dropped from the tree of industry, and to barter truth, love, and honor for traffic in wool, beetroot sugar, and potato spirits." Might I suggest that we bring our minds to bear on how to ensure that truth, love, and honor do not continue to be bartered? Is it possible to dance a passionate dance of development, to turn development into a means for social justice for all? We urgently need to do so.

Notes

1 Chomsky, Noam. (1959) "A Review of B. F. Skinner's Verbal Behavior," *Language*, 38(1): 26–59. (Reprinted in J. A. Fodor and J. J. Katz (eds) (1964) *The Structure of Language*, Upper Saddle River, NJ: Prentice-Hall, pp. 547–578.)

2 Ray, Satyajit. (1984) *The Home and the World*, screenplay and direction by Satyajit Ray (based on the novel *Ghare Baire* by Rabindranath Tagore), Mumbai: National Film Development Corporation of India.

3 Jensen, Arthur R. (1969) "How much can we boost IQ and scholastic achievement?" *Harvard Educational Review*, 39: 1–123.

4 Coard, Bernard. (1971) *How the West Indian Child Is Made Educationally Sub-Normal in the British School System: The scandal of the black child in schools in Britain*. London: New Beacon Books.

5 Webber, Frances. (2009) "Bad science?" Institute of Race Relations: Comment, posted 24 September 2009. http://www.irr.org.uk/2009/september/ha000014.html

6 Hull, Gloria T., Patricia Bell Scott, and Barbara Smith (eds) (1982) *All the Women Are White, All the Blacks Are Men, But Some of Us Are Brave*, Old Westbury, NY: Feminist Press; Moraga, Cherríe, and Gloria Anzaldúa (eds) (1984) *This Bridge Called My Back: writings by radical women of color*, Latham, NY: *Kitchen Table/Women of Color Press*.

7 Bhavnani, Kum-Kum. (1991) *Talking Politics: a psychological framing of views from youth in Britain*, Cambridge: Cambridge University Press.

8 Bhavnani, Kum-Kum. (2001) "Editor's Introduction," *Meridians: feminism, race, transnationalism*, 1(Spring): ix–xiv.

9 http://www.theshapeofwatermovie.com

10 Some key works include *On the Edges of Development: cultural interventions*, edited by Kum-Kum Bhavnani, John Foran, Priya Kurian, and Debashish Munshi (New York: Routledge, 2009), which includes "Dancing on the Edge: women, culture, and a passion for change" (with Krista Bywater); *Feminist Futures: reimagining women, culture and*

development, edited by Kum-Kum Bhavnani, John Foran, and Priya Kurian (London: Zed Press, 2003), which includes Light Carruyo's essay, "Dreams and Process in Development Theory and Practice"; "The Red, the Green, the Black, and the Purple: reclaiming development, resisting globalization," by Kum-Kum Bhavnani, John Foran, and Molly Talcott, in *Critical Globalization Studies*, edited by R. Appelbaum and W. I. Robinson (New York: Routledge, 2004); and "From Critical Psychology to Critical Development Studies," by Kum-Kum Bhavnani and Peter Chua, in *International Journal of Critical Psychology*, 1(1) (2000): 62–78.

11 New York: *Monthly Review*, 1987.
12 "THEY CAME FIRST for the Communists, and I didn't speak up because I wasn't a Communist. THEN THEY CAME for the Jews, and I didn't speak up because I wasn't a Jew. THEN THEY CAME for the trade unionists, and I didn't speak up because I wasn't a trade unionist. THEN THEY CAME for the Catholics, and I didn't speak up because I was a Protestant. THEN THEY CAME for me, and by that time no one was left to speak up."

Index